1981

University of St. Francis
GEN 320.973 K193
Katznelson, Ira.
The politics of

W9-ADS-659

ԵԵԵ4022 3

SECOND EDITION

the
politics
of
power

**A CRITICAL INTRODUCTION
TO AMERICAN GOVERNMENT**

the politics of power

A CRITICAL INTRODUCTION TO AMERICAN GOVERNMENT

Ira Katznelson
University of Chicago

Mark Kesselman
Columbia University

SECOND EDITION

HARCOURT BRACE JOVANOVICH, INC.

New York   San Diego   Chicago   San Francisco   Atlanta

LIBRARY
College of St. Francis
JOLIET, ILL.

Copyright © 1979, 1975 by Harcourt Brace Jovanovich, Inc.

All rights reserved. No part of this publication may be reproduced
or transmitted in any form or by any means, electronic or mechanical,
including photocopy, recording, or any information storage and
retrieval system, without permission in writing from the publisher.

Requests for permission to make copies of any part of this work should
be mailed to: Permissions, Harcourt Brace Jovanovich, Inc., 757 Third
Avenue, New York, N.Y. 10017

ISBN: 0-15-570746-9

Library of Congress Catalog Card Number: 78-71479

Printed in the United States of America

320.973
K193

To the memory of Paul Kesselman,
to Anne Kesselman
and to
Ephraim and Sylvia Katznelson

101,733

preface

Our aim in this book is to introduce students to American government and to explore how the interplay of politics and power influences their lives. We examine the country's major institutions and practices, how they have evolved and changed over the years, and how they function today. However, rather than presenting what exists as natural and desirable, we attempt to describe the politics of American power from a coherent, critical perspective. We stress that fundamental inequalities—political, economic, social, and educational—exist among groups and classes in the United States and question what these inequalities mean in terms of a democratic order.

Although we discuss in detail the workings of the major American political institutions, we go beyond formal institutions and procedural democracy to place primary emphasis on the relationship between American capitalism and politics. Even in periods of economic expansion, the requirements of capitalism limit democratic practice and relegate democracy largely to the sphere of selecting government officials. In the developing political, economic, and social crisis of the present era, the fundamental question of the relationship among capitalism, socialism, and democracy is even more apparent. In this book, we have attempted to study the politics of American power from a coherent perspective that, although it will surely not be shared by all, will, we hope, provoke students to develop their own approach to American politics.

Many people contributed generously to the writing of this book. Deborah Socolow Katznelson's and Wendy Kesselman's enthusiastic encouragement, critical assistance, and love helped in the most important ways. In addition to the friends, colleagues, and students whom we thank in the first edition, we would like to express our gratitude to Donald W. Allan, Amrita Basu, Alan Draper, Kevin Gleason, James Greer, and Patrick V. Peppe.

We are once again the fortunate beneficiaries of the superb craftsmanship and professionalism of the editorial and production staff at Harcourt Brace Jovanovich. In particular we wish to thank Joanne Daniels, Lee Shenkman, and Thomas Williamson.

IRA KATZNELSON
MARK KESSELMAN

contents

4

the corporate complex and crisis   84

5

workers and work   112

public policy and political control
at home and abroad   139

6

competition without representation:
political parties and elections   141

7

the welfare state   182

conclusion   367

12

capitalism, socialism, and democracy   369

thinking about politics

1

capitalism and democracy

Had the title *Capitalism, Socialism, and Democracy* not been used by Harvard economist Joseph Schumpeter in his classic treatment of these subjects in 1942, we would have selected it for this book.[1] For, in *The Politics of Power*, we explore the relationship between the capitalist economic and social system of the United States; its democratic politics, government practices, and public policies; and the possibilities for fundamental change.

The connections between these subjects raise the most interesting and pressing questions about political life in all the advanced industrial societies of Western Europe and North America. Indeed, the central questions confronting modern social theory and political philosophy for the past century have been about the tensions inherent in societies that are simultaneously capitalist and democratic. The political content of debate in most of these countries has been shaped principally by these questions. Even when these questions are not overtly on the agenda, the relationship between capitalism—which routinely generates inequalities in life conditions—and democracy—which posits equal rights and re-

[1] Joseph Schumpeter, *Capitalism, Socialism, and Democracy* (New York, 1942).

3

sponsibilities for all citizens—affects major features of political life. In the United States, it is impossible to understand the politics of power—and powerlessness—without attention to these concerns, because American society is both the most capitalist and one of the most procedurally democratic of all the countries of the West.

The way people organize the production and distribution of necessities and other goods is a critical factor shaping organized human life. The particular form that production takes divides members of a society into different groups depending on their relationship to the means of production. The process of producing goods thus involves more than producing material articles; it also involves producing and reproducing through time relationships connected with production. In a feudal order, for example, the process of production created anew in each generation the relationship of serf to feudal lord.

In the United States, production is organized within a capitalist framework. The central relationship in a capitalist order is "the relation of capital and labor itself, of capitalist and worker." [2] Most members of the community contribute their labor to producing goods and services. But the tools of production—the factories, machines, and raw materials—are privately owned and controlled by a small minority.

The relationship between these classes is systematic and relatively stable and constitutes a social structure. The most important feature of this structure is the fundamental contradiction between the interests of the dominant minority who own and control the production apparatus and the interests of workers who must sell their labor for a wage. Those in control make decisions that shape the lives of all Americans. They are also the principal beneficiaries of capitalist production and receive substantially more of the material rewards and social benefits from the process. Those who work for wages have little say over the broad shape of the society or over major decisions affecting their lives, and they receive a lesser share of capitalism's rewards and benefits.

In a capitalist system, there are two related areas of economic inequality: income and wealth. In the United States, the pattern of income distribution has remained virtually unchanged in this cen-

[2] Karl Marx, *Grundrisse*, translated by Martin Nicolaus (New York, 1974), p. 458.

tury. In 1910, the top fifth of income earners received 46 percent of the national income; today, the richest fifth's share is still over 40 percent. The share of the bottom fifth has actually declined from over 8 percent in 1910 to just over 5 percent today.[3] This pattern of inequality in income is tied directly to even greater disparities in the distribution of wealth—ownership of corporate stock, businesses, homes and property, cash reserves, government and corporate bonds, and retirement funds. Roughly 20 percent of personal wealth in the United States is owned by one-third of 1 percent of the population; the richest 1 percent own over 28 percent of the wealth; and the top 10 percent of Americans own over half (56 percent). The bottom 10 percent actually owe more than they own.[4]

This basic structure underpins the complexity of everyday life in the United States. Although Americans have diverse ethnic and racial backgrounds, work in different kinds of jobs, live in different places, and hold widely different political opinions, all are part of the class structure and are affected by it. Capitalist production interpenetrates virtually every aspect of American society, including the place of racial minorities and women, the quality of city neighborhoods, and the political choices made by government officials and citizens.

These choices are made by citizens in the world's oldest political democracy. All adult American citizens today have the right to vote. The party system invites citizen participation, and parties compete actively to win the electorate's support. Interest groups lobby to defend the interests of their members. Newspapers and television provide regular reports of government activities, debate the wisdom of government policies, and expose wrongdoing by high government officials. In few countries is political debate as open, free, and extensive.

[3] Charles Anderson, *The Political Economy of Social Class* (Englewood Cliffs, N.J., 1974), chapter 4; Douglas Dowd, *The Twisted Dream: Capitalist Development in the United States Since 1776* (Cambridge, Mass., 1974), pp. 117–21; Carolyn Shaw Bell, "Another Look at Distribution of Income," *Wall Street Journal*, November 12, 1976, p. 10.

[4] Frank Ackerman, Howard Birnbaum, James Wetzler, and Andrew Zimbalest, "Income Distribution in the United States," *Review of Radical Political Economics* 3 (Summer 1971): 24–26; Thomas Weisskopf, "Capitalism and Inequality," in Richard Edwards, Michael Reich, and Thomas Weisskopf, eds., *The Capitalist System* (Englewood Cliffs, N.J., 1972), pp. 125–32.

PARADOXES OF CAPITALIST DEMOCRACY

Upon examining American capitalism, one puzzling aspect becomes immediately apparent. It is in the interest of members of the capitalist class to use their resources to maintain their position, protect existing arrangements, and thereby freeze inequalities. At the same time, logically, it is in the interest of noncapitalist groups and classes to direct their resources toward fundamental change. From this perspective, widespread challenges against the basic social structure should dominate American politics. Yet, obviously, these challenges do not occur. Much of the everyday political life we observe—speechmaking, elections, congressional debates—does not appear to reflect the fundamental antagonisms of interest. We are thus confronted by our first paradox of American politics and society—political stability despite structural class inequality.

This paradox is expressed clearly in taxation policy. The most progressive tax is the federal income tax. The more income an individual or family earns, the higher percentage they pay in taxes. Yet the income tax has virtually no effect on the overall distribution of income in the United States. For example, the Congressional Joint Committee on Taxation found that the richest fourth of households in America took home 55.5 percent of the income in the country in 1977 and yet still had 53.2 percent after paying income taxes.

Other taxes are mostly regressive; they take more proportionately from those least able to pay. In 1977, state and local sales taxes and excise taxes, for example, took under 4 percent of a $50,000 income while taking almost 11 percent of the earnings of a household earning $5,000. The very minor degree of redistribution caused by the federal income tax is thus offset by state, local, and social security taxes; the result is that those earning from $8,000 to $30,000 a year category pay approximately 30 to 32 percent of their income in taxes.[5]

Nevertheless, there is a noticeable lack of enthusiasm among

---

[5] Art Pine, "Income Tax Doesn't Redistribute U.S. Wealth," *The Washington Post*, March 27, 1978, p. A14; U.S. Department of the Treasury, Internal Revenue Service, "Individual Income Tax Returns, Preliminary Statistics of Income, 1976" (Washington, D.C., 1978).

most Americans for a more equitable tax system. Although Americans are often cynical about the ways tax dollars are spent and think taxes are too high, "when redistributive issues are clearly raised, . . . it appears that most Americans do not want steeply progressive taxation." In responding to the questions of researchers, Americans say they favor tax breaks that disproportionately aid the wealthy and prefer sales to income taxes.[6] These findings strongly indicate that political and social stability in the United States, fashioned in the face of a high degree of inequality (higher than anywhere else in the West)[7], is based principally not on a high degree of repression, though such coercion exists, but on a high degree of consent.

Democratic institutions and political freedom in the United States make America's strong political stability particularly noteworthy. No other nation, among the nearly two hundred existing today, has been governed by the same Constitution since the eighteenth century. Although there have been opposition movements calling for fundamental change in the United States, they have been relatively rare. In light of the freedom to organize, the weakness of opposition political movements suggests that there is substantial popular support for existing arrangements. In a public opinion poll of citizens in England, Italy, Germany, Mexico, and the United States, Americans expressed most pride in their political institutions.[8]

But popular support for American political institutions provides a clue to the persistence of inequality. In contrast to the United States, in every European country workers and the poor have organized political parties and long-term social movements to pressure government to respond to their needs. Large worker-based political parties in these countries have been responsible for obtaining benefits from governments for the working class. The absence of a strong working-class political movement in the United States means that workers and the poor have no regular organized way to press political demands. Government policies are bound to be less responsive to the working class if it fails to organize and use

[6] Benjamin I. Page, "Taxes and Inequality: Do the Voters Get What They Want?" unpublished manuscript.

[7] For a discussion, see Ira Katznelson, "Considerations on Social Democracy in the United States," *Comparative Politics* 11 (October 1978): 77–99.

[8] Gabriel Almond and Sidney Verba, *The Civic Culture* (Princeton, N.J., 1963).

its political resources effectively. But what explains the relative political quiescence of the American working class? Why have those groups suffering systematic unequal treatment not used their right to vote and other political resources to press not only for modest but for substantial social change as well?

The second paradox is that of want and insecurity amidst plenty. Although, as we shall see, the kind of market capitalism that many economists assume to exist does not, in fact, operate in the United States, there are far fewer government constraints on the operation of the private economy than elsewhere in the capitalist world. No industries have been nationalized. No mechanisms of national economic planning exist. The American welfare state is fairly small.

This relatively unbridled capitalism produces goods and services in abundance. One hundred years ago, most of the technological innovations that now make for material ease did not exist. Automobiles, airplanes, computers, plastics, modern medicine, synthetic fabrics, indoor plumbing, cheap printing, television, washing machines, and telephones were all invented in the twentieth century—most of them in the United States. This country pioneered the mass-production techniques that make it possible to produce goods cheaply so that the fruits of modern science and industry can be distributed widely.

But far from equally. Although American industry churns out a vast quantity of products—two trillion dollars ($2,000,000,000,000) yearly—millions of citizens lack adequate health care, housing, safe working conditions, even the chance to get a job. In the last several years, there has been a combination of rising prices—usually a sign that there are not enough workers available to produce needed goods—along with from seven million or more unemployed workers unable to find jobs, and others so discouraged from looking that they are not even included in the official counts of the unemployed. One in ten families, and one in four individuals not living in families, earn incomes below the level of poverty as defined by the federal government; for blacks, the relevant figures are one in four, and two in five, respectively. The routine operation of American capitalism also produces regional disparities. While large cities in the Northeast and Midwest are decaying, suffering fiscal crises, and have many poor and unemployed workers, industries are spending heavily in other regions of the country. One may reasonably ask, why, in the most affluent nation in world history, is there so inadequate a provision of employment and public services, and so skewed a distribution of opportunities?

Our third paradox concerns the activities of government. It has rightly become a commonplace to comment on the growth of government. Total government spending in the United States accounted for 7 percent of the Gross National Product in 1902; 10.6 percent in 1927; 25.6 percent in 1955; and 36.5 percent in 1976. At the turn of the century, 4 percent of all employed Americans worked for the government; today the equivalent figure is 20 percent. Social welfare expenditures—defined as "cash benefits, services, and administrative costs of all programs operating under public law that are of direct benefit to individuals and families"—rose from a per-capita level of $211 in 1950 (in 1967 dollars) to $934 in 1975. Such spending, much of it directed at alleviating hardship and inequalities, is approximately fifty times greater than it was at the turn of the century, and at least five times what it was during the height of the New Deal of President Franklin Roosevelt in the 1930s.[9]

Yet this massive expansion in government activity has not changed the distribution of wealth and income, has not provided for an alleviation of unemployment, and has not eliminated, or even substantially reduced, the experience of poverty. To be sure, the distribution of income in the United States is more equal after government benefits are calculated; but, as a recent Institute for Research on Poverty study undertaken at the University of Wisconsin demonstrates, even after these benefits are calculated, the "distribution of income changed very little between 1950 and 1970, despite the large growth in taxes and government services during these years." It may well be, the Institute's director speculates, that the ordinary operation of the economy generates a "distribution of income that has become more unequal over time. Just like Alice, the government has had to run faster (tax and spend more) to keep up."[10] Why has massive government intervention failed to reverse inequalities of wealth, income, and power, or assure that minimum social needs are met?

[9] Alfred Skolnik and Sophie Dales, "Social Welfare Expenditures, 1950–1975," *Social Security Bulletin* 39 (January 1976): 3–20; G. Warren Nutter, *Growth of Government in the West* (Washington, D.C., 1978); James L. Clayton, "The Fiscal Limits of the Welfare-Warfare State," *The Western Political Quarterly* 29 (September 1976): 364–83.

[10] Morgan Reynolds and Eugene Smolensky, *Public Expenditures, Taxes, and the Distribution of Income: The United States, 1950, 1961, 1970* (New York, 1977); Irwin Garfinkel, "Foreword," in Reynolds and Smolensky.

STANDARDS OF DEMOCRACY

In 1961, political scientist Robert Dahl published an influential study of politics in New Haven, Connecticut. By commonly accepted standards, he argued, the city was a democracy, since virtually all its adult citizens were legally entitled to vote, their votes were honestly counted, and "two political parties contest elections, offer rival slates of candidates, and thus present the voters with at least some outward show of choice." Although the city's residents were legally equal at the ballot box, they were substantively unequal. Economic inequality in New Haven contrasted sharply with its formal political equality. Fewer than one-sixteenth of the taxpayers owned one-third of the city's property. In the wealthiest ward, one family out of four had an income three times the city average; the majority of the families in the poorest ward earned under $2,000 per year. Only one out of thirty adults in the poorest ward had attended college, as contrasted to nearly half of those in the richest ward.[11]

Is the combination of legal equality and class inequality democratic? Dahl put the question this way, "In a system where nearly every adult may vote but where knowledge, wealth, social position, access to officials, and other resources are unequally distributed, who actually governs? . . . How does a 'democratic' system work amid inequality of resources?"[12] He placed quotation marks around the term *democratic* because its meaning in this situation is unclear. Should a democratic system be measured only by legal standards of equality, such as fair and open election procedures, or should it be measured by substantive standards, according to the control and distribution of resources? What, in short, is the relationship of capitalism and democracy?

PROCEDURAL DEMOCRACY: STRUCTURE IGNORED

In his study of New Haven, Dahl argued that, rather than one elite group making political decisions, different elite groups determined

[11] Robert Dahl, *Who Governs? Democracy and Power in an American City* (New Haven, Conn., 1961), pp. 3–4.
[12] *Ibid.*, pp. 1, 3.

policy in different issue areas, such as urban renewal, public education, and the nomination of candidates for office. In each area, however, there was a wide disparity between the ability of politically and economically powerful people and average citizens to make decisions. As a result of such disparities, Dahl noted, New Haven was "a long way from achieving the goal of political equality advocated by the philosophers of democracy and incorporated into the creed of democracy and equality practically every American professes to uphold."[13]

Nevertheless, he concluded that "New Haven is an example of a democratic system, warts and all."[14] Dahl never resolved the problem of capitalist inequalities in a "democratic" system. Rather, he reached his conclusion by assessing democracy only according to the procedural test (Can citizens vote? Do they have a choice between candidates? Are elections honest and conducted freely?). The structure of society and class inequalities are ignored.

This approach has dominated much recent thinking about democracy. As mentioned at the start of this chapter, the most influential twentieth-century discussion of the relationship of capitalism and democracy is by Joseph Schumpeter in *Capitalism, Socialism, and Democracy*. Schumpeter defines democracy wholly in procedural terms. Even though we reject his proposed standard of democracy, it is important to review his arguments here because his work underpins the way that most American social scientists think about democracy and because the issues he raises are basic to the elaboration of the approach to democracy we propose in this chapter.

Schumpeter began his discussion by rejecting the "classical view of democracy," which held that democracy exists when the people decide issues in the interest of the common good of all. This view assumed that there exists a "common good"—that all the members of the political system share basic interests. Since all members of the polity share these interests, it is possible to talk of "the people" who actually make decisions—either directly by themselves or indirectly through representatives whose job it is to accurately reflect the "common good."

Schumpeter powerfully questioned the existence of these assumed entities in a capitalist society. He wrote, "There is . . . no such thing as a uniquely determined common good that all people

[13] *Ibid.*, p. 86.
[14] *Ibid.*, p. 311.

could agree on or be made to agree on by the force of rational argument."[15] A "common good" does not exist in societies characterized by basic structural inequalities because of the absence of shared interests. So long as patterns of inequality persist, it is impossible to speak of a "common good," since the good of some depends on the subordination of others.

Hence it is also impossible to speak of "the people," for when members of a society have different interests, there is no single, natural direction their will can take. Rather, "the people" are divided into groups that reflect the unequal distribution of power. Schumpeter thus concluded that "both the pillars of the classical doctrine inevitably crumble into dust."

Because he found the classical approach to democracy out of touch with reality Schumpeter proposed that we accept "another theory which is much truer to life and at the same time salvages much of what sponsors of the democratic method really mean by this term."

Whereas the classical doctrine saw democracy as a set of institutional arrangements for reaching decisions to realize the people's common good, Schumpeter viewed democracy as "that institutional arrangement for arriving at political decisions in which individuals acquire the power to decide by means of a competitive struggle for the people's vote." Democracy thus becomes a set of rules for choosing, by election, among competing political leaders; the substance of what is decided by those selected is only secondary. Schumpeter's alternative to the classical doctrine of democracy is also rooted in a profound distrust of the governed. Indeed, for Schumpeter, it is best that political elites, not "the people," make decisions, because the people are incompetent:

> The typical citizen drops down to a lower level of mental performance as soon as he enters the political field. He argues and analyzes in a way which he would readily recognize as infantile within the sphere of his real interests. He becomes a primitive again.[16]

For Schumpeter, and for the vast majority of American social scientists who have accepted his approach, a political system is democratic when citizens are provided with an opportunity to vote

[15] Schumpeter, p. 251.
[16] *Ibid.*, p. 262.

either for the political leaders in office or for a set of competing leaders who wish to get into office. Democracy is seen as a method, a set of formal procedures by which citizens can select among a limited number of alternative sets of leaders. The role of voters in this conception resembles the role of consumers in a market economy. Much as consumers choose among competing products packaged by business people, so voters choose among competing candidates packaged by political parties. "The psycho-technics of party management and party advertising," Schumpeter wrote, "slogans and marching tunes, are not accessories. They are of the essence of politics."[17] Since neither major party challenges the basic structure of capitalist inequality, the act of choice, a legal right, replaces the substance of choice at the heart of democratic theory.

This purely procedural definition of democracy has become an ideological tool of social control. Those who benefit most from the capitalist social structure may maintain, since citizens can choose their leaders, that they have little cause for grievance. The system, by definition, is open and democratic. Those with complaints can express them in the next election. In this way, the procedural approach to democracy requires and promotes a relatively passive citizenry.

"Democracy" emerges from Schumpeter's discussion without its cutting edge. The classical view of democracy, however flawed by its reliance on the concepts of "common good" and "the people," was concerned fundamentally with the substance of political decision making and the rule of the many against the powerful few. For this reason, democracy commanded far from universal acceptance. The emasculation of the term by Schumpeter has made it far more acceptable to dominant interests. Democracy is not a standard against which existing practice can be measured critically but is rather an uncritical, incomplete description of present electoral arrangements. Not surprisingly, almost all those who define democracy in wholly procedural terms find that there is no clash between democracy and capitalist inequality.

In rejecting the classical definition of democracy, Schumpeter had three alternatives. The first was to abandon the term *democracy* altogether as hopelessly utopian. The second, which he opted for, was to retain the term but redefine it to conform to existing

[17] *Ibid.*, p. 283.

realities. The third alternative, which we support, was to maintain the term *democracy* as a yardstick against which to measure and test reality. Thus, in a preliminary way, we define *democracy* as *a situation in which all citizens have relatively equal chances to influence and control the making of decisions that affect them.* This alternative recognizes that although formal democratic procedures are essential to democracy, they do not guarantee it. For democracy approached this way does not depend simply on a set of rules, important though rules may be, but on the nature of the social structure within which the rules of procedural democracy operate.

Broadly, we may distinguish three different, though related, approaches to our definition of democracy. The first stresses popular participation in decision making; the second, the representation of interests; and the third, the transformation of the social structure itself. Let us examine each of these approaches in turn.

THE IMPORTANCE AND LIMITS
OF DIRECT PARTICIPATION

Citizen participation in decision making has traditionally been regarded as the centerpiece of democracy. Convincing arguments for a participatory form of democracy were put forward by Jean Jacques Rousseau, an eighteenth-century French philosopher. His influential political theory hinged on the *direct* experience of political participation. For Rousseau, participation has objective and subjective components. The objective component is that citizens exercise control by participating in decision making; the subjective component is that, because they feel they have been able to participate authentically in the making of decisions that affect them, citizens come to identify with the decisions taken and develop feelings of loyalty to the society. In addition, citizens learn to participate effectively. As social theorist Carole Pateman put it in her interpretation of Rousseau's *The Social Contract*, "the more the individual citizen participates, the better he is able to do so. . . . He learns to be a public as well as a private citizen."[18]

---

[18] Carole Pateman, *Participation and Democratic Theory* (Cambridge, Mass., 1970), p. 25.

One of the byproducts of authentic participation is that citizens learn to identify and interpret their own interests accurately and need not depend on the interpretations of others. Conversely, if participation is inauthentic, if individuals are given the feeling of participating in decision making but are not accorded the power to actually control the decision-making process, the inevitable short-term result is that they are prevented from arriving at an accurate perception of their interests. Though eighteenth-century New England town meetings were examples of direct democracy, many were dominated by a small elite who controlled the agenda and often successfully manipulated the group discussions. The key issue is thus not whether people participate in the political system but what the *terms* of their participation are.

In the past fifteen years, many organizations—including communes, antiwar protest groups, and women's-rights groups—have been founded on classical, Rousseauian democratic principles. They reject the formal procedural approach to democracy and run themselves, instead, as participatory democracies. Their members have self-consciously sought to create open, democratic communities in which all members participate directly in decision making. For many political activists, this kind of direct democracy provides a model for how democracy should be practiced in American society as a whole.

The leap from the small group to the society, however, is impossible to make. The program of participatory groups, including face-to-face unanimous decision making and absolute equality of status and power, is actually based on principles of friendship. As political scientist Jane Mansbridge notes

> friendship is an equal relation, it does not grow or maintain itself well at a distance, and its expression is in unanimity. . . . As participatory democracies grow from groups of fairly close acquaintances to associations of strangers, friendship can no longer serve as the basis of organization. Distrust replaces trust, and the natural equality, directness, and unanimity of friendship are transformed into rigid rules whose major purpose becomes the prevention of coercion and the protection of the individual.[19]

In small groups where people know each other intimately and are present voluntarily, the principles of direct, unanimous democracy

[19] Jane Mansbridge, "The Limits of Friendship," unpublished manuscript, pp. 1–2.

may work to produce a natural, organic consensus of the group's will. Beyond such small groups, however, consensus is likely to be the result of manipulation, since shared values and mutual respect can develop only in situations where group members share interests. Small groups may constitute a "people" with a "common good," but as Schumpeter demonstrated, these entities in a capitalist society are fictions on a larger scale.

If democracy is to be used as a yardstick to assess both what exists and what is possible, the direct-participation approach is ruled out, because society as a whole does not provide the "friendship" basis that direct democracy requires. Hence a second approach to our definition of democracy argues that the crucial issue is not whether people participate directly, but whether all groups of the capitalist social structure and their interests achieve political *representation*.

REPRESENTATIVE DEMOCRACY

There are four dimensions of representative democracy that provide us with an immediately useful yardstick against which to test present realities. The first is *procedures*. It is essential in a democracy that individuals and groups be able to make their views known and fairly select their leaders and public officials. Hence civil liberties are essential. Free speech, free assembly, and freedom of the press are basic aspects of procedural representation. When these procedural guarantees are suppressed, it is extraordinarily difficult for people to formulate and express their interests.

The electoral mechanisms available to citizens for selecting their representatives are also an important factor in procedural representation. How wide is the electorate? How is party competition organized? What, in short, are the rules of the electoral process? As we have seen, electoral choice is at the heart of the formal procedural standard of democracy developed by Schumpeter.

But, unlike those who advocate procedural democracy, we believe that it is a mistake to limit the discussion of procedures of representation to elections. Rather, we must consider the nature of all of the rules that determine whether an individual or group has access to the political system and whether that access is likely to have an effect on decision-making. Thus the traditionally narrow focus of issues raised about the procedures of representation must be widened. Are workers permitted to join unions? How are congressional committee chairmen selected? How does an elected mayor exercise control over nonelected city bureaucrats? To whom and how is a school system's personnel formally accountable? How are key foreign-policy decision makers chosen? How, if at all, are they formally held accountable? What are the procedures for representation in areas such as the space program, where expertise is available only to a few? Who selects the experts and to whom are they accountable? What are the procedures of leadership selection in interest groups (unions, farmers' organizations, professional associations)?

The list could easily be extended. The procedural dimension of representative democracy depends not only on equitable electoral procedures but more broadly on the mechanisms of access, influence, and accountability in government and in organizations that claim to represent the interests of their constituents. It is essential that the "rules of the game" ensure that the line that divides representatives and represented not harden and that access to ruling positions be open to all and not limited by racial, class, sexual, or other forms of discrimination.

Let us briefly consider an historical example. In the early 1900s, the Democratic party Tammany Hall machine dominated politics in New York City. During this period, most of the city's population consisted of European immigrants and their children. Because the populations of ethnic neighborhoods were relatively homogeneous, the ethnic groups gained control over the Tammany political clubs in their area. Blacks, however, were excluded from these organizations. They participated in party affairs through a citywide organization called the United Colored Democracy, whose leaders were selected by the white leaders of Tammany Hall, not by other blacks. Not surprisingly, studies of political patronage in the period indicate that blacks did the least well of all the groups in the city in securing political jobs; and the jobs they did get were the least desirable.[20]

---

[20] Ira Katznelson, *Black Men, White Cities* (New York, 1973), chapter 5.

Thus both the blacks from the South and the white ethnics from Europe joined the Democratic party, but on very different procedural terms. Although both groups could vote, the differences blacks experienced in the rules of access to the Democratic party severely limited their chances of reaping the rewards of municipal patronage.

The second dimension of representation is *personnel*. Irrespective of the way in which representatives have been selected, those who govern may or may not accurately reflect the demographic characteristics of class, race, ethnicity, sex, and geography of those they formally represent. During the Cuban missile crisis of 1962, for example, which was resolved when the Soviet Union removed its offensive missiles from Cuba after an American blockade of the island had been imposed, fewer than twenty individuals made the decisions that, by their own account, might have resulted in 150,000,000 casualties. The executive committee of the National Security Council met regularly in the two-week period of crisis to recommend courses of action to President Kennedy. Almost all of the council's members were Protestant, all were white, male, and wealthy. They included an investment banker, four corporation lawyers, a former automobile company president, and a number of multimillionaires.

In this instance, a very small group of men, hardly representative of the population as a whole, had the power to make decisions of the highest consequences. Judged by the personnel dimension of representation, the absence of democracy in this case is beyond doubt. The demographic representativeness of those who make political decisions is not important just in order to fulfill abstract numerical quotas of representation. Rather, the personnel dimension of representation is important because the more demographically representative a political system is, the more likely it is that the interests of the basic groups of the social structure will be adequately and substantively represented. It is highly unlikely, for example, that a group of business leaders will accurately represent the interests of workers or that the interests of blacks will be best represented by whites. This might occasionally be the case, but group members are much more likely to represent their own interests than those of their structural antagonists. It is not surprising, therefore, that workers in unions earn better wages than those whose wage levels are entrusted to the discretion of their employers; nor is it surprising that Southern blacks have been treated more equitably by police since the passage of the Voting Rights Act of 1965 than they had been when they had to depend on the goodwill of the white community.

To represent group interests adequately, representatives must also fulfill the dimensions of *consciousness*—they must be aware of and responsive to their constituents' concerns. In this respect, subordinates often find it much more difficult than the privileged to achieve representation of their interests, since those with more resources tend to perceive their interests more accurately than subordinates. The privileged are also in a better position to put pressure on their representatives than those who are politically powerless. Thus representation concerns not only *who* rules but also the *uses* to which power is put by those who rule. The first two dimensions of representation—procedures and personnel—refer to the first of these two issues. But the dimension of consciousness asks how representatives see the interests of their constituents and how they act on behalf of these interests. To satisfy the requirements of representative democracy, those who formally represent the population must use the power conferred by their positions to promote the interests of the represented.

But even where the first three dimensions of representation are satisfied, political democracy cannot be said to exist. The last dimension that must be realized is *effectiveness*—the ability of representatives to produce the results they desire. A system cannot be democratically representative if effectiveness is distributed very unequally among representatives. For example, given the fact that most congressional legislation is decided by the various committees, it would be difficult to argue that Polish working-class citizens who select a Polish working-class representative will be democratically represented if the representative is placed on committees irrelevant to their concerns.

Thus representative democracy is achieved only when all four dimensions are satisfied: when leaders are selected by regular procedures that are open to all people and all groups have relatively equal access to the political system; when representatives reflect the demographic composition of the population as a whole; when they are conscious of and responsive to their constituents' interests; and when they can effectively act on behalf of those interests.

SUBSTANTIVE DEMOCRACY:
STRUCTURE TRANSFORMED

Unlike the purely procedural approach to democracy, the standard of representative democracy does not simply endorse present practices as democratic. Rather, it allows us to measure the degree of representative democracy that exists and, conversely, shows us how much needs to be done to achieve a fully representative democracy. As such, this standard is the best available to test the democratic content of existing political institutions and processes.

Nevertheless, it is limited. It leaves us with the basic dilemma posed earlier in the chapter: in Dahl's words, "How does a 'democratic' system work amid inequality of resources?" What is the relationship between a political system based on equality of representation and an economic system based on the inequality of capital and labor?

The answer to this question is that the two systems may coexist, as they have in much of the West for more than a century, but the routine operation of a capitalist economy prevents the full achievement of representative democracy: a situation in which all citizens have relatively equal chances to influence and control the making of decisions that affect them. This demanding, critical standard of democracy—a standard of substantive democracy— is based not only on the dimensions of representation but on the criterion of structural change. The basic contradictions between capitalism and democracy can be finally resolved only by the transformation of the social structure.

The issues discussed in this chapter provide a framework for the analysis of American politics. The organization of *The Politics of Power* is governed by the attempt to make sense both of the three paradoxes discussed at the outset of this chapter as well as the more general relationship between capitalism and democracy in the United States. This introductory discussion, however, is not yet complete. For much of political life is informed by the ways people see the social reality in which they live. What people do is shaped by how they think. Before proceeding to our discussions of the organization of production, government institutions, public policy, and political behavior, we turn first to the ways Americans think about politics.

2

ideology and the creation of consciousness

"Our behavior is a function of our experience. We act according to the way we see things."

R. D. LAING, *The Politics of Experience*[1]

"The ideas of the ruling class are in every epoch the ruling ideas. . . . The class which has the means of material production at its disposal, has control at the same time over the means of mental production."

K. MARX and F. ENGELS, *The German Ideology*[2]

What people think strongly influences what they do. Yet how can the political significance of culture be studied? How do people develop political beliefs, define political reality, and come to believe what is politically right and wrong?

---

[1] R. D. Laing, *The Politics of Experience* (New York, 1967), p. 28.
[2] Karl Marx and Frederick Engels, *The German Ideology*, in Robert C. Tucker, ed., *The Marx-Engels Reader* (New York, 1972), p. 136.

21

22   CREATION OF CONSCIOUSNESS

The proposition by Marx and Engels cited above provides a trenchant (if oversimplified) description of the political relevance of culture. According to Marx, the power to define reality, just as economic and political power, is unequally distributed. The ideas held by rulers—what they pronounce to be accurate and right—will generally be the prevailing ideas of society at large. British scholar Frank Parkin suggests that Marx's proposition

> rests on the plausible assumption that those groups in society which occupy positions of the greatest power and privilege will also tend to have the greatest access to the means of legitimation. . . . Dominant values are in a sense a representation of the perceptions and interests of the relatively privileged; yet by virtue of the institutional backing they receive such values often form the basis of moral judgments of underprivileged groups. In a way, dominant values tend to set the standards for what is considered to be objectively "right."[3]

DOMINANT, ACCOMMODATIONIST, AND RADICAL IDEOLOGY

More important than the specific political beliefs within a particular ideological orientation are the problems and priorities identified by the ideology—the political agenda. Political scientist E. E. Schattschneider points out that the "definition of alternatives is the supreme instrument of power."[4] By defining alternatives, a political ideology highlights some issues and ignores others, "both focuses attention and diverts it," in the words of sociologist Alvin Gouldner.[5]

Although ruling groups have more power than other groups to shape the political ideology generally prevailing in a society, they meet resistance to their control of the ideological sphere as they do in the spheres of material production and politics. Parkin has suggested a way to understand the ideological struggle. Three

---

[3] Frank Parkin, *Class Inequality and Political Order* (New York, 1971), pp. 82–83.
[4] E. E. Schattschneider, *The Semi-Sovereign People* (New York, 1960), p. 68.
[5] Alvin W. Gouldner, *The Dialectic of Ideology and Technology* (New York, 1976), p. 83.

ideological orientations can be identified: dominant, accommodationist, and radical. (We are adapting Parkin's scheme for present purposes and modifying his terminology slightly.)

The dominant ideology is what Marx meant by the term *ruling ideas*. Put forward by established authorities, the dominant ideology praises traditional arrangements, denies the existence of conflicts of interest between authorities and subordinates, and opposes political change. The dominant ideology makes alternatives to established arrangements appear risky and irresponsible and thus undercuts dissent.

In contrast to the dominant ideology, the accommodative ideology perceives a host of problems, deficiencies, and evils in America, ranging from low wages, poverty, unemployment, bad housing, poor health, and racial and sexual discrimination, to excessive spending for military purposes, political corruption, inflation, high taxes, the squandering of natural resources, and pollution. Far from being satisfied with things as they are, the accommodative ideology seeks improvement in these diverse areas. It advocates bringing pressure to bear on authorities in order to remedy the deficiencies in American society. Taken together, the problems identified by the accommodative ideology add up to a powerful indictment.

The weakness of the accommodative perspective, however, is that it does not add these problems together. The various difficulties are perceived as separate and unrelated, each requiring its own solution. Therefore, demands by different groups within the accommodative framework are not coordinated and often clash. Thus workers in the corporate sector seek higher wages at the same time that consumer movements seek lower prices. Neither group recognizes that the two demands clash within a system of corporate price-fixing. In such a framework, there is no way to assign priorities and to plan an effective strategy of change. Particular changes may be made—the Truth in Lending Law, the Highway Safety Act, civil-rights legislation, the Environmental Protection Act, and improvements in particular cities or in the situation of particular groups (women, homosexuals, blacks)—but continued control by corporate producers and political leaders goes unchallenged.

The accommodative ideology accepts the basic structure of inequality as natural and inevitable. At the same time, it offers a way for the discontented to express grievances. Thus, although the accommodative ideology may raise issues that prove unsettling to established arrangements, it does so in a way that permits adjustments to be made and discontent to be defused without basic change.

The third ideology—what we will term the radical ideology—shares with the accommodative ideology a stress on the problems that exist in the United States. But the radical critique reaches further: it regards them not merely as evils in themselves but as a manifestation of systematic structural inequality. From the radical perspective, not only are problems linked but they are cumulative—those who have little education are unable to obtain good jobs and their children have less chance to get adequate education. Low-paying jobs go along with poor housing, poor health, and a lack of other resources; these problems in turn are linked to a system of corporate capitalism in which inequality is inherent in the capital-labor division.

How can this situation be changed? The radical ideology believes that piecemeal reforms do not address the basic problem of inequality and that a strategy of fundamental change must be devised to overcome the contradictions of corporate capitalism.

Poverty: Contrasting Views

To illustrate the differing perspectives, let us examine attitudes toward poverty in America. In the dominant American ideology, poverty hardly exists. The United States is one of the world's richest countries and has a higher per capita income than most other countries. Even the poor in America live better than much of the world's population. But even if one admits that many Americans live far from well, it is doubtful whether government action can be helpful in alleviating poverty. And since public programs may only make matters worse (for example, by causing inflation and the growth of government), the best policy is to do nothing unless political challenge from the poor makes a response by government absolutely necessary. But if political action is needed, those in government and other leadership positions are best qualified to diagnose the problem and sponsor a solution.

The accommodative ideology argues that poverty not only exists but that it is widespread. It specifies that a certain proportion of the population—too large a proportion in its view—does not share in the affluence of American society and that government help should be given to those falling below the poverty line. It is a disgrace that many Americans should go hungry in a country that produces two trillion dollars of goods and services per year. However, from the accommodative perspective, poverty is an isolated social ailment that can be engineered away through government programs, such as food stamps, public housing, welfare payments, and coordinated antipoverty attacks. No basic change is needed in the organization of production or the political sphere.

The radical critique refuses to define the problem as one of poverty per se, for this implies that poverty is amenable to treatment as a separate problem from corporate capitalism and inequality of wealth and power. In the radical view, poverty is viewed not as an isolated problem but as part of the uneven process of capitalist development. Capitalist production systematically reproduces inequalities in political and economic resources. These inequalities are especially great in the United States, where the working class has not directed sustained pressure toward the goal of achieving equality. In the radical view, accommodationist attacks on poverty will at most alleviate only its worst manifestations without resolving the larger problem of inequality. And, since addressing the more fundamental issue would require broad structural change, programs tailored to the specific problem of poverty will probably fail. The arsenal of innovations in the antipoverty programs of the 1960s did little to diminish inequalities of income in the United States, and these programs were abolished (and inequality increased) when the political threat that produced them had subsided. In the radical view, what needs to be confronted is not poverty, but the power of the corporate complex and structural inequality.[6]

It appears that, in the competition among the three ideologies, most Americans have chosen the dominant or accommodative ideology. The democratic verdict seems to be for the continuation of present arrangements. At least until recently, the observa-

---

[6] Labelling an ideology as dominant, accommodative, or radical does not determine its accuracy or validity. Some established arrangements may be worth preserving, and the dominant ideology may accurately describe them. On the other hand, adopting a radical ideology is no guarantee of accuracy. But we believe that a radical analysis potentially provides the best tool for understanding contemporary America. The other two modes have built-in limitations both because they ignore some of the largest features of politics and because they defend inequity.

/01, 733

College of St. Francis Library
Joliet, Illinois

tion by political scientist V. O. Key was quite accurate: "The great political triumph of large-scale enterprise has been the manufacture of a public opinion favorably disposed toward, or at least tolerant of, gigantic corporations."[7] However, as we will see in Chapter 6 (on political participation), alternatives to the dominant ideology rarely gain a full hearing. In the competition among the three ideologies, the dominant ideology has the decided advantage, the accommodationist has some chance of being heard, and the radical ideology is rarely discussed. Marxist scholar Ralph Miliband has observed, "For indoctrination to occur it is not necessary that there should be monopolistic control and the prohibition of opposition: it is only necessary that ideological competition should be so unequal as to give a crushing advantage to one side."[8]

IDEOLOGY AND DEMOCRACY

A number of studies by political scientists suggest that the political beliefs of most Americans are diffuse and inadequately thought out. On the basis of public-opinion surveys, political scientist Philip Converse has concluded that of all Americans only 3 percent (most of whom are wealthy and educated) can be said to adhere to a political ideology. (Converse defines ideology as a logically coherent set of principles explaining political reality and justifying political preferences.) The opinions of the average citizen appear shifting and inconsistent. When asked a series of questions about attitudes toward government, few people display stable attitudes over a period of time.[9] Thus, Converse finds a large gap between the educated elite and the general public. When political scientist Robert Lane interviewed New Haven workers, he found that they did not have a firm sense of justice and an articulate set of principles that could be considered an ideology.[10]

Findings such as these, combined with other studies showing that most Americans are politically uninformed, have led scholars to conclude that the mass public is poorly equipped to participate

[7] V. O. Key, Jr., *Politics, Parties, & Pressure Groups*, 5th ed. (New York, 1964), p. 96.

[8] Ralph Miliband, *The State in Capitalist Society* (New York, 1969), p. 182.

[9] Philip E. Converse, "The Nature of Belief Systems in Mass Publics," in David E. Apter, ed., *Ideology and Discontent* (New York, 1964), pp. 206–61.

[10] Robert Lane, *Political Ideology* (New York, 1962).

in politics and that the American people cannot be trusted to rule themselves. Hence, these scholars argue, it is just as well that voting turnout rates are low and that few people are politically active.

The assertion that Americans do not have a clear conception of ideology implies that most Americans do not rationally perceive their interests. In part this is correct. Recall Marx's proposition that the prevailing ideas of a society are those of the ruling class. The general electorate is constantly barraged with messages reinforcing the dominant ideology. Most Americans get fragmented, low-quality information. They are misled about their interests by schools, media, and government. Since they lack the resources, education, and time to analyze their interests in depth, they are often misinformed. An important consequence of the dominant ideology is to mask the connection between the problems people encounter in their daily lives and the actions of government. Politics seems remote from their personal situation.

By contrast, those with greater resources consistently receive superior information—not only do they listen to television news broadcasts but they read one or several newspapers, subscribe to specialized journals, and hire experts to provide additional information and watch over their interests. The wealthy and powerful are better equipped to perceive and defend their interests. They utilize political activity and government help as a matter of course.

However, there is evidence that the broad spectrum of Americans are quite aware of their interests and are neither as witless nor as nonideological as leading studies suggest. When ideology is defined in terms meaningful to average Americans, they display attitudes that are rational in terms of their particular situation. Political scientist Lewis Lipsitz interviewed the poor in Durham, North Carolina, and found:

> The dominant theme is the sense of being cheated: one's government is not concerned enough with one's well-being; one's government is willing to spend money on what appears to many of these men as frivolous or illegitimate enterprises [military spending] while it fails to meet their own deeply felt day-to-day needs.[11]

These opinions are hardly irrational. What is missing, however, is the link between people's perceptions and political action. But

---

[11] Lewis Lipsitz, "On Political Belief: The Grievances of the Poor," in Philip Green and Sanford Levinson, eds., *Power and Community: Dissenting Essays in Political Science* (New York, 1970), p. 165.

this, too, is reasonable in light of the slender resources many people have (time, wealth, skill) and the lack of viable alternatives available.

Studies showing that Americans lack a firm ideology are often construed to mean that people are basically content with existing public policies. But in a study based on public-opinion data, sociologist Richard Hamilton concludes that this belief is a myth. A large proportion of Americans favor measures for redistributing income and providing public support to low-income groups. Years before these issues were discussed by political officials as serious possibilities, many Americans favored public health insurance, guaranteed employment, and a minimum annual wage.[12] Political analyst Louis Harris has found that 71 percent of Americans want the tax laws rewritten to raise taxes for the wealthy and reduce them for Americans with lower incomes.[13] Hamilton's study suggests why alternative policies do not reach the political agenda. The reason is not that existing policies reflect the interests and wishes of the majority: this is an illusion fostered by the leaders of the media, community organizations, and political parties, who are more conservative than the majority of citizens. But this illusion also serves to isolate citizens for they may come to believe the myth that the majority of people favor the status quo.

In the absence of political movements that articulate workers' grievances and press for radical change, the tendency is to internalize and privatize problems. Americans are troubled, but they keep their worries to themselves and do not see the political relevance of their unhappiness. Or they take individual action borne from despair—America has the highest crime rate among industrialized nations, surely a sign of political discontent, as well as the highest rate of divorce and mental illness.

When questioned about their cares, many Americans express anxiety about economic problems, health, and family matters.[14] On the basis of interviews with workers, sociologists Richard Sennett and Jonathan Cobb find that most workers are unhappy and feel personally defeated. Although they have achieved some success in American society, they blame themselves for not having climbed even higher—into a middle-class professional position.

---

[12] Richard Hamilton, *Class and Politics in the United States* (New York, 1972), pp. 89–93.
[13] Louis Harris, *The Anguish of Change* (New York, 1973), p. 10.
[14] Hamilton, p. 85.

They share a common feeling of being mistreated, of not having control over their lives. Yet the grievances workers feel, based in large part on accurate perceptions of their situation, do not lead to a radical ideology and movement, or even to an accommodationist outlook.[15] The result is that grievances remain segregated within different sectors of the society. Anger is not based on a radical analysis linking the various inequalities to a structure of exploitation and is not integrated into a mass-based movement. It is often turned against others at the bottom, not those in positions of dominance.

THE DOMINANT IDEOLOGY

The dominant ideology can be considered the "official" creed; it is what most of the people hear most of the time. The dominant ideology is more powerful in the United States than in any other capitalist democracy. Most political debates in the United States take place within the framework of this ideology, a situation related to the absence of a broadly based working-class movement pressing for fundamental change. So powerful is the dominant ideology in this country that existing economic and political arrangements frequently appear not merely as the best possible arrangements but as the only possible ones.

American history has been punctuated by waves of protest. However, these protests generally have not presented demands that challenged dominant values. Political protest in the United States may occasionally have pushed the dominant ideology to its limits and even posed accommodative demands, but protest movements have rarely put forward an alternative ideology for reorganizing political and economic arrangements.

Political disagreements do not necessarily signify that the dominant ideology is under challenge. In fact, vigorous debate can be a sign of the vitality of the dominant ideology, so long as disagreements occur within its boundaries and various contenders do not question the existing framework. For example, current

[15] Richard Sennett and Jonathan Cobb, *The Hidden Injuries of Class* (New York, 1972). Also see Studs Terkel, *Working* (New York, 1974).

debates about energy policy generally remain within the dominant ideology; only a few critics of this policy challenge the fact that energy corporations monopolize America's resources and dictate the policy itself. A rare instance when debate took an accommodative turn was during the 1930s, when the federal government created the Tennessee Valley Authority—a government authority sponsoring an integrated program of flood control, rural electrification, fertilizer production, and low power rates in the Tennessee Valley. Yet this innovation in public power has never been repeated in the United States, largely because of the determined opposition of private power companies. The example of the TVA enlarged the ideological horizon in an accommodative direction, yet it remains unique within the United States.

The Four Elements of the Dominant Ideology

The specific values of the dominant ideology may change through time. As we will describe later in the chapter, dominant values are presently under severe stress. However, the following four clusters of values taken together can be considered elements of the current dominant American political ideology. Given its role in American politics, we shall devote considerable attention in this chapter to the dominant ideology and only briefly sketch the accommodative and radical ideologies.

1. Materialism, consumerism, and possessive individualism. Although the word *capitalist* is rarely used to describe the United States, capitalist values are one of the key elements in the dominant ideology. As we will show in later chapters, the needs of capitalism play a central role in shaping the American political agenda. British scholar C. B. MacPherson has suggested that capitalist values imply a particular view of society and human nature—what he calls possessive individualism.[16] According to MacPherson, in a capitalist society people are deemed free to treat their bodies as property. This makes it possible to bargain away their life (measured in terms of the working day) for a wage. Within this framework, the most appropriate activity outside work is striving to attain the material goods to achieve private satisfaction.

A capitalist system legitimizes itself through the promise of material abundance (as opposed to nonmaterial values like com-

[16] C. B. MacPherson, *The Political Theory of Possessive Individualism* (New York, 1973).

munity or autonomy). Nowhere in the world have consumer satis-
factions been emphasized as much as in the United States. Political
economist Herbert Gintis has explained that "people emphasize
consumption in capitalist society because it's the best thing going,
and it is the area over which they have the greatest degree of
control."[17] Gintis points out that, in a capitalist society, other areas
of possible fulfillment—for example, work, community, and
education—are rarely as rewarding.

The United States has not only promised material abundance;
it has to a considerable extent fulfilled the promise by pioneering in
mass production and mass consumption. Although most Americans have not enjoyed the material ease that America's productive
capacity potentially makes possible, there has been a widespread
distribution of consumer goods. The dominant ideology has gained
support through its promise of ever-greater material abundance.

2. Procedural democracy and freedom. Democratic arrangements were part of the dominant ideological creed in the
United States earlier than in any other nation. Elsewhere, dominant values were anti-democratic and upheld aristocratic privilege;
democracy and liberty were part of the accommodative or radical
ideologies of these nations.

Legitimation that rests on universal participation and the
freedom to express dissent is potentially dangerous to the status
quo, since the broad majority may use their freedom to demand
more responsive government policy. However, democratic values
have been a powerful means for sustaining established arrangements in the United States. One reason for this, according to
the dominant view, is that since there is freedom to participate in
the political arena, the resulting system must represent the
reasoned choice of the majority. As Alexis de Tocqueville, a
French observer of the United States, remarked more than a
century ago, democracy can be used to suppress minority opinion
and prevent serious consideration of alternatives to the existing
system.[18] For, as was shown in Chapter 1, there is the illusion in
the United States that existing arrangements are democratically
chosen when, in fact, democracy is confined to a narrow sphere of
decision-making. The result is the appearance of democratic
legitimacy despite the fact that democracy is actually quite limited

---

[17] Herbert Gintis, "Consumer Behavior and the Concept of Sovereignty," *The
American Economic Review* 62 (May 1972): 267–78.
[18] Alexis de Tocqueville, *Democracy in America* (New York, 1969), pp. 246–61.

in scope. All forms of dissent thus appear to be in opposition to the democratic verdict.

3. Patriotism. There is a fierce value placed by the dominant ideology on the power of the American nation. Patriotism in the United States often attains a religious intensity. It includes virulent doses of chauvinism and *machismo* and brashly asserts American superiority over other nations. Patriotism and national security are often used to limit criticisms of existing arrangements.

4. Technology. An inaccurate analogy is often made between technology and politics. Just as there is said to be "one right way" in technological matters, the same is true in politics—according to the dominant ideology. The result is to avoid discussion of alternatives and to focus discussion on limited techniques for piecemeal improvement. For example, President John F. Kennedy declared in 1962, "What is at stake in our economic decisions today is not some grand warfare of rival ideologies which will sweep the country with passion, but the practical management of a modern economy. What we need are not labels and clichés, but more basic discussions of the sophisticated and technical questions involved in keeping a great economic machinery moving ahead."[19]

The dominant ideology is greater than the sum of its parts. It can be considered a secular religion: the "American way of life." Like a religious creed, the dominant ideology is not usually subjected to rational analysis but is put forward to be accepted on faith.

SOCIALIZING TO DOMINANT VALUES

Ideologies, whether dominant, accommodative, or radical, do not float in air. They are part of broader political struggles whose outcome determines how a society is organized. Dominant values have the edge over the two other ideological orientations in part because key institutions support the dominant approach. Dominant values are taught in elementary school, high school, and college; they are presented over television and in newspapers, and

[19] Quoted in Gouldner, p. 250.

are proclaimed at presidential press conferences and during congressional elections by candidates of both parties. They serve as weapons in an ongoing political struggle. To understand how dominant values are disseminated and the ends they serve, it is useful to focus on the three institutional mechanisms of schools, media, and government.

Schools and Domination

Schools have been called a "model of society," and, along with television, they constitute a child's first sustained contact with the wider society outside the home.[20]

The hidden curriculum   Since there is little formal instruction in American history, politics, or civics until the later grades of elementary school, one might suppose that it is not until this point that schools affect children's political beliefs. Yet what children learn is not confined to the content of their courses. Indeed, some scholars argue that school may exercise its greatest political influence in the earliest years, before children have even the haziest conception of American politics.[21]

Two aspects of schooling need to be distinguished. On the one hand, there is the formal curriculum: the three R's, civics, science, and the like. Most school boards and teachers consider that formal subject teaching is what school is all about. To be sure, students do spend time grappling with the mysteries of multiplication and division. Much of their school day, however, is spent in ways that are irrelevant to the formal curriculum. Philip Jackson, a professor of education who carried out extended case studies of several elementary-school classrooms, points out that, in the typical school, relatively large numbers of children are brought together into a relatively small room and confined there most of the school day. Academic learning in such a situation is difficult at best. Children spend an inordinate amount of time in "noneducational" activities—lining up, waiting to get the teacher's attention, pledging allegiance to the flag, taking tests, pretending to study, lunch

[20] Joseph Grannis, "The School as a Model of Society," in Norman Adler and Charles Harrington, eds., *The Learning of Political Behavior* (Glenview, Ill., 1970), pp. 137–48.
[21] David Easton and Jack Dennis, *Children in the Political System* (New York, 1969), chapters 4–6.

period, play, and listening to the teacher scold.[22] According to Professor Jackson, "From kindergarten onward, the student begins to learn what life is really like in the company."[23] Let us delve into this hidden curriculum to understand its message.

The first political lesson of school is that attendance is compulsory. Jackson notes, "There is an important fact about a student's life that teachers and parents often prefer not to talk about, at least not in front of students. This is the fact that young people have to be in schools, whether they want to be or not."[24]

Once in school, children learn that they are subject to the teacher's authority. Underlying the hidden curriculum is the importance of obedience and hierarchy. Teachers rarely get angry, Jackson notes, when a child does not know the right answer. But they often lose their temper when they consider that a child is breaking the rules of proper classroom conduct. Jackson points out, "The several rules of order that characterize most elementary school classrooms all share a single goal: the prevention of 'disturbances.'"[25]

The formal curriculum   The political instruction that children receive is consistent with the message of the hidden curriculum. Children are schooled in the dominant ideology as a matter of course. A greater proportion of elementary-school time is devoted to political indoctrination in American than in Soviet schools.[26] In civics courses, the dominant ideology is presented as if it were an accurate description of reality. America is a democracy in which the people rule. Government exists to help people solve their problems. The good citizen supports the government and acts through established institutions. Little is said about poverty, conflict, violence, militarism, corporate power, or racism in America. When particular minority groups are mentioned, their "good" leaders are praised: Dr. Martin Luther King, Jr., and Jackie Robinson, not Malcolm X or Eldridge Cleaver.

Although children may become disenchanted in later life, a strong residue of patriotism remains that reinforces the dominant

---

[22] Philip Jackson, *Life in Classrooms* (New York, 1968).
[23] *Ibid.*, p. 73.
[24] *Ibid.*, p. 9.
[25] *Ibid.*, p. 104.
[26] G. Z. F. Bereday and B. B. Stretch, "Political Education in the U.S.A. and the U.S.S.R.," *Comparative Education Review* 7 (1963): 9–16.

ideology.[27] In a study of political attitudes in five nations, the United States had the highest proportion of citizens who expressed pride in their country's political institutions.[28] This finding has been interpreted as evidence of the excellence of American institutions, but it might with equal validity be used as evidence of the effectiveness of American political indoctrination.

Reproducing the social structure: differential socialization
The dominant ideology argues that the road to social advancement in our technological society is through educational attainment. And, since access to education is presumably open to all as a result of equal educational opportunity, it follows that schools serve as an equalizing and democratizing instrument in America.

In fact, however, a review of education suggests that access to education is heavily influenced by a student's social origins. Students from different classes receive a different symbolic message, different amounts of education, and, in fact, a different kind of education. As a result, schools act as a mechanism to reproduce existing social inequalities in the next generation. Economist Samuel Bowles observes:

> In modern America the school has replaced the frontier and the Horatio Alger type as the ultimate repository of that "equality of opportunity" which was promised to all. Yet the educational system does not and cannot lead to much greater equality of opportunity or of income under capitalism. The American school system is in fact instrumental in the legitimation of inequality and its transmission from one generation to the next.[29]

The amount of education that lower- and middle-class children get differs sharply. On the average, children from relatively well-to-do backgrounds receive four more years of education than do children from poor backgrounds. Since a person's occupation and future income usually depend on the length of time he or she has stayed in school, the additional education middle-class children receive assures that they will get better positions in the future.

---

[27] It should be noted that most studies of children's political attitudes derive from studies of white middle-class children. The few studies based on children from other backgrounds are not conclusive.

[28] Gabriel Almond and Sidney Verba, *The Civic Culture* (Boston, 1965), p. 64.

[29] Samuel Bowles, "Unequal Education and the Reproduction of the Hierarchical Division of Labor," in Richard C. Edwards, Michael Reich, and Thomas E. Weisskopf, eds., *The Capitalist System* (Englewood Cliffs, N.J., 1972), pp. 218–19.

36   CREATION OF CONSCIOUSNESS

Thus, the class structure is reproduced from one generation to the next.

Particularly important is the question of higher education. The expansion of college enrollment has been dramatic. In 1935, 12 percent of all college-age youths were in college; in 1970, the comparable figure was 40 percent.[30] Ten million youths are presently attending institutions of higher education. Yet this expansion and the upgrading of employers' educational requirements may not signify an upgrading of jobs. Many jobs that formerly required only a high-school diploma now demand a college degree. Many students graduating from college face an uncertain future due to the lack of sufficient jobs requiring advanced training.

Moreover, college attendance still depends less on ability than on parental income. In 1967, only 20 percent of high-school graduates from poor economic backgrounds enrolled in college compared to 87 percent of graduates from well-to-do backgrounds.[31] Among children of equal IQ or academic achievements, those from well-to-do backgrounds stand a far better chance of attending college. Statistical analyses by Samuel Bowles and Herbert Gintis suggest that social-class background and the number of years spent in school (which is also related to social class) count for more than IQ in explaining later economic success.

Nor, despite the rise in the average amount of schooling, is access to education becoming more egalitarian. The amount of schooling a student obtains in the present period is as closely tied to his or her social background as was the case a half century ago. The generalization that emerges from the research conducted by Bowles and Gintis is that it is better to be born rich than smart. Equal opportunity in education is largely a myth.

Yet the myth of equal educational opportunity serves an important political purpose within the dominant ideology: it "demonstrates" to those who do not secure good positions that they do not deserve them. Political theorist John Schaar has suggested that the belief in equal educational opportunity

> breaks up solidaristic opposition to existing conditions of inequality by holding out to the ablest and most ambitious members of the disadvantaged groups the enticing prospect of rising from their

---

[30] Daniel Bell, *The Coming of Post-Industrial Society* (New York, 1973), p. 318.
[31] Bowles, p. 224. This section draws on the excellent research of Samuel Bowles and Herbert Gintis, *Schooling in Capitalist America: Educational Reform and the Contradictions of Economic Life* (New York, 1976).

lowly state into a more prosperous condition. The rules of the game remain the same: the fundamental character of the social-economic system is unaltered. All that happens is that individuals are given the chance to struggle up the social ladder, change their position on it, and step on the fingers of those beneath them.[32]

The Consciousness Industry

The media are an influential means of communicating dominant ideology among adults: nine American homes in ten have at least one television receiver. The daily circulation of American newspapers is sixty-seven million. Each night over fifty million American families watch television network news. On the whole, television is quite timid in its criticism of prevailing arrangements and reluctant to question the official ideology. One reason lies in the fact that, through government licensing, control over most of the air waves—a community resource as public as air and water—is granted to private business to use for a profit.

Television and radio networks and local stations are corporate behemoths. NBC is owned by the Radio Corporation of America, the twentieth largest industrial corporation in the United States. CBS and ABC, which also rank among the few hundred largest corporations, are immense communications empires; each controls record companies, motion picture studios, movie theaters, and publishing companies. All three networks have major Pentagon contracts for radar, electronics, and communication equipment. As one student of television has pointed out:

> Since the controllers of the broadcast media, generally, represent corporate and business orientations, and find the present broadcasting and economic systems profitable, they have a special stake in the continuation of the present situation. They therefore view as disruptive, radical, subversive, or even unpatriotic, forces, materials and programs which might, however indirectly, disrupt the present arrangement. It is natural that the voices of the media should speak the language of business, for their masters are big business.[33]

Television is first and foremost a big prosperous business. The television stations in the fifty most populous markets average 36

---

[32] John H. Schaar, "Equality and Opportunity, and Beyond," in Herbert G. Reid, *Up the Mainstream: A Critique of Ideology in American Politics and Everyday Life* (New York, 1974), p. 240.
[33] Harry J. Skornia, *Television and the News: A Critical Appraisal* (Palo Alto, Calif., 1968), p. 70.

percent profit on gross revenues and a rate of return on capital as high as 200 to 300 percent. Thus, each year a television station may earn several times what its broadcasting equipment and other capital are worth.[34]

Not only is television big business but it is also dependent on the advertising dollar of big business for its profits. Four billion dollars each year is paid by corporate advertisers to television stations. The networks generally follow the adage: don't bite the hand that feeds you. Thus, the desire to please corporate sponsors makes for a system of informal private censorship.

Television news   The media present a hidden message very different from their official attitude of "let the chips fall where they may." The point can be illustrated by an analysis of television news, which, according to polls, is the news medium attracting the widest following and greatest confidence. Television news presents distant activities with a clarity and drama no scholarly analysis or newspaper can match. But television news has characteristics that inhibit reflection and analysis. First, the quantity of information that can be presented is limited: fewer words are spoken during a half-hour news telecast than are printed on one page of a daily newspaper. Television compresses items, presents them in rapid-fire thirty-second sequences, and thus is forced to oversimplify.

Second, television news is superficial. News items focus on the unusual, anecdotal, and photogenic, no amount of which is sufficient to provide a basis for public awareness or knowledge of critical issues. "In the news land of television," communications specialist Harry Skornia notes, "where the showman is king, the news is expected to entertain rather than primarily to inform."[35] A spectacular mine disaster, airplane crash, or traffic accident gets prominent coverage; but the day-to-day conditions that make work unrewarding, difficult, and dangerous generally go unreported.

The media thus shape reality as much as they reflect it. Each evening, CBS anchorman Walter Cronkite ends his newscast with, "That's the way it was." But that's not the only version or the truest version of the day's political events. A more accurate closing would be, "That's the way the CBS news staff decided it was."

---

[34] Ronald H. Coase, "The Economics of Broadcasting and Public Policy," in Paul W. MacAvry, ed., *The Crisis of the Regulatory Commissions: An Introduction to a Current Issue of Public Policy* (New York, 1970), p. 95.
[35] Skornia, p. 29.

Journalist Edward Epstein asks, "Why, a couple of years ago, did ecology stories come into favor while black-militant stories seemed to die out? It is impossible to say how new categories of news emerge."[36] It is a commonplace that bias in news presentation is unavoidable. Among the myriad of events that occur each day, only a few items will be selected for presentation in a newscast. Moreover, the same event can be presented in as many different ways as there are points of view. What kind of bias shapes television news in America?

It should come as no surprise that the bias underlying television newscasts is that of the dominant ideology. Political scientist Robert Dahl points out, "The amount of time and space devoted by the mass media to views openly hostile to the prevailing ideology is negligible. . . . Hence the general effect of the mass media is to reinforce the existing institutions and ideology."[37]

Governmental pressure also influences networks and stations to stay within the dominant ideology. The government has a potent weapon to brandish against radio and television broadcasters through the authority of the Federal Communications Commission (FCC) to grant, renew, or refuse to renew broadcast franchises and issue broadcast regulations. Although the FCC is prohibited from exercising censorship of news broadcasts, the government's life-and-death hold over television and radio broadcasters makes them especially careful not to antagonize the government. Self-censorship has the same effect as official censorship.

Entertainment: the hidden political message   In terms of prime time, total hours of programming, and (probably) the impact of television on political attitudes, entertainment far outweighs news in importance. Entertainment programming provides even greater support to dominant values. The political impact of entertainment is heightened because the distinction between fact and fiction is often masked in television: much entertainment consists of "real life" serials purportedly based on "actual cases from the files of" the New York City or Los Angeles police departments, or a particular hospital or law firm. No effort is spared to make the presentation appear true to life—uniforms, surround-

---

[36] Edward Jay Epstein, "The Selection of Reality," *The New Yorker*, March 3, 1973, p. 52.
[37] Robert Dahl, *Political Opposition in Western Democracies* (New Haven, Conn., 1966), pp. 47–48.

ings, and professional jargon all convey the impression that the program is an accurate reflection of reality.

In fact, entertainment programs glamorize and slant reality. Authorities are usually warm, concerned, and sincere people attempting to help the community. Although facing manifold difficulties, they usually manage to come out on top. In the strange world of television, crimes never go unsolved, patients rarely die, and defendants are almost never convicted of crimes they did not commit. As for those at the bottom, they are beset by problems, but none so great that—thanks to the good will of authorities—they cannot be solved within their half hour of allotted television time. The possibility of rebellion against the status quo is never evoked, except by a radical, a hippy, or a militant black—whose harebrained schemes are proved wrong by the patient efforts of wise moderate authorities. Even more than in news broadcasts, the message of entertainment programs is that there is no reason for fundamental change, since dominant institutions are responsive to individual grievances—and serious group grievances of class and race do not exist. (The fact that only 1 percent of the nation's radio and television stations are controlled by ethnic minorities helps explain the inaccurate portrayal of black and other minority groups by the media.)

Advertising   Perhaps television's greatest impact is through advertising—the reason why commercial broadcasters are in business in the first place. Like entertainment, advertising describes a world that does not exist. Automobile ads portray their wares in the tranquil setting of country lanes and green fields. One would never know that automobiles cause traffic jams, fatal accidents, and pollution.

Advertising oversimplifies and stereotypes the world. A woman's chief cares are dirty dishes, floors, and shirt collars; preparing meals for her children and husband; and looking like a model. Blacks are smiling, cheerful, and middle class—just like white Americans. True, many television ads are replete with anxiety—pharmaceutical companies see to that. But sleeplessness, indigestion, headaches, nervous tension, anger—the difficulties that afflict Americans living in the stressful conditions of corporate capitalism—soon vanish after swallowing pills thoughtfully provided (at exorbitant prices because of the high cost of advertising) by the American drug industry.

Consistent with the dominant ideology, television advertising suggests that the answer to one's problems is to be found in material goods—political change is never the answer. Thus, you have no friends? Use our mouthwash or deodorant. Fed up with your job? Sneak a week in the Caribbean. Unable to pay your bills? "Consolidate" your debts with a loan or a credit card. The advertising political parties sponsor at election time provides an exact parallel to this approach. Want to solve the country's problems? Vote for our party and everything will be fine.

Television advertising begins to have an impact early in life—children no longer sing nursery rhymes, they sing Kellogg's Frosted Flakes jingles. Children log more time watching television than they spend in school. An average child sees seventy television commercials a day—25,000 each year.[38]

The constant barrage of television advertising can be considered political propaganda that infects American culture with materialism, competitiveness, a manipulative attitude toward one's own body and toward others, and an acceptance of corporate capitalism.

The Government as Socializer

Government officials at all levels—from the president to the local police officer—represent an important socializing influence. Government does not simply reflect and respond to public opinion, as the dominant imagery of procedural democracy suggests. Instead, government is constantly concerned with shaping and manipulating public opinion. A presidential press conference is better understood as an attempt to build support for the president's policies than an exercise in clarification. A screaming police car is delivering a symbolic message: opposition to authorities brings quick reprisal.

Among the government's major concerns are how to package its image, manage the news, subdue political opinion, and suppress dissent. For government officials, according to one observer, "Public opinion is simply one more problem that demands skillful management."[39] To this end, the federal government earmarks about $400 million each year to cover public information activities—double the entire amount spent for newsgathering by the two major wire services (AP and UPI), the ten largest newspa-

[38] *New York Times*, May 12, 1974.
[39] Richard J. Barnet, *Roots of War* (New York, 1972), p. 267.

pers in the country, and the three major television networks.[40]

By changing people's perception of reality rather than the reality itself, the actual adjustments that might erode authorities' power need not be carried out. When a mine caves in, the government expresses sympathy for the victims and sponsors an "investigation"—which soothes public distress but often does not require owners to improve safety conditions. When a group's discontent boils over into actual protest, the president appoints a "blue ribbon" study commission of "distinguished citizens"—a symbolic gesture that takes the place of meeting the group's demands. In recent years, official commissions have been appointed to study problems of youth, campus disorders, aging, urban discontent, and violence. The recommendations of these commissions either are politically "safe" (which is to be expected, given the composition of the panels) or, in the rare event they require substantial reform, are ignored by the government.

The extent of the government's attempt to harness symbols to its own ends can be savored merely by enumerating terms used in official parlance: *urban renewal, the war on poverty, Office of Economic Opportunity, the independent regulatory commissions, and the Department of Defense.* Their reality is very different from the implied meaning. For example, the war on poverty mainly benefited not the poor but professional welfare bureaucrats, scholars carrying out urban research, and (above all) local business people—physicians benefiting from medicare and medicaid, slum landlords who end up with a high proportion of welfare money, and road contractors who received much of the appropriations for Appalachia. And one could never tell from its title that the Department of Defense is among the foremost forces for militarism in the world.[41]

The institutions and procedures of democracy, notably political parties and elections, deliver the dominant ideological message that established arrangements are freely chosen by American citizens. Political scientist Dan Nimmo suggests that election "campaigns are a significant form of symbolic reassurance contributing to the stability of democratic regimes. . . . By voting we acquire the feeling that we as citizens are participating in governing the

[40] William Rivers and Wilbur Schramm, *Responsibility in Mass Communications* (New York, 1969), p. 97.
[41] See Murray Edelman, *The Symbolic Uses of Politics* (Urbana, Ill., 1964), and *Politics as Symbolic Action* (Chicago, 1971).

political system."[42] Thus, the normal functioning of democratic institutions is probably more influential in strengthening dominant values than any possible conspiracy by political authorities.

Schools, the media, and government have been analyzed in detail because they are the most important institutions through which dominant values are communicated to the population. However, *all* institutions in the United States that do not challenge existing structural arrangements can be considered as socializing instruments of dominant values. Socialization occurs on the job and in the armed forces, where hierarchy and authoritarian values predominate.

The ability of schools, media, and government to shape people's political consciousness should not be exaggerated, however. The complex process by which individuals and groups develop political attitudes cannot be reduced to a simple formula. People are not passive agents, easily manipulated. Children display a healthy suspicion of schools and teachers. And citizens frequently distrust or ignore what they are told by politicians and television. People learn not only from dominant socializing institutions but from their daily experience under capitalism: from the tedium of work and school, the deterioration of neighborhoods, and the commercialism paraded in the media. As a result, there is a gap between most people's views and the "official" ideology.

Cynicism is a common response in the United States to this situation. Cynicism represents an attempt to keep an arm's length away from the false promises of the dominant ideology. But, if it represents less than fervent support for existing arrangements, it does not challenge dominant institutions in an effective manner. Ultimately, in fact, cynicism provides indirect support for the dominant ideology since it accepts that things cannot be much different than they are.

The Decline of the Dominant Ideology

In the 1970s, the dominant ideology has come under severe challenge—a challenge that will continue into the 1980s. A constant theme of this book will be the current crisis of dominant American institutions. This crisis is reflected in the ideological sphere by popular questioning of the four major elements of the dominant ideology reviewed earlier.

[42] Dan Nimmo, *The Political Persuaders* (Englewood Cliffs, N.J., 1970), pp. 5–7.

The capitalist economies of Western Europe, the United States, and Japan are in severe difficulty. There has been an abrupt end to the wave of prosperity originating after the Second World War. Capitalist economic institutions can no longer guarantee ever-higher standards of living to most workers and are less able to attract support on the basis of their technological performance. Generations of capitalist production and technological advances have led straight to high prices, unemployment, depleted resources, devastated urban and rural areas, and pollution.

In the political sphere, the dominant ideology is less able to attract support through an appeal to procedural democratic values. Patriotism has become a hollow word for many Americans following both the disastrous invasion of Indochina during the 1960s and early 1970s as well as the revelations of government wrongdoing covered up in the name of patriotism and national security. Further, as government has become more active in trying to assure capitalist prosperity, it has been held responsible for economic crisis.

The overall result has been a sharp rise in the number of Americans questioning the dominant ideology. Even the dry statistics of public-opinion polls are eloquent. Between 1966 and 1972, the proportion of Americans agreeing with the statement: "People who run the country don't care what happens to people such as myself," went from 26 percent to 50 percent.[43] In 1964, one-fifth of the population said that government could not be trusted to do what is right all the time; in 1973, the proportion of the population expressing this opinion was over three-fifths.[44] In 1964, 28 percent of the electorate felt government helped special interests more than general interests; by 1973, two-thirds of the electorate were in this category.[45] Among college youth, 37 percent agreed in 1969 that "big business needs reform or elimination"; four years later, 54 percent agreed with this statement.[46] A Gallup poll reported that the proportion of Americans "dissatisfied with the way this nation is being governed" went from 54 to 66 percent between 1971 and 1973.[47]

[43] Louis Harris, *The Anguish of Change* (New York, 1973), p. 10, and unpublished data from Harris.
[44] Norman H. Nie, Sidney Verba, and John R. Petrocik, *The Changing American Voter* (Cambridge, Mass., 1976), p. 278.
[45] *Ibid.*
[46] Daniel Yankelovich, Inc., poll reported in *New York Times*, May 26, 1974.
[47] *New York Times*, October 14, 1973.

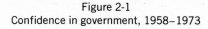

Figure 2-1
Confidence in government, 1958–1973

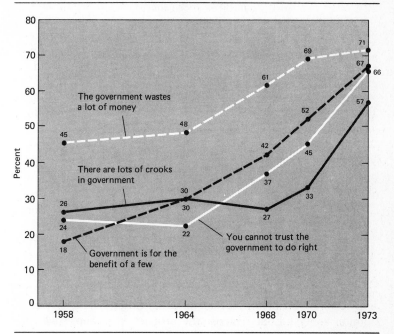

Source: Norman H. Nie, Sidney Verba, and John R. Petrocik, *The Changing American Voter* (Cambridge, Mass., Harvard University Press, 1976), p. 278. Copyright © 1976 by the Twentieth Century Fund.

The general drop in confidence accorded established leaders can be seen from the following trend: whereas in 1966, a majority of Americans expressed high confidence in five out of twelve leadership groups; by 1977 not one of the twelve groups attracted the confidence of a majority of Americans.[48] (See Table 2–1.)

That Americans are not quite as trustful of their leaders can also be seen from the fact that nearly half of those who were questioned in a poll agreed that "most political parties care only about winning elections and nothing more," and a majority agreed that "most politicians are looking out for themselves above all else" and that "most politicians are bought off by some private interests."[49] Such feelings have led to an increased sense of aliena-

[48] Harris, p. 12, and *The Harris Survey*, March 14, 1977.
[49] Herbert McClosky, "Consensus and Ideology in American Politics," *American Political Science Review* 58 (June 1964): 361–82.

Table 2-1
Drop in confidence for leadership groups and institutions
(among American adults)

Have "great deal" of confidence in people in charge of running:	Feb. 1966 %	Sept. 1973 %	Feb. 1977 %
Medicine	73	57	43
Major companies	55	29	20
The military	62	40	27
Higher education	61	44	37
Organized religion	41	36	29
U.S. Supreme Court	50	33	29
Executive branch of government	41	19	23
Congress	42	29	17
The press	29	30	18
Television news	25	41	28
Organized labor	22	20	14
Advertising agencies	21	11	7

Source: Louis Harris, *The Harris Survey*, March 14, 1977. Used by permission.

tion from government. According to a scale devised by public-opinion analyst Louis Harris, the proportion of those who felt alienated increased from 34 to 46 percent between 1966 and 1972. As one might expect, satisfaction is highly correlated with income: in 1972, only 30 percent of those with incomes of $15,000 or more felt alienated compared to 63 percent of those with incomes below $5,000.

The Right Turn in the Dominant Ideology

How have those supporting the dominant ideology attempted to adapt to the new conditions of economic crisis and political challenge? The Trilateral Commission is one of the groups trying to reshape the dominant ideology. Founded in 1973 by David Rockefeller, Chairman of Chase Manhattan Bank, the commission is composed of political officials, corporate executives, and professors from the United States, Western Europe, and Japan. Although formally a private organization, the commission is a more powerful and authoritative policymaking body for the capitalist world than most government agencies. For example, among the American members of the commission when it was created were a little-known Georgia governor named Jimmy Carter and Senator Walter Mondale.

The commission has attempted to reduce conflicts among capitalist nations as well as between the industrialized capitalist world and Third World nations. It analyzed the crisis of the dominant ideology within capitalist democracies in a report entitled *The Crisis of Democracy*.[50]

The Crisis of Democracy sees the major problem as a decline in governmental authority, due to the reduced "legitimacy of hierarchy, coercion, discipline, secrecy, and deception [by government]. . . ."[51] The problem has been compounded by a surge in democratic participation. Does the commission welcome the increase in political participation, more intense commitment to the "democratic and egalitarian values of the American creed," and increased vitality of democracy?[52] Quite the contrary: this is the very problem that it believes must be alleviated. The ultimate danger, the report asserts, comes not from external aggression or internal subversion but from "the internal dynamics of democracy itself. . . ."[53]

The remedy, according to the authors of the report, is "a greater degree of moderation in the practice of democracy," and "limits to the indefinite extension of political democracy."[54] One of the aims of the commission is to reconstruct a dominant ideology in the United States that legitimates a roll back in democracy and an increase in government repression. The commission justifies the principle of democratic participation while calling for its restriction in practice. Democracy is fine as a means of legitimation on condition that it is not truly practiced.

It is still an open question whether the attempt will succeed to reshape dominant values by curtailing the commitment to democracy. This issue will be analyzed in the last chapter.

---

[50] The Trilateral Commission, *The Crisis of Democracy* (New York, 1975). Although the report was not officially approved by the entire commission, it provides a good indication of the commission's search for a new ideological direction.
[51] *Ibid.*, p. 93.
[52] *Ibid.*, p. 112.
[53] *Ibid.*, p. 115.
[54] *Ibid.*, pp. 113, 115.

THE ACCOMMODATIVE IDEOLOGY

The accommodative ideology generally accepts dominant values as a guide but points to their shortcomings in practice. For example, capitalist production is faulted for its inefficiencies and hazards; political institutions are criticized for falling under the control of private interests. But the goal of the accommodative ideology is to eliminate these difficulties while preserving the overall system of corporate production and procedural democracy. The accommodative ideology may thus act as a safety valve for discontent, thereby strengthening dominant institutions and the dominant ideology in the long run.

Yet the accommodative ideology, when extended and deepened in its critical bite and made part of an ongoing movement for change, can lead to a more wide-ranging challenge. It may thus serve as a bridge toward a radical perspective. However, whether the accommodative approach leads backward to a dominant perspective or forward to a radical perspective cannot be answered in the abstract. Much depends on whether accommodative reforms appease discontented groups and encourage resignation to the political status quo, or help stimulate a movement for wider political change.

The three institutions that disseminate the dominant ideology may also play a limited role in fostering accommodative values. Schools may expand students' horizons, encourage the sharpening of critical skills, and provide access to materials that question the dominant ideology. The media thrive on controversy, dissent, and exposure of official wrongdoing. For example, newspapers were influential in exposing Richard Nixon's deception in the Watergate affair—exposure that led to his resignation in 1974. Government officials, too, may act in an accommodative mode, especially if they have been elected as the result of mobilization by aggrieved groups.

There are also other institutions that may provide support for the accommodative message. Most foundations, for example, provide financial support for politically safe activities, including cultural affairs (orchestras, museums, opera companies), medical research, and education. However, some foundation support goes for accommodative activity. Notable in this regard is the Ford Foundation, the country's largest foundation, which has sponsored voter-registration drives aimed at expanding the number of black voters in the South, and school decentralization and preschool programs that provide benefits for racial minorities and the poor. The Ford Foundation illustrates the thin line that separates the dominant and accommodative ideologies. By attempting to anticipate and identify problems, publicize them, and propose new alternatives, the Ford Foundation has sometimes been criticized for engaging in controversial activities. Yet the aim of this accommodative activity is to devise reforms to make the system work better. Political scientist Jeffrey M. Berry studied Washington-based groups who claimed to represent public interests such as environmental action groups. He found that these groups had received large contributions from the Ford Foundation and he noted, "The Ford Foundation's generosity reflects a phase in its larger philanthropic effort to encourage social change. . . . Through its financial contributions, the Ford Foundation has not only directed political activism into meaningful channels 'within the system,' but has also helped legitimize interest groups as beneficial components of the governmental process."[55] Far from undermining established arrangements, the ultimate effect is probably to strengthen them.

Groups such as the American Civil Liberties Union, the National Association for the Advancement of Colored People, the Americans for Democratic Action, Ralph Nader's various organizations, Friends of the Earth, Common Cause, and organized labor (the AFL–CIO) often focus criticism on particular problems, voice specific grievances, and educate many to question the dominant ideology.

But protest directed at particular issues and criticism of prevailing arrangements within the United States are mostly within the dominant or accommodative mode. Newspaper and television accounts question specific wrongdoing, but the private ownership of the media makes a radical critique unlikely. Universities permit students and faculty to enjoy freedom of thought—so long as it remains "responsible" and does not threaten to spill over into disruptive action. Foundations and public-interest groups mute their criticism for fear of jeopardizing their financial support and tax status.

Working-class protest may have an accommodative bite, es-

[55] Jeffrey M. Berry, *Lobbying for the People: The Political Behavior of Public Interest Groups* (Princeton, N.J., 1977), p. 73.

pecially when it becomes militant and challenges existing institutions. A good example of this pattern was a nationwide coalminers strike in the winter of 1977 that lasted more than three months, despite the pleas by President Carter and union leaders to return to work.

The ecology movement has mounted extensive protests in recent years to oppose nuclear power plants. For example, during the summer of 1977, one thousand protesters were arrested in a demonstration at Seabrook, New Hampshire. The tactics of civil disobedience marked this as an accommodative challenge.

A series of segmented protests by individual groups provides the seeds for a radical movement, but it does not by itself constitute such a movement. Unless the accommodative ideology enlarges its perspective to include a structural critique, dominant values and institutions are not likely to be shaken. In fact, the most likely result is that they will be strengthened. The dominant ideology and institutions in the United States have displayed a remarkable ability in the past to absorb and coopt protest.

In other capitalist democracies, a broadly based powerful socialist movement has prevented the absorption of accommodative protest by connecting specific grievances to a general analysis and strategy for change. The absence of such a movement in the United States probably means that for the foreseeable future protest will remain confined to accommodative channels.

THE RADICAL IDEOLOGY IN
HISTORICAL PERSPECTIVE

Compared to countries in Western Europe, a sustained radical movement and ideology are weakly represented in the United States. Some of the reasons are discussed in later chapters. The lack of a feudal past and the widespread distribution of property in the United States made for a more fluid social structure. With the notable exception of permanently suppressed black and ethnic minorities, Americans generally calculated that social betterment could come through efforts to change their individual situation rather than the whole political and economic system.

What would be a radical ideology appropriate for the United

States? For reasons to be discussed in the conclusion, a socialist perspective is the major radical ideology offering an alternative to capitalism. Other proposals for radical change promote the claims of particular groups; only socialism promotes the interests of the broad working majority. This entire book attempts to provide a radical critique of existing arrangements; the conclusion will suggest how American society might be reorganized in a socialist manner.

The radical ideology links inequality and injustice in the United States to the tension between capitalist production and procedural democracy. It argues that the dominant ideology is inaccurate, self-serving for the privileged groups who disseminate it, and opposed to the interests of most Americans. The accommodative ideology risks strengthening the very system that causes inequality and injustice. The radical ideology argues that reforms should not be rejected out of hand but neither should they be accepted uncritically; instead, as stated earlier, the standard for judgment should be whether or not such reforms contribute to mobilizing a broad movement for deeper change.

Despite their relative weakness, the radical ideology and movements have not been absent from the American past. Three recent periods can be identified when radical movements began to emerge. In all three cases, authorities reacted by using repression at variance with procedural democracy. Authorities may tolerate dissent within the accommodative perspective (although even this is far from certain), but when criticism of prevailing arrangements takes on a radical hue, authorities try to crush the emerging movement.

The Populist and Socialist movements prior to the First World War presented radical critiques of the growing power of corporations. Both movements offered intelligent analyses and feasible alternatives. Both attracted widespread support and elected candidates to political office. (In the first decades of the twentieth century, the Socialist party elected eighty state legislators and mayors in a number of cities, including Milwaukee, Wisconsin; Schenectady, New York; and Butte, Montana.) Moreover, the Socialist party opposed United States entry into the First World War in the name of pacifism, antimilitarism, and anticapitalism. As the only organized opposition to the war, it attracted further support.

The Socialist party was soon made the target of government

retaliation under the Espionage Act of 1917. The government declared many Socialist publications illegal and refused them the use of the mails. It illegally tapped the telephones of Socialist party leaders, expelled from the country aliens who were party members, and imprisoned Socialist editors and party leaders (most notably Eugene Debs, the party's candidate for president). As with later attacks on opposition movements, the government used an arsenal of illegal procedures: police surveillance and violence, judicial repression, and the passage of laws designed to trap opposition members (in violation of the constitutional prohibition on bills of attainder). The government's counterattack was successful and, at a critical juncture—during the period of corporate consolidation—a potentially effective opposition to the corporate complex was shattered.[56]

During the depression of the 1930s, when the country was plagued by economic stagnation, widespread unemployment, and poverty, a number of radical opposition movements again began to develop, including the Socialist party, the Communist party, and others. The threat was met first by New Deal welfare programs for the poor, which undercut the opposition and helped save capitalism. Later, during the Second World War and the 1940s and 1950s, nationalism, patriotism, and loyalty were used against the left. A "red scare" was instituted in schools, government, media, and industry, partly at the instigation in the late 1940s of Senator Joseph McCarthy of Wisconsin (hence the term *McCarthyism* often used to characterize the period). Government and private "loyalty" programs were established for the purpose of denying jobs to suspected critics of American institutions. The threat of bolshevism and the Soviet Union was used to suppress opposition within the United States, and, for generations, dissent in America was equated with a lack of patriotism.

The 1960s represent the third period containing the seeds of a radical movement. Many subordinate groups engaged in protest—blacks, chicanos and other Spanish-speaking groups, American Indians, women, homosexuals, and students. The demands voiced by a host of individual groups often remained within the accommodationist ideology. Groups attempted to improve their own status without confronting more generalized patterns of inequality.

[56] James Weinstein, *The Decline of Socialism in America, 1912–1925* (New York, 1967).

Yet a particular group's criticism can take a radical turn if the focus of discontent broadens to include analysis of wider political arrangements. The antiwar movement began by criticizing the American invasion of Vietnam; but accommodationist analysis turned radical when it argued that the causes of the war were not simply the result of mistakes and miscalculations by American political leaders, but were rooted in basic internal arrangements in America (the military-industrial complex) and America's self-appointed position abroad as guardian of the status quo.

The new left was the first major opposition movement in America since the 1930s, and, according to journalist Kirkpatrick Sale, it was "the first really *homegrown* left in America."[57] It emerged from two angry accommodationist protests of the 1960s: the civil-rights movement in the beginning of the decade and the antiwar protest beginning in the mid-1960s. Among its organizational antecedents were the Student Nonviolent Coordinating Committee (SNCC), founded in 1960, which played a leading role in the civil-rights protest and organized freedom rides and sit-ins in the South; and Students for a Democratic Society (SDS), also founded in 1960, which supported teach-ins, antiwar rallies, draft resistance, campus opposition to the Vietnam war, and community control. (A related movement—black militancy—is described in Chapter 12.)

The opposition movement was extremely widespread in the late 1960s. Two hundred and forty-nine civil disturbances occurred throughout the United States in 1967. In April 1968 alone, following the assassination of Martin Luther King, Jr., there were 237.[58] In addition to black rebellion, antiwar protest reached nationwide proportions. The peace movement went far beyond the few universities that received much of the media's attention. Occupation of campuses and large-scale demonstrations occurred not only at Berkeley, Chicago, Columbia, Cornell, and Wisconsin but also at the University of Colorado, University of Kentucky, Vanderbilt, Duke, Missouri, and the University of Washington. More than half the large American universities experienced demonstrations against corporate and military recruiters on campus dur-

---

[57] Kirkpatrick Sale, *SDS* (New York, 1973), p. 8.
[58] Adam Yarmolinsky, *The Military Establishment* (New York, 1970), p. 189.

ing the fall of 1967.[59] One million students boycotted classes during an antiwar moratorium on April 26, 1968. In 1969 alone, the police were called in at over one hundred colleges.

The peak of antiwar protest occurred after the United States invasion of Cambodia in April 1970, when four-fifths of all American colleges and universities had demonstrations and five hundred universities and colleges were closed down.[60] In two campus demonstrations during May 1970—at Kent State in Ohio and at Jackson State in Mississippi—police and National Guard opened fire on striking demonstrators, killing and wounding students.

The new left of the 1960s was quite different from the "old left" of the 1930s. Members of the new left aimed to achieve large-scale changes—the end of the Vietnam war, the elimination of racist practices in America, and the overturn of corporate dominance at home and abroad. But members of the new left also sought ways to transform their own lives in the present, rather than waiting for overall changes in society. They rejected the organized, regimented, hierarchical life of corporate capitalism and many experimented with drugs, sex, and communal living styles. They sought to regain control over their own lives by stressing personal responsibility and demanding to participate in decisions that affected their everyday lives. They attempted to democratize institutions like the school, family, and local community.

In their zeal to transform the present, members of the new left had an important impact on values and political practice. The new left encouraged a freedom in personal relations and life styles. It succeeded in applying massive pressure to reduce American involvement in the Vietnam war. University links to the military-industrial complex were weakened: classified research became prohibited on many campuses, military training units were dissolved, and military recruiting was ended. President Johnson's decision not to seek a second full term in 1968 was in good part a result of the opposition to his war policies mounted by the new left and the peace movement. The new left (along with the women's movement and black militancy) was responsible for a cultural upheaval in America and a questioning of long-established values. The new left demonstrated that changes could be effected through the dedicated efforts of an opposition.

After initially being caught off guard, authorities soon responded to the opposition challenge. In *Counterrevolution and*

---

[59] Sale, p. 380.
[60] Harris, p. 219; Sale, p. 636.

Revolt, critical theorist Herbert Marcuse has described what he calls a preventive counterrevolution, waged by the government against a revolution that never occurred.[61] Official repression took a variety of forms.

Much of the anticipatory counterrevolution consisted of an attempt to smash the credibility of the radical ideology and demonstrate the superiority of the dominant ideology. Dominant institutions, including government and universities, participated in the crackdown. For example, government agencies were directed to root out opposition organizations. In May 1968, the director of the FBI directed all FBI offices to attack organizations and individuals "who spout revolution and unlawfully challenge society to obtain their demands."[62] The FBI's Cointelpro (Counterintelligence Program) was a massive fifteen-year program of subversion against domestic critics. The program "actively sought to undermine the activities of dissident political groups."[63] Cointelpro activities were directed against urban groups, Puerto Rican nationalists, leftist groups like the Socialist Workers party, and black militants. The FBI contacted employers of political critics and tried, often successfully, to get the critics fired. The FBI wiretapped the telephones and spied on the personal lives of political activists. It wrote scurrilous letters charging its opponents with sexual misconduct. It infiltrated opposition organizations to gain information to discredit the organization and foment factional strife. The *New York Times* later commented that the FBI and the CIA "seemed to have turned into instruments of a police state."[64]

Government agencies, including the FBI and intelligence units of the armed forces, compiled computerized files on fifteen million Americans. The Pentagon alone had one thousand agents assigned to domestic surveillance in the fall of 1967.[65] The FBI assigned two thousand agents to the new left, and by 1970 every college campus in the country had its own undercover FBI agent (usually posing as a student). University officials expelled student leaders who organized student protest movements. On the local level, municipal authorities created their own "red squads," with their personnel numbering 14 in Columbus, Ohio, 40 in Boston, 70

---

[61] Herbert Marcuse, *Counterrevolution and Revolt* (Boston, 1972), chapter 1.
[62] *New York Times*, December 7, 1973.
[63] *New York Times*, November 24, 1977.
[64] *New York Times*, April 30, 1978.
[65] Sale, p. 406.

in Detroit, 84 in Los Angeles, 123 in New York, and 500 in Chicago.[66]

As a result of these measures, dissent was crushed in the United States. There was an apparent return to the easygoing apathetic ways of the 1950s—illustrated on college campuses by the revival of proms, fraternities, and beer drinking. University officials encouraged these harmless practices—for the harried college president, they were infinitely preferable to a campus takeover. Other evidence that the political challenge had been quelled included the decrease in funding of government programs for the poor, the decline of black enrollments in college after their expansion in the 1960s due to black protest, and a reduction of corporate contributions to "responsible" black organizations (like the Urban League), which had been supported in the 1960s as a counterweight to radical black organizations.[67]

We can sum up and simplify what occurred in the recent past as follows: political conflict in the United States normally takes the form of competition among interest groups committed to the dominant ideology, although there is some accommodative protest as well. However, during the unusual period of the 1960s, a more basic cleavage began to develop between dominant interests and an emergent radical movement. Whereas authorities may accept or reject accommodationist demands, they always seek to destroy a radical movement.

The least costly way is through symbol manipulation— appointing a commission, controlling the media, or adopting the form but not the substance of reform (as when black lingo became popular in the media, or when Lyndon Johnson vowed that "we shall overcome"). The next step is the adoption of accommodative reforms—those that do not pose a basic threat to the alliance of corporate and government officials. In practice, authorities rarely accept even these demands—they are often diluted when applied and thus transformed into merely symbolic concessions. Nonetheless, accepting accommodative demands provides a safety valve for discontent, enlarges the constituency of the dominant, and puts authorities in a favorable light—by making them appear receptive to criticism and generous to the disadvantaged. If these gestures do not disarm the opposition, authorities take the further step of

[66] *Ibid.*, p. 544.
[67] *New York Times*, February 3, 1974.

active repression—the dark side of authorities' responsiveness to accommodationist demands.

By the end of the 1970s, aided by the withdrawal of the United States from Vietnam, the weakness of the opposition, a harsh crackdown on dissent, and the economic crisis, those in authority appear to have regained control. Yet, as we will show in the last chapter, the breakdown of control by institutions like political parties, the failure of corporate capitalism, popular disillusionment with political and corporate leaders, and the rise of sexual and racial liberation movements suggest that a potential exists for a new radical movement.

capital, labor, and government

3

capitalism as private government

On September 19, 1977, disaster struck at Youngstown, Ohio, with effects as devastating as an earthquake, flood, or hurricane. Yet this was not a natural disaster. It was the announcement by the management of the Lykes Corporation, which owned the Youngstown Sheet and Tube steel company, that it had decided to close the local steel mill.

At one stroke, 4,000 steelworkers in the area lost their jobs. One commented, "We'll just about lose it all," referring to the life his family had built during the eight years he had worked for Youngstown Sheet and Tube.[1] The effects of the closing reverberated throughout the Mahoning Valley, harming thousands of other area residents. Food, clothing, furniture, and other retail stores whose business depended on steelworkers experienced a drop in sales, which resulted in further layoffs. Schools and other public services were cut back as a result of the decline in tax revenues from the company and its employees. The blow that was dealt to the area will last for years to come.

[1] *New York Times*, September 21, 1977.

It is rare that the social effects of management decisions can be pinpointed so precisely. Yet the case of Youngstown is far from unique. In the steel industry alone, Bethlehem, Johnstown, and Conshohocken in Pennsylvania, as well as cities in New York and Ohio, have been crippled by layoffs of thousands of steelworkers. The cutback in steel production is part of larger changes going on worldwide. The abrupt slowdown of the American and other capitalist economies has reduced the demand for steel. Further, American steel plants are at a particular disadvantage: they are technologically backward, since American steel executives have been slow to introduce the latest steelmaking techniques. As a result, American steel companies are being squeezed by foreign competition, especially Japanese firms using modern methods. American steelworkers are bearing the burden of management misjudgment.

The crisis at Youngstown graphically illustrates the fundamental conflict of interest between management and workers in a capitalist society. For this reason capitalism can be considered as a system of private government.

What was the basis on which management reached its decision to close the steel mill at Youngstown? How much did it take into account the interests of workers and other community residents? It is a safe guess that the management of the Lykes Corporation decided on the basis of what would be best for the Lykes Corporation, not what would be best for workers or the community. Nor are the managers of Lykes any more greedy or villainous than other corporate executives. Marx's description of the basic rule guiding capitalist decision-making remains as true today as a century ago.

> [The capitalist] shares with the miser the passion for wealth as wealth. But that which in the miser is a mere idiosyncrasy, is, in the capitalist, the effect of the social mechanism, of which he is but one of the wheels. Moreover, the development of capitalist production makes it constantly necessary to keep increasing the amount of capital laid out in a given industrial undertaking, and competition makes the immanent laws of capitalist production to be felt by each individual capitalist, as external coercive laws. It compels him to keep constantly extending his capital, in order to preserve it, but extend it he cannot, except by means of progressive accumulation. Accumulate, accumulate! That is Moses and the prophets![2]

[2] Karl Marx, *Capital* (New York, 1967), Vol. I, pp. 592, 595.

The management of Lykes did not intend to harm the workers whose lives were disrupted by their decision. As the passage in Marx suggests, management had nearly as little choice as the workers affected by the decision. So long as they chose to be managers, they had to act like managers.

It was not the personal intentions of corporate management but the imperatives of profit-seeking in a capitalist system that dictated the decision. Following the logic of capitalism, steel company executives ignored the costs to workers, their families, and the community of closing down the steel mill. Indeed, management was forced to ignore these human costs if it was to secure maximum profits for the company. The costs were an unintended by-product of management's attempt to secure maximum profits. In the same way, the large proportion of American coalminers afflicted by black lung disease, the polluted air, water, and soil of America's natural environment, and scores of devastated American cities are by-products of the day-to-day functioning of American corporate capitalism.

The Youngstown case illustrates how the enormous power wielded by private management in a capitalist society is used to benefit companies, not communities. A *New York Times* reporter observed that executives of the Lykes Corporation

> made the decision in private the day before [it was announced]. They were under no obligation to give any notice or to assume any responsibility for the consequences in the areas from which they were drawing labor and resources. . . . Lykes was exercising a traditional and jealously guarded right of the management of American business: to be the sole determiners of when a plant should be built, expanded or closed.[3]

What was government's role in the decision? In a democracy, do not the people or their elected representatives make the important decisions that affect the whole community? The answer is: not in a capitalist democracy. Although the decision vitally affected the citizens of Youngstown, they had no say in the matter, nor did their local government, their congressional representatives, the Ohio state government, or federal officials.

Yet the crisis of the American steel industry did elicit government action. But, as described by economists Gar Alperovits and Jeff Faux, "The political response to the Youngstown layoffs has

[3] *New York Times*, December 26, 1977.

not centered on saving the town, but on saving the *steel industry*."[4] The federal government has provided steel companies with tax credits to modernize their equipment. Most of the new investment will go into "labor-saving" technology, which is another way of saying that it will go for machines, not workers. The residents of Youngstown have little to hope for from the government's efforts on behalf of the steel industry. Thanks to past struggles by labor unions, the government does provide benefits for a limited period to unemployed workers.

The Youngstown disaster illustrates in microcosm the workings of a capitalist system. This chapter explores the broad outlines of capitalism.

CAPITALISM AS A SYSTEM OF PRIVATE GOVERNMENT

Capitalism may be defined as a system in which production is privately controlled and carried on for sale and profit rather than for consumption (use). The functioning of capitalism consists of production, sales, and investment. Those who own and control the means of production—the factories, machines, and raw materials used to produce commodities for sale—set the process in motion by hiring workers to carry on the actual work of production. The aim of the capitalist in doing so is to make a profit, which can then be used for further investment and the accumulation of additional profits. Economist Paul Sweezy, following Marx, suggests that capital can be defined as self-expanding value: "Capitalism therefore can exist only if there is some way that capitalists can regularly sell their products for more money than they had to lay out to produce them."[5]

The difference between the cost of production and the sale price is profit, or surplus value. Profit derives from the fact that workers produce more value than the wages they receive for their labor (after other costs of production are subtracted).

---

[4] *New York Times*, November 3, 1977. Italics in original.
[5] Paul Sweezy, "The Present Stage of the Global Crisis of Capitalism," *Monthly Review* 29 (April 1978): 9.

The second phase of the process is the realization of profit through the sale of the commodities workers produce. Unless goods are sold, profits cannot be realized. Thus, the capitalist attempts to maximize profits by organizing production at the lowest possible cost (for example, by squeezing workers to work hard) and selling the commodities that are produced at the highest possible price.

The third phase of the capitalist production process is investment in new means of production. The penalty for failing to renew and expand the means of production is that competitors gain an edge and eventually the capitalist will be forced to close down operations (like at Youngstown). Thus, expanding production— capital accumulation and new investment—is a necessity if capitalist production is to continue.

This analysis of the capitalist system raises many questions. Why do capitalists have the legal right and the material resources to hire others to work at their direction? Why are they entitled to take the surplus created by workers? Why do most members of the society have to work for a wage or salary and follow the dictates of capitalist management? A crucial assumption underlying capitalist production is that most people do not control the means of production and are forced to work for those who do in order to earn the necessities of life. Further, capitalism requires a political framework that protects the right of capital to both hire workers and appropriate the surplus value workers create. These assumptions have pervasive consequences for the way that the community is organized. And any analysis of politics would be incomplete if it did not study the way that capitalist production is organized.

No matter how democratic the formal political institutions, the exploitation of workers is inherent in a capitalist society. Exploitation occurs through the process by which workers produce surplus value that is appropriated by capital and used to reproduce a society where the means of production are privately owned and controlled and where, in order to survive, workers are forced to enrich capital. Although these harsh facts are rarely noted, they are the daily reality of capitalist society. It is only at unusual moments, like at Youngstown, that this situation becomes painfully clear. In most cases, the inner reality of a capitalist society is obscured by the illusion (and, to some extent, the reality) of free choice and democratic government.

A fuller picture of capitalism as a system of private government can be gained by reviewing some of the rights conferred by control of capital.

Where to produce   In a capitalist system, those who own and control the means of production are free to decide the geographic location where production will be carried on. This decision is made strictly on the basis of which location will reap the greatest profits or (another way of describing the same thing) which location will minimize the costs of production and maximize sales. Among the different factors taken into account are proximity to suppliers, raw materials, and markets, as well as adequate transportation facilities.

Two factors affecting the attractiveness of plant sites are especially relevant for political analysis. One is the tax advantages and other benefits promised a company by local and state governments. Local governments bid against each other in an attempt to attract private industry, offering companies low taxes, custombuilt factories, roads, and waste treatment facilities. Who pays for these inducements? The answer is local residents, mostly workers.

The second, and more important, factor in determining a company's choice of plant location is the characteristics of workers. Companies search for areas where workers are willing to work for low wages. Wage rates and the militance of workers (for example, their readiness to strike) vary in different sections of the country. Where workers are unionized, wages are higher. A company may prefer to hire nonunion labor to keep wages low and workers divided. (However, as we will see in Chapter 5, labor unions may provide other attractive benefits to company management.) The amount management saves by paying low wages represents an additional contribution capital extracts from working people.

The Youngstown case illustrates what can happen to a community in a capitalist society, in which management is free to decide where to invest. A pattern of decisions by many corporations has nationwide consequences. Scores of companies have closed down in the Northeast and Midwest and are moving South, leaving behind a trail of blight. Many corporations have found that the wage bill is lower yet if they invest in manufacturing facilities outside the United States. (The process of multinational expansion abroad will be examined in Chapter 8.) Not only do corporations not have to pay for the damage they cause when they shut down operations in an area; the federal government provides tax breaks for new investments, which acts as an incentive for corporations to move.

But capitalism is not a static system, the same at all times and places. In other capitalist nations, working-class pressure has limited the freedom of corporate producers to close factories. For example, in France, Sweden, and West Germany, which are all capitalist nations, government approval is required before a plant can close. In addition, companies must contribute to the cost of retraining and relocating workers affected by a shutdown. These benefits provide a cushion for workers; they have been obtained as a result of sustained demands put forward by working-class movements and parties in these nations. As Chapters 5 and 6 will analyze, the absence of a working-class party in the United States puts workers at a double disadvantage.

What to produce   Investment decisions, especially major ones, made by giant corporations, determine the kinds of goods available in the society. In a capitalist society, those controlling capital are free to decide what they wish to produce. As with the choice of where production will occur, the decision about what to produce is determined on the basis of what promises to fetch the most profit. Although the situation is irrational from the standpoint of a society with vast social needs, it is rational from the standpoint of profitable investments. For example, given a highly unequal distribution of income in the United States, many Americans lack adequate housing because they cannot afford it. Consequently, the fact that there is a pressing need for decent housing does not mean that it is profitable to provide it.

The whole community is affected by the capitalist investment decision. When investment lags, then production lags, wages stagnate, and many workers are unable to find jobs. When investment booms, then production booms, jobs are plentiful, and wages rise as employers compete for workers.

How production is carried on   In a capitalist society, management has substantial control over the production process. Management decides who will be hired, promoted, and fired; the level of wages that will be offered; the length of the working day; and the kind of technology used in production. As the result of working-class struggle, culminating in government regulation of some of these questions, management is no longer wholly free. If it were, the working day would continue to be fourteen to sixteen hours long, as it was for the average steelworker as recently as the period before the First World War. More generally, there is a continual struggle between management and workers concerning control of the workplace. In a capitalist society, the workplace is not organized democratically. Workers are paid to take orders, not to exercise initiative.

The price of commodities   In a capitalist system, people acquire most goods and services by purchasing them in the market. Those owning and controlling capital are free to set the level of prices they charge. Of course, consumers are free to refuse to purchase. But this becomes a hollow right when people are dependent on capitalist production for food, energy, clothing, shelter, and other necessities. In a situation of free competition, prices are set at a level just slightly higher than the costs of production. American capitalism is organized differently: a relatively few corporations produce the bulk of what is manufactured and this enables them to charge higher prices.

What does all this mean? From the standpoint of capitalists, it means business as usual, the normal calculations of profit and loss that guide capitalist investment, production, and sales. Yet from the viewpoint of the majority, it is a system of private government in which the basic contours of the society are shaped by private business firms pursuing their self-interest. As economist Charles Lindblom points out, "Because public functions in the market [capitalist] system rest in the hands of businessmen, it follows that jobs, prices, production, growth, the standard of living, and the economic security of everyone all rest in their hands."[6]

This book attempts to study the conflict between the needs of capitalist production and the needs of the whole society, as well as the tension between the undemocratic organization of the economy and the formally democratic character of the political system. The sphere of democratic politics is limited in the United States by the capitalist organization of the economy. The most far-reaching decisions are not made by citizens on the basis of what will be best for the community but by corporate management on the basis of what will be best for the corporation. In the next section, we will review the overall characteristics of the private government exercised by corporate capitalism in the United States.

[6] Charles E. Lindblom, *Politics and Markets: The World's Political-Economic Systems* (New York, 1977), p. 172.

CORPORATE CAPITALISM

Suppose it was learned that a small group had obtained critical power in the United States. Imagine that, in a country with a population of 210,000,000, several thousand Americans— unrepresentative, not democratically chosen nor even known to most people—had control over some of the most important aspects of American life. This small group decided what kinds of products Americans would manufacture. It owned and controlled the factories in which production occurred. It not only employed but could also promote or fire a large proportion of Americans. This group produced dangerous and expensive weapons for the military. It controlled radio and television networks and deeply influenced Americans' values and attitudes. It dominated the companies that produce the automobiles, television sets, and electric appliances found in many American homes.

Because this group controlled much of the country's productive capacity, its decisions affected all Americans. Yet members of the group based their decisions not on what the country needed but on what would be profitable for the small controlling group. As a result, some Americans were saturated with a profusion of possessions, while many others could barely obtain basic necessities, such as food, housing, and medical care.

Further, this group was also able to influence political decisions. Its contributions to political parties were vital for a candidate to be nominated and elected to office. It developed close ties to Congress, the president, and government agencies. Most government policies were designed to help this group retain its favored position.

One can imagine the outcry that would greet the announcement that such a group existed. After all, its existence would not only make democratic government an illusion but would also prevent many Americans from achieving the benefits America promises.

And yet, such a group does exist. All that has been described is fact, not fiction. A convenient shorthand label for the process of production, distribution, and consumption, over which this group exerts control, is corporate capitalism. What makes it such a powerful force in America?

There are approximately twelve million economic enterprises

Table 3-1
The 20 largest industrial corporations, 1977 (ranked by sales)

Rank '77	'76	Company (Headquarters)	Sales ($000)
1	2	General Motors (Detroit)	54,961,300
2	1	Exxon (New York)	54,126,219 *
3	3	Ford Motor (Dearborn, Mich.)	37,841,500
4	5	Mobil (New York)	32,125,828 *
5	4	Texaco (White Plains, N.Y.)	27,920,499
6	6	Standard Oil of California (San Francisco)	20,917,331
7	8	International Business Machines (Armonk, N.Y.)	18,133,184
8	7	Gulf Oil (Pittsburgh)	17,840,000*
9	9	General Electric (Fairfield, Conn.)	17,518,600
10	10	Chrysler (Highland Park, Mich.)	16,708,300
11	11	International Tel. & Tel. (New York)	13,145,664
12	12	Standard Oil (Ind.) (Chicago)	13,019,939 *
13	15	Atlantic Richfield (Los Angeles)	10,969,091
14	13	Shell Oil (Houston)	10,112,062 *
15	14	U.S. Steel (Pittsburgh)	9,609,900
16	16	E. I. du Pont de Nemours (Wilmington, Del.)	9,434,800
17	17	Continental Oil (Stamford, Conn.)	8,700,317
18	18	Western Electric (New York)	8,134,604
19	20	Tenneco (Houston)	7,440,300
20	19	Procter & Gamble (Cincinnati)	7,284,255
		Total	**395,943,963**
		Total, 500 largest industrial corporations	**1,086,609,167**

* Does not include excise taxes.
** Reflects a credit.
† Average for the year.

Source: *Fortune*, May 8, 1978, pp. 240–41. Reprinted by special permission from the

in the United States, from small family farms and shoe repair shops to the United States Steel Corporation and Gulf Oil Corporation. In terms of value, their individual net worth ranges from several hundred dollars to the $90 billion in assets controlled by American Telephone and Telegraph (AT&T).

One can distinguish between two sectors of private production: corporate capital, which includes the largest mining and

Assets ($000)	Rank	Net income ($000)	Rank	Employees Number	Rank
26,658,300	2	3,337,500	1	797,000 †	1
38,453,336	1	2,422,964	3	127,000 †	4
19,241,300	4	1,672,800	4	479,300 †	2
20,575,967	3	1,004,670	8	200,700	7
18,926,026	6	930,789	9	70,646	37
14,822,347	7	1,016,360	6	38,283	105
18,978,445	5	2,719,414	2	310,155	5
14,225,000	8	752,000	10	59,400	51
13,696,800	9	1,088,200	5	384,000 †	8
7,668,200	18	163,200 **	66	250,833 †	6
12,285,522	11	550,667	15	375,000	4
12,884,286	10	1,011,575	7	46,667	79
11,119,012	12	701,515	12	51,666	66
8,876,754	14	735,094	11	33,548	124
9,914,400	13	137,900	84	165,845 †	8
7,430,600	19	545,100	16	131,317	13
6,625,229	21	380,626	26	43,141	90
5,875,543	23	490,076	18	162,000	9
8,278,300	15	426,900	21	93,000	25
4,487,186	31	461,463	19	53,700	58
281,022,553		**20,548,813**		**3,873,201**	
803,698,430		**52,558,835**		**15,298,292**	

1978 Fortune Directory; © 1978 Time Inc.

manufacturing corporations, banks, retail chain stores, insurance companies, utilities, television networks, and law firms; and small-scale capital, which includes restaurants, local newspapers, clothing stores, small construction companies, and small manufacturers (such as garment factories). In terms of the number of workers employed, the two sectors are nearly equal. However, that is about all they have in common. Productive resources are owned, organized, and managed very differently in the two sectors: the sphere of corporate capital is far more productive, centralized, and powerful than the sphere of small-scale capital. Measured by the ability to shape the major decisions regarding the organization of society and the distribution of benefits, corporate capital far outdistances small-scale capital.

Some idea of the power concentrated within the corporate sector can be conveyed by the following figures. Among the over 400,000 manufacturing concerns in the United States, a fortunate few—about 200—have assets worth over $1 billion. They are the industrial giants of America, whose names are household words: Ford, General Electric (GE), Exxon, International Business Machines (IBM), Chrysler. These corporations are immense individually; their combined worth and power are staggering. The top 500 corporations control three-quarters of all industrial assets in the United States—leaving the remaining one-quarter to the other 400,000 firms. The same 500 corporations had $1.1 trillion in sales in 1977—over half the total sales of the entire American economy.

Yet, even within the top group of 500 there are further inequalities between the biggest and smallest corporations: the largest (General Motors—GM) had sales in 1977 that were 150 times greater than the smallest corporation (McCormick). The 200 largest corporations control nearly two-thirds of all manufacturing assets in the United States, and the top 10 alone account for about one-seventh of America's total annual Gross National Product (GNP).

These statistics indicate the overall dimensions of corporate capitalism. Some additional important features of corporate capitalism include:

Size   The largest corporations, which dominate production in the United States, are immense. For example, General Motors employs 800,000 people, has assets of $27 billion, annual sales that are twice as great, and profits exceeding $3 billion. General Electric employs over 400,000 workers in 240 factories in over 20 countries. GE produces 230,000 different products.[7] The output of GE, GM, and Exxon exceeds the total national product of hefty countries like Austria, Denmark, or Yugoslavia.

[7] William Serrin, *The Company and the Union: The Civilized Relationship of the General Motors Corporation and the United Automobile Workers* (New York, 1973), chapter 3; John Woodmansee et al., *The World of a Giant Corporation* (Seattle, Wash., 1975), p. 4.

Most of the products Americans buy, from toothpaste to automobiles, are produced by corporate capitalism. The top 500 corporations employ fifteen million workers—about two-thirds of the industrial workers and one-third of all workers in the United States.[8] Many Americans who are not directly dependent on giant corporations for their livelihood are indirectly dependent. Small manufacturers produce parts and other supplies that they sell to these corporations. Retail dealers sell and repair workers service what corporate capitalism produces. Many local retail stores, gasoline stations, bus companies, and banks would not exist were it not for the economic activity of the corporate giants. Newspapers and television stations also would not survive without the advertising revenue they receive from corporate capitalism.

A typical mammoth corporation constitutes a powerful force in American politics. Together, the few hundred largest corporations control most of the country's productive resources. The requirements of corporate capitalism are a first priority on the American political agenda.

Concentration   Economists call an industry *concentrated* if a few large firms dominate production and sales. Automobile production is one such industry. Four companies—GM, Ford, Chrysler, and American Motors—produce 95 percent of the nine million automobiles made in the United States each year. (More than half of these—about five million—are produced by GM.)

Firms in a concentrated industry behave differently than firms in a competitive industry. The critical difference is the extent of their power. In a competitive industry, many small companies compete with each other and none get a large share of the market. In a concentrated industry, firms enter into long-term arrangements with other firms to stabilize their supplies and sales. In a process known as administered prices, they informally cooperate to set prices high enough to assure profits even when demand for their products may lag. (One study found that the average rate of profit before taxes was 20 percent in concentrated industries, but only 13 percent in nonconcentrated industries.[9])

Large firms in concentrated industries have also evolved a different pattern of relationships with their employees. In contrast

---

[8] James O'Connor, *The Fiscal Crisis of the State* (New York, 1973), p. 34, footnote 7. This section owes much to O'Connor's excellent study.

[9] Howard Sherman, *Radical Political Economy: Capitalism from a Marxist Humanist Perspective* (New York, 1972), p. 108.

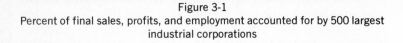

Figure 3-1
Percent of final sales, profits, and employment accounted for by 500 largest
industrial corporations

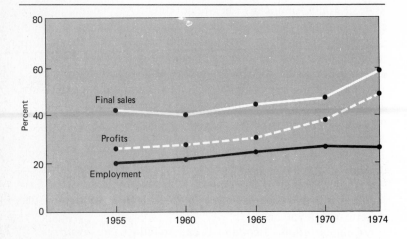

Note: Sales as percent of final sales (sales of top 500 include intermediate and foreign sales); profits as percent of all non-financial corporate profits; employment as percent of civilian labor force.

Source: *Fortune*, "The Fortune Directory of the 500 Largest Industrial Corporations," July 1956, July 1961, May 1966, May 1971, May 1974; and *Survey of Current Business*, October 1975 and 1973 Business Statistics Supplement; in Richard C. Edwards, Michael Reich, and Thomas E. Weisskopf, eds., *The Capitalist System: A Radical Analysis of American Society*, 2nd ed. (Englewood Cliffs, N.J.: Prentice-Hall, Inc.), 1978, p. 122.

to workers in competitive industries, workers in large corporations often belong to labor unions. Corporations have always tried to prevent their employees from organizing a union, since unions secure higher wages for their members. However, many corporations have come to recognize that unions may provide benefits in return for the higher wage costs they exact—which, in any case, corporations can pass along to consumers thanks to administered prices. Unions help stabilize management-employee relations— for example, they can minimize unexpected work stoppages. Corporations and unions often develop what journalist William Serrin ironically refers to as a "civilized relationship."[10]

When production becomes concentrated, in brief, control over the society's productive resources becomes centralized. Giant corporations are powerful, stable institutions, able to exer-

[10] Serrin, *op. cit.*

Figure 3-2
Percent of all manufacturing assets held by top manufacturing corporations

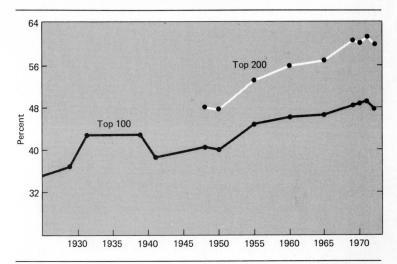

Source: Richard C. Edwards, Michael Reich, and Thomas E. Weisskopf, eds., *The Capitalist System: A Radical Analysis of American Society,* 2nd ed., © 1978, p. 133. Reprinted by permission of Prentice-Hall, Inc., Englewood Cliffs, N.J. Sources listed in original.

cise considerable control over their environment—including consumers, workers, and (as we shall see in the next chapter) government. The trend toward concentration in the American economy has been rapid. In the period from 1948 to 1968, the 200 largest corporations increased their share of total manufacturing assets in the United States from 46 to 60 percent.[11] The same proportion of sales that the top 200 firms controlled in 1950 was controlled by only half as many firms twenty years later. (As can be seen in Figure 3-2, the trend slowed during the 1970s.)

Concentration thus occurs not only within given industries but in the economy as a whole. The American economy has become nationalized, integrated, concentrated, and centralized around a cluster of privately owned industries and firms. In describing the contours of concentrated industries, we are also describing the results of private decisions about the allocation of resources in the United States.

[11] John Blair, *Economic Concentration* (New York, 1972), p. 64.

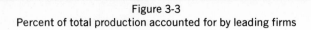

Figure 3-3
Percent of total production accounted for by leading firms

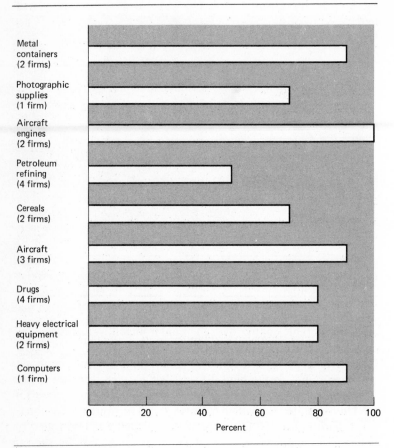

Source: William G. Shepherd, *Market Power and Economic Welfare: An Introduction* (New York: Random House, 1970), pp. 152–54. Reprinted by permission.

Expansion and contraction   Economist Douglas Dowd has pointed out, "Expansion may be seen as the essence of the capitalist *process*, as the heartbeat of capitalism."[12] One aspect of this expansion is that corporate capital has extended its control beyond the traditional spheres of industrial and mining activity.

[12] Douglas F. Dowd, *The Twisted Dream: Capitalist Development in the United States Since 1776*, 2nd ed. (Cambridge, Mass., 1977), p. 36.

WHO OWNS AMERICA?   77

Corporations have moved into the entertainment and leisure fields, including motion picture companies, hotels, travel and tour companies, and restaurants (Howard Johnson's and McDonald's, rather than the corner drugstore, now supply Americans with hamburgers). In the field of agriculture, "agricorporations" are fast replacing the family farm, centralizing the production, processing, and distribution of food. (By 1966, the 100 largest food manufacturers accounted for nearly half of all food commercially marketed.[13])

Yet the expansion of corporate capital means the contraction of job opportunities. One reason for the current high rate of unemployment is that corporate production has replaced workers with machines. As the corporate sector grows larger, there are relatively fewer jobs available. Although the corporate sector accounts for an ever-larger share of total production, it provides jobs for a dwindling share of the total labor force.

The process is illustrated by the corporate takeover of agriculture. Since 1940, as agriculture has become penetrated by corporate capital and transformed into agribusiness, the resulting mechanization has forced 20 million people off the land. Since 1950, mechanical harvesters have eliminated jobs for 2 million of the 4.3 million farm workers.[14] The remaining farmers are becoming hired hands for large agricorporations that produce farm machinery, pesticides, and fertilizers and then process the food, which is grown to their specifications. Corporations have also been moving onto the land directly. Among the nation's largest "farmers" are Boeing, Dow Chemical, and Tenneco.

WHO OWNS AMERICA'S PRIVATE GOVERNMENT?

The answer to this question begins with tracing the ownership of stock in giant corporations. In the corporate form, people who invest money receive shares in the assets or stock of the corporation. They share in the corporation's profits in proportion to the amount of stock they own. Stockholders are entitled to vote for the

[13] James Hightower, "The Case for the Family Farmer," *Washington Monthly* (September 1973), p. 28.
[14] Douglas Zoloth Foster, "Weeding Workers: How the University of California is Underwriting the Loss of 170,000 Jobs," *In These Times*, May 10–16, 1978, pp. 12–13.

board of directors of the corporation. As with profits, the number of votes stockholders get is proportional to the amount of stock they own. The board of directors chooses the corporation's top management and reviews management decisions. Since corporations control most of America's productive assets (means of production), those who control corporations are influential in deciding what America will produce and consume.

To begin with, only one family in six owns stock. Most Americans must use their income for necessities; few families have money left over to invest. In fact, through the lure of installment buying, a majority of Americans spend more than they earn. Rather than having savings to invest, they have debts to pay. Only the wealthy have the surplus necessary to purchase stock. Over half of all savings in the United States is supplied by the richest 5 percent of the society.

Even among the small group owning stock, the distribution of stock ownership is highly unequal. Two-thirds of all stockholders own less than $10,000 in stock, a negligible investment compared to what is needed to gain a voice in a large corporation. For participation in the corporation depends not only on owning stock in the corporation but on how *much* one owns: a person owning one share has one vote at the annual stockholders' meeting, while a person with one hundred shares has one hundred votes, and a person with ten thousand shares has ten thousand votes. Small stockholders are lavishly praised at the annual meeting, but they are "owners" of a corporation only in legal appearance. In reality, it requires many thousands of shares of stock in a corporation to have an *effective* voice.

Most stock is held by a tiny proportion of Americans. An examination of the upper range of the stock-owning pyramid indicates that less than one-tenth of all stockholders own 80 percent of all stock. In 1969, 1 percent of the population owned over half of all corporate stock.[15] In a nation of 210,000,000 people, the means of production are owned by a group no larger than the population of a small city.

---

[15] J. D. Smith and S. D. Franklin, "The Concentration of Wealth, 1922–1969," *American Economic Review*, May 1974, p. 166; cited in Richard C. Edwards, Michael Reich, and Thomas E. Weisskopf, eds., *The Capitalist System: A Radical Analysis of American Society*, 2nd ed. (Englewood Cliffs, N.J., 1978), p. 166.

The Professionalization of Capital

Despite their strategic position, the fabulously wealthy upper class does not rule corporate capitalism by itself. (For one thing, there just are not enough members to do so.) In recent decades, there has been a trend toward professionalizing the management of capital. The new breed of corporate managers are usually engineering or business school graduates trained to apply modern methods to furthering the search for corporate profits. Relatively anonymous bureaucrats, the new managers are quite different from the colorful magnates of an earlier era. And because they are out of the public eye, they are less likely than old-time tycoons like J. P. Morgan or John D. Rockefeller to provide a target for popular discontent. (Has anybody heard of Reginald Jones? He is chairman of GE.)

Most corporate executives, even those not in the ranks of the superwealthy, own large blocks of shares in the corporations they manage. About one-half of an executive's pay is in the form of stock bonuses and options, deferred compensation, and profit sharing rather than straight salary. (This is not to say that corporate executives do not receive handsome salaries: the country's highest-paid corporate executives have an annual salary of about $1 million.) A study of ninety-three top executives in the country's largest corporations found that nearly half owned $1 million apiece in stocks in their corporation.[16] Although this amount is not sufficient to provide a controlling interest in the corporation, it does mean that top management has similar interests to the corporation's other large stockholders.

It seems to make little difference for corporate performance whether a corporation is controlled by large stockholders, as was typical for corporations in the past, or whether, as is becoming more common, professional managers play a dominant role. A study conducted by economist Robert J. Larner compared the performance of two such groups of corporations and found little difference between the two.[17] Contrary to the view of those who have asserted that manager-controlled corporations in the modern era are more "mature," less aggressive, less interested in profits, and more interested in stability than were owner-controlled corpo-

---

[16] Robert J. Larner, "The Effect of Management-Control on the Profits of Large Corporations," in Maurice Zeitlin, ed., *American Society, Inc.* (Chicago, 1970), pp. 251–62.

[17] *Ibid.* For a similar view see Edward S. Mason, "Corporation," in *International Encyclopedia of the Social Sciences* vol. 3 (New York, 1968): 396–403.

rations in the past, Larner finds that both types of corporations act about the same.

In the present period, capital is organized in collective units rather than by individual capitalists. Economists Paul Baran and Paul Sweezy suggest that "the real capitalist today is not the individual businessman but the corporation."[18] That corporations have become increasingly large and complex, drawing on the skills of diverse technical specialists, and run by professional managers, means that they are more effective in pursuing the quest to cut costs and increase profits. But it does not alter the fundamental rule by which they operate: "Accumulate, accumulate! That is Moses and the prophets!"

New Sources of Capital

The savings of wealthy individuals have not been sufficient to assure enough capital to fuel corporate growth. Corporations have devised new sources, enabling a greater expansion of corporate capitalism. Capital increasingly comes from institutionalized sources.

Retained earnings   Giant corporations in concentrated industries have found a more reliable source of new capital than individual investors: themselves. A common corporate practice, called retained earnings, is for the corporation to save some of its profits rather than distributing them all to stockholders. In general, only large firms in a concentrated industry can charge high enough prices to make retained earnings possible. Retained earnings thus represent "forced savings" corporations extract from consumers. (The estimated yearly cost of higher prices to consumers from corporate concentration is over $40 billion.[19]) In 1973, about half of the $70 billion after-tax corporate profits was retained; the rest was distributed as dividends to stockholders.[20]

Government subsidy   An important source of capital for the corporation is government subsidy. (This subject will be discussed more fully in Chapters 4 and 8.) The largest capital grants by government have gone to military contractors. The government has provided billions of dollars for research and development, for

[18] Paul Baran and Paul Sweezy, *Monopoly Capital* (New York, 1966), p. 47.
[19] Mark J. Green, with Beverly C. Moore, Jr., and Bruce Wasserstein, *The Closed Enterprise System: Ralph Nader's Study Group Report on Antitrust Enforcement* (New York, 1972), p. 14.
[20] *New York Times*, January 2, 1974.

building and equipping factories, and for a loan guarantee to keep Lockheed in business.

Financial institutions   Banks, insurance companies, investment bankers, trust funds, pension funds, and mutual investment funds have come to constitute an important source of corporate capital. Banks are the largest institutional investors. A growing part of banking business comes from managing pension funds for corporate workers as well as trust funds, a device used by wealthy individuals to minimize inheritance taxes. It was estimated in 1973 that banks controlled $170 billion in corporate stock.[21] By 1977, bank trust departments held 25 percent of all corporate stock in the United States.[22] Much of this derives from union pension funds managed by bank trust departments. American capitalism works in mysterious ways: banks have gained a leading voice in major corporations through stock purchases made with union pension funds representing the savings of workers employed by these very corporations! One analyst dubs this process "pension fund socialism."[23]

A bank that invests in a corporation or makes a large loan to the corporation expects to get a say in the company. A common practice is for one of the bank's officers to be made a member of the corporation's board of directors. This is called an interlocking directorate, and it gives the bank a direct voice in the corporation's affairs. One study found that the largest banks have interlocks with 286 of the 500 largest corporations.[24] Economist Robert Sheehan has estimated that one-fifth of the 500 largest corporations are controlled by banks and other financial institutions.[25]

Through control of stock in competing corporations, banks, insurance companies, and law firms serve as the hub of a wheel connecting many giant corporations. For example, the Morgan Guaranty Trust (a leading investment bank) controls more than 7 percent of the stock in American Airlines, United Airlines, and TWA, the three largest domestic airlines. Chase Manhattan Bank

[21] *Business Week* (June 2, 1973), p. 58.
[22] *Trusts and Estates*, March 1974, p. 145; cited by David M. Kotz, "Finance Capital and Corporate Control," in Edwards et al., p. 153.
[23] Peter F. Drucker, *The Unseen Revolution: How Pension Fund Socialism Came to America* (New York, 1976).
[24] U.S., Congress, House, Committee on Banking and Finance, Subcommittee for Domestic Finance, Staff Report, *Commercial Banks and Their Trust Activities*, 90th Cong., 2d sess., 1968, in Zeitlin, p. 75.
[25] Robert Sheehan, "Proprietors in the World of Big Business," in Zeitlin, p. 79; Kotz estimates that the total is even larger.

holds over 5 percent of all stock in fou competing airlines, six railroads, and seventeen industrial companies.[26] One recent study finds that these two giant banks alone exercise substantial control over 36 of the 200 largest industrial corporations.[27]

Coordination and Competition

Interlocking directorates, whether under bank control or directly among corporate producers, are one mechanism by which corporations try to coordinate their activities and minimize competition. It is common for corporations to have interlocking directorates with large suppliers of parts and raw materials, with favored customers, and even (although this is illegal) with competitors. Interlocking directorates create a tight network reaching throughout corporate capitalism. One study notes, "Less than 4,000 managers of large corporations hold the directorships that interconnect the elite classes of officers and managers of the major corporations that employ most of the workers and do most of the business in American life."[28] Economist Peter Dooley found that by 1965 all but 17 of the 250 largest corporations had interlocks with each other.[29] A study prepared for a Senate subcommittee in 1978 found that interlocks are especially high among the very largest corporations. Each large corporation is directly or indirectly interlocked with nearly every other giant corporation.[30] To illustrate, in 1978 John D. deButts, chairman of AT&T (the world's largest corporation) was on the boards of GM (the nation's largest automobile producer), Citicorp (the nation's second largest bank), and U.S. Steel (the nation's largest steel producer).

Additional informal coordination among corporations occurs through trade associations in a given industry and through "umbrella" organizations like the National Association of Manufacturers, the National Industrial Conference Board, the United States Chamber of Commerce, and the Committee for Economic Development. These organizations act as spokespersons for broad sectors of business and define the common interests of corporate

[26] U.S., Congress, Senate, Committee on Government Operations, *Disclosure of Corporate Ownership*, 93rd Cong., 1st sess., December 27, 1973, p. 22.
[27] Kotz, pp. 147–58.
[28] L. Lloyd Warner, *The Emergent American Society* (New Haven, 1967), p. 157.
[29] Peter C. Dooley, "The Interlocking Directorate," *American Economic Review* 59 (June 1969): 315.
[30] *New York Times*, April 23, 1978.

capitalism, which David Rockefeller, chairman of the Chase Manhattan Bank, has defined as "a community of interests and search for stability in which business can thrive and capital be protected."[31] Whatever differences exist within corporate capitalism, there is internal agreement on perpetuating a capitalist economy based on private ownership and control of the means of production organized within large corporate units.

Yet, however united corporate producers may be on fundamentals, they remain hopelessly divided on the particulars of *who* shall profit. No matter how concentrated, corporate production continues to be characterized by competition and anarchy. The hallmark of capitalist production is the absence of a collectively determined assessment of what the community needs. Individual corporations continue to make this decision on the basis of what will best serve their own interests. This fact is key to understanding the unstable character of capitalism, for there are forces constantly at work tending to tear capitalism apart from within.

The anarchy of capitalist production, as well as resistance from workers, creates a need for government coordination. If public government did not serve the needs of capitalism, the two would go down together. The next chapter analyzes the built-in instabilities of capitalist production, how government in the United States has attempted to stabilize this chaotic situation, the process by which this has led to an ever-larger role for government, and the failure of government measures to resolve the latest crisis of capitalism.

[31] *New York Times*, November 7, 1973.

4

the corporate complex and crisis

For two decades after the Second World War, the most noteworthy feature of American society was its sustained economic growth, reflected in the outpouring of consumer goods—automobiles, homes, television receivers, and kitchen appliances—that made the United States the most prosperous society in the world. It was soon forgotten that for ten years before the war, the United States had experienced the most severe depression in its history.

During the growth years of the 1950s and 1960s, it seemed that hard times were a thing of the past. In a few short years, this optimism was seen to be as outmoded as the oversized automobiles of that period. In the 1970s the economy slowed to a crawl; in 1974–75, for the first time since the Second World War, Gross National Product (GNP) actually fell.

The crisis of the 1970s suggests the need for a return to basics to understand, both in theory and by an historical examination of the United States, the unstable crisis-prone tendencies inherent in capitalism and how government has played a critical role in attempting to moderate these tendencies. The current crisis is rooted in cyclical movements of boom and bust that have both short- and long-term components. In past periods when capitalism exhibited a tendency toward breakdown, it was transformed and strengthened—in part thanks to government help. What is striking about the current crisis of capitalism is the lack of solutions on the horizon, short of changes that would drastically alter or even eliminate capitalist production.

Capitalism is not necessarily on the way out. A tendency toward breakdown does not signify that breakdown will actually occur. But if past history is any guide, the present crisis signifies that we are living in a transitional period in which the future will look fundamentally different from the past.

THE UNSTABLE CHARACTER OF CAPITALISM

As we saw in the last chapter, in a capitalist society those controlling portions of capital compete with each other to secure maximum profits. It follows, then, that maximum profits require continued economic growth. Yet capitalism is incapable of sustaining growth. In order for capitalist production to flourish, periods of contraction must alternate with periods of growth. There are three reasons why this is so. All stem from the fact that the competition inherent in a capitalist system means that there is no way to assure economic stability. The economy is thus constantly oscillating from one crisis to the next. In particular, periods of economic expansion are eventually followed by periods of economic contraction and recession. One reason is that there is a constant tendency for productive capacity to outstrip demand. During periods of economic growth, capitalists estimate that the chances of making a profit are high and they invest in new equipment to expand output. But this eventually leads to overproduction because workers (who, along with their families, form a majority of the society) are paid such low wages that they cannot afford to purchase the commodities that the system is capable of producing. As economist Roger Alcaly points out, "The small incomes of the majority of the population limits their ability to consume the output that the economy is increasingly capable of producing."[1] When production exceeds demand, factories begin to run at partial ca-

[1] Roger E. Alcaly, "An Introduction to Marxian Crisis Theory," in Union for Radical Political Economics, *U.S. Capitalism in Crisis* (New York, 1978), p. 18. This section draws heavily on Alcaly.

Figure 4-1
Changes in output and employment in the U.S., 1890–1975

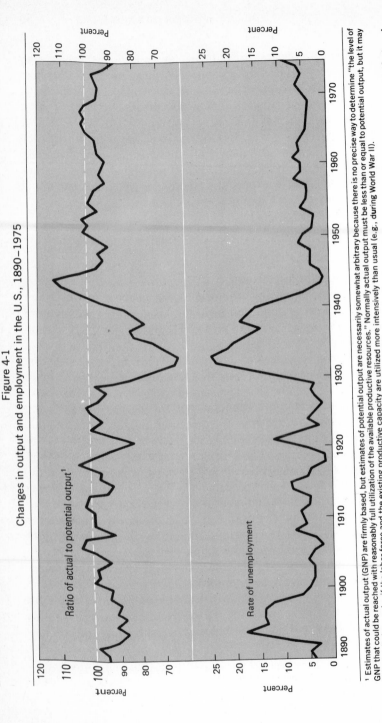

[1] Estimates of actual output (GNP) are firmly based, but estimates of potential output are necessarily somewhat arbitrary because there is no precise way to determine "the level of GNP that could be reached with reasonably full utilization of the available productive resources." Normally actual output must be less than or equal to potential output, but it may temporarily be greater if the labor force and the existing productive capacity are utilized more intensively than usual (e.g., **during World War II**).

Source: Thomas E. Weisskopf, "Sources of Cyclical Downturns and Inflation," in Richard C. Edwards, Michael Reich, and Thomas E. Weisskopf, eds., *The Capitalist System: A Radical Analysis of American Society*, 2nd ed., © 1978, p. 444. By permission of Prentice-Hall, Inc., Englewood Cliffs, N.J. Sources listed in original.

pacity, workers are laid off, thus further reducing the demand for goods, and a downward spiral toward recession begins.

A second way in which an economic boom turns to a recession is through workers demanding higher wages. When the economy is expanding, more workers are hired in order to produce more goods. When the number of people looking for work goes down, employers are forced to raise wages to attract new workers. The result is to increase the cost of producing commodities. When profits are squeezed beyond a certain point, workers begin to be laid off, contributing to the downward spiral.

A third way that prosperity generates recession under capitalism is that machines are used to replace workers: technological innovation and mechanized production are central to capitalism. In a society where all shared in the gains from technological innovation, no one would be harmed by technological advances. But in a capitalist society, mechanization spells unemployment, with those replaced by machines forced to absorb the costs of mechanization. Thus, under capitalism, mechanization tends to produce unemployment and recession.

Although the driving force of capitalism is the search for profitable investments and, hence, expansion, it is paradoxical that inner tendencies periodically drive capitalism toward contraction and stagnation. This phenomenon of boom and bust, what is referred to as the business cycle, is a universal tendency of capitalism. Hard times are often incorrectly interpreted as the result of bad luck or exceptional circumstances. In reality, inner tendencies counteract the capitalist drive to expand, forcing the economy to stagnate. The tendency to contract is as central to the functioning of a capitalist economy as the tendency to expand.

Thus, a recession is both a logical outcome of capitalist production and, within limits, even beneficial for capitalism. A recession sets the stage for a new period of profitable investment and economic growth. First, it weeds out inefficient producers; firms that cannot turn a profit during the harsh conditions of a recession are forced out of business. Second, a recession weakens the working class and thereby strengthens the dominance of capital. During a recession, the working class is divided, more ready to accept low wages, and compliant. As some workers lose their jobs, all workers begin to fear the coming of hard times, to appreciate what they have gained, and to demand less of their employers.

However, a recession can go too far. When the economy slides from a mild recession to a deeper and more durable depression, the costs to capital begin to outweigh the benefits. All capitalist firms, not only the least efficient, are damaged by the economic collapse. Further, the working class begins to resist the sacrifices that it is being called upon to make.

One of the major goals of the federal government is to moderate the extremes of the business cycle. Although the government has officially been committed to pursuing a policy of full employment since the 1946 Employment Act, in fact the government has attempted to "manage" recessions: to guide the economy through periodic mild recessions (and the resulting unemployment) that produce benefits for capitalism but to prevent recessions from developing into a depression. However, the government's ability to prevent a depression may collide with the fundamental tendencies of a capitalist economy to slide into a major depression at periodic intervals. Just as there are inherent tendencies toward recession every five to ten years, so there are deeper tendencies, which apparently push the economy to the brink of crisis as the result of a fifty-year cycle of expansion and stagnation.

N. D. Kondratieff, a Soviet economist in the 1920s, was the first to detect long waves of growth and stagnation within capitalist economies, moving in approximately fifty-year cycles from the early nineteenth century. During the first half of a fifty-year cycle, there is a steady, often vigorous, economic expansion; during the second half, there is the onset of stagnation, deepening into depression and crisis toward the end of the cycle. The movement of long historical waves is associated with fundamental changes in the economic, social, and political spheres.

Scientific and technological breakthroughs that make possible major shifts in a society's patterns of production and consumption set the stage for long waves. During the expansionary phase, major new investments shape the society's future development. The boom is set off by the discovery of new sources of energy and locomotion, cheap sources of labor and raw materials, and advances in transportation, communication, and production. These innovations involve the whole society, creating a demand for the new products made possible by the breakthrough. The period of expansion produces a spirit of optimism, vitality, and commitment. For several decades, the society experiences prosperity and purpose. Class struggles temporarily take a back seat to the pursuit of happiness. The society works hard and lives well.

However, like the self-limiting tendencies of the short-term business cycle, there are inherent limits to long periods of expansion. Fewer new outlets for profitable investments remain as the new infrastructure is completed. Economist David Gordon suggests that the "size and inflexibility [of infrastructural booms] channel economic growth along increasingly unprofitable paths."[2] In a long wave, the tendency toward stagnation occurs slowly, not all at once. It is overlaid by the short-term swings of the business cycle, where periods of upswing continue to occur, though with less frequency than declines. (By contrast, during the expansionary phase of a long wave, the upturns of the business cycle are more durable than downturns.) The downward slide does not occur all at once, although the arrival of crisis may be heralded by a dramatic event, such as "Black Friday," the outbreak of the financial panic in October 1929 that devastated the New York Stock Exchange, or the tripling of petroleum prices imposed by the Organization of Petroleum Exporting Countries (OPEC) in 1973. The economic stagnation may be obscured by short-term prosperity, government measures, and popular misconceptions. Yet the crisis eventually becomes more pervasive as growth is replaced by stagnation, good times turn to bad, and optimism to pessimism.

When the society experiences a major crisis, the future becomes increasingly problematic, and dominant institutions are challenged as people find that they are serving the system rather than the system serving them. In the past, crises have been resolved by major changes in economic and political institutions. After each crisis, there has been increased centralization and interpenetration of economic and political institutions. Government intervention has helped bring an end to the crisis and has facilitated a new period of growth.

LONG WAVES IN AMERICAN HISTORY

There have been three long waves of expansion and stagnation in American history since the early nineteenth century. In the present era, a long wave of expansion began around the time of the

[2] David M. Gordon, "Up and Down the Long Roller Coaster," in *U.S. Capitalism in Crisis*, p. 31.

Second World War, peaked in the 1960s, and turned downward in the early 1970s. While the outcome of the present period cannot be accurately predicted, the most likely characteristics of the next decade appear to be instability and deepening crisis. In the account that follows, we will focus on the changing role of government in facilitating the economic transformation of American capitalism.

The expansionary phase of the first long wave in American history, starting in the 1840s, was based on a shift in power sources from water-driven devices to the steam engine. New transportation facilities—canals, roadways, and especially railroads—made it economically feasible to produce for regional and even national markets.

According to historian Morton Keller, "The postwar economic boom [following the Civil War] was sparked by government-supported railroad construction."[3] The federal government contributed 100 million acres of land and $100 million to subsidize the building of railroads. In ten years, trackage doubled to 74,000 miles, making possible the vast westward expansion.

Economist Douglas Dowd sums up the new developments:

> The transportation network . . . constituted an enormous demand for a whole range of products—most importantly, metals and machinery and coal, the heart of nineteenth-century industrial development. A new technology was required to dig canals, to tame the plains and mountains with rail and powerful locomotives, and to exploit the surface and subsurface resources of America's varied lands. All this, taken together with a persisting labor shortage, meant that the United States became the first of all industrial nations to develop a comprehensive machine technology for all aspects of production—agriculture, mineral, manufacturing, and transportation.[4]

This was the classic era of competitive capitalism. Government's role was mainly limited to providing the framework in which competitive capitalism could develop. Not that government's role was negligible. It brutally suppressed working-class strikes and challenges as well as Indian opposition, and it provided business with extensive subsidies of land and capital. But government's role was mainly limited to providing law and order within a capitalist setting, which included guaranteeing the sanctity of contracts and protecting private property.

[3] Morton Keller, *Affairs of State: Public Life in Late Nineteenth Century America* (Cambridge, Mass., 1977), p. 165.
[4] Douglas F. Dowd, *The Twisted Dream: Capitalist Development in the United States since 1776*, 2nd ed. (Cambridge, Mass., 1977), pp. 63–64.

It was the competitive nature of early capitalism that led to the downturn of the late nineteenth century and, eventually, a new configuration of economic and political institutions. Fierce competition meant that new efficient production methods were quickly translated into falling prices. Beginning in 1873 and lasting until the end of the nineteenth century, there was an era of sagging employment, prices, profits, and production. The railroads, once hailed as an engine of progress, were a major target of popular wrath. The late nineteenth century was the first major crisis of American capitalism. The Granger, Populist, Free Silver, and other popular movements called not only for extensive reforms but also challenged the manner in which industrialization was carried out under the control of private business, with government a cooperative junior partner.

The crisis was resolved in a way that permitted a surge of growth under capitalist auspices. The second long wave, which began in the late nineteenth century, was sparked by technological developments based on new power sources—notably the electric motor and internal combustion engine—and their application to transportation and manufacturing.

Intertwined with the new technological developments was a centralization of production in the corporation. Corporate concentration made possible the limiting of competition, the control of prices, and greater stability of profits. Historian David Noble points out that in such varied industries as petroleum, steel, rubber, and transportation, "the systematic introduction of science as a means of production presupposed, and in turn reinforced, industrial monopoly."[5] The movement toward mergers and industrial concentration represented a social and organizational transformation as significant as the shift in technology.

The federal government also played a critical role in the change, helping to protect and stabilize corporate concentration under the guise of limiting and regulating corporations.

Government Regulation and Corporate Production

As long as there were many manufacturers in a given industry, they had no choice but to compete. But the corporate form offered a means of thwarting the free market. A large company could profit from its power over the market to undercut its competitors,

---

[5] David F. Noble, *America by Design: Science, Technology, and the Rise of Corporate Capitalism* (New York, 1977), p. 6.

monopolize sources of supply, and coerce or buy out smaller competitors. A further extension of the trend was the creation of trusts, in which many producers within an industry were merged into a single large firm. The result was a monopoly in which, unrestrained by competition, the trust could raise prices and achieve huge financial gains.

Small businessmen and farmers tried to unite in the face of the corporate threat to their survival. The Greenback, Granger, and Populist parties were moderately successful. Many state governments passed laws that regulated the new monopolies. For example, Wisconsin, New York, and other states prohibited railroad freight carriers from giving rebates (lower rates) to large shippers. Nationally, the Sherman Antitrust Act of 1887 prohibited "combinations in restraint of trade." The law empowered the federal government to break up conspiracies among competitors. Yet a pattern originated with the Sherman Act that was repeated often in the future. When public opposition was strong, the government stepped in to curb the worst excesses of business and to provide the appearance of regulation—without mortal damage to business interests. As described by historian Richard Hofstadter, the Sherman Act was "recognized by most of the astute politicians of that hour as a gesture, a ceremonial concession to an overwhelming public demand for some kind of reassuring action against the trusts."[6]

The Critical Period: 1897 to 1912

That the Sherman Act failed to prevent combinations in restraint of trade can be seen from the fact that the largest merger movement in American history (to that time) began in 1897, ten years *after* its passage.

By 1900, however, the merger movement began to slow. Moreover, the giant corporations that developed from the merger movement do not appear to have outperformed their smaller rivals. The point of diminishing returns in achieving efficiency through large size seems to have been reached in the early 1900s. The best example was the United States Steel Corporation, organized in 1901 under the leadership of J. P. Morgan, leading financier of the period. It was the largest industrial corporation formed until then.

---

[6] Richard Hofstadter, *The Age of Reform* (New York, 1960), p. 245.

Figure 4-2
Acquisitions of manufacturing and mining companies 1895–1972

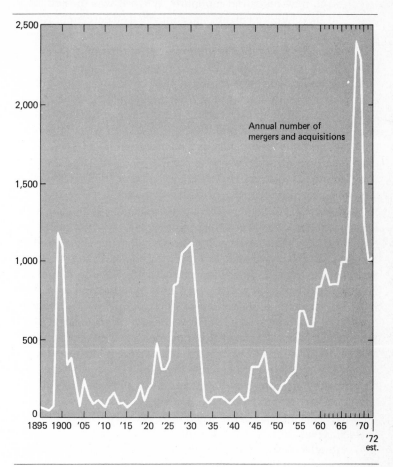

Source: Tom Cardamone for *Fortune* Magazine; © 1973 Time Inc.

Its assets of over $1 billion made it bigger than other leviathans
organized during this period, such as Standard Oil of New Jersey,
American Smelting and Refining Company, and Consolidated Tobacco Company. J. P. Morgan created U.S. Steel not to achieve
greater efficiency but to eliminate competition. There were already
a number of large, efficient steel companies. The most notable of

these was Andrew Carnegie's, which Morgan was successful in buying out and merging with the other companies he had captured to form the new industrial monolith. When it was formed, U.S. Steel had eight hundred plants and controlled 60 percent of American steel production. It was a gigantic test of whether bigness and near-monopoly conditions could prevent competition.

In fact, however, U.S. Steel was neither more efficient nor more profitable than its remaining competitors; and it was not even able to prevent new competition from arising in the steel industry. In the years following its creation, the price of U.S. Steel's stock declined, and its share of total steel output fell from over 60 percent to 40 percent. Its failure was due mainly to its large size, which made it inflexible and slow to innovate, compared to its smaller competitors. Moreover, U.S. Steel was unable to persuade other steel companies to abide by price-fixing agreements.[7]

What happened in the steel industry occurred in other industries in which there were huge new trusts. After its creation, Standard Oil failed to increase its control over the petroleum industry. In the automobile, copper, telephone, and meat industries, trusts were unable to outperform their competitors or dominate the industry. They, too, were unable to prevent new firms from entering the industry and to enforce price-fixing agreements among competitors. If it had not been for government intervention, the breed of industrial giant might have continued to decline. Thus, technological innovations and government-regulated protection for the emergent corporate giants helped make possible renewed economic expansion in the early years of the twentieth century. The irony is that government has often been perceived as being directed against big business when in fact government contributed to its survival.

Gabriel Kolko, the first historian to analyze this crucial transition in American history, notes: "The dominant fact of American politics at the beginning of this century was that big business led the struggle for the federal regulation of the economy. . . . Federal economic regulation was generally designed by the regulated industry to meet its own ends, and not those of the public." Kolko adds that the method used by big business to secure dominance over small business, agrarian interests, and labor was "the utilization of political outlets to attain conditions of stability, predictabil-

[7] This account draws on Gabriel Kolko, *The Triumph of Conservatism: A Reinterpretation of American History, 1900–1916* (New York, 1963).

ity, and security."[8] To cite one example, the Interstate Commerce Commission, created in 1887, has often been perceived as a move to curb and regulate the railroads. Yet "the intervention of the federal government not only failed to damage the interests of the railroads but was positively welcomed by them."[9] As in other comparable cases of government "regulation" of industry, the railroads used the government to control competition, calm an outraged public, and limit competition—ends that they could not achieve by themselves. The assurance given by Attorney General Richard Olney (himself a former railroad company executive) in a letter in 1892 to a disturbed railroad president suggests the value of regulation to railroad interests:

> The [Interstate Commerce] Commission, as its functions have now been limited by the courts, is, or can be made, of great use to the railroads. It satisfies the popular clamor for a government supervision of railroads, at the same time that the supervision is almost entirely nominal. Further, the older such a Commission gets to be, the more inclined it will be found to take the business and railroad view of things. It thus becomes a sort of barrier between the railroad corporations and the people and a sort of protection against hasty and crude legislation hostile to railroad interests.[10]

Thus, the turmoil of the late nineteenth century ended in the triumph of big business and conservatism—under the guise of reform: "By 1918 the leaders of the large corporations and banks emerged secure in their loose hegemony over the political structure."[11] The contrast with the earlier period could not have been greater. Manufacturers had never constituted a cohesive group in America; instead, they had consisted of many competing small producers, split by regional and economic rivalry. Moreover, business had been only one economic interest in the United States, no more powerful—probably less powerful—than farmers and merchants. The shift to corporate capitalism signified a fundamental transformation of the political and economic structure. A centralized economy (particularly following the New Deal in the 1930s), controlled by large corporate producers with the help of big

---

[8] *Ibid.*, pp. 3, 57–58.
[9] Gabriel Kolko, *Railroads and Regulation, 1877–1916* (Princeton, 1965), p. 3.
[10] Marver H. Bernstein, *Regulating Business by Independent Commission* (Princeton, 1955), p. 265.
[11] James Weinstein, *The Corporate Ideal in the Liberal State, 1900–1918* (Boston, 1968), p. 3.

government, replaced an economy divided by conflicting interests and controlled by none. This new alliance of giant corporate producers and an interventionist government can be called the corporate complex.

The combination of new technology, corporate concentration along with government regulation and a sharp increase in demand, led to sustained economic growth during the period of the First World War. The expansion transformed American society. The mass-produced automobile gave rise to related industries, including glass, rubber, and paint. Along with the radio and telephone, the automobile changed consumer patterns and, thanks to the birth of the advertising industry, helped produce the first consumer society. During the period following the First World War, the United States became the world's leading power, accounting for about half the world's total production.

Yet toward the end of the 1920s there were already signs of an approaching economic collapse. The downturn was obscured by financial trickery and frantic speculation. But, beginning with the collapse of the stock market in 1929, there erupted the worst depression ever for American capitalism. At the height of the Great Depression in 1933, production plunged to half its former level and unemployment soared to 25 percent. For ten years, under presidents of both parties, the government sought a way out; but all approaches failed. Republican president Herbert Hoover followed the traditional course of limiting government expenditures, balancing the federal budget, and hoping that the downturn would eventually reverse itself. Instead, the crisis deepened, and he was swept from the presidency in the 1932 elections.

Democrat Franklin Roosevelt promised a New Deal and bravely proclaimed in his inaugural address, "The only thing we have to fear is fear itself." However, his attempts to use government power to check the depression failed in the short run, although they led to a new pattern of government-corporate cooperation. Roosevelt first worked directly with business in an attempt to coax a revival. The National Recovery Administration (NRA), launched in 1933, developed codes of business conduct designed to reduce competition and keep prices high enough to assure profits. The NRA was declared unconstitutional by the Supreme Court, dominated by justices who harked back to the days of small business and competition. Roosevelt's next approach, known as the second New Deal, was to grant relief directly to the poor and unemployed. The measures Roosevelt sponsored looked like a direct attack on business and the individualist values of capitalism. However, although Roosevelt's program of government assistance to retired workers, the poor, and the unemployed was partly a response to the militant protest developing in the 1930s, the New Deal was far from constituting a fundamental attack on corporate capitalism.

The New Deal accepted the basic legitimacy of corporate dominance. Aside from the government's one notable attempt to organize production directly (the Tennessee Valley Authority, which developed a system of flood control, and electric power and fertilizer production), the New Deal did not challenge corporate production. The top 100 corporations increased their control of all corporate assets during the New Deal, and the highest income group increased its share of the country's personal wealth.[12] The New Deal was an innovative attempt to save corporate capitalism from the crisis of its own making. As political scientist David Greenstone observes, "In general, the New Deal may have functioned to forestall radical change by eliminating the most unpopular features of American capitalism."[13]

Nonetheless, peacetime government expenditures failed to end the depression. "The Great Depression of the thirties never came to an end," economist John Galbraith has pointed out. "It merely disappeared in the great mobilization of the forties."[14] Only in 1940 did per capita income climb back to the peak reached in 1929.

The New Deal, as well as the requirements of production for total war, led to government assuming responsibility for regulating overall demand in the economy, with the goal of preventing economic crisis. As a result of the tremendous expansion of the federal government, its taxing and spending pattern (fiscal policy) began to have a significant impact on the entire economy. And, thanks to the technological developments and investment possibilities made

[12] Kenneth Prewitt and Alan Stone, *The Ruling Elites: Elite Theory, Power, and American Democracy* (New York, 1973), p. 45.
[13] J. David Greenstone, *Labor in American Politics* (New York, 1969), p. 46.
[14] John Kenneth Galbraith, *American Capitalism: The Concept of Countervailing Power* (Boston, 1952), p. 69.

possible by the Second World War, the United States entered the third long wave of economic growth.

Second World War to the Present

Following the Second World War, the United States experienced the greatest period of growth that the world had ever seen. The massive war effort stimulated innovations in electronics, tele-communications, radar, data processing, aircraft, and nuclear power. These developments, along with a backlog of consumer demand from the war, triggered a postwar surge in civilian produc-tion. Another factor in the long wave of growth was the privileged position of the United States, described in chapter 8, which enabled the United States to gain access to foreign markets for American goods and to obtain new materials abroad at cheap prices. In addition, following a postwar wave of strikes by workers in major industries, a new pattern of collective bargaining devel-oped, described in the next chapter, which provided labor stability for corporate producers. A final factor stimulating the boom was the enthusiastic commitment of the federal government to foster-ing capital accumulation by the corporate complex. A consensus developed between both major political parties on the need for an interventionist government to keep the economy on an expansion-ary course. The federal government played a key role in assuring the development of the third long wave. The next section reviews the new measures directed to assuring economic expansion and stabilization.

But government intervention cannot provide a cure-all for a capitalist economy. The expansion of the 1950s and 1960s has ended, and the current era is characterized by meager growth, high prices, and high unemployment. The present crisis will be dis-cussed at the end of the chapter.

GOVERNMENT AND THE ECONOMY

Although most basic decisions in a capitalist society are made by the "private government" that owns and controls capital, govern-ment plays a central role as well. In each of the long waves of economic change in American history, government played a vital and expanding role. In the United States, the major political trend of the twentieth century is toward larger and more powerful government. There is now one federal official for every sixty citizens. Few areas of human activity escape government involvement. To some extent, the balance of power between government and business has drifted toward government, as tax revenues and government expenditures have grown and business has become more dependent on government assistance.

However, the growth in government power has not been at the expense of business. As we have seen, there have been a massive expansion and centralization of corporate power in the twentieth century. Since government does not directly control production, it is forced to rely on corporate capital to perform the functions essential for the survival and prosperity of the society.

So long as production remains privately controlled by corporate producers, government will always put the needs of corporate capitalism at the top of the political agenda. "Not many Government officials are so witless as to overlook their own dependence on business," observes economist Charles Lindblom. "If business is not induced to perform, the result is economic distress. When the economy fails, the Government falls. . . . Hence, no category of persons is more attentive to the needs of business than the Government official."[15]

Yet government is not simply a blind captive of business, ready to do its bidding. If it were, capitalism would have long since disappeared. Government must be free to oppose individual corporations or even, on rare occasions, the whole business community if it is to preserve the larger framework within which profitable corporate production (what is also called capital accumulation) can occur. No single corporation or business organization possesses government's central vantage point to judge what is needed for the whole capitalist system. For example, automobile producers bitterly opposed federally imposed gasoline efficiency requirements on the grounds that they would cut into auto sales. Yet these requirements, aimed at achieving reduced energy consumption, were in the long-term interest of American capitalism and of the automakers themselves.

Economist James O'Connor has distinguished two broad functions of a capitalist government: assisting capital accumula-

[15] Charles E. Lindblom, "The Business of America Is Still Business," *New York Times*, January 4, 1978.

tion (which will be studied in the remainder of this chapter) and maintaining a framework of social control so that capital accumulation can occur. [16] Social control (which O'Connor calls legitimization) consists of obtaining popular assent within the United States for the capitalist system—for example, through mobilizing electoral majorities, providing government welfare payments, and using force (as a last resort if peaceful means fail). Social control abroad (which will be discussed in Chapter 8) is also necessary if American capitalism is to flourish.

Regulating Demand

Government uses an arsenal of techniques in attempting to counteract the most extreme tendencies toward boom and bust of a capitalist economy. In the period following the Second World War, the government's major aim has been to maintain a rising level of total (aggregate) demand that was in rough balance with rising productive capacity. It did so through monetary and fiscal policy.

Monetary policy   The Federal Reserve Board regulates the amount of money in circulation by varying the interest rates it charges to private banks within the Federal Reserve system. Although the Federal Reserve Board is a government agency, private banks choose most of the members of the regional Federal Reserve Bank boards. The Federal Reserve Board is closely allied with the banking industry and its monetary policies often have the effect of restricting economic growth and raising unemployment.

Fiscal policy   Fiscal policy refers to the taxing and spending activities of the government. Government expenditures increase the demand for privately produced goods and services when government spends more than it receives in tax revenues, a process that is called deficit spending or (more informally) pump priming. When government collects more in tax revenues than it spends, the result is a budget surplus. This reduces purchasing power (demand) and thus slows up economic activity. Since the Second World War, federal spending has been at a high level and government-created demand was one of the major sources of the long expansionary wave in the postwar years.

The collection of taxes is another element in fiscal policy. The importance of government can be appreciated from the fact that

---

[16] James O'Connor, *The Fiscal Crisis of the State* (New York, 1973).

Figure 4-3
Tax table showing progressive feature of income tax

SCHEDULE X—Single Taxpayers

If the amount on Schedule TC, Part I, line 3, is:

Enter on Schedule TC, Part I, line 4:

Not over $2,200............ —0—

Over—	But not over—		of the amount over—
$2,200	$2,700	14%	$2,200
$2,700	$3,200	$70+15%	$2,700
$3,200	$3,700	$145+16%	$3,200
$3,700	$4,200	$225+17%	$3,700
$4,200	$6,200	$310+19%	$4,200
$6,200	$8,200	$690+21%	$6,200
$8,200	$10,200	$1,110+24%	$8,200
$10,200	$12,200	$1,590+25%	$10,200
$12,200	$14,200	$2,090+27%	$12,200
$14,200	$16,200	$2,630+29%	$14,200
$16,200	$18,200	$3,210+31%	$16,200
$18,200	$20,200	$3,830+34%	$18,200
$20,200	$22,200	$4,510+36%	$20,200
$22,200	$24,200	$5,230+38%	$22,200
$24,200	$28,200	$5,990+40%	$24,200
$28,200	$34,200	$7,590+45%	$28,200
$34,200	$40,200	$10,290+50%	$34,200
$40,200	$46,200	$13,290+55%	$40,200
$46,200	$52,200	$16,590+60%	$46,200
$52,200	$62,200	$20,190+62%	$52,200
$62,200	$72,200	$26,390+64%	$62,200
$72,200	$82,200	$32,790+66%	$72,200
$82,200	$92,200	$39,390+68%	$82,200
$92,200	$102,200	$46,190+69%	$92,200
$102,200	....	$53,090+70%	$102,200

$600 billion—one-third of the entire amount of Gross National Product (GNP—the entire national output)—is collected by federal, state, and local governments in tax revenues and then redistributed through government expenditures.

As with its other activities, government tax policies serve the

Table 4-1
Combined effect of federal individual income and payroll taxes
on the distribution of income, 1972

Income quintile	Percentage distribution	
	Total income before taxes	Total income after income and payroll taxes
Total population		
Lowest 20	1.7	1.8
20 to 40	6.6	7.0
40 to 60	14.5	14.8
60 to 80	24.1	24.4
80 to 100	53.1	51.9
Total	100.0	100.0

Source: Adapted from Edward R. Fried, Alice M. Rivlin, Charles L. Schultze, and Nancy H. Teeters, *Setting National Priorities: The 1974 Budget* (Washington, D.C., 1973), p. 50. © 1973 by the Brookings Institution, Washington, D.C.

dual (and conflicting) purpose of assisting business and building popular support for the economic and political system. On the one hand, the tax system is designed to assist capital accumulation. Special tax breaks are provided for income derived from profits. (This is called capital gains, and it is taxed at a lower rate than wages and salaries.) Corporations are thus given incentives to encourage investment.

On the other hand, in an attempt to build popular support, the tax system is often said to help redistribute income from the wealthy to the poor. The principle is given expression in the progressive federal income tax, which requires the wealthy to pay a higher proportion of taxes than the poor. Prominent display is given each year to the federal income-tax rates on the tax forms sent to millions of families. The table shows that the tax rate for the lowest income groups is 14 percent, and it gradually increases to reach a hefty 70 percent for all taxable income earned over $100,000.

A simple way to measure how well the progressive income tax redistributes income is to compare the distribution of income among different income groups before and after they pay taxes.

The surprising result is that tax laws have little effect on the relative distribution of income among most income groups. Most Americans—those earning between $2,000 and $30,000 annually—pay about the same proportion of their income in taxes (about one-quarter). Those earning more than $30,000 pay a slightly higher tax—but nowhere near the rate given in the tax table. The cruelest irony is that the lowest income group, those with incomes under $2,000, also pay a higher proportion of taxes than many Americans.

What accounts for the discrepancy? First there are a bewildering variety of other taxes beside the federal income tax. Most are regressive: instead of levying a higher rate on the wealthy, they levy a lower rate. One important example is payroll (social security) taxes, which are deducted directly from an employee's salary by his or her employer. Since social-security taxes are collected only on the first $17,700 of one's income, those earning above this amount pay proportionately less tax. (Nor is this a minor example: 31 percent of all federal tax revenue is now raised through payroll taxes.[17]) Local sales taxes, levied on clothing and other necessities, also fall more heavily on the poor.

Special features of the tax laws further permit the wealthy to shelter earnings from the progressive income tax. Such provisions, which result in a lower tax bill, are equivalent to granting a subsidy to affluent taxpayers. One example is a lower tax rate on income that comes from the sale of stocks (capital gains). If this income were taxed at the same rate as wages, it would produce $5 billion more in federal tax revenue. Who gets this $5 billion bonus? Three-quarters of it goes to .5 percent of the population—one in two hundred families.[18] Another example: dividends from state and municipal bonds—two-thirds of which are owned by .1 percent of the population—are not taxed at all.[19] Through such devices, the wealthy exempt much of their income from high tax rates. Rather than redistributing income to the poor, two economists conclude that tax laws "provide a vehicle of redistribution to the wealthy."[20] Since the wealthy do not need to spend all their income

[17] Charles L. Schultze et al., *Setting National Priorities: The 1973 Budget* (Washington, D.C., 1972), p. 7.
[18] Martin Pfaff and Anita Pfaff, "How Equitable are Implicit Public Grants? The Case of the Individual Income Tax," in Kenneth E. Boulding and Martin Pfaff, eds., *Redistribution to the Rich and the Poor* (Belmont, California, 1972), p. 191.
[19] Philip M. Stern, *The Rape of the Taxpayer* (New York, 1973), p. 62.
[20] Pfaff and Pfaff, p. 201.

Table 4-2
Spending by all levels of government, 1902–1974

Year	Billions of dollars	Percent of GNP
1902	1.7	7.7
1913	3.2	8.2
1922	9.3	12.5
1929	10.3	10.0
1934	12.9	19.8
1939	17.6	19.4
1944	103.0	49.1
1949	59.1	23.0
1954	96.7	26.5
1959	131.0	27.1
1964	175.4	27.7
1969	290.1	31.2
1974	460.9	33.0

Source: 1902, 1913, and 1922 are from Thomas A. Dye, *Understanding Public Policy,* © 1972, p. 186. Reprinted by permission of Prentice-Hall, Inc., Englewood Cliffs, N.J. 1929–1974 are calculated from tables in *Economic Report of the President,* 1971 and 1975.

on current needs, they invest part in corporate production. The tax system thus functions to assist capital accumulation, with control of the process as well as the profits remaining in the hands of a small minority of Americans.

Government expenditures   Government spending has been climbing steadily throughout the twentieth century: from less than one-tenth of GNP at the turn of the century, it now constitutes one-third of GNP. (As the late Senator Everett Dirksen once said, "A billion here and a billion there and pretty soon it adds up to real money.")

In recent years, although there continue to be annual increases in federal government spending, these increases have kept pace with the rise in GNP. (Federal government expenditures now constitute about one-fifth of GNP.) The major reason that government spending continues to absorb a rising share of national output has been a sharp increase in state and local government expenditures. In 1957, state and local governments collected one-fourth as much in tax revenues as the federal government; by 1977, the proportion of tax revenues collected by state and local governments increased to more than one-third of federal tax revenues.[21] This helps account for the "tax revolt" occurring in many states and communities.

Total federal government expenditures since the Second World War have been immense. Between 1946 and 1975, the federal government purchased $2 trillion of goods and services.

What was obtained by the colossal sums spent by the federal government in the postwar period? Three major categories of federal expenditures can be identified. By far the largest amount—three-quarters of the total—has gone for military purposes. The second largest category has been welfare-state payments. Both of these can be considered expenses to obtain social control—the first, abroad; the second, within the United States. They are analyzed in later chapters.

Socializing the Costs of Production

Most remaining federal government expenditures go for physical facilities and services that can be considered a direct or indirect subsidy to affluent citizens and business. Business is the largest beneficiary of most government-provided services and facilities, including government statistical services, transportation facilities, and subsidies for R&D. However, these government outlays are financed by all taxpayers. Were it not for public largesse, private business would have to pay for many of these services directly. The costs of production are thus paid for by the whole society, but the major benefits go to private producers. Government-provided benefits can consist of a direct subsidy to private producers—a subsidy to develop new products that can be patented and sold by a private firm, for example—or facilities available to all but which benefit business disproportionately—the interstate highway system, for example. The interstate highway system was built at a cost to taxpayers of $80 billion (the largest public works project in history). The system represents an indirect subsidy to corporate producers—the major users—for it enables them to ship their products quickly and cheaply throughout the country.

[21] *Dollars & Sense*, no. 40, October 1978, p. 4.

DIMENSIONS OF THE PRESENT CRISIS

It is a measure of the present crisis that massive government expenditures have not been able to assure continued economic expansion in the 1970s. Despite extensive government intervention since the Second World War, the expansionary phase of the third long wave lasted no longer than the two previous long periods of growth of American capitalism in the nineteenth and early twentieth centuries.

During the long expansion beginning in the 1940s, severe economic crisis seemed a thing of the past, although there continued to be periodic ups and downs of the business cycle. Then, ominous warning signs began to appear on the horizon: a slowdown of corporate profits in the late 1950s, an international trade deficit beginning in the 1960s (signifying that other nations were producing more efficiently than the United States), and persistent inflation throughout the 1960s.

The full extent of the crisis was obscured for several years. The Vietnam war kept the economy booming when it would probably have otherwise begun to turn slack. Moreover, the financial costs of the war were concealed by President Lyndon Johnson, who decided not to raise taxes for fear of provoking public opposition to the war. The result was to fuel inflationary pressures as government competed with business and consumers for scarce resources.

A tripling of petroleum prices by the Organization of Petroleum Exporting Countries (OPEC) in 1973 along with soaring food prices made the dimensions of the crisis dramatically clear. Since then, despite a short period of recovery for business after 1975 (whose impact was negligible for most Americans), it has been apparent that we are coming to the gravest crisis since the depression of the 1930s.

Stagflation In the 1970s, unemployment rates have been higher than at any time since the 1930s while prices have risen faster than at any period in American history. A new term—*stagflation*—had to be coined to describe the unprecedented coexistence of *stag*nation and *inflation*. Among the elements of the crisis are extensive layoffs of public employees, deteriorating public services, stiff competition from foreign producers, and public discontent with the performance of government and business.

Figure 4-4
Inflation and unemployment rates, 1953–1975

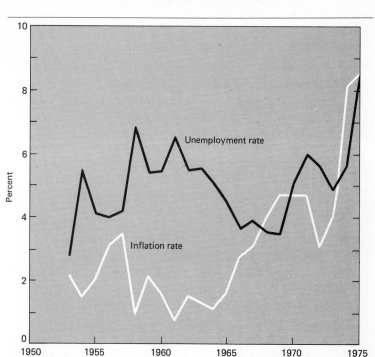

[a]Private nonfarm deflator (excluding 1974 and 1975 energy contribution).

Source: George L. Perry, "Stabilization Policy and Inflation," in Henry Owen and Charles L. Schultze, eds., *Setting National Priorities: The Next Ten Years* (Washington, D.C., 1976), p. 300. © 1976 by The Brookings Institution, Washington, D.C. Official unemployment rate provided by U.S. Bureau of Labor Statistics, adjusted from 1953 to 1966 by the author to make series consistent with the 1967 BLS revision; deflator from *Economic Report of the President, January 1976*, table B-30, p. 206.

An illustration of the crisis is that there have been three recessions in the 1970s compared to only one in the 1960s. Whereas in the 1950s and 1960s, wages were continually rising, wages were lower in 1976 than at the beginning of the decade. A price rise of 3 percent annually was considered high prior to the 1970s. Since 1968, prices have risen more than 3 percent every year—with the *lowest* rise being 6 percent.

A meager upswing in 1975–78 came mainly from government and consumer spending, while investment continued to lag. But no sustained surge has ever occurred without substantial business investment.

High rates of unemployment are thus rooted in the reluctance of business to invest. In the present period, factories are closing down or running at partial capacity. Also, unemployment increases as mechanized methods of production eliminate much human labor. Another reason for high unemployment is that American corporations are exporting jobs: foreign investment means fewer jobs for American workers. Further, the demand for American goods abroad has declined because in some industries—steel, for example—American production methods have lagged behind those used by competitors like Germany and Japan. Finally, the international crisis of capitalism has reduced the demand for American products.

Several factors have contributed to the persistent inflation of the present period. Much of the economic growth in the 1950s and 1960s was financed by credit. But banks have reached the limit of their lending capacity and, in the words of the editors of the *Monthly Review*, are "skating on thin ice." Bank loans as a proportion of bank deposits increased from 39 percent in 1950 to 84 percent in 1974. One major failure by a bank or corporation could trigger a wave of failures throughout the business world.[22]

Corporate concentration, too, contributes to inflationary pressures, since corporations maintain high prices even in slack periods. Thus, during one recent recession, prices fell 6 percent in a group of nonconcentrated industries but rose by the same amount in a group of concentrated industries.[23]

The fiscal crisis   Although the purpose of government spending has been to stimulate economic prosperity, it has come under increasing attack as a factor contributing to the crisis. Government has been unable to gain sufficient popular support to raise taxes. As a result, the federal government ran deficits exceeding $60 billion annually throughout the late 1970s. When government spending goes beyond a certain point, it contributes not to economic expansion but to excess demand, rising prices, and inflation. That is the situation during the current period.

On the local level, taxpayers have begun to revolt against their

[22] Editors of the *Monthly Review*, "Banks: Skating on Thin Ice," in *U.S. Capitalism in Crisis*, pp. 115–22.
[23] John M. Blair, "Market Power and Inflation: A Short-Run Target Return Model," *Journal of Economic Issues* 8 (June 1974): 458.

growing tax bill. The most dramatic example was a statewide referendum in California in June 1978, when voters approved a limitation on state property taxes that sent state revenues falling from $14 billion to $5 billion. The result was a cutback in state services and the layoff of thousands of state employees. However, since the bulk of the tax cutbacks benefited large companies and wealthy residents, most voters have experienced the costs of the retrenchment but have not received much tax relief.

Government Response to Crisis: The Politicized Economy

The limits of fine-tuning   Government efforts to keep the economy on a stable course have been described as fine-tuning. The economy is likened to a powerful, delicately balanced machine, with government making precise adjustments to keep the machine on course. This analogy is hardly adequate during the present period of stagflation, when the economic machine has lurched out of control. Traditional fiscal and monetary policies have proved ineffective, and government has been forced to consider more drastic measures. As in past crises, the form this takes will make government even more responsible for the economy and expose it to greater political challenge.

In a search for a way out of the crisis, government has recently become more closely involved in the actual production process. A prime example is the setting of wages and prices, traditionally considered one of the central prerogatives of private management in a capitalist society.

Wage and price control   Beginning in 1962, President Kennedy attempted to control inflation by exerting pressure on corporate management and labor to limit price and wage increases. Through "jawboning" (the use of persuasion, negotiations, and threats), Kennedy tried to prevent wage and price rises from exceeding guidelines established by economic advisers. The most famous case was in 1962, when Kennedy forced the United States Steel Corporation and other steel producers to postpone steel price rises.

Presidents Kennedy and Johnson were moderately successful in using jawboning to slow inflation. When President Nixon took office, however, a number of factors converged to produce galloping inflation. (The annual rise in the cost of living during the 1970s doubled from the decade before.) At first, he insisted that government should keep hands off "private" decisions such as the setting of wages and prices. But when prices shot up and consumer demand and employment fell, Nixon completely reversed his policy. In August 1971, he acknowledged the failure of government nonintervention and adopted the "New Economic Policy." Going far beyond the jawboning approach, the new program gave government power to prohibit wage and price increases it judged excessive. The federal government thus became closely involved in one of management's chief tasks in a capitalist economy: setting wages and prices. Critics noted that, unlike wages and prices, corporate profits were exempt from government control. As a result, corporate profits in the early 1970s rose three times faster than wages. Nonetheless, government controls failed to control inflation and prices continued to rise throughout the 1970s twice as fast as during the previous two decades.

Regulating supply   The federal government has also begun to assume responsibility for assuring an adequate supply of raw materials for American industry, symbolized by the creation of the Department of Energy in 1977. In 1978, President Carter proposed an energy plan that established federal priorities for energy sources and uses. Carter's plan also provided tax measures and mandatory controls to achieve government objectives. The plan illustrates how the federal government has gone beyond regulating aggregate demand to regulating the supply of key elements of production.

Planning   The United States is the only capitalist nation without some planning apparatus. Planning in other capitalist nations does not impose rigid directives or eliminate private control of the economy. Much like the United States planning of energy sources and uses, economic planning in a capitalist economy seeks to anticipate and eliminate supply bottlenecks, coordinate government policies, and foster a more stable economic climate. Introducing planning in the United States might reduce the extent of the crisis, although the example of capitalist nations of Western Europe who have introduced planning suggests that planning cannot overcome the instability inherent in capitalism.

However, planning goes against the grain of the dominant American ideology. It suggests that the society's overall needs can be analyzed and public action taken to meet the most pressing needs. Conservatives oppose planning because it potentially undermines the logic of capitalism, which assumes the anarchy of production and frees private producers from undue government interference. "But what the conservatives fail to see," points out economist Robert Heilbroner, "is that there is no alternative to planning if capitalism is to be kept alive at all." [24] Another difficulty in introducing planning is that it runs counter to the typical political pattern of interest-group politics and the clientelistic bureaucracy in the United States, to be described in Chapter 9.

Planning is an attempt to minimize the worst costs without a fundamental change in capitalist production. Yet increasing government involvement in the economy poses risks for capitalism, with no guarantee that government can accomplish its objective of overcoming the crisis. The larger government's role becomes, the more the particular advantages or misfortunes of groups are seen to depend not on blind fate or the impersonal workings of the market but on government action. Thus, as control over the economy becomes more centralized, corporate capitalism becomes more exposed—and potentially vulnerable to political challenge. A central requirement of capitalism is to insulate the workings of the economy from democratic control. The separation of the economy and the political sphere is eroded when government attempts to bail out corporate capitalism in crisis. Thus, as the economy sinks deeper into crisis, government is drawn deeper into the quagmire and increasingly becomes a target for political challenge.

However, the particular form that political conflict takes depends on how the working class and other groups are organized.

5

workers and work

Alexis de Tocqueville arrived in the United States from France in 1831. Like other travellers to pre-Civil War America, when the country was mostly agrarian and the cities were unindustrialized, he was impressed most by the absence of class divisions. "Among the novel objects that attracted my attention during my stay in the United States," he wrote, "nothing struck me more forcibly than the general equality of condition among the people."[1]

Similarly, on his trip to the United States in 1842, the English novelist Charles Dickens discovered that even in the newly established textile mills of New England, conditions contrasted sharply with those in factories in Great Britain. Describing factory life in Lowell, Massachusetts, where virtually all the employees were teenage farmgirls, he wrote:

> The girls, as I have said, were all well dressed; and that phrase necessarily includes extreme cleanliness. They had serviceable bonnets, good warm cloaks, and shawls; and were not above clogs and patterns. . . . They were healthy in appearance, many of them remarkably so, and had the manners and deportment of young women; not of degraded brutes of burden. . . . The rooms in which they worked were as well ordered as themselves. In the windows of some there were green plants, which were trained to shade the glass;

[1] Alexis de Tocqueville, *Democracy in America* (New York, 1945), p. 3.

112

in all, there was as much fresh air, cleanliness, and comfort as the nature of the occupation could possibly admit of.[2]

Dickens, like Tocqueville, devoted much of his account to a discussion of the consequences of relative economic and social equality. The analyses of both chroniclers (especially of Tocqueville) have been influential in shaping the popular view of America's social structure. But their accounts documented an era that was coming to a close. In the 1840s and 1850s, the country's social structure began to undergo fundamental change. The development of early industrial capitalism created new class divisions that were soon to supplant the more egalitarian, individualistic democracy Tocqueville and Dickens observed.

THE DECLINE OF THE INDEPENDENT MIDDLE CLASS

By the late 1840s, the paternalism of the Lowell factories was a quaint memory. Had Dickens returned to Massachusetts in 1850, he would have had to confront a very different industrial reality. During the decade, the wages of the mill workers became severely depressed. Historian Norman Ware has found:

> In 1846 the wages of weavers in Newburyport were reduced 10 percent and in Lowell it was said that never since the beginning of the industry had the operatives received lower wages, though "they are compelled to do all of one-third more work and, in some cases, double." Whereas in 1840 weekly time wages were from 75 cents to $2 per week and board, in 1846 they ran from 55 cents to $1.50, making a 25 percent reduction in spite of the fact that they were doing 33 percent more work.[3]

There were sporadic strikes throughout the decade, in opposition both to more work at lower wages and to the length of the work day, which averaged twelve hours. Without exception, all the strikes, including one that lasted six months in the winter of 1850–51, were broken by the employers. When Dickens had visited Lowell, it was possible "for the New England women who lived isolated lives in farming communities to feel, when they went to Lowell, as if they were going to boarding-school, in spite of the

[2] Charles Dickens, *American Notes* (London, 1972), p. 115.
[3] Norman Ware, *The Industrial Worker, 1840–1860* (Chicago, 1924), pp. 113–14.

long hours." But, according to Ware, as the logic of profit replaced this genteel paternal tradition

> the older amenities had to go . . . the boarding-school dream faded. The girls were no longer able to relieve one another at their work, to snatch a rest of fifteen minutes, to read a book propped up on the frame. They ceased the cultivation of window flowers—in fact, they left the mills altogether and were replaced by new workers.[4]

By the end of the 1840s, the deterioration of working conditions drove the women out. They were replaced by immigrants escaping the Irish famine of 1848.

By the outbreak of the Civil War, the basis for conflict between workers and industrialists was developing rapidly. In community after community, the events that occurred in Lowell in the 1840s were replicated. By the end of the nineteenth century, as the Western frontier closed, capitalist class divisions overtook an older America of self-employed merchants, artisans, farmers, professionals, and traders.

The impact of these changes on everyday life was overwhelming. In their study of Muncie, Indiana, between 1890 and 1924, sociologists Helen and Robert Lynd documented the massive shift in social relationships that resulted from the development of industrial capitalism. Traditional craft patterns broke down under the impact of machines and assembly-line techniques in the local factories; skilled labor was now unnecessary for most jobs. As self-employed craftsmen and local entrepreneurs were forced out of business, workers' traditional neighborhoods lost their cohesiveness and autonomy. The city as a whole lost its sense of autonomy as well, since most of the urban economic changes were the result of national forces outside the city's control. The businessman, not the independent craftsman, was now at the top of the town's wealth, status, and power hierarchies.[5] In short, the division between the capitalist class and the working class came into being.

People became divided by class not only at the work place but also in their daily lives in the community and in politics. New institutions, including unions and businessmen's associations, developed that became vehicles for the expression and containment of the new structural antagonisms of interest. Unlike regional or religious distinctions, class distinctions underpinned the experience of living in a total, inescapable way.

---

[4] *Ibid.*, pp. 120–21.
[5] Robert S. Lynd and Helen Merrell Lynd, *Middletown* (New York, 1929).

Tocqueville and Dickens visited an America of *independent* workers; after the Revolution, four out of five workers (excluding slaves) were farmers, artisans, merchants, doctors, traders, small businessmen, lawyers, and craftsmen. Property was a liberating force. Because property, especially land, was distributed relatively equally, it provided a basis for a more substantive level of democracy than any country had known before. In this respect, the United States was truly a revolutionary society. Thomas Jefferson's dream of a dynamic agrarian democracy had been put into practice for white American men (excluding, however, a politically invisible majority of the population, made up of blacks, women, and Indians).

By 1900, however, the independent middle class had declined in size and was replaced by a growing percentage of Americans who did not own their tools of production but sold their labor for a wage. Whereas in 1780, only 20 percent of the work force were paid employees, in 1900, 68 percent were wage earners; the independent middle class had shrunk to less than one-third of all workers.[6]

Today, the demise of the independent property-owning middle class is virtually complete. Fewer than 3 percent of Americans are farm owners, and fewer than 7 percent are self-employed. Thus, with the development of industrial capitalism, ownership of the tools of production has come to divide Americans rather than unite them. As a result of the dual trend of the decline of the independent middle class and the development of a working-class majority, almost all Americans belong to one of two basic classes: those who own and control the means of production and workers—from dishwashers to skilled engineers—who sell their labor for a wage.

The decline of the independent middle class was no accident. Rather, it was required by the development of industrial capitalism. Mass production had two effects: one was to force independent craftsmen and entrepreneurs out of business; the second was to standardize the labor force. As factories grew rapidly in size at the turn of the century, working conditions became more uniform and impersonal. Technological innovations mechanized work and undermined the need for skilled craftsmen. In the automobile industry, for example, skilled mechanics and work gangs were replaced by semiskilled assembly-line workers.

[6] Michael Reich, "The Evolution of the United States Labor Force," in Richard C. Edwards, Michael Reich, Thomas E. Weisskopf, eds., *The Capitalist System: A Radical Analysis of American Society* (Englewood Cliffs, N.J., 1972), p. 175.

The skills needed in one industry became similar to those needed in others. As a result, "workers became members of an increasingly faceless mass of indistinguishable factory labor."[7]

WORK

Today, two major trends characterize the nature of work: the growth of white-collar (professional, clerical, and sales) employment and the transition to a situation in which most workers produce services rather than goods.

As American industry has continued to mechanize and automate, fewer workers are needed to produce increasing amounts of goods. In 1965, coal production was up 38 percent over 1950, yet employment in the mines fell by 10 percent. In the same period, total manufacturing output went up 79 percent, with only a 7 percent increase in production workers. By contrast, white-collar employment increased more than 60 percent in the mining industry, and 70 percent in manufacturing as a whole.

This trend is caused by the growing organizational complexity of contemporary corporations and the government. As economist Michael Reich notes:

> With the development of far-flung corporate sales and distribution networks and corporate divisions specializing in research and development and overall corporate coordination, more white collar workers—managerial, professional, technical, clerical and sales—are needed.[8]

In high-technology industries—particularly in electronics— scientists, technicians, and engineers comprise the majority of employees. Indeed, two very different fields of white-collar jobs have developed since the Second World War: clerical jobs (two-thirds of which are held by women) and technical and professional jobs. The increase in both types of white-collar employment is linked to the shift in the economy from manufacturing to service occupations.

The word *services* applies to a number of distinct kinds of

---

[7] David M. Gordon, Richard Edwards, and Michael Reich, "Labor Segmentation in American Capitalism," unpublished manuscript.

[8] Reich, in Edwards, Reich, and Weisskopf, p. 178.

Table 5-1
The changing occupational structure of the labor force

Occupational group	1910	1920	1930	1940	1950	1960	1970[a]	1976[a]
Managers, Officials and Proprietors (except farm)	6.6%	6.6%	7.4%	7.3%	8.8%	8.5%	10.5%	10.7%
White-Collar Workers	14.7	18.3	22.0	23.8	27.7	33.8	37.8	39.4
Professional and Technical	4.7	5.4	6.8	7.5	8.5	11.4	14.2	15.2
Clerical	5.3	8.0	8.9	9.6	12.3	15.0	17.4	17.9
Sales	4.7	4.9	6.3	6.7	6.9	7.4	6.2	6.3
Blue-Collar Workers	38.2	40.2	39.6	39.8	41.2	39.5	35.3	32.9
Craftsmen and Foremen	11.6	13.0	12.8	12.0	14.5	14.3	12.9	12.7
Semi-skilled	14.6	15.6	15.8	18.4	20.9	19.7	17.7	15.3
Unskilled	12.0	11.6	11.0	9.4	6.8	5.5	4.7	3.9
Service Workers	9.6	7.8	9.8	11.8	10.3	11.7	12.4	13.7
Agricultural Workers	30.9	27.0	21.2	17.4	11.8	6.3	4.0	3.3
Farmers and Farm Managers	16.5	15.3	12.4	10.4	7.5	3.9		
Farm Laborers	14.4	11.7	8.8	7.0	4.3	2.4		
Total[b]	100.0	100.0	100.0	100.0	100.0	100.0	100.0	100.0

[a]Date for 1970 and 1976 refer to employed persons only.
[b]Individual items are rounded independently and therefore may not add up to totals.

Sources: Michael Reich, "The Evolution of the United States Labor Force," in Richard C. Edwards, Michael Reich, and Thomas E. Weisskopf, eds., *The Capitalist System: A Radical Analysis of American Society* © 1972, p. 178. Reprinted by permission of Prentice-Hall, Inc., Englewood Cliffs, N.J.; and U.S. Department of Commerce, Bureau of the Census, *Statistical Abstract of the United States* (Washington, D.C., 1976), p. 372.

employment, all of which are expanding. As sociologist Daniel Bell notes, "in the very development of industry there is a necessary expansion of transportation and of public utilities as auxiliary services in the movement of goods and the increasing use of energy, and an increase in the non-manufacturing but still blue collar force."[9] Thus the first kind of service employment is an integral part of the industrial process. This is not a new service sector.

[9] Daniel Bell, *The Coming of Post-Industrial Society* (New York, 1973), p. 127.

With the growth of the population and mass consumption of goods, more and more people are involved in the distribution of goods and in the fields of insurance, real estate, and finance. This cluster of activities provides the supportive services needed to keep goods circulating and to provide capital for industrial expansion.

Personal services have also expanded numerically, but their organization has changed. Chains of restaurants, hotels, and automobile garages as well as the entertainment and sports industries carry out functions that were once fulfilled by independent entrepreneurs. Today, the production and distribution of personal services is increasingly in impersonal corporate hands.

The fourth major area of services are those provided by government, including education, health care, and welfare. Government service employment has grown enormously; for example, there were 1,254,000 teachers in the United States in 1950; in 1966 the number had risen to 2,353,000.

Stratification and Class

Given the differentiation in the work force, some observers argue that the class division between capital and labor has been superseded by a more complex, stratified, occupational order in which there are numerous gradings of material rewards, status, and power. A related proposition is that the shift in employment from the production of goods to the production of services has fundamentally transformed American capitalism. Daniel Bell, for one, has suggested that we have entered a new age in which the basic antagonism is not between capitalist and worker in the context of the factory but between the white-collar professional expert and the rest of the population. These views are only partial truths at best. Perhaps most importantly, they overstate the distinctiveness of white-collar and service occupations.

In 1870, there were only 82,200 clerical workers in the whole country (less than 1 percent of the work force). These bookkeepers, secretaries, bank tellers, payroll and postal clerks, and stenographers more often than not had the status of craftsmen and were very well paid. In 1900, economist Harry Braverman reports, "clerical employees of steam railroads and in manufacturing had average annual earnings of $1,011; in the same year the average annual earnings of [blue-collar] workers in these industries was

$435 for manufacturing and $548 for steam railroads."[10] The division between the large mass of blue-collar workers and the tiny number of white-collar workers was great. If this gap had continued, the rapid expansion of white-collar clerical work would have been significant indeed.

But the very process of clerical expansion has made office work more and more like blue-collar work. Indeed, according to the Bureau of Labor Statistics, weekly clerical wages today are lower than those for every type of blue-collar work, including unskilled labor. Moreover, clerical work is now depersonalized. It has been stripped of its craft status, routinized, and systematized. The tasks of most clerical workers have come to resemble those of shopfloor workers. Common office tasks have been precisely quantified so that corporate offices may be run as large, efficient machines. The Systems and Procedures Association of America, for example, has published a guide based on information provided by General Electric, the General Tire and Rubber Company, and other enterprises, which presents a standard for office performance: "File drawer, open and close; no selection, .04 minutes; . . . desk drawer, open side drawer of standard desk, .014 minutes," and so on.[11] As sociologist C. Wright Mills concluded in his study of office work, except for hard physical labor, there are few characteristics of blue-collar work that are not also true for at least some white-collar work. "For here, too, the human traits of the individual, from his physique to his psychic disposition, become units in the functionally rational calculations of managers."[12]

Even skilled and professional white-collar work has changed. Engineers, scientists, and technicians have lost their traditional independent craft status. Like manual laborers, they work for others who control the aims and conditions of their labor. Lawyers and doctors—the best-paid and most respected white-collar workers—have also lost a significant amount of their traditional independence. Year after year, a diminishing proportion of lawyers are engaged in their own practices, as a larger number work for big law firms or are employed directly by government or corporations on a salary basis. Similarly, an increasing proportion of doctors

[10] Harry Braverman, "Labor and Monopoly Capital," *Monthly Review* 26 (July–August 1974): 51.
[11] *Ibid.*, p. 74.
[12] C. Wright Mills, *White Collar* (New York, 1954), pp. 226–27.

work for a salary in large urban research centers, clinics, and hospitals.

Undeniably, the rapid growth in the production and distribution of services has changed American capitalism. But it has not eliminated or transformed the most fundamental distinction between capital and labor. Although the content of production has changed, its class character has not. Like factory workers, service workers (both blue and white collar) remain wage earners without control over the means of production or the work process.

Discontent, Division, and Struggle

The majority of American workers are profoundly discontented with their work. A recent task force report to the secretary of the Department of Health, Education and Welfare found that only 40 percent of white-collar workers and 20 percent of blue-collar workers would choose to do the same work if they had a choice.[13] After having spent three years interviewing people in depth about their work, Studs Terkel wrote of the "scars, psychic as well as physical, brought home to the supper table and the TV set":

> There are, of course, the happy few who find a savor in their daily job. . . . For the many, there is hardly a concealed discontent. The blue-collar blues is no more bitterly sung than the white collar moan. "I'm a machine," says the spot-welder. "I'm caged," says the bank teller, and echoes the hotel clerk. "I'm a mule," says the steelworker. "A monkey can do what I do," says the receptionist. "I'm less than an implement," says the migrant worker. "I'm an object," says the high fashion model. Blue collar and white call upon the identical phrase: "I'm a robot."[14]

Such discontent, which includes dissatisfaction over the diminishing buying power of the pay packet, poses a threat to the stability of the current order, for it is the raw material of political struggle. But the discontent of most workers often does not achieve political expression beyond individualistic solutions (such as high absenteeism) and a low level of craftsmanship. Essentially this is so because the characteristics that divide workers from each other have prevented collective action, because the trade union movement has been integrated into the economic system in the past four decades on terms that do not challenge the hegemony of

---

[13] Special Task Force to the Secretary of Health, Education, and Welfare, *Work in America* (Cambridge, Mass., 1973), pp. 15–16).
[14] Studs Terkel, *Working* (New York, 1974), pp. xi–xii.

the American capitalist system, and because the trade unions are not part of a predominantly working-class political party that organizes people's discontents not only at work but outside of the work place.

THREE HISTORIES

Americans are not a homogeneous lot. In particular, today's working class of wage earners consists of three broad groups, each with its own distinct history, each having entered the industrial work force at different periods of American economic development, and each of which today plays an economic role different from the others. These three groups are blacks and other non-European minorities, white Europeans, and women.

Blacks and Other Non-European Minorities

The experience of America's non-European minorities—blacks, Indians, Asians, Mexicans, and Caribbean Hispanics—has been considerably different from that of other Americans, including European immigrants. With the notable exception of Indians and some Chicanos, minorities came to the United States for the same reason as European immigrants: to work. But the answers to where and under what circumstances they worked were quite different for the two groups.

The native North American Indian tribes, many of whom were mobile hunters, withstood the attempts made by the New World colonists to force them into dependent labor relationships, including slavery. They resisted agricultural peonage and fought for their lands. South of the Rio Grande, where Indian settlements were dense, the Spanish succeeded in subjugating the Indians economically and in capturing their labor. By contrast, in the territories that eventually became the United States, Indian settlements were sparse and thus difficult to colonize for labor. Instead, a process of genocide drove Indians off their lands to make room for European settlements.

Today, the surviving remnant live on reservations and, increasingly, in middle-size and large cities. Their living conditions are more depressed than those of any other American minority group. Indian unemployment is over 40 percent, and an over-whelming number of those who work have low-paid menial jobs.

In the American South, neither Indian nor white labor was sufficient to meet the demands of large-scale plantation agriculture. Slaves were imported to meet that need. There, as in other parts of the continent, property ownership was largely restricted to whites. "White men, even if from lowly origins and serf-like pasts, were able to own land, property and sell their labor in the free market." [15] Even the most degrading "free labor" jobs of the developing capitalist sectors of the economy were for whites only. Blacks and the other racial minorities were channelled into a secondary labor market that was both noncapitalist and unfree. The correlation between color and "free" work was nearly exact.

After the Civil War, as America rapidly industrialized, the manpower needs of the factories were not filled by newly freed blacks but by white ethnics from Europe.

> American captains of industry *and* the native white proletariat preferred the employment of despised, unlettered European peasants to that of the emancipated Negro population of the South. Low as was the condition and income of the factory laborer, his status was that of a free worker. [16]

Black Americans became sharecroppers and tenant farmers on Southern plantations, little removed from their former conditions of slavery.

A similar pattern of work relations was created in the Southwest in the nineteenth century. After the Mexican defeats in the Texas war of independence in 1836 and the Mexican War of 1846 to 1848, a new pool of dependent Mexican labor was available to the colonizers. This work force was usually bound to contractors and landowners in a status little above peonage. Asians, too, especially the Chinese, were contract rather than "free" laborers in the Southwest, where they were used in work gangs to build railroads and mines.

In our discussion of class relations, we emphasized the basic distinction between those who own and control capital and those who sell their labor for a wage. The colonized minorities, however, at least until well into the twentieth century, were outside of this class dynamic. Workers in capitalist enterprises, including the European immigrants, worked within the wage system, whereas

---

[15] Robert Blauner, *Racial Oppression in America* (New York, 1972), p. 58.
[16] *Ibid.*, p. 59.

the minorities filled jobs in the least advanced, most industrially backward sectors of the economy. As a result, sociologist Robert Blauner notes:

> In a historical sense, people of color provided much of the hard labor (and also technical skills) that built up the agricultural base and mineral-transport-communication "infrastructure" necessary for industrialization and modernization, whereas the Europeans worked primarily within the industrialized modern sectors. The initial position of European ethnics while low, was therefore strategic for movement up the economic and social pyramid. The placement of nonwhite groups, however, imposed barrier upon barrier on such mobility, freezing them for long periods of time in the least favorable segments of the economy.[17]

A dual labor market, in which whites are distinguished from nonwhites, continues to exist in the United States at present. Although the following discussion examines the particularities of the black experience, the same general trends hold for Indians, Chicanos, Asians, and Caribbean Hispanics.

A wide disparity between the incomes of whites and blacks is the most obvious indicator of the continuing existence of racial inequality at the work place. The most exhaustive study published on the subject in the past decade reported that "median family income for nonwhites in 1966 was $4,628 and for white families $7,722, giving a nonwhite to white median income ratio of 59.9 percent." Since then, although there has been a slight improvement in the ratio of black to white income, the dollar gap has actually widened. Although black families earned $9,321 a year in 1975, white family income had increased to $14,268; hence the average black American still earns roughly $6 for every $10 earned by his or her white counterpart. Only 10 percent of white families earned under $5,000 in 1975, but more than one in four black families had such meager incomes.[18]

Moreover, the higher the wage and prestige of an occupation, the lower the percentage of black workers in that occupation. Blacks represent about 12 percent of the labor force, yet only 5 percent of professionals, 3 percent of managers, 6 percent of clerks, and 3 percent of salespeople. By contrast, blacks make up

[17] *Ibid.*, p. 62.
[18] Albert Wohlstetter and Sinclair Coleman, "Race Differences in Income," Report Prepared for the Office of Economic Opportunity, October 1970, mimeographed manuscript; Institute for Research on Poverty, "Statistics of Poverty," August 1977, mimeographed manuscript.

half the country's domestic household workers, and one-quarter of the unskilled laborers.[19]

The majority of blacks work for small business firms, not the big corporations, or are unemployed (the unemployment rate for blacks has been approximately double the rate for whites in the 1970s). And within the relatively depressed sector of the economy in which most blacks work, a significant amount of discrimination limits blacks to the meanest, lowest-paid, most transient work, or to black service firms that sell goods and services to the ghettoes. A recent study of Chicago's labor market found that 70 percent of small firms did not employ any blacks; of the 30 percent that did, virtually all had a majority of black workers.

In the past decade some of the great class and economic differences between blacks and whites have gradually been eliminated. For example, as late as 1950 only 16 percent of black males were employed as craftsmen, foremen, or on white-collar jobs; 21 percent worked as semiskilled workers; the rest were either unskilled, working in lower-class service jobs, or unemployed. By 1970, over 30 percent of black males worked in white-collar jobs and almost 30 percent were semiskilled workers.[20] Much of this was due to gains achieved by the civil rights movement of the 1960s, which broke barriers to black employment in many corporate and government jobs. However, one ironic result has been a widening of the gap between middle- and lower-income blacks, the latter still being the majority confined to semiskilled and unskilled jobs, unemployment, or welfare. As a *New York Times* survey concluded:

> The decade produced the most extensive gains for the most favored segments of black America—the middle class and working class blacks. Blacks who entered the decade with educational and marketable skills were in a better position generally to exploit the newly created opportunities. . . . Those mired in rural poverty and the urban welfare system derived peripheral benefits of food stamps, improved health care and larger dependency payments, but on the whole remained poor, unskilled, and disaffected.
>
> These deepening divisions created a new generation of haves and have-nots in black America. . . . If middle class blacks complained about the widening gap with whites, lower income blacks

---

[19] *New York Times*, July 24, 1974.
[20] William Julius Wilson, *The Declining Significance of Race* (Chicago, 1978), pp. 126–29.

bitterly pointed to the widening gap between them and the black middle class.[21]

Half of all the black poor, as defined by federal government standards, are under eighteen, and—given their skill levels and the patterns of discrimination—they are likely to remain poor for a long time. Indeed, as sociologist William Wilson stresses, "the chances for economic improvement for the black poor are rapidly decreasing." In support of this finding, he cites the sharp rise in the black unemployment rate for young and poorly trained ghetto blacks, evidence that many blacks have given up looking for work altogether, and the elimination of jobs in areas where many blacks live. "In short," he concludes, "there are clear indications that the economic gap between the black underclass . . . and the higher income blacks will very likely widen and solidify."[22]

If the growing division in the black community is the most significant trend affecting non-European minorities in this decade, the second most important is the dramatic increase in the number of illegal aliens who now live in the United States. Accurate estimates of their numbers are hard to come by, but a recent informed guess placed this population at approximately 8 million. About 60 percent are Mexicans who crossed the border without being seen; the next largest group is Central and South Americans. These immigrants, who generally come from desperately poor situations, work at very low-status, low-paid jobs. A 1975 survey found that Mexican aliens earned $2.34 an hour on average, with more than one in five workers being paid below the minimum wage. These newcomers live in fear of being caught, rarely use public services, and are targets for gross exploitation. As a group, they have replaced blacks at the bottom of the social structure. Language barriers and their illegal status make resistance or protest virtually impossible.[23]

White Europeans

The United States is a nation of immigrants, most of whom have come from Europe. With the exception of American Indians (the country's real native Americans), virtually all Americans came

---

[21] *New York Times*, August 26, 1973.
[22] Wilson, pp. 129–34.
[23] Elizabeth Midgley, "Immigrants: Whose Huddled Masses?" *The Atlantic Monthly*, April 1978, pp. 6–26.

from overseas, or their ancestors did, no earlier than the seventeenth century. Colonial America was largely settled by Protestant English, French, and Dutch settlers. Their descendants today (sometimes referred to as WASPs, for White-Anglo-Saxon Protestants) do not often think of themselves as immigrants or as an ethnic group. Yet, they too have been an integral part of the massive migration of European ethnics to the United States during the past four centuries. Hence they are included in this discussion of white European workers.

Factory capitalism, however, did not develop during a period of mass Protestant European immigration, but during a period of Catholic and Jewish immigration. Thus, while many white Protestants joined the industrial labor force from the farms and smaller cities of rural America, the newer, late nineteenth and early twentieth century, European immigrants entered the industrial work force directly. In 1850, 11.5 percent of the population was foreign-born; in 1890, 16.6 percent, a figure that remained roughly constant until the passage of restrictive immigration legislation in the early 1920s. Major industrial centers were mosaics of numerous distinct ethnic communities.

In late nineteenth-century America, class and ethnicity interpenetrated each other. Before 1880, when the large-scale migration from Southern and Eastern Europe began, the members of the newly developing working class consisted of the following basic ethnic elements: (1) native-born white Protestant artisans who continued to work in handicraft industries that predated the American revolution; (2) a small number of white native-born farmers who came to the cities and factories of the Northeast instead of joining the larger migration westward to new agricultural lands; (3) skilled Northern European immigrants—German, French, English, Welsh, and Scotch-Irish—who had craft occupations in the new factories; and (4) Irish and Chinese peasants who "were propertyless in the historical sense of possessing neither capital nor land, as well as in the modern sense of possessing no skills that would give them status within the industrial system."[24] Most were employed in railway construction, which required large numbers of unskilled laborers.

As the economy developed in the late nineteenth century, work that had been done by skilled mining, textile, and steel

[24] Stanley Aronowitz, *False Promises* (New York, 1973), p. 146.

workers could now be done by unskilled workers tending machines. The massive migration from Southern and Eastern Europe brought the millions of unskilled workers needed to staff the developing corporate industries. In 1880, only 4 percent of the miners in the coal fields of eastern Pennsylvania were from Southern or Eastern Europe; but as the coal industry was mechanized and skill levels were reduced, immigrant workers poured into the mines from Italy, Poland, Russia, Czechoslovakia, Austria, Hungary, and Lithuania. Similar changes in the work force occurred in textile, iron, and steel plants. By 1900, the new ethnic immigrants provided the core of productive factory labor.

As more and more factory jobs became unskilled and were filled by the white-ethnic immigrants from Southern and Eastern Europe, native-born and Northern European skilled workers established formidable craft-union barriers to protect their jobs from incursion by the rest of the labor force. Especially by the use of separate seniority lists, unskilled workers were barred from skilled jobs even when they accumulated company seniority. Until the 1930s, in many industries only the skilled workers were represented by trade unions; the unskilled remained without union protection.

Hence, at least until the late 1930s, there was little occupational mobility available to the newer ethnic immigrants who had joined the industrial work force at the bottom rungs. There were exceptions—mainly Jewish and Greek—who had arrived with experience as artisans and proprietors that facilitated their entry into small business as owners. The great bulk of Catholic immigrants, on the other hand, had no such entrepreneurial preparation.

Most of the newer ethnic immigrants were peasants from societies that were sharply stratified along hierarchical, semifeudal lines. The inheritance of semifeudal social relations was a major factor in fragmenting the developing industrial working class and in dividing workers from each other. As sociologist Stanley Aronowitz has noted:

> Contrary to the commonly held belief that the success of our economic development has been due, in large measure, to the absence of a feudal past, it is evident that the genius of American capital consisted in its ability to incorporate the institutions of rank and obligation, the separation of mental and physical labor, the distinction between town and country, and the authority relations that

marked feudalism. Feudalism was not denied, but transformed and used by employers in the development of capitalism.[25]

Today, children and grandchildren of the newer European immigrants provide the bulk of the work force for the country's largest industrial corporations. Indeed, with the development of industrial unionism in the 1930s and the relative prosperity of the corporate sector of the economy, these white ethnics as a group are better off economically than women workers and racial minorities. Although ethnic categories are an important basis for the organization of the daily lives of many Americans (ethnic schools, churches, neighborhoods, and shops continue to provide a sense of solidarity and identity), the distinctions between old and new ethnics no longer differentiate workers from each other in terms of either their wages or their occupations. With minor exceptions, the Southern and Eastern European ethnics have achieved an occupational profile remarkably like that of the society as a whole. Proportionately, roughly as many ethnics are managers, white-collar workers, blue-collar workers, and farmers as the American population as a whole.

Women

In his report on manufacturers in 1796, Alexander Hamilton proposed that women and children be put to work in developing industries to save them from the "curse of idleness." In Lowell, Massachusetts, and in other New England mill towns, unmarried women were recruited to meet the labor needs of the new factories. But it was assumed that married women would stay in the home. As the country industrialized in the middle and late nineteenth century and the economic world of the independent middle class was shattered, an increasing number of men began to work in impersonal factory surroundings beyond the immediate embrace of home and community. Ideas about women conformed to this new reality:

> With men removed from contact with children during the lengthy and exhausting day, women had to fill the breach. Simultaneously, [capitalist] economic policies which emphasized individualism, success and competition replaced the old puritan ethic which emphasized morality, hard work and community. Men who worked hard and strove for success required wives who could competently supervise the household and exercise supportive roles as well. . . .

[25] *Ibid.*, p. 183.

In what Bernard Wishy calls a reappraisal of family life that took place after 1830, motherhood rose to new heights, and children became the focus of womanly activity.[26]

But this new ethos applied almost exclusively to white, native-born American women. Immigrant and black women were driven into the labor force by need and, from 1850 on, took jobs in the burgeoning industries. The prevailing feminine ideal of domesticity, however, "provided employers with a docile labor force of women who, for the most part, were convinced that their real calling lay in marriage and child-rearing, and had only a transient interest in their jobs."[27] In complementary fashion, since women "really" belonged at home, employers were permitted to treat them as if their earnings were not necessary for family survival. Thus, from the very entry of women into the mainstream work force to the present, women's wages have been considerably lower than men's (a tendency that has been reinforced by consistently lower rates of union membership by women).

During the last decades of the nineteenth century, the place of women in the labor force began to undergo considerable change. Before then, most clerical workers were men. But with the growing concentration of American industry and the expansion of corporate capitalism, the demand for clerical workers rose rapidly, and the number of available literate men was inadequate. A large pool of educated women was tapped.

In this century, the entry of women into office work has increased at such a rate that clerical labor has become feminized: many jobs are labeled "women's work" and entail services of a sex-stereotyped nature. Indeed, as sociologist Margery Davies points out, the work of a secretary came to be compared functionally with the role of a wife.

> Secretaries began to be expected to remind their bosses of birthdays and other social occasions, go out to buy sandwiches or coffee, and even run such personal errands as buying Christmas presents. All clerical workers were expected to dress nicely and be personable to visitors to the office; in other words, to be conscious and careful of their female roles as decorative sex objects and practitioners of the social graces.[28]

---

[26] Alice Kessler Harris, "Women, Work, and the Social Order," unpublished manuscript.

[27] *Ibid*.

[28] Margery Davies, "Woman's Place Is at the Typewriter: The Feminization of the Clerical Labor Force," *Radical America* 8 (July–August 1974): 19.

Women have thus come to occupy low-wage white- and blue-collar jobs. Collectively, they make up a marginal, exploited labor force. Only just over one-third of women work full time; the many women who work on a part-time or temporary basis never achieve seniority or fringe benefits. Women are readily fired in periods of economic recession and rehired when employers need them. Because many must stop working to look after their families, they have high turnover rates in the work force and are more exposed than men to the risks of unemployment. They are discriminated against in being promoted to supervisory jobs. And they are paid significantly less than men.

In 1939, the median income of men was $1,419, as compared to $863 for women, or 60.8 percent of men's wages. Thirty-five years later, the median income of working women had decreased to 57 percent of the median wage for men, as women earned $6,957 compared to $12,152 for men. Even comparing workers of the same age and education, women are still paid about a third less than men. And as more and more women enter the labor force with higher educational qualifications, the outlook for improvements in the relative standing of women workers is not good. The next decade, *The Wall Street Journal* predicts, will produce few professional and even more low-skill jobs for women. Because of declining birth rates, the market for teachers and social workers, two fields where women have long outnumbered men, is dwindling. At the same time, the market for clerical workers, whose jobs are increasingly routinized, is growing because of the growth of corporate and governments staffs as well as the increasing use of data-processing equipment.[29]

EARLY UNION STRUGGLES AND REPRESSION

July 16, 1877 is a landmark date in American labor history. On that date, the Baltimore and Ohio railroad cut wages by 10 percent. In protest of the move, the crew of a cattle train in Martinsberg, West Virginia, abandoned the train, and other trainmen refused to

[29] June Kronholtz, "Though More Women Work, Job Equality Fails to Materialize," *The Wall Street Journal*, July 6, 1976, pp. 1, 16.

replace them. By the end of the month, the first mass strike in America had spread across the country. "Strikers stopped and seized the nation's most important industry, the railroads, and crowds defeated or won over first the police, then the state militias, and in some cases even the Federal troops" who were called out to deal with the class insurrection. In a dozen major cities, all industrial activity was stopped by general strikes. The strikes were eventually put down by employers with the help of police and military authorities, but the Great Upheaval, as the event came to be known, was profoundly important in two respects. First, it reflected the workers' sense of their new structural position in American society in face of the decline of the independent middle class. ("There was no concert of action at the start," the *Labor Standard* wrote. "It spread because the workmen of Pittsburgh felt the same oppression that was felt by the workmen of West Virginia and so with the workmen of Chicago and St. Louis.") Second, the strikes highlighted the need for workers to organize if they were to successfully resist the repression of workers' movements by employers and the government.[30]

By the middle 1880s, the Knights of Labor, the most important national union organization of the period, was growing at a phenomenal rate. In July 1884, it had just over 71,000 members; two years later it had over 729,000. The Knights sought to link all workers, skilled and unskilled, black and white, men and women. But the Knights' leadership was opposed to the strike weapon and to the wage system as a whole. Instead, they developed a fundamentalist religious perspective that eschewed wage struggles and promoted a cooperative fellowship among workers. The Knights' opposition to strikes proved to be the cause of their undoing, because strikes were the only weapon workers had to resist collectively the hardships inflicted by the developing factory economy. Hence, by the turn of the century, much strike action was spontaneously organized, outside of the formal structure of unions.

By the First World War, two very different kinds of unions had emerged. The American Federation of Labor (AFL), which had been founded in 1881 and was led by Samuel Gompers, organized skilled craft workers, the most well paid of the new proletariat. The

[30] Jeremy Brecher, *Strike!* (San Francisco, 1972), pp. 1–21.

AFL was a conservative union force. It did not challenge the developing distribution of resources or the basic structure of industrial capitalism. Rather, the AFL sought to defend the relatively privileged position of the craftsmen it represented and limited its demands to higher wages and shorter working hours. By contrast, the Industrial Workers of the World (IWW), which was founded in 1905, appealed to the interests of all workers, especially those who were most exploited. By the end of the First World War, the IWW had been smashed, and the AFL was gaining in strength. What accounts for the difference in their relative success?

The key factor was the response of management and government authorities to the two unions. The AFL was tolerated and even welcomed by some employers because, by representing only skilled craft workers, it divided workers from one another. But the IWW, which sought to articulate the interests of all workers as a class and which posed socialist alternatives to prevailing economic arrangements, presented a far greater threat both to capitalist industry and the social order as a whole. Thus, between 1905 and the outbreak of the First World War, IWW activities were systematically countered by government action:

> In Pennsylvania, the state police, which had been originally created by reformers "anxious to abolish the use of private police forces during industrial conflicts" constantly worked for the employers, not for the strikers. In San Diego, Washington State, and Arizona vigilante mobs . . . took direct repressive action against the IWW. Contacts between the mobs and leading state figures made such actions official government policy. . . . Vigilante action was frowned on, however, by some state officials who felt that there were "cleaner" ways to repress the organization. A public safety committee in Minnesota, a council of defense in Washington State, and a Commission on Immigration and Housing in California became official bodies seeking official solutions for the elimination of the IWW.[31]

Many of these local organizations urged the Wilson administration to take federal action to repress the IWW. There followed a campaign of federal action that included the deportation of many IWW leaders who were aliens and the trial of hundreds on conspiracy charges (conspiracy against industrial production). In one instance, after deliberating less than an hour, a Chicago jury found

---

[31] Alan Wolfe, *The Seamy Side of Democracy* (New York, 1973), pp. 26–27.

more than one hundred defendants guilty of four counts of conspiracy each.[32]

The demise of the IWW was also closely linked to the legitimization of the AFL. In particular, Gompers, Felix Frankfurter (who was later to become a justice of the Supreme Court), and Ralph Easley of the National Civic Federation campaigned actively for recognition of the AFL as a "safe" alternative to more threatening workers' organizations. One manufacturer urged that workers should be granted the "shadow of industrial democracy without the substance" to keep them "contented and productive."[33]

The repression of the IWW, of course, was not the only response of capitalists and the government to the militancy of the new industrial working class. Ideological propaganda, the reliance on state militias to protect strike-breakers, and the fostering of antiunion violence were among the common techniques of the day. And among these strategies were the manipulation of existing ethnic, racial, and sexual divisions in the work force and the creation of new divisions between kinds of workers (clerical versus managerial, white collar versus blue collar). Indeed, these strategies were related, since the antagonisms based on personal characteristics were exacerbated in order to legitimize new divisions between levels of work in the firm. As two historians have noted:

> Within the shop immigrants and Negroes did almost all unskilled and some semiskilled work, whereas the skilled jobs and minor administrative positions were reserved for native white Americans. "That job is not a hunky's job, and you can't have it," was the answer given to intelligent foreigners who aspired to rise above the ranks of common labor. Thus a wedge of racial discrimination was driven into the labor force.[34]

And as white-collar work increased, discrimination against women was used to solidify emerging lines of division within the office between jobs with and without managerial career potential. "In the office as well as the plant, organizing internal segments around externally sanctioned divisions—white over black, men over women, native American over immigrant—apparently reinforced the emergent lines of authority within the industrial hierarchy."[35]

[32] *Ibid.*, p. 29.
[33] *Ibid.*
[34] Thomas Cochran and William Miller, *The Age of Enterprise: A Social History of Industrial America* (New York, 1961), pp. 230–31.
[35] Gordon, Edwards, and Reich, "Labor Segmentation in American Capitalism."

UNIONS JOIN THE CORPORATE ECONOMY

Until the 1930s, as a result of the divisions in the work force and in the union movement, the vast majority of American workers were without union protection or representation. Between 1930 and 1940, however, the number of unionized workers more than doubled from 3.1 million to 7 million. In that decade, unions affiliated with the Congress of Industrial Organizations (CIO), founded in 1935, succeeded in unionizing the most important mass-production industries in the country, including steel and automobiles.

But their success came only after bitter, protracted struggles, in which class antagonisms were raw and palpable. "Four men were killed and eighty-four persons went to hospitals with gunshot wounds, cracked heads, broken limbs or other injuries received in a battle late this afternoon between police and steel strikers at the gates of the Republic Steel Corporation plant in South Chicago" as the United Steel Workers of America successfully sought recognition, the *New York Times* reported in May 1937.[36] In January 1936, automobile workers demanding recognition of the United Automobile Workers (UAW) staged sit-ins and took control of General Motors automobile plants in Flint, Michigan; Atlanta, Georgia; Anderson, Indiana; Norwood, Ohio; and Kansas City, Missouri. On the forty-fourth day of the sit-in and strike at Flint, General Motors gave in and recognized the UAW, but only after massive police violence and cooperative attempts between the governor and the company had failed to dislodge the workers.

Thus in the late 1930s, workers, through union-led mass actions, seemed to be moving rapidly to achieve a significant amount of substantive representation and fundamental structural change.

In 1973, however, thirty-six years after the Flint sit-in, *Business Week* editorialized:

> The unions have become an established institution, well financed and run by highly professional managers. These officers are paid on much the same basis as businessmen. . . . And they deal with many of the same problems—budgets, investments, taxes, even bargaining with staff and office worker unions.[37]

[36] Melvyn Dubofsky, ed., *American Labor Since the New Deal* (Chicago, 1971), p. 113.

[37] *Business Week*, August 18, 1973, p. 88.

The editorial also noted that the unions were "acting responsibly" and that strike figures had reached "the lowest level in years." In the same year, the steelworkers (led by a president who earned an annual salary of $70,000) signed a contract that pledged the union to fight wildcat strikes by its members. They also agreed—in advance of a wage settlement—not to strike, but to settle all wage disputes by arbitration. A major study of the UAW concluded:

> The relationship between the General Motors corporation and the United Automobile Workers has altered—they are not enemies, nor, in any large sense, adversaries. It is true . . . that the two, General Motors and the UAW, have *a greater community of interest than of conflict*.[38]

What had happened to produce the shift in less than four decades from militant class organization and confrontation to "responsible" routinized cooperation?

The development of a relatively conservative AFL-CIO (they merged in 1955) was made possible by the growing divisions between the corporate and small-capital sectors of the American economy. Unlike small-capital industries, whose major costs are wages and who have to absorb wage increases at the expense of profits, the corporate-sector industries are largely able to pass along wage increases in the form of higher prices. In the corporate sector, wages, prices, and profits are not determined by the operation of a traditional competitive market but are planned by the corporations and government. Hence corporate-sector companies, whose major expenses relate to technology, not men and women, have been able to accept the emergence of mass industrial unionism as one more element among many to be planned for in advance. Indeed, corporate-sector firms gain tangible benefits from the existence of a unionized work force because the unions guarantee that, outside of strike periods, the companies will have a predictably available work force at predictable wages.

By the end of the Second World War, most industrial unions had entered into permanent collective bargaining agreements with the largest corporations in the corporate sector. The unions succeeded in obtaining higher wages for their members, but not without relinquishing much in return. In addition to agreeing to increased productivity, union leaders began to collaborate with company managements to introduce technologically advanced

---

[38] William Serrin, *The Company and the Union* (New York, 1972), pp. 305–06.

production methods, which usually are resisted by the rank and file. Overall, from the standpoint of those who own and control corporate capital, "the main function of unions was (and is) to inhibit disruptive spontaneous rank and file activity (e.g., wildcat strikes and slowdowns) and to maintain labor discipline in general. In other words, *unions were (and are) the guarantors of managerial prerogatives.*"[39]

The union movement, to be sure, has supported progressive welfare-state legislation; in particular, unions have vigorously promoted the expansion of the social security system, unemployment and disability insurance, and other protections against economic insecurity (national health insurance is a present important target). But as we will see in Chapter 7, none of these programs threaten major corporate firms; indeed, to the extent that they make workers more secure and provide them with state, rather than corporate, benefits, the corporations stand to gain a more contented, productive work force. For this reason most major advances in social insurance since the New Deal have been supported by large industrial employers.

Thus, in terms of their economic welfare, the growth of industrial unionism has made a very real difference to corporate-sector workers. But the costs of these gains have been high. In particular, the union movement has left workers without the ability to control decisions that affect them at the work place. Political scientist David Greenstone notes, "the crucial fact is that the workers neither own nor control—*that they exercise no substantial economic authority over*—the firms in which they work."[40] In fact, the growth of industrial unionization, by conceding management prerogatives, has often made the conditions of work much more difficult. As companies introduce new technological innovations, individual workers have to bear the brunt of the speed-up of the work process.

For example, in 1966, General Motors opened a new Chevrolet plant at Lordstown, Ohio, that turned out 60 cars per hour, the company's usual production rate. In late summer 1971, the company brought in a new management team that introduced production methods aimed at increasing the number of cars produced to 110 per hour. The pace of work, which traditionally had been rapid, became maddening. A worker whose assembly-line job

[39] James O'Connor, *The Fiscal Crisis of the State* (New York, 1973), p. 23. Emphasis added.

[40] J. David Greenstone, in *The Nation*, September 8, 1969, p. 214.

was the installation of front seats was now expected to perform eight different operations — walking about twenty feet to a conveyor belt that transported the seats, lifting the seat and hauling it to the car, lifting the car's carpet, bending to fasten the bolts by hand, fastening them with an air gun, replacing the carpet, and putting a sticker on the hood signifying that the job had been properly done — in a total period of thirty-six seconds.

In the winter and spring of 1971–72, plant workers, mainly high-school graduates in their twenties, began to sabotage the work process. The workers began to pass many cars down the production line with bolts and parts missing. Unassembled engines were passed along, covered by their outer shells. More than half the cars that came off the production line had to be returned for major repairs.

This situation was threatening both to General Motors and to the leadership of the workers' union, the United Automobile Workers (UAW). The company's production and profits were jeopardized; even more importantly, the command authority of the plant's management to regulate the work process was directly challenged by the workers' in-plant protests. Similarly, the UAW had much to lose, since the workers' sabotage bypassed the union completely and implicitly raised issues of worker control that transcended the routine pattern of wage bargaining between the company and the union.

Thus, it was in the interests of both the company and the union officials to regain control over the workers. When 350 workers were dismissed for "efficiency" reasons in February, the UAW stepped in and called for a strike vote. In March, Lordstown's workers walked off the job. The strike did not revolve around the issue of the debilitating work process, but concentrated instead on wages, layoffs, and back pay for those who had been fired. The spring strike ended with a proclaimed victory by the union. The real victory belonged not to the strikers but to company and union officials who had succeeded in restoring normal patterns of bargaining and in cooling the workers' discontent by channeling it in traditional directions. The union bargained *for* wages and job security; control of the work process was bargained *away* in return. Working conditions were unchanged.

Although the union leadership claimed "total victory" at the end of the strike, some workers were not so sure. One bitterly complained, "Before the strike the union was in favor of not working faster than you could. Now people are afraid not to work.

The company and the union say everything is settled, we had a strike. But what did we achieve for it?"[41]

The growth of industrial unionism has been achieved at a high cost for nonunionized workers as well. Although unions are seen as the representatives of workers, most workers are not represented by unions and do not receive the benefits of collective bargaining. Yet they have to pay the higher prices companies charge to offset wage increases. Nonunionized labor literally pays the price of unionized workers' gains. Thus, by representing only a portion of the working class, unions splinter workers into opposing groups that are more conscious of antagonisms that divide them than of long-range interests that bind them together.

The percentage of American workers who are members of trade unions has declined sharply. There are now about 20 million dues-paying union members in the country, about 500,000 fewer than five years ago. They account for just over 20 percent of the work force; yet approximately twenty years ago, nearly 35 percent of the work force belonged to unions.[42] Although union leaders, *Business Week* notes, are "by and large nonradical bread-and-butter unionists . . . who negotiate contentedly, though militantly, within the free enterprise system, and agree with the staunchest capitalist that private investment generates jobs and growth," many businessmen have concluded that they would rather do without a unionized work force, and they fight union organizers' attempts to expand their organization's membership.[43] Especially in the South, where only about one in ten workers belong to unions, this resistance has been very successful, often as the result of intimidation, mass firings, and unlawful restrictions on the rights of union officials to place their case before a plant's workers. Today, the union movement is weaker than at any time since the Second World War. In part, this declining influence is the result of the failure of workers to fashion a working-class political party of the kind commonly found in Western Europe. It is to the nature of the country's political parties and mechanisms of political participation, therefore, that we now turn.

[41] Aronowitz, p. 43.
[42] *New York Times*, February 24, 1978, p. A12.
[43] *Business Week*, September 22, 1975, p. 109.

public policy and political control at home and abroad

6

competition without representation: political parties and elections

Presidential elections are reported more extensively than virtually any other event in the entire gamut of American politics. Television coverage begins years before the nominating conventions, with endless speculation about the prospects of rivals for the nomination in the two major parties. The conventions and the presidential campaigns are televised in exhaustive detail. Yet the most important choices have been made long before the conventions: the alternatives presented by parties do not accurately reflect the interests or wishes of the broad majority of the population. The party system obscures the lack of representation by the fig leaf of competition.

One of the central features of American politics this book is attempting to analyze concerns the coexistence of legal equality and procedural democracy in the political sphere, and substantive inequality of resources—economic, political, and social—possessed by different groups of Americans. Elections are the foremost institution of procedural democracy. Citizens are presumably able to elect representatives responsive to their interests. Yet they do not do so. Instead, voters regularly elect representatives who tolerate the persistence of deep-rooted inequality.

In order to understand why, an examination of the American electoral process must be broadened to include political parties. The significance of elections depends on the nature and the extent of the alternatives offered to voters and how the alternatives get organized. This in turn requires analyzing the central role of political parties in nominating candidates for office, developing policies, and thereby organizing electoral choice.

One reason for the failure of procedural democracy to alter (or even challenge) structural inequality is that political parties do not offer viable alternatives to the status quo. The two major parties are more similar in their policies than they are different. In the twentieth century, with the partial exception of the New Deal, both parties have been united in their support for corporate capitalism. Conflict between the parties has concerned relatively minor matters, including the rivalry of candidates for office, the differing tactics each party advocates to achieve the same objective of maintaining and stabilizing conditions favorable to corporate dominance, and the marginal benefits each party promises its slightly different constituency.

However, even in cases where candidates are virtually indistinguishable from each other, elections are not trivial. Their significance lies in the fact that they encourage the belief (part truth mixed with a good dose of illusion) that established arrangements are freely chosen by the American people and serve their interests. A vote for a candidate represents more than an expression of confidence in a person: it symbolizes an expression of confidence in the *system* of parties, elections, and, ultimately, the American political structure. As political scientist Murray Edelman points out, political parties and elections "quiet resentments and doubts about particular political acts, reaffirm belief in the fundamental rationality and democratic character of the system, and fix conforming habits of future behavior."[1]

[1] Murray Edelman, *The Symbolic Uses of Politics* (Urbana, Ill., 1964), p. 17.

As described in earlier chapters, there is a fundamental class cleavage in American society. But this cleavage is not reflected within the party system. Only about half the adult population goes to the polls in a typical presidential election. Even fewer vote in off-year elections, when there is no presidential contest. Among the ranks of nonvoters are found a disproportionate number of blacks, unemployed, elderly, uneducated, and poor, although the number of educated, involved—and alienated—nonvoters is growing. Political scientist E. E. Schattschneider has called nonvoting

> by a wide margin the most important feature of the whole system, the key to understanding the composition of American politics. . . . It is profoundly characteristic of the behavior of the more fortunate strata of the community that responsibility for widespread nonparticipation is attributed wholly to the ignorance, indifference and shiftlessness of the people. This has always been the rationalization used to justify the exclusion of the lower classes from any political system. There is a better explanation. Abstention reflects the suppression of the options and alternatives that reflect the needs of the nonparticipants.[2]

In order to understand the largest significance of American political parties, one needs to broaden the focus beyond day to day partisan disputes or even the quadrennial presidential elections. Viewed from the perspective of their overall impact on the political system, American political parties reflect and thereby reinforce the existing distribution of political and economic power. Although they differ somewhat in terms of their electoral constituencies and policy preferences, both major parties are conservative forces that blur cleavages and strengthen the status quo.

More concretely, this means that political parties reinforce the dominance of business. As political scientist Andrew Martin puts it, "In the absence of any political party independent of business . . ., American business elites remain effectively insulated from political challenge through the democratic process."[3]

The fact that American political parties do not challenge business control suggests that parties are relatively weak. Moreover, recent trends, which will be discussed in this chapter, point to a

[2] E. E. Schattschneider, *The Semi-Sovereign People* (New York, 1960), pp. 103–05.

[3] Andrew Martin, *The Politics of Economic Policy in the United States: A Tentative View from a Comparative Perspective* (Beverly Hills, Cal., 1973), p. 31.

further weakening of the party system. The result renders parties both less able to challenge business dominance and less effective in fostering the impression of popular support for business dominance. Yet the parties' lack of independence does not signify that the subject of political parties and elections should be ignored. Political parties and elections potentially provide an arena for mobilizing popular movements. And in the absence of popular mobilization, the electoral sphere provides an important symbolic boost to the existing distribution of power. By fostering the belief that existing arrangements are freely chosen and desirable, the party system endows them with legitimacy and deters alternative majorities from seeking change.

POLITICAL PARTIES AS DEMOCRATIC FORCES

Parties were once a democratizing force in the United States. During the late eighteenth century, when other nations were governed by narrowly-based oligarchies, political parties originated in the United States and contributed four democratizing elements that leavened traditional political arrangements.

American political parties expanded political *participation*, both in the choosing of government officials and in the ruling process itself. Parties first mobilized eligible voters in the period before the Civil War, when restrictions on the suffrage were (compared to other countries) few; and they helped break down the deferential system of politics in which only the socially privileged and wealthy could participate.

This does not mean to suggest that America started out as a pure democracy. For several decades after the Constitution was ratified, the suffrage extended only to white male landowners. In most states, the poor were excluded from participation by a property qualification until the 1820s, and slaves, Indians, and women were excluded even longer. Moreover, the sphere of electoral politics was limited. Within the federal government, the only officials chosen by popular elections were members of the House of Representatives. Senators and the president were indirectly elected: senators, by state legislatures, which were themselves chosen by popular election; the president, by members of the electoral college, who were also chosen by state legislatures. And yet, despite numerous qualifications, the United States had the first popular government in the world, and citizen interest in politics ran high.[4] In the presidential election of 1840 (which by then was an election where the outcome in the electoral college directly reflected the popular vote), 80 percent of the eligible voters turned out to vote, a figure far higher than current turnout rates.[5]

Political parties represented *contending social and political forces*. By linking groups that were geographically separated, parties made it possible for people to organize and defend their interests within the national arena. This did not happen overnight. The first national governments were physically and functionally remote from popular forces. It was not until political parties extended their organization to the grass roots—beginning in Andrew Jackson's time (1820s to 1840s)—that one can begin to speak of a national constituency.

American political parties institutionalized *opposition* to the government. In other countries, the men holding public office might organize themselves into a group. But what made the American party system unique was that officeholders were organized into *several* groups, that these groups developed links to popular forces outside the government, and that one of these early groups (the Republicans under Jefferson's leadership) represented an open, organized opposition to the government's policies.

However, neither of the first two party groupings accepted the legitimacy of opposing parties. As historian Richard Hofstadter notes, "the creators of the first American party system on both sides, Federalists and Republicans, were men who looked upon parties as sores on the body politic."[6] In fact, the Federalists, the first party to rule, tried to destroy Republican opposition by passing the Alien and Sedition laws. The Sedition Act made it a crime to express criticism of the government, and the Federalists used it to indict the editors or publishers of fourteen major Republican newspapers. (Their humorless approach can be inferred from their indicting, convicting, and fining one editor "for expressing the

---

[4] The French Revolution of 1789 ushered in universal manhood suffrage earlier than in the United States. But Napoleon's coup d'état and the Restoration ended France's brief democratic experiment.

[5] William Nisbet Chambers, "Party Development and the American Mainstream," in William Nisbet Chambers and Walter Dean Burnham, eds., *The American Party Systems: Stages of Political Development*, 2nd ed. (New York, 1975), p. 12.

[6] Richard Hofstadter, *The Idea of a Party System: The Rise of Legitimate Opposition in the United States, 1780–1840* (Berkeley, Calif., 1969), p. 2.

wish that the wad of a cannon discharged as a salute to President Adams had hit the broadest part of the President's breeches."[7]) The Federalists not only failed to destroy the Republicans, however, but the attempt cost them office—they were turned out in 1800 when Jefferson was elected president—and was influential in leading to their ultimate disappearance from the political scene.

Parties facilitated *alternation* in office. The replacement of Federalist President John Adams by Thomas Jefferson, a Republican, was the first case of peaceful transference of power from one party to another as a result of election returns. Parties thus made it possible for the principle of majority rule to determine the composition of the government.

On the whole, American political parties and elections in the early years represented a substantial advance in democratic practice over other countries. But what was a democratic—and even influential—system in one epoch may not be equally so in another. During the last century, political parties became both less democratic and less influential as forces affecting the course of American politics.

THE DOMINANT LIBERAL TRADITION

During the course of American history, the party system has rarely been the only forum for the expression of political conflict, nor has it always been the major forum. As political scientist Robert Dahl points out, "From the very first years under the new Constitution American political life has undergone, about once every generation, a conflict over national politics of extreme severity."[8] In addition to the Civil War, when there was outright warfare between opponents, conflict in the United States has found expression through protest activity, political violence, demonstrations, and strikes. Clashes have occurred among organized agencies, such as

[7] Henry Jones Ford, *The Rise and Growth of American Politics* (New York, 1898), p. 112, cited in V. O. Key, Jr., *Politics, Parties, & Pressure Groups* (New York, 1964), p. 205.

[8] Robert A. Dahl, *Political Oppositions in Western Democracies* (New Haven, Conn., 1966), p. 50.

interest groups, business organizations, and labor unions; and among regional, ideological, and ethnic groups. A more violent form of conflict has been the official repression of Indians and the generations of subjugation of blacks.

Yet, with the important exception of the Civil War, the extremes of conflict that characterize other countries have been less apparent in the United States. In contrast to Europe, conditions in early America fostered relative equality, discouraged class consciousness, reduced the need for violent disruptions, and provided a framework for a democratic party system. Foremost was the lack of a powerful hereditary aristocracy. Alexis de Tocqueville, who visited the United States in the 1830s, observed in *Democracy in America* that Americans were born equal rather than having to fight a revolution to achieve equality. Men were not frozen into a fixed station, in which they grew up, lived, and expected to die; what counted was individual effort. According to sociologist Seymour M. Lipset, in *The First New Nation*, the leading cultural values in America came to be individualism, equality, and achievement. A second condition that differentiated the United States from Europe was the pluralism of American society, which embraced a gamut of occupational, regional, ethnic, and religious subcultures; encouraged toleration; and splintered power. Third, unlike most Europeans, Americans had a way of escaping from the old life and finding a new one: they could move. Land was plentiful and cheap, and the lure of the frontier was strong.

Lastly was the fact that suffrage requirements were minimal. In eighteenth-century Europe, workers, merchants, and entrepreneurs were legally excluded from political power. As a result, they organized their own political parties, which were illegal and revolutionary, operating against (not within) the political system. In America, where universal male suffrage was achieved before the industrial revolution, political parties were less class oriented and represented coalitions of social, economic, and regional interests. Groups did not have to struggle to gain admission to the system: they were already inside the political arena. However, as class divisions hardened after the industrial revolution, American parties became less and less representative of the existing social structure.

The same conditions that acted to moderate conflict in the United States contributed to the acceptance of a basic ideology, which political theorist Louis Hartz has called the liberal tradition.[9] This ideology was based on the views of English philosopher John Locke, who believed that individual freedom flourished through private property and limited government—a view ideally suited to the simple conditions of early America.

Capitalism was not seriously challenged in the United States, as it was by socialists and anarchists in Europe and Chartists in England. Nor—again in contrast to Europe—was there a powerful preexisting conservative establishment consisting of the Church, the army, and the aristocracy to oppose the rise of capitalism.

Procedural democracy came early in the United States in part because of the triumph of capitalism. The framers of the Constitution used procedural democracy to protect the interests of private property. In contrast to the feudal system of fixed status and obligations, capitalism required legal equality and freedom: the freedom of citizens to acquire private property, choose an occupation, and sell their labor for a wage; to enter the market, produce whatever was demanded, and buy and sell the commodities thereby produced.

So long as agriculture predominated, manufacturing was rudimentary, and there were relatively few extremes of wealth, capitalism and procedural democracy could be defended as having expanded freedom in comparison with the feudal system. But when conditions changed toward the end of the nineteenth century—the end of the frontier, an increase in population, technological innovations, and the development of corporate capitalism—procedural democracy and capitalism paved the way to a new oppression.

THE EVOLUTION OF POLITICAL CLEAVAGES

As the United States changed, one can distinguish several periods, each characterized by the dominance of a particular cluster of economic and regional forces. Such forces are usually grouped within a ruling political party and opposed by a minority party containing groups and regions on the defensive. The cleavage

[9] Louis Hartz, *The Liberal Tradition in America* (New York, 1955).

between parties both shaped and reflected the major conflicts within the society at that time.

The degree to which American political parties have been able to attract stable electoral followings seems to follow a cyclical pattern. Political scientist Walter Dean Burnham has described contrasts in the party system during stable and unstable periods. American parties thrive during stable periods, when they can count on a large loyal constituency and when they can express (and at the same time blur) important political differences of the time. During such periods, one party is usually somewhat dominant, able to unite leading economic, social, and regional interests in a broad majority consensus on important issues.

But, as Burnham points out, " 'Politics as usual' in the United States is not politics as always."[10] At periodic intervals, when economic and social crisis looms, parties become unable to adapt to the new conditions. As a crisis gathers momentum, issues develop that cut across existing party lines, alienating voters, heightening their attention to issues and their discontent with the alternatives offered them by the existing parties. At these times, voters begin to seek answers outside the existing party system, and the parties are ripe for realignment. It is during these periods of crisis that new political movements and leaders have arisen outside the two-party system (third parties, popular movements, protests, and strikes). Their success leads the existing parties to seek ways to adjust to the situation. The result has been a shifting of parties—in terms of the issues they emphasize and positions they take—as well as a shuffling of the parties' constituencies, as voters (especially younger voters without long-standing partisan attachments) gravitate to the party whose position they favor. A new party may emerge to replace one of the leading parties (as the Republican party replaced the Whigs in the 1850s), or the minority party may become the majority party (as the Democratic party did in the 1930s), or the majority party may capitalize on the new issues to regain its dominance (as the Republican party did in 1896 and the Democrats may be doing at the present time). During past crises, at some point a new alignment crystalized and a new period of stability began, issues sank into the background, and voters

---

[10] Walter Dean Burnham, "The End of American Party Politics," in Joseph Fiszman and Gene S. Poschman, eds., *The American Political Arena: Selected Readings,* 3rd ed. (Boston, 1972), p. 250.

again relied on partisan identification rather than the parties' policies to guide their voting choice.

This model provides a useful way to organize the discussion of changing political cleavages in the United States, if one keeps in mind that the American party system overrepresents dominant social groups and underrepresents subordinate groups. To summarize what follows: the history of the American party system consists of the early defeat of the Federalists, followed by the dominance of Jefferson's Republican party (the forerunner of today's Democratic party), whose support rested on Southern and agrarian interests. Following the Civil War, control shifted back to the North and, with greater velocity during the industrial revolution at the end of the nineteenth century, to commercial and then corporate power. The Republican party (as it is still known today) held office nearly without interruption from the Civil War to the New Deal by making itself the spokesman for ascendant industrialism and corporate capitalism.

The New Deal represented another major shift, with the formation of a majority coalition within the Democratic party consisting of organized labor, ethnic and urban groups, and the South. Currently, this coalition has been torn by new social tensions, and there is evidence of a general decline in the parties' control over the electorate.

The Founding Period Until the Civil War

The first broad cleavage pitted mercantile, financial, and manufacturing interests, which were centered in the North and formed the backbone of the Federalist party under Alexander Hamilton's leadership, against agrarian, planter, and small landowning interests, which were concentrated in the South and West and grouped in the Republican party led by Jefferson.

The two parties had different views of government, in line with their different constituencies. The Federalists favored a strong national government acting to develop the country's economy. They sponsored tariffs (beneficial to industry), public roads and canals (which increased commerce), and the creation of a national bank (helpful for financial interests). The Republicans, responsive to their agrarian constituents, favored low taxes and simple, frugal government, and they were distrustful of a strong national government as potentially tyrannical.

Yet party differences should not be magnified. Both parties were true to the Lockean liberal tradition described earlier in this chapter. And, once in office, Jefferson's actions belied his earlier philosophy. In keeping with the Republican belief in limited government, he proposed only a few measures; but the effect was to leave in operation the elaborate commercial system erected by his Federalist predecessors. The single most important achievement of his administration—the Louisiana Purchase—opened up vast new commercial possibilities (as well as providing land for small farmers who supported the Republicans).

Despite George Washington's fear, as expressed in his farewell address, that the spirit of party "agitates the community with ill-founded jealousies and false alarms, kindles the animosity of one part against another, foments occasionally riots and insurrection," political parties soon came to have just the opposite effects. They proved a powerful instrument for moderating differences, reducing conflict among groups, and preventing riots and insurrection.

Federalist dominance ended with Jefferson's election in 1800. In large part, this was preordained: a party resting mostly on commercial and mercantile interests was bound to fail in a country with few cities and a large agricultural population. Moreover, the Federalists did not conceal their disdain for the lower orders, a mistake in a country where the spirit of egalitarianism ran high and an aristocratic political approach was sure to unleash widespread opposition. Jefferson's success rested on the fact that, unlike the Federalists, he (and the Republicans) accepted popular government.

Parties languished in the Era of Good Feeling that followed Jefferson's presidency. Then, in 1828, Andrew Jackson's election created a fresh impetus to party organization. Jackson was the first president to be nominated by a national convention, rather than by a congressional caucus in which congressmen selected a candidate and lobbied in the states to get him elected. Furthermore, in most states during this period, popular election of pledged presidential electors replaced their election by state legislators. Jackson popularized politics. He revitalized Jefferson's party, creating a party organization that reached throughout the country. He provided a vital link between government and the people and offered voters a sense of participation that had largely been lacking in Jefferson's day and virtually absent in the years following. The number of voters soared from one-half million in 1824 to five million by the time of the Civil War. Voting turnout (the proportion of eligible voters who turn out to vote) jumped from 27 percent in 1824 to 78 percent in 1840.[11]

Jackson's presidency called into existence an opposition party, the Whigs, which, if it inherited the Federalists' constituency of manufacturing interests, was careful not to make the Federalists' mistake of ignoring popular sentiment. In fact, the Whigs (and their successors, the present Republican party) demonstrated how successful a conservative business-oriented party could be in currying popular favor. The Whigs' stress on the image of the common man was symbolized by their nomination of popular military heroes for president: four of their six candidates after 1832 were generals. In similar fashion, the Republicans' only success in presidential elections between 1932 and 1968 was the eight years of General Eisenhower's presidency between 1952 and 1960.

By the end of the Jacksonian period, the party system was formed in a mold that, in many respects, persists to this day. The two parties then in existence are the direct ancestors of the present two major parties. During Jackson's time, the two became more competitive, with the average difference between their vote declining from 36 percent in 1828 to 9 percent in 1844.[12]

Republicans in Power: 1860 to 1932

As the early party system became more competitive and national in scope, it was torn apart by bitter sectional rivalry revolving around slavery, which opposed Northern commercial interests to Southern planter interests. The party system was too weak to contain the conflict between two economic systems, one based on free labor, the other based on slave labor. The slavery issue destroyed the Whig party, which tried to straddle the fence. A new party was formed, which called itself the Republican party (not because it resembled Jefferson's Republicans, but because it wanted to evoke his popularity). Based in the North, it was created to serve as the vehicle for antislavery commercial interests and abolitionists. When the Republican candidate, Abraham Lincoln,

[11] Everett Carll Ladd, Jr., *American Political Parties: Social Change and Political Response* (New York, 1970), p. 96; Chambers, in Chambers and Burnham, p. 32.
[12] Richard P. McCormick, "Political Development and the Second Party System," in Chambers and Burnham, p. 99.

was elected president in 1860, the South seceded from the union and war began.

The Civil War ended in a victory for Northern urban industrial business, which used free labor, over Southern commercial agriculture, which was based on slave labor. The end of slavery did not usher in a social revolution in the South. The efforts of the Radical Republicans (a splinter group) to break up plantations and distribute land to the former slaves failed—thus creating the conditions for the tenant-farming system that kept blacks in a state of semiservitude.[13] For the United States as a whole, the Civil War ended in a victory for procedural democracy and industrial capitalism and put the Republicans in firm control of the federal government. The Democratic party, the dominant party of the previous period, was in no position to challenge the Republicans after the defeat of the South.

The Republicans presented themselves as the guardians of rising urban and industrial interests, and in the post-Civil War period the economic balance of power swiftly tipped toward industry. Whereas in 1850, two-thirds of the work force was engaged in agriculture, by 1870 a majority of the working class was in nonagricultural occupations. Between 1860 and 1930, the number of industrial workers swelled from one million to eight million. From 1860 to 1920, the urban population doubled every two decades; it took the entire period for the rural population to double. Cities grew especially fast. Before the Civil War, only New York had over 250,000 inhabitants. By the First World War, twenty-three other cities had reached this size.

At this critical turning point in the nation's history, the Republican party was able to represent the thrust to industrialization and insure that it was carried out under the guidance of private business interests. Thanks to their control of the Republican party, rising industrial and manufacturing interests were able to resist the protest of agrarian groups against exploitation by railroads, financiers, and middlemen, and prevent political challenge from the growing urban proletariat.[14] Thus, although the Republican party did not advertise itself as a class-based party, it reflected a major regional and historical cleavage that served class interests. After 1896, the Republican party was alone in enthusiastically embracing the in-

[13] Barrington Moore, Jr., *Social Origins of Dictatorship and Democracy* (Boston, 1966), chapter 3.

[14] James L. Sundquist, *Dynamics of the Party System: Alignment and Realignment of Political Parties in the United States* (Washington, D.C., 1973), chapters 6–7.

dustrial boom. The Republicans' success—they were virtually unchallenged during the entire period from the Civil War until well after the First World War—meant that the industrial revolution in the United States was carried out by private interests that were relatively unrestrained by opposition from within the party system. Neither the Democratic party nor a series of protest parties (Greenback, Farmers' Alliance, Populist) were successful in their attempts to overturn Republican and business dominance.

In a feeble attempt to rival the Republicans, the Democratic party first tried to emulate them. However, only Grover Cleveland, a conservative Democrat whose probusiness policies were indistinguishable from the Republicans', was successful in winning presidential elections (in 1884 and 1892). Until 1896, "on the fundamental question of the time—the role of government in a modern industrial society—the two national parties had no quarrel. Both saw an identity of interest between the government and the great banking, manufacturing, and railroad corporations."[15] Beginning in 1896, the Democrats tried to forge a rival coalition based on Western and Southern agrarian interests, but the party failed dismally in three electoral defeats (in 1896, 1900, and 1908) under the banner of William Jennings Bryan. Bryan summed up the weakness of the party. His major proposal was for monetary policies favoring farmers and debtor interests. He represented the fundamentalist Protestant values of the declining rural areas; as such, he held little appeal for the Northern workers and immigrants (mostly Catholics) whose ranks were swelling in the late nineteenth century.

Rather than attempting to challenge the *manner* in which the Northeastern industrial and financial elite was directing industrial expansion, the Democrats, under Bryan, evoked a nostalgic but outmoded rural past. In a critical election in 1896, Northern workers and immigrants gave their support to Bryan's conservative and victorious opponent, William McKinley. Thus, during a crucial period in its expansion and consolidation, the American working class became organized within rather than against the existing party system.

During the critical years of industrialization, the costs of industrial expansion were financed mostly by the working class:

[15] *Ibid.*, p. 140.

between 1890 and 1914 wages hardly rose, despite a huge industrial boom and massive increases in productivity, total output, profits, and capital investments. As late as 1920, some steelworkers worked a twelve-hour day, 363 days per year.[16] The party system failed to reflect the cleavage between those benefiting and those being harmed by industrialization. The system ignored the plight of industrial workers in the North, where the Republicans were dominant; and it ignored poor whites and blacks in the South, where the Democratic party became an instrument for the defense of regional and often racial interests.

The party system performed a conservative function by its influence over the millions of immigrants pouring into the country. As many immigrants arrived between 1890 and the First World War as had come during the whole preceding century. Given universal suffrage, the new immigrants potentially posed an immense threat to established arrangements. However, the urban political machine proved an efficient device for socializing and pacifying immigrants.

When reform efforts were launched by the Progressives in the early twentieth century, they addressed the symptom and not the cause. The Progressives identified corruption as the primary problem and attacked the political machine as the primary cause. Their reforms aimed to end the purchase of votes, political patronage, and graft. Yet, corrupt as the urban machine was, it was a far lesser evil than the brutal conditions of industrial production. (Indeed, the machine flourished on graft it received from the industrial sector.) Nonetheless, instead of attacking corporate capitalism, the Progressives accepted the trend toward corporate concentration. Progressive reforms did little to improve conditions for those suffering from industrial expansion; instead of democratizing electoral participation, they served mainly to cripple political parties. The nonpartisan ballot in municipal elections, direct primary, and personal voter registration requirements resulted in a weaker and depoliticized party system. Voting turnout, one measure of political vitality, was far higher before the Progressive reforms than it has ever been since (although other factors contributed to the decline). The party system was permanently undermined by the reforms of the Progressive era, not only as an instrument of man-

---

[16] Ladd, p. 125; J. David Greenstone, *Labor in American Politics* (New York, 1969), p. 19.

ipulation and control but also as a potential agency for mobilizing popular majorities against corporate dominance.[17]

The New Deal and Its Legacy

The first major sign that the Democratic party was no longer acting simply as a spokesman for the rural past was the nomination of Alfred E. Smith for president in 1928. Smith was as different from Bryan as could be imagined. He was a Catholic New Yorker, an immigrant, and a world away from Bryan's rural fundamentalism. Smith proved as unappealing to rural areas and the South as Bryan had been to cities. Able to win only the deep South (pro-Democratic for generations), Massachusetts, and Rhode Island, he lost the election to Herbert Hoover.

Franklin D. Roosevelt, an urbane patrician, was better able to bridge the gap between rural and urban interests in 1932. He was helped by the fact that the Republicans were saddled with responsibility for the Great Depression, which began in 1929. A whole generation identified the GOP (Grand Old Party) as the party of the depression and viewed the Democrats as the party that took power confidently proclaiming, in the words of Roosevelt's first inaugural address, "The only thing we have to fear is fear itself." Generations after the industrial revolution occurred in the United States, the Democrats reached for the constituency that had been the victims of industrial growth—labor, ethnic, and urban groups.

In his recruiting efforts, Roosevelt worked with the fast-rising labor unions in the Congress of Industrial Organizations (CIO). In return for Roosevelt's support, organized labor—officially nonpartisan until the 1930s—came to play a role within the Democratic party comparable to the role played by large labor unions in Western Europe: unions provided funds, personnel, organization, and research for the party. During elections, unions often proved "a valued and integral part of the Democrats' normal campaign apparatus."[18]

---

[17] Walter Dean Burnham, *Critical Elections and the Mainsprings of American Politics* (New York, 1970), *passim.* See Philip E. Converse, "Change in the American Electorate," in Angus Campbell and Philip E. Converse, eds., *The Human Meaning of Social Change* (New York, 1973), pp. 263–337, for a critique of Burnham's position.

[18] Greenstone, p. 9.

Yet the realignment that began with Smith's candidacy in 1928 and stretched through Roosevelt's election campaigns of 1932 and 1936 was far from forging a class-based party system: the representation of class divisions was blurred by historical traces persisting from the Civil War. Both New England and the South remained true to past tradition: New England, to the party of Lincoln (despite the inroads Smith made there); the South, to the Democrats. Both parties formed quite diverse coalitions; neither party represented the working class majority nor challenged capitalist dominance.

The New Deal softened the edges of industrialism, repaired its worst damage, and used the government's power to provide benefits to the urban and rural poor hit hardest by the depression. This was a program that the Republican party, a backward-looking captive of business interests, could not match. Yet, in part because of the powerful role conservative Southern Democrats played within the party, in part because Roosevelt "never entertained any idea of a fundamental alteration of the structure of ownership and control of business enterprises," the New Deal did not represent a frontal assault on corporate capitalism—regardless of what many outraged business executives thought at the time.[19] Quite the contrary. It was under the liberal auspices of the New Deal (and successive programs sponsored by Democratic presidents since Roosevelt) that the corporate complex experienced its greatest expansion, prosperity, and power. The benefits provided workers by the New Deal, such as Social Security, unemployment insurance, workmen's compensation, and legal recognition for labor unions, helped stabilize industrial production. In addition, the government provided lavish benefits to industry in the form of political protection, regulation, tax benefits, grants, and military spending.

Although corporate capitalism was forced to share power with the burgeoning federal government in Washington, the new alliance did not threaten corporate interests so long as the government remained under the control of "cooperative" forces. Before discussing present-day political cleavages, it is useful to explore how party compliance with the corporate complex has been assured.

[19] Ladd, p. 188.

MONEY AND POLITICS

If political parties accurately represented the interests of voters, elections would challenge established arrangements. Given the large majority of Americans whose interest lies in change, one party or the other would find it electorally profitable to unite this majority around the banner of fundamental change. Yet the routine pattern is for parties to differ in only minor respects and to propose only marginal reforms.

An important reason is that parties need more than votes to succeed; they also need money. Especially today, elections are costly. The 1972 elections cost well over $400 million. (This was a record and, with public financing of presidential elections beginning in 1976, it will probably not be equalled.) Of this amount, $110 million was spent to nominate and elect candidates for president, most of the money going for media and advertising costs. President Nixon spent $60 million in his election campaign. Democratic candidates for the nomination spent $26 million in the preconvention campaign, and George McGovern spent $27 million in the election campaign itself. Another $100 million went to elect congressmen and senators; about $100 million went to elect state officials, such as governors and state legislators; and the remaining $100 million was spent in local elections.[20] Election costs are high in nonpresidential years as well: $64 million was spent in the 1974 congressional elections.

Who gives political contributions? According to Senator Russell Long, chairman of the Senate Finance Committee, "It would be my guess that about ninety-five percent of campaign funds at the congressional level are derived from businessmen."[21] Although some money is raised through small contributions, a substantial proportion comes from large gifts. In 1968, nearly half the publicly-reported funds raised by the major presidential candidates came from contributions of $500 or more.[22] Political scientist David Nichols found that, in Cleveland, nearly all large political

[20] Unpublished data kindly made available by Herbert Alexander.
[21] Philip Stern, *The Rape of the Taxpayer* (New York, 1973), p. 388.
[22] Herbert E. Alexander, *Financing the 1968 Election* (Lexington, Mass., 1971), p. 167.

contributors were affluent businessmen, usually corporate executives or lawyers.[23]

Wealthy donors support both parties, although most of their gifts go to the Republicans. Campaign finance specialist Herbert Alexander found that nearly all large contributions by top corporation executives go to Republican candidates. The result is that, despite the financial support given to the Democrats by labor unions, the Democratic party raises less than the Republicans.

The major consequence of the high costs of campaigning, however, is not to favor one party over the other but to maintain the dominance of *both* parties. The parties' dependence on private contributions means that political conflict takes place within limits acceptable to wealthy donors.

Parties and candidates must prove their "reliability" before they can attract sizeable donations. Since candidates need money before they can even attempt to gain the nomination, political gifts influence the selection of who is to run long before the election campaign itself. As Will Rogers remarked, "It takes a lot of money to even get beat with."[24] While having lavish campaign funds does not guarantee nomination or election—there are numerous examples of candidates who outspent their rivals and still lost—political aspirants who cannot recruit affluent patrons are pursuing a nearly impossible dream. The role played by money in party politics goes a long way toward nullifying any possible challenge parties might pose to established arrangements.

As a result of widespread public disgust following revelations about political corruption in the 1970s, culminating in the Watergate scandal (see Chapter 9), a series of federal election campaign reforms were adopted in 1971, 1974, and 1976. The laws regulate election campaigns for the presidency and Congress; in addition, nearly all states passed similar laws to regulate campaign finance for state and local elections. The 1971 Federal Election Campaign Act provides for:

Public disclosure of campaign contributions. Candidates and political parties must periodically make available the names of all donors who contribute $50 or more.

[23] David Nichols, *Financing Elections: The Politics of an American Ruling Class* (New York, 1974), pp. 77–78.
[24] Congressional Quarterly, *Dollar Politics* (Washington, D.C., 1971), p. 3.

Spending limits. No individual can give more than $1,000 to a candidate each year. Candidates and parties are also limited in how much they can spend in both the primary- and general-election campaigns for congressional and presidential races. However, no limit is placed on the amount that candidates can spend from their personal funds.

Public financing of presidential elections. Qualified candidates for the presidency are given public funds for their campaign (to qualify, candidates must obtain $5,000 in small gifts in each of twenty states); qualified political parties are given money to finance their nominating conventions. Candidates who receive public funds for their general-election campaigns are prohibited from raising additional money from private sources.

The money provided for public campaign financing is substantial. In 1976, fifteen candidates for the two major parties' nominations received $24 million. The two major parties each received $2 million to underwrite their conventions. After their nominations, Gerald Ford and Jimmy Carter each received $22 million for their presidential campaigns.[25]

Although the campaign-finance reforms have partially achieved their stated aim of shedding light on the sources of political contributions and cleaning up the corruption involved in campaign finance, they have not much diminished the parties' dependence on wealthy patrons. They have other effects, however, that are quite important. One is to provide the major political parties with a boost at a time when they are sagging badly, both by the financial benefits they receive at taxpayers' expense and by the added legitimacy the laws provide through the impression that the parties' finances are now above reproach. Another important consequence of the reforms is to penalize all parties other than the Democrats and Republicans: no minor party or candidate qualified for public funds in 1976, and it is unlikely that any will in the foreseeable future. Thus, while the two major parties and their candidates were receiving $72 million in public funds in 1976, not a nickel went to other parties and candidates. The result is to freeze the two-party system and to benefit both major parties at the expense of other parties.

Since the spending limits do not apply to contributions made

---

[25] Herbert E. Alexander, *Financing Politics: Money, Elections and Political Reform* (Washington, D.C., 1976), p. 246.

by candidates to their own campaigns, wealthy candidates are given a substantial edge. Spending limits also favor incumbents, who have less need to buy media exposure. Thus, the trend toward reduced competition in congressional races (see Chapter 10) is heightened by the campaign reforms.

Most important is that the reforms do not alter the dependence of political parties on private wealth. In some ways, this has even increased, for example, by the authorization in 1974 of corporate-sponsored political action committees that can solicit contributions from employees and distribute them to cooperative candidates.

Political parties will be broadly responsive to the interests that provide them with financial support. In a capitalist society, this generally means business interests. There are, however, two alternatives to this situation (in addition to public financing, which simply stabilizes the two-party system in its present mold). One is to gather large numbers of small contributions. Barry Goldwater in 1964 and George McGovern in 1972 succeeded in raising substantial amounts in this way. But so much energy needs to be diverted to fund-raising that the campaign to reach voters suffers.

The other alternative to business financing is the labor movement. Trade unions provide funds, mostly for the Democratic party (for example, $6 million in the 1974 congressional campaigns) and their organizational resources can be a vital source of services for the Democratic party.[26] But labor is at a decided disadvantage in the United States. For example, contributions exceeding $500 by private donors as well as contributions by lobbies and trade associations amounted to more than four times labor's contributions in 1974.[27] Although the Democratic party is often considered the party of the people, large gifts to the Democratic party by wealthy individuals substantially exceed labor's contribution. The result is that both major parties are directly beholden to business and professional interests. It is no surprise that party policies are responsive to dominant interests and that the parties are hardly inclined to challenge these interests.

The campaign-finance reforms have led to new circuits through which business funds flow to the parties. But these reforms have had little impact in democratizing the party system. Far

---

[26] Greenstone, chapters 8, 10.
[27] Alexander, *Financing Politics*, p. 228.

more significant than outright political corruption—cash delivered in unmarked envelopes—is the perfectly legal process by which the party system is shaped by private capital.

The conclusion of a study analyzing California's supposedly tough campaign-finance reform might be applied to the whole range of federal and state reform in this area: the author concludes that political money in California continues "to be raised largely in the same old ways—from corporations, other special interests, and wealthy individuals." [28]

It would be surprising if the results were otherwise: there is a convergence of interests between the legislators who write the laws regulating political finance and business interests, who are the major donors and beneficiaries of a friendly government. In order for a major alternative to the present system of party finance to exist, there would need to be a major alternative to the present party system and the policies it fosters.

REALIGNMENT OR DECAY OF POLITICAL PARTIES?
THE 1970s

During stable periods, a party's electoral following tends to remain loyal through time. Most voters develop a sense of psychological attachment to a party when they are young, and this identification persists despite changes in the parties' candidates and stands on particular issues. A sense of partisan identification is thus transmitted from one generation to the next. Electoral studies carried out by the Survey Research Center of the University of Michigan find that this affective attachment of voters to one party or the other acts as an important influence on the voting decision. It can be distinguished from voters' perceptions of the candidates nominated by each party and the stands the parties take on campaign issues. Unless voters strongly prefer the opposite party's candidates or issue position, they will probably vote for the party with which they identify, especially if their sense of party identification is strong. The parties' ability to develop a sense of partisan identification among the electorate is an indication of their strength, or "reach."

[28] William Endicott, "California: A New Law," in Alexander, *Campaign Money*, p. 111.

One result of the New Deal realignment was that the Democratic party attracted a majority of party identifiers. In election after election since 1932, the Democrats had only to mobilize their natural majority to win. After nearly forty years in which the Democratic party and the New Deal coalition dominated presidential elections (save for the presidency of Eisenhower, a soldier-hero not closely associated with the Republican party) and most congressional elections, the 1970s represent another period of upheaval and transition. The New Deal coalition has been shaken by the rise of new social issues that are related to fundamental demographic changes in American society, in particular the movement of blacks to the North, the suburbanization of American politics, and the growth of a new middle class.

As a result of the industrialization and the fading of Civil War memories in the South, black migration to the North, and the national media's dominance over communications, regional differences in the United States have declined and political life has become nationalized.

Take the movement of Southern blacks northward, for example. Between 1940 and 1970, a total of five million blacks moved to Northern cities. One result was to force into the open the racial issue that the Democratic party had submerged during the New Deal. Before the 1960s, Southern Democrats had succeeded in preventing outside interference with the system of racial injustice in the South. When President Truman was nominated for reelection in 1948 on a mild civil rights plank, Southern Democrats bolted the convention and sponsored their own candidate. Although Truman won reelection, Southern Democrats and conservative Republicans in Congress blocked attempts to pass civil rights legislation.

But after a sizeable number of blacks had achieved the vote in Northern cities, the race issue came into prominence. Seeking to attract black and liberal votes in the North, Presidents Kennedy and Johnson (especially Johnson) sponsored far-reaching civil rights legislation. For the first time in recent American history, federal legislation was used to reduce racial discrimination in education, voting, and public accommodations. These policies set in motion the South's swing away from the Democratic party. During the Johnson landslide of 1964, the South abandoned its historic Democratic affiliation, and conservative Southern whites proved a major source of support for Barry Goldwater. The trend continued under Presidents Nixon and Ford, whose opposition to school busing and general conservatism contributed to the Southern shift toward the Republican party.

Republican gains in the South are matched by their gains among Northern groups that were traditionally Democratic. George Wallace's success in 1968 as a third-party candidate and a general decline in support for the Democratic party among Catholics and workers suggest the wisdom of political analyst Samuel Lubell's observation: "Always in the past the assumption has been that the South, as it changed, would come to resemble the North more and more. . . . [Instead], the North as it changes, may be southernized."[29] Catholic support for the Democratic party has steadily declined from a high of 82 percent in 1960 (when John F. Kennedy, a Catholic, was the Democratic candidate) to 43 percent in 1972. Organized labor's support has also declined: from 75 percent in the 1930s and 1940s, to 46 percent in 1972.[30] Many Catholic, white ethnic, and unionized workers have become increasingly restive as they experience the brunt of racial strife and urban dislocation and decay. Workers who had achieved a decent but difficult existence saw their new gains threatened by rising taxes, inflation, and the deterioration of property values when neighborhoods became racially mixed; they saw their way of life threatened by radical political movements, the free life styles adopted by youth, the rising incidence of violence in American society, and black insurrection.

Although the Democratic party has lost some of its traditional sources of support, it has gained others. The Northeast has moved toward the Democratic party; New England is no longer a one-party (Republican) region. Black migration to Northern cities has created additional support for the Democratic party. Although the suburban vote has increased by 37 percent between 1952 and 1968, those with Democratic loyalties who have moved to the suburbs have not shifted to the Republican party. Protestants have shifted away from the Republican party and divide their vote more evenly between the two parties. A new middle class of pro-Democratic, college-educated professionals has emerged. Youth, particularly college students (who represent nearly half of those in the college-age bracket) are pro-Democratic: among college students identify-

[29] Samuel Lubell, *The Hidden Crisis in American Politics* (New York, 1971), p. 86.
[30] Richard L. Rubin, *Party Dynamics: The Democratic Coalition and the Politics of Change* (New York, 1976), pp. 32, 56.

ing with a political party in 1970, 65 percent identified with the Democrats. By 1974, there was a further shift toward a Democratic party identification among all youth: three-quarters of the 18–24 year old age group identifying with a political party were pro-Democratic.[31]

Decline of the Democratic Coalition

A major reason that the Democratic party usually dominated the federal government since the 1930s is that Democratic domestic policies provided benefits to a majority of citizens, including minimum-wage legislation and pensions under the Social Security System. Given the alternative of conservative Republican government (Republican leaders often opposed the Democratic-sponsored welfare programs), it was logical for the Democrats to win most of the time.

The Democratic party coalition more accurately mirrors the whole society, with minority groups present in substantial numbers as well as professional and other middle-class supporters. Beginning in the 1930s, the Democratic party gained electoral majorities through five straight presidential elections by a liberal economic appeal to disadvantaged groups who were suffering from the Great Depression. The party could also count on a solid bloc of states in the one-party South and therefore accorded a privileged role in party councils to white Southern politicians.

While the two parties agree on fundamentals, they do display somewhat different approaches, in part reflecting their different constituencies. Although there is a factional and ideological conflict in the Republican party between Eastern and Midwestern liberal corporate interests against conservative interests from the Sunbelt, the Republicans are more socially and ideologically united than the Democrats. The Republican party attracts few blacks, Catholics, Jews, or workers and takes a straightforward conservative line. New issues emerging since the 1960s have been especially divisive for the Democratic party. The race issue has done the most to split the Democratic coalition, provoking, in turn, other explosive cleavages within both the Democratic party and the whole society.

Black militance in the 1960s resulted in Democratic-

---

[31] Warren E. Miller and Teresa E. Levitin, *Leadership and Change: The New Politics and the American Electorate* (Cambridge, Mass., 1976), p. 194.

sponsored programs of civil rights and economic benefits to blacks. The first antagonized the white South; the second, the white North. In the years between 1964 and the early 1970s, the percentage of native white Southerners identifying themselves as Democrats fell from 71 percent to 47 percent.[32] As Democratic president Lyndon Johnson tried both to pacify rebellious blacks in the North as well as to consolidate black support for the Democratic party in Northern cities, traditional white sources of support for the Democratic party were jostled. Rising welfare costs, busing to achieve racial integration in Northern schools, and crime rates served to feed racial resentments of the white working class and led to its partial defection from the Democratic party in 1968. On the other hand, black Americans have given increasing support to the Democrats; blacks now make up about one-fifth of the Democrats' national support.

Tensions within the Democratic coalition were also intensified by foreign-policy issues during the 1960s. Political analysts John Judis and Alan Wolfe have suggested the term *cold-war liberalism* to describe how domestic liberals in the Democratic party during the 1940s and 1950s favored militarist and interventionist policies abroad during this period.[33] American involvement in Vietnam represented the culmination of this approach. The Democratic coalition was split down the middle on the issue of the war in Vietnam: most labor union leaders supported the war to the end, while many of the party's youthful supporters were bitterly opposed.

Yet the tax revolt of the 1970s is potentially the most dangerous issue of all for the Democratic coalition, for it splits the coalition between groups who continue to favor government intervention and welfare programs—the hallmark of New Deal liberalism—and groups who attribute their economic difficulties to government wastefulness. Although large majorities of voters continue to favor traditional welfare programs, there is also widespread and growing opposition to an activist government and high taxes.

The Democratic party has been the object of particular criticism on all these issues. It sponsored many of the reform programs

[32] Norman H. Nie, Sidney Verba, and John R. Petrocik, *The Changing American Voter* (Cambridge, Mass., 1976), p. 221.
[33] John Judis and Alan Wolfe, "American Politics at the Crossroads: The Collapse of Cold-War Liberalism," *Socialist Revolution* 32 (March-April 1977): 9–37.

in the domestic field that are the target of attack. And many of the criticisms come from within its own ranks.

Since the New Deal, except for the unusual candidacy of soldier-hero Dwight Eisenhower in the 1950s, the Democratic party merely had to mobilize its loyal followers to win elections. (And even during Eisenhower's presidency, the Democrats were dominant in Congress.) In the presidential elections of 1968 and 1972, Democratic candidates took opposite courses as they attempted to build a majority—yet a move toward one side of the fragmented party only alienated potential supporters on the other side. In 1968, Hubert Humphrey appealed to the traditional New Deal coalition of labor, Catholics, and urban interests, but antagonized the youthful liberals in the party who identified him with the Vietnam war and the same old politics. In 1972, George McGovern appealed to the new left, but he was deserted by organized labor (the AFL-CIO refused to endorse the Democratic candidate for the first time in years) as well as local Democratic party leaders.

In 1976, Jimmy Carter pulled off the feat of gaining support from both wings of the party. Carter did this through a campaign in which issues were hardly mentioned. Instead, he ran as an outsider against the federal government in Washington, which corresponded to the public mood of disquiet with government. (Carter was also helped by Republican responsibility for the Watergate scandal as well as the dismal economic situation, which developed during the Republican administration.) Carter won not by mobilizing an enthusiastic majority but by being deft enough to avoid antagonizing any large bloc of voters. But this technique is far from being an innovative attempt to deal with the current crisis, as Carter's subsequent lackluster performance as president made clear.

The Democratic party has reacted to voter opposition to high taxes by moving in a conservative direction. (A columnist in the *Wall Street Journal* suggested that President Carter's "instincts on budget matters are more conservative than those of any Democratic President in modern times."[34] By this means, the Democratic party attempted to forestall the criticism that it was pro-spending. The conservative drift was rewarded by voters in the 1978 congressional elections. But, in the longer run, it is bound to conflict with

---

[34] Norman C. Miller, "Perspective on Politics," *Wall Street Journal*, October 12, 1978.

voters' demands for government help in face of the growing cost of
basic services like food, housing, and medical care, as well as the
scarcity of employment.

So great is the edge enjoyed by the Democratic Party that the
United States can be considered to have a one and one-half rather
than a two-party system. For example, in the 1978 elections,
although the Republican party achieved small gains in elections for
both houses of Congress, state legislatures, and governorships, the
Democratic party continues to control the large majority of these
offices. The Democrats' recent success has been based on emulat-
ing the Republicans' conservative approach: under President Carter, the Democratic party followed two previous Republican presidents in rolling back reform programs originally sponsored by
Democratic administrations in the 1930s, 1940s, and 1960s. At the
present time, the two parties are more indistinguishable than ever;
and both channel popular discontent in a conservative direction.

Although the Democratic party stands a better chance of
dominating future elections, neither party has been able to develop
a program that attracts a stable majority. The existing party system
becomes increasingly less capable of generating popular
enthusiasm. In the process, it has been losing its ability either to
serve as an instrument of domination (by producing steady support
for the political system) or to serve as a vehicle for mobilizing a new
majority around a program for fundamental reform.

Nominating and Electing a President

The last arena in which political parties have often played a major
role is elections: both in the designation of candidates and in
election campaigns. Yet even in this last remaining stronghold of
party activity, the party system has lost its monopoly of control.
Moreover, parties have been increasingly less able to convince the
public that elections matter.

To simplify our examination of elections, attention will be
centered on the office of president. However, about 500,000 public
officials are elected in the United States, and voting also takes
place on bond issues, referenda, and the like. Thus, while important, presidential elections are only one example of the American
electoral process.

The closest American parties come to the annual congresses

held by major European parties is the national convention held every four years to nominate a president and a vice president and draft a party platform. Since Jackson's time, the national convention has represented the sovereign party, meeting in all its majesty. That picture is changing, however; the convention as a television special has supplanted the convention as a decision-making body.

The party platform is the authoritative guide to the party's policies. Try designating which two of the following planks were in the Democratic platform of 1968, and which two in the Republican:

> The forty-hour week adopted 30 years ago needs re-examination to determine whether or not a shorter work week, without a loss of wages, would produce more jobs, increase productivity and stabilize prices.

> Use the defense dollar more effectively through simplification of cumbersome, overcentralized administration of the Defense Department, expanded competitive bidding on defense contracts, and improved safeguards against excessive profits.

> Our aim is to strengthen state and local law enforcement agencies so that they can do their jobs.

> In this endeavor [to eliminate poverty], the resources of private enterprise—not only its economic power but its leadership and ingenuity—must be mobilized.

If you guessed that the first two were from the Democratic platform and the second two from the Republican, your grand score is zero: the order was the opposite. This little exercise tells something about platform writing. Each party tries to court the opposite party's electorate, with the result that they both usually drive toward the center. While on the one hand, parties attempt to attract distinctive constituencies, they will seek votes wherever they can find them, without regard to ideology.

Public opinion polls repeatedly show that the broad electorate is unable to distinguish between the policy stands of opposing candidates. Yet responsibility for the electorate's ignorance lies in good measure with the candidates themselves, who take pains to minimize their policy differences and maximize ambiguity. For example, in 1968 the country was wracked by the Vietnam war. To what extent did the Democratic and Republican presidential candidates offer alternative policies toward the war? Not much, according to political scientists Benjamin Page and Richard Brody.

> It is possible for scholars, after reading all their [the candidates']
> speeches and statements, to arrive at judgments about what their
> "real" positions were; but the ordinary citizen may be forgiven if he
> failed to penetrate the haze of vague hints which alternated with
> total silence about Vietnam in most of the candidates' rhetoric.[35]

Yet voters did correctly perceive the positions of George Wallace and Eugene McCarthy, candidates for the presidential nomination who took clear stands on the war; and voters' attitudes toward Wallace and McCarthy were highly correlated with their own policy position. Page and Brody conclude that "when the American people are presented with a clear choice, they are able and willing to bring their policy preferences to bear."[36]

Their lack of a distinctive program led political scientist Otto Kirchheimer to characterize American parties as "catch-all" parties. Catch-all parties are more concerned with gaining office than with putting policies into effect once they get there. They claim that anything the other party can do, they can do better—but they refuse to engage in an analysis of what needs to be done.[37]

Political conventions are also losing control over the choice of a presidential candidate. The use of public-opinion polls competes with the expert judgment of local politicians and convention delegates regarding the grass-roots popularity of different candidates. The candidates themselves have begun to develop elaborate preconvention campaigns, such as those of John F. Kennedy in 1960, Barry Goldwater in 1964, Richard M. Nixon in 1968, George McGovern in 1972, and Jimmy Carter in 1976. The result is that the choice of a candidate has usually been made even before the convention meets. The convention merely ratifies the results of the informal preconvention selection process, puts on a show for television (the convention is staged to have the maximum nationwide impact on prime time), and disperses. In every presidential convention from 1956 to 1976, both parties nominated a presidential candidate on the first ballot; in previous years, except when there was an incumbent president, a first-ballot nomination was a rarity.

---

[35] Benjamin I. Page and Richard A. Brody, "The Vietnam War Issue," *The American Political Science Review* 66 (December 1972): 987. Also see Stanley Kelley, *Political Campaigning* (Washington, D.C., 1960), pp. 50–84.

[36] Page and Brody, p. 993.

[37] Otto Kirchheimer, "The Transformation of the Western European Party Systems," in Joseph La Palombara and Myron Weiner, eds., *Political Parties and Political Development* (Princeton, N.J., 1966), pp. 177–200.

Who gets nominated? An analysis of the candidates illuminates the general significance of political parties and elections. To
begin with, potential nominees are usually confined to the vice
president, senators, and governors; and all but two major candidates in the past half century have been white, male, Protestant,
relatively affluent, and married with a family. The exceptions are
John F. Kennedy, a Catholic, and Adlai Stevenson, who was
divorced (both were probably hurt by having these "deviant"
characteristics). Put another way, any one of the following characteristics has (until now) been sufficient to disqualify one from
consideration: female, black, Jewish, known to have had psychiatric treatment, poor, or atheist. The list could be extended but the
point is clear: presidential candidates are chosen out of a small pool
from which the vast majority of Americans are excluded. In terms
of the criteria of representation described in Chapter 1, the
nominating process recruits from a socially unrepresentative segment of the electorate.

An important consideration in choosing a nominee is the
ability of a candidate to attract large contributions at the prenomination stage. It is probably at this point that political money makes
its influence felt most—for "unreliable" candidates are not apt to
be considered a wise investment. Potential candidates are particularly sensitive to the wishes of wealthy donors at this early
stage—for without this initial support a candidate cannot even
wage a decent fight for the nomination. The advice Sam Rayburn,
a powerful Speaker of the House of Representatives, gave
freshmen congressmen puts the point more bluntly: "To get along,
go along."

Occasionally, candidates do make proposals that antagonize
the business community, with results that serve to prove the rule.
In 1964, Barry Goldwater was a frank throwback to an earlier era:
he speculated about abolishing the social security program, turning over TVA to private interests, and rolling back government
regulations. Goldwater claimed that he represented "a choice not
an echo" in relation to the New Deal tradition. He was promptly
abandoned by a traditional bastion of Republican support—
businessmen—who did not want the clock turned back. In 1972,
George McGovern was made to appear a "radical" (a term Hubert
H. Humphrey pinned on him in the California primary—and virtually the kiss of death in American politics). Yet McGovern
represented at most a moderate challenge to established institutions. His proposal to cut the military budget would still have left

the United States with the largest military budget in the world. His "radical" welfare proposals were more modest than programs *already* existing in European countries with *conservative* governments (including England, France, and Italy).[38]

The decline of the parties' power can be seen from their diminished role in the campaign itself. Three mechanisms have replaced parties as the dominant instruments in election campaigns: the candidate's own campaign organization, the media, and professional consulting firms.

Candidates for offices at all levels—from president to town alderman—prefer to develop their own campaign organizations, manned by their personal supporters, separate from the official party and working in uneasy alliance with it. A bewildering array of groups may be formed to work for the candidate's election (there were 222 national-level committees in the 1968 presidential race—many created simply to evade campaign-finance laws).[39] Within the overall campaign organization, the regular party apparatus ranks low, for candidates have more trust in, and control over, organizations staffed by their personal associates.

Although professional party organizations may be on the wane, political activism in the electoral process may be on the rise, as witnessed by the large number of volunteers in recent election campaigns. In contrast to the professional politician or member of a party machine, who entered politics in search of a job, the new (often youthful and educated) amateurs are motivated to participate because of enthusiasm for a candidate's personality or policies. They participate irregularly—mostly at election time, both in the prenomination drive and the election campaign. Their enthusiasm motivates them to perform without pay the tedious but necessary jobs of getting names for a nomination petition, ringing doorbells, manning telephones, and stuffing envelopes. That dedicated volunteers can make a difference is shown by the nomination of Barry Goldwater in 1964, the rapid rise of Eugene McCarthy in 1968 (after thousands of college students poured into New Hampshire to campaign for him in the primary), and the nomination of George McGovern in 1972. The continuing tendency of many

---

[38] For example, these countries require that employers provide workers with several weeks annually of paid vacations, and all three have virtually free cradle-to-the-grave medical service for all citizens. Far from being ahead of his time or radical, McGovern would have been regarded as a conservative in most European countries.

[39] Alexander, *Financing the 1968 Election*, p. 117.

political activists to channel their energies through the party and electoral system checks the decline of parties.

The media, especially radio and television, play a fundamental role in political campaigning. It has become commonplace that a candidate can reach more people in one television "spot" than in weeks of arduous campaigning. Reliance on the media reduces the need for elaborate grass-roots party machinery. Assuming the candidate has the money—no small matter as we have seen—the media make possible a campaign blitz, and under conditions of the candidate's own choosing. Television makes the "selling of the president" possible as no other medium can.[40]

Another recent development tending to make the party organization obsolete is professional campaign consultants. According to political scientist Frank Sorauf, the parties' "fairly primitive campaign skills have been superseded by a new campaign technology, and more and more they are finding themselves among the technologically unemployed."[41] There have always been specialists in the art of political organizing: people who knew how to get a press conference scheduled, prepare campaign literature, set up a public rally, and resolve the numerous crises that arise in a political campaign. In the past, these people were connected with a party organization and they always worked with only one party.

But in recent years, there has developed whole campaign organizations for hire: the rent-a-car principle applied to politics. The new industry of professional campaign consulting has boomed and now numbers around three hundred firms. In contrast to the former free-lance campaign specialist, the consulting firm handles the entire political campaign: speechwriting, polling, data processing, organizing rallies, and on and on.

On balance, the net effect of the new election mechanisms is to shift more power into the hands of those who have been dominant in the past. The costs of the new style campaigning make parties even more dependent on wealthy donors.

Decline of the Parties' Electoral Reach

One of the principal activities of American parties has been to mobilize and control the electorate. Yet a number of trends suggest that here, too, the party system is coming apart. Reviewing shifts

---

[40] Joe McGinnis, *The Selling of the President, 1968* (New York, 1969).
[41] Frank J. Sorauf, *Party Politics in America*, 2d ed. (Boston, 1972), p. 411.

Figure 6-1
Distribution of population on political beliefs, 1956 and 1973

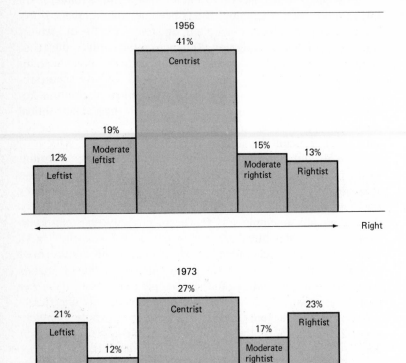

Source: Norman H. Nie, Sidney Verba, and John R. Petrocik, *The Changing American Voter* (Cambridge, Mass., Harvard Univeristy Press, 1976), p. 143. Copyright © 1976 by the Twentieth Century Fund.

in voter alignments since the 1960s, Walter Dean Burnham sees "a change of revolutionary scope" in progress.[42] Whereas previous electoral realignments strengthened the party system, the present shift is apparently away from political parties altogether.

The American electorate presently displays characteristics

---

[42] Walter Dean Burnham, "American Politics in the 1970's: Beyond Party?" in Chambers and Burnham, p. 308.

that are in marked contrast to the recent past. With some early exceptions, the first major studies of the American electorate that relied on public-opinion–poll data were carried out in the 1950s, a period of unusual political quiescence. In these circumstances, it is not surprising that election studies found voters to be relatively uninvolved in politics, hazy about differences between the parties, more clear about their partisan affiliation than their stand on political issues, and trustful toward government. During this period, voters paid little attention to issues, changed their position frequently, but voted with great regularity for the same political party. In retrospect, the 1950s represent a digression from the polarized conflicts that came before and after.

The 1960s ushered in a period of sharp bitter polarization. As the New Deal coalition began to erode under the double strain of an unpopular war abroad and domestic tensions, candidates began to put forward sharper ideological alternatives. Barry Goldwater's conservative candidacy in 1964 was a major catalyst in awakening political interest, prompting ideological self-examination, and dividing opinion. Reform programs sponsored by Democratic presidents in the 1960s further polarized politics and increased public awareness of issues and alternatives. Responses to questions about political beliefs changed drastically between the 1950s and the 1970s; the proportion of those who regard themselves as centrists declined and those who regard themselves as leftists or rightists increased.

Younger voters (those in their twenties) were especially affected by the turbulent conflicts of the 1960s. They did not judge these events from the perspective of a stable partisan attachment. Instead, their formative political years occurred as the present crisis began to emerge. When political parties provided little help in understanding or coping with the crisis, young voters saw no reason to give their allegiance to one party or the other—or, for that matter, the whole party system. Thus, in contrast to 1952, when only one-quarter of the youngest voters considered themselves independents, in 1974, more than half of the youngest voters considered themselves independents.[43]

Young voters displayed a new kind of political stance in the 1970s: more independent of political parties, skeptical of government, and involved and coherent in their approach to political

[43] Nie, Verba, and Petrocik, p. 60.

issues. The search for an attractive ideological alternative now rivals or exceeds traditional partisan loyalty as a guide to voting choice. The new-style voters tend to split their votes between candidates of different parties, switch from one party to the next in successive elections, and may not vote at all, given the unsatisfactory alternatives that parties offer.

If young educated voters led the way in the issue-oriented politics of the present period, voters of all ages and social groups have joined in. Political scientists Norman Nie, Sidney Verba, and John Petrocik comment, "Perhaps the most dramatic political change in the American public in the past two decades has been the decline of partisanship."[44]

The result has left parties floundering as they are no longer able to count on a large stable following. Factional divisions within the parties have increased and candidates often abandon reliance on the party altogether once they gain its nomination, preferring to mount their own campaign and downplay their party affiliation.

The future is wide open in this fluid situation. Millions of voters presently withhold their support from the party system and either remain detached and critical or participate in issue-oriented grass-roots movements. What it would take for parties to reach these voters may be beyond the parties' capacity: a meaningful program for change. Meanwhile, the parties limp along in an ever weakened form.

The crisis of the party system is part of the larger crisis of the political and economic system. Voters are angry at being asked to make increasing sacrifices when they receive fewer benefits in return. Their political opinions are complex and contradictory. For example, in 1978, three-fourths of the electorate believed that the government should guarantee a job for everyone seeking work. Four-fifths of the electorate wanted the government to assure low-cost medical care. Two-thirds of the electorate called for government regulation of safety conditions in factories. These measures imply an activist role for the federal government and a more restricted role for business. Yet a majority of the electorate also believed that the government had gone too far in regulating business.[45] In this volatile situation, the possible future alternatives are endless. We will discuss some of these alternatives in the last chapter.

[44] *Ibid.*, p. 47.
[45] *CBS/New York Times* News poll, unpublished, January 21, 1978, partially reported in the *New York Times*, January 22, 1978.

Decline of the Party System

The decline of the party system can be documented by several related phenomena.

First, voter turnout is falling. Through the end of the nineteenth century, voting turnout sometimes exceeded 80 percent of the eligible voters. Nowadays, half the voters or less seem to think it worth the trouble to vote.

One reason for the sharp drop in voting turnout after the turn of the century was the Progressive reform requiring people to register in order to vote, defended by the Progressives as a way to end election malpractices and improve the quality of the electorate. However, the emergence of personal registration requirements "coincided with the mass immigration of foreign-born newcomers in American cities and the move to disenfranchise Blacks in the South."[46] Thus, the registration requirement proved an effective technique, then and now, for reducing the number of voters. Professor of journalism Penn Kimball observes that registration "discriminates most particularly against the poor. . . . Voter registration operates as an effective system of political control."[47]

Who are the nonvoters? Not surprisingly, those who do not vote are frequently among the less advantaged. The largest groups of nonvoters are found among the rural and urban poor, blacks, Mexican-Americans, Puerto Ricans, and the elderly. Another large group includes youth and those who have recently changed residence (and are therefore not eligible to register). As Frank Sorauf points out, "the parties find it easier to be moderate and pragmatic because the electorate to which they respond is largely settled in and committed to the present basic social arrangements."[48]

Voting turnout has continued to decline in recent decades. Less than half the potentially eligible electorate voted in the 1976 presidential election, down from 55 percent in 1972. And the turnout rate in off-years, without a presidential election to bring out voters, is even smaller. Commenting on the 1976 election returns, Governor Edmund G. Brown of California said, "The biggest vote of all in November was a vote of no confidence." That 70 million citizens—about half the entire electorate—failed to vote in the

---

[46] Penn Kimball, *The Disconnected* (New York, 1972), p. 4.
[47] *Ibid.*, pp. 3–4.
[48] Sorauf, p. 203.

Figure 6-2
Party identification, 1920–1974

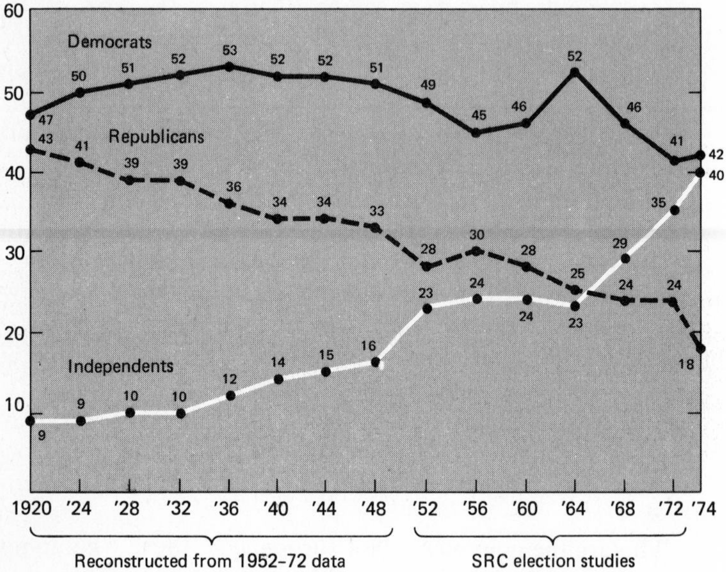

Source: Norman H. Nie, Sidney Verba, and John R. Petrocik, *The Changing American Voter* (Cambridge, Mass., Harvard University Press, 1976), p. 83. Copyright © 1976 by the Twentieth Century Fund.

presidential election amounted to a veritable electoral boycott.

The lessening importance of the party as a guide to candidate selection is another reason for the decline of the party system. In 1952, half the citizens interviewed by the Survey Research Center of the University of Michigan mentioned the party affiliation of the presidential candidates as a reason for liking or disliking them; in 1972, only one-fifth of voters interviewed mentioned the candidates' party affiliation in explaining their evaluations.[49]

The rise of vote switching and ticket splitting is also important to an understanding of the parties' decline. As voters judge on bases other than the candidates' party label, there is increased switching from one party to the other. This can be seen in the growing number of citizens who vote a split ticket, casting their

[49] Nie, Verba, and Petrocik, p. 68.

ballot for the presidential candidate of one party and the congressional candidate of the other party. The party label seems to have lost its unifying force. Professor Burnham calls this a four-party system in which voters remain loyal to congressional candidates in election after election but shift their vote in presidential elections. The result is that there is ever-greater stability in voting for congressional candidates (and high rates of incumbency, as analyzed in Chapter 10) along with erratic swings in the two parties' presidential vote.[50]

Finally, there is the rise of independents. In the 1950s, most citizens identified themselves as followers of one of the two major parties. Partisan identification was stable through time and was transmitted from one generation to the next. Starting in the early 1960s, the number of voters identifying themselves as independents began to rise sharply. Independents now rank as the second largest "party," ahead of the Republicans and close behind the Democrats.

THE FUTURE OF
AMERICAN POLITICAL PARTIES

Less and less organized political activity is taking place within the party system. A large minority of Americans either have been ignored by political parties or have decided to turn their backs on the party system altogether, judging that parties offer little hope for change. Others have engaged in volatile voting behavior, reflecting their anger at not getting what they want from the parties. Political candidates find that other instruments are more efficient than parties in manipulating voters. And groups that do challenge established institutions work through channels outside the two major parties. Parties are increasingly old-fashioned and outmoded. They have proved to be blunt, unwieldy instruments. Even within their remaining area of dominance—the nomination and election of public officials—parties are being pushed aside by professional polling agencies, the media, campaign consulting firms, and the personal organizations of the candidates.

Paradoxically, although parties have been conservative instruments of political control, their decline may signify an addi-

[50] Burnham, in Chambers and Burnham, pp. 317–40.

tional step away from democratic participation. French political scientist Maurice Duverger suggests that "a regime without parties is of necessity a conservative regime."[51] A leading sociologist, Robert Michels, wrote in *Political Parties*, "Organization is the weapon of the weak against the strong." However undemocratic and unresponsive, parties offer a potential for organizing opposition to established arrangements.

Thus the decline of parties does not signify a decline in political control. Walter Dean Burnham, among the first to describe broad historical changes in the evolution of the party system, notes:

American electoral politics is undergoing a long-term transition into routines designed only to fill offices and symbolically reaffirm "the American way." There also seems to be tendencies for our political parties gradually to evaporate as broad and active intermediaries between the people and their rulers, even as they may well continue to maintain enough organizational strength to screen out the unacceptable or the radical at the nominating stage. . . . Their disappearance as active intermediaries, if not as preliminary screening devices, would only entail the unchallenged ascendancy of the already powerful, unless new structures of collective power were somehow developed to replace them.[52]

American party competition can be likened to professional sports contests with now one team winning and now the other. In both cases, the stakes are high and the competition is tough—and sometimes dirty, as Watergate demonstrated.

However, as with the rivalry of professional sports teams, dirty competition is rare; conflict between American political parties usually takes place within a context of shared interests. Underlying the particular interest of each contender in winning the game is a deeper interest in seeing the game continue. In this sense, as noted earlier, the real contest is not between Democrats and Republicans, but between those who are represented by the party system and those who are not. The disintegration of political parties suggests that this is a sports contest with ever fewer participants. Professor Burnham speculates that, "If 'partisan decomposition' continues under these conditions of pervasive public discontent, democracy will be progressively emptied of any opera-

[51] Maurice Duverger, *Political Parties* (New York, 1963), p. 426.
[52] Burnham, in Fiszman and Poschman, p. 257.

tional meaning as executive-bureaucratic imperatives come to dominate the political system." [53]

This chapter has studied why the potential conflict between procedural democracy and structural inequality does not emerge more openly. Elections hold out the possibility of democratizing the social structure. Since procedural democracy provides for legal equality, with every citizen entitled to vote, an electoral majority might be fashioned uniting subordinate groups, in order to challenge dominant interests. In practice, elections have had an opposite effect: most of the time they have stabilized existing arrangements.

Among the reasons for the conservative bias of the electoral system are the lack of alternatives presented by parties to the electorate, the organization and financing of parties, and the higher rate of participation by the well-to-do. Other factors, analyzed in other chapters, include the operation of political institutions (the presidency, Congress, local government, and the courts) and ideological attitudes in America.

Yet as social tensions increase, political parties may be losing their capacity to control and limit political choice. To some extent other agencies, including government, the media, and private campaign firms, may be picking up the slack. However, the voters' growing attention to issues, increasing political independence, and rising dissatisfaction with limited political choices suggest the potential for an opposite development. If the party system continues to decay, the possibility expands for either increased control by dominant groups or, alternatively, popular mobilization by subordinate groups.

However, the decline of the present two-party system need not lead to reduced political participation and even fewer alternatives to the status quo. The more open situation creates new possibilities for broadening the ideological and political agenda to embrace wider choices. Rather than lamenting the present situation, thoughtful political participants may be in a better position to shape the future.

---

[53] Burnham, in Chambers and Burnham, p. 354.

7
the welfare state

No major political party in the United States is committed to the growth of government. Indeed, most politicians, most of the time, talk of cutting out unnecessary programs, eliminating waste, and controlling the share of the Gross National Product taken by public spending generally, and by the welfare state in particular. And yet, social-welfare expenditures—the cash benefits, services, and administrative costs of government programs, such as social security, Medicare, and public assistance, that directly benefit individuals and families—continue to rise under Republican and Democratic administrations alike. At the close of the Eisenhower administration, about 10 percent of GNP was accounted for by welfare-state spending. Five years later, when President Johnson was in office, the proportion was up to 12 percent. Under President Nixon in 1970, 15 percent of GNP went for such programs; and at the beginning of the Ford administration in 1974 almost 18 percent of GNP was spent in this way.[1] How are we to understand this continuous growth?

When this experience is compared to that of the other western capitalist democracies, however, it is not so much the growth of the United States welfare state that is puzzling but its relatively

[1] Robert J. Lampman, "Changing Patterns of Income, 1960–1974," in David Warner, ed., *Toward New Human Rights: The Social Policies of the Kennedy and Johnson Administrations* (Austin, Texas, 1977), p. 118.

small size. For as we noted in Chapter 1, the United States has consistently spent a lower proportion of its resources on social-welfare programs than any other western society. We thus must ask, how are we to make sense both of the growth of the American welfare state and of its relatively small size? In this chapter we shall see that the routine functioning of the corporate complex produces welfare-state growth to maintain social peace and the dual economy.

The comparatively slow growth of welfare spending in the United States is accounted for largely by the absence of a working-class party or movement that regularly promotes such programs. As a result, the main expansions in the size and character of the welfare state have come in periods of major social unrest, as angry social movements have pressed their claims on government. In more quiet times, a "nonpolitical" problem-solving orientation governs the growth of the welfare state.

THE DUAL WELFARE SYSTEM: SOCIAL CAPITAL AND SOCIAL EXPENSES

It is necessary to distinguish two quite different, though related, categories of welfare-state programs. The first provides tangible benefits to better-off workers in the corporate and state sectors of the economy. Most of these programs take the form of social insurance. Old-Age and Survivors and Disability Insurance under Social Security are the best known and most inclusive. The second category consists of programs directed mainly at the poor in the small-capital sector. The most important of these programs is Aid to Families with Dependent Children (AFDC), the heart of which is commonly referred to as welfare.

As differentiated by economist James O'Connor, the first category, which he calls *social capital*, directly or indirectly serves the interests of private corporations. By using tax money to provide benefits and insurance for workers, social-capital expenditures lower labor costs for corporations and thus increase corporate productivity and profitability. The second category, which O'Connor calls *social expenses*, is not productive or profitable, but is equally necessary to corporate capitalism because it maintains the social order. The routine operation of the economy creates economic dislocations, including unemployment, underemployment, and a high proportion of workers whose wages are at or near subsistence levels. The resulting discontent threatens social stability. Thus, there are programs such as the AFDC that are "designed chiefly to keep social peace among unemployed workers."[2]

As we shall see, there are basic inequities between the two parts of the dual welfare state. Compared with social-insurance programs, social-expense programs provide recipients with lower levels of support; they are called by less legitimate names (relief vs. compensation); they tend to be administered by state and local governments; and they stigmatize the poor. These differences are no accident. The two kinds of programs service the needs of different sectors of American capitalism. Yet they spring from the same historical roots.

HISTORICAL FOUNDATIONS

The history of state involvement in social welfare can be variously interpreted. On the one hand, it can be seen as an account of the growing liberalization of provisions for the poor and of developing attempts to address the causes of poverty. Before 1935, the United States lacked even a basic social-security program of the sort that had long been adopted in the capitalist countries of Western Europe. By 1964, the government's involvement in social welfare had expanded to such an extent that an American president declared unconditional war on poverty; five years later, a conservative president proposed a guaranteed minimum income for all Americans. But, on the other hand, the growth of the welfare state can be seen as the continuation of basic historical traditions that "include repression, local financing and administration, a minimization of the amount of money spent on the poor, an emphasis on the work ethic, a distinction between the deserving and the undeserving poor, and a stigma attached to those who are dependent on relief."[3] As a result, the major innovations in public-welfare policy in this century have consistently been paternalistic at best, and often punitive to the poor.

[2] James O'Connor, *The Fiscal Crisis of the State* (New York, 1973), p. 7.
[3] Bruno Stein, *On Relief* (New York, 1971), p. 43.

Twentieth-century American welfare programs are rooted in the assumptions and practices of the English Poor Law of 1598. The act was passed in response to the social problems created by the shift from feudal to early capitalist patterns of agriculture, which drove many agricultural laborers off the land. Under the provisions of earlier laws, wandering paupers were punished with whipping, branding, enslavement, and even death. Yet these repressive measures became inadequate in controlling the rapidly increasing numbers of dispossessed workers. A British historian captured the mood of the period, which is remarkably similar to that of contemporary America in many respects:

> Wanderers were feared in the sixteenth century as likely to be thieves and rogues, and if in any number to cause more serious trouble, perhaps even political disturbances. . . . [M]obility of labour was to be feared. As Tawney has said, the sixteenth century lived in terror of the tramp. . . . The combination of fear and feeling can be detected in the preamble to the Elizabethan statute of 1598:
>
> *whereas a good part of the strength of this realm consisteth in the number of good and able subjects . . . and of late years more than in time past there have been sundry towns, parishes and houses of husbandry destroyed and become desolate, whereof a great number of poor people are become wanderers, idle and loose, which is the cause of infinite inconvenience . . .* [4]

The Poor Law attempted to deal with this breakdown of social control by mandating that local governments maintain their *own* poor at the smallest level of government, the parish. Local officials were given wide latitude in determining the level of benefits and how they would be disbursed. All able-bodied people, including children, were compelled to work. A refusal to work was a punishable crime.

The principles of the Poor Law, and of the subsequent amendments to it that usually followed periods of mass unrest in Britain, were transplanted to the American colonies and became the basis of American social welfare. The autonomy of localities produced widely different eighteenth- and nineteenth-century welfare policies for the poor. It also enabled localities to reduce their tax burdens by making nonresidents ineligible for welfare (such residency requirements were only ruled unconstitutional by the Supreme Court in 1969). Regulations that made work compulsory

---

[4] Maurice Bruce, *The Coming of the Welfare State* (New York, 1966), pp. 24, 26.

provided an ample low-paid work force for developing capitalist enterprises. And like English Poor Law practices, which often segregated the poor in workhouses and poorhouses, American social-welfare policies were administered in such a way as to stigmatize the poor and distinguish between the deserving and undeserving poor.

Local welfare systems could not survive the ravages of the depression, nor were they compatible with the basic shift in the economy from small-scale, largely local or regional capital to corporate capital. As more and more Americans became poor (most of whom had little experience with hard-core poverty), the federal government nationalized welfare policy by funding and setting standards for traditionally autonomous local welfare programs. Nevertheless, many of the system's basic characteristics continued to prevail.

The Social Security Act of 1935 created a countrywide framework for a dual welfare state. It established the basic programs of social capital and social expenses. The social-capital expenditures included Social Security and a federal/state system of unemployment compensation. The bill's most significant program of social expenses was Aid to Dependent Children (ADC), which has developed into today's AFDC. Augmented by programs of public health, food stamps, public housing, and other services, it remains the core of the social-expenses welfare state.

SOCIAL WELFARE AND THE NEW DEAL

The Social Security Act was not passed in an economic or political vacuum. With the election of Franklin D. Roosevelt in 1932, the federal government began to respond more actively to the massive economic upheaval of the depression. The first response of the New Deal to soaring unemployment rates was the substitution of work relief for direct cash relief. By mid-January 1934 the Civil Works Administration (CWA) had put four million Americans to work, thus making the federal government the largest employer in the country.

But by the spring of 1934 the CWA was closed down. It had drawn the widespread opposition of the corporate community, whose members feared the CWA threatened the private-enterprise system. "Work relief raised the specter of government activity in areas hitherto reserved for private enterprise, and CWA minimum wage scales raised the specter of government interference in the conduct of private enterprise."[5] The abolition of the CWA signified that Roosevelt sought to win support from businessmen (albeit unsuccessfully) in the first year of the New Deal and to restore their confidence in American capitalism.

By the congressional elections of 1934, growing business opposition to the Roosevelt regime made it necessary for the president to seek to save capitalism and members of the corporate order in spite of themselves. As *Fortune* magazine noted in 1935, it was "fairly evident to most disinterested critics" that the New Deal had "the preservation of capitalism at all times in view." A small minority of the corporate community agreed with this assessment and played a major role in the administration, but in the main Roosevelt had to build his political constituency of farmers, workers, and homeowners without overt business support.

The defection of much of his minority business support from Roosevelt's political coalition eliminated political cross-pressures in the administration and freed it to deal with mass discontent more directly than might otherwise have been possible. With the end of the CWA in 1934, millions of Americans who had been given jobs now found themselves again dependent on the largesse of private, local, or state relief agencies. Their restiveness was palpable. Many, at the time, thought the United States was in a prerevolutionary situation:

> For discontent had not evaporated with the elections of 1932; rather, it was stilled for a moment by the promise of a new regime, the confidence a new leader inspired. However, as the Depression wore on, with conditions showing little improvement, unrest surfaced. By 1934, various dissident leaders were drawing upon this unrest, giving it organizational form and coherence, aspiring to build political movements that would change the face of America.[6]

Roosevelt responded by promoting social-welfare legislation that undercut these growing dissident movements and acted to restore stability. In his January 4, 1935, State of the Union message, Roosevelt proposed sweeping reforms, including redistribu-

[5] Frances Fox Piven and Richard Cloward, *Regulating the Poor: The Functions of Public Welfare* (New York, 1971), p. 82.
[6] *Ibid.*, p. 85.

tive tax laws, new labor legislation, the restoration of national work relief, and programs of social insurance. The proposals were largely gutted by the Congress, but the passage of diluted versions had a larger symbolic importance: it convinced many of the discontented that the federal government was acting vigorously on their behalf.

The measure that had the most direct impact on the unemployed was the restoration of massive publicly-funded employment under the Works Progress Administration (WPA). Millions of Americans were once more put to work, a fact that more than anything else eased the threat of civil disorder. But after 1936, as the most important dissident movements of the period (including the Townsend Old People's Movement, the Workers Alliance, and other populist organizations of the left and right) declined in membership and influence, the New Deal quickly reduced its concessions to the poor, and the number of federally-paid jobs was sharply cut. Once the threat of a civil uprising had passed, the government withdrew from the employment picture in order to restore the traditional prerogatives of private capital.

Hence the most enduring welfare innovation of the depression was not work relief but the Social Security Act. It provided the basic framework for the modern American welfare state, and its provisions meshed with, rather than challenged, the dominant corporate system. Unemployment insurance, social security pensions, and categorical aid to mothers and families with dependent children have been with us ever since. These programs have continued to grow in size, and they have been joined by such new government undertakings as food stamps, and Medicare and Medicaid. How do these programs mesh with the corporate complex? What accounts for their growth and their limitations?

THE DUAL WELFARE SYSTEM
AND THE CORPORATE SECTOR

We have seen how the major innovations in America's welfare-state policy were utilized to defuse discontent in the period of the New Deal. But the welfare state also has economic and political functions in more quiet times. Since the welfare state is not an undifferentiated whole, however, it is necessary to explore these functions with reference to the dominant corporate sector of large capital and local and regional small capital. Each of these two sectors is serviced differently by the welfare state. First let us consider the relationship of the welfare state to the corporate sector.

The distinction between the two kinds of welfare-state programs dates back to the Social Security Act of 1935. The social-insurance provisions of the bill, which insure against old age, retirement, and unemployment—as well as similar programs adopted in the 1940s, including veteran's life insurance and insurance against work-related accidents—directly support the needs of the corporate complex. Paradoxically, although these insurance payments go to workers, "the fundamental intent and effect of social security is to expand productivity, production, and profits. *Seen in this way, social insurance is not primarily insurance for workers but a kind of insurance for capitalists and corporations."* [7] What does this statement mean?

Most corporate leaders would probably agree that the relatively better-off workers in large-capital firms will work harder if they are more secure economically. Thus, many industries instituted systems of workmen's compensation well before such insurance was mandated by law. Although the passage of most landmark pieces of social legislation was primarily the result of political activity by powerful organized workers, corporate leaders of the largest, most economically advanced industries have often been in the vanguard of those demanding the expansion of the social-insurance system.

Today, social-insurance programs enjoy the enthusiastic support of both business and labor in the corporate sector. A look at Social Security indicates the reasons. Retired workers in the 1970s share about $45 billion each year in Social Security payments, up from $19 billion in 1964. [8] Workers are taxed to pay for these benefits at the rate of 6.1 percent of the first $22,900 they earn each year. An identical tax is paid by the employer. But most economists believe that, in the case of corporations, the employer's share is passed along to the worker in the form of lower wages. Thus, while corporate employers largely escape having to

[7] O'Connor, p. 138.
[8] Charles L. Schultze et al. *Setting National Priorities: The 1972 Budget* (Washington, D.C., 1972), p. 21.

make a real contribution to the social-security system, corporate workers in effect pay a tax (both direct and indirect) of more than 12 percent of their income. Hence the corporation profits at their expense.

In turn, however, corporate-sector workers gain at the expense of the lower-paid workers in small-capital industries. Although all workers are taxed equally up to the first $22,900 they earn (income over this figure is exempt), the more an individual earns while working, the higher his or her retirement payments. Moreover, millions of people who have been unemployed for long periods do not accumulate the required work-time and receive no benefits at all when they retire, even though they paid taxes when they worked.

In spite of the fact that the social-security tax is America's most regressive tax (exempting interest, profit, rent, capital gains, and all payroll income over $22,900), this and other programs of social insurance, like unemployment insurance and workmen's compensation, favor the corporate worker and thus are supported by organized labor as well as by corporate management. The corporations are enabled to keep wage costs down, and corporate-sector workers gain by what economist Milton Friedman has called "the poor man's welfare payment to the middle class."[9] As O'Connor noted:

> Organized labor is more or less satisfied because the system redistributes income in its favor. Monopoly capital is also relatively happy because the system insures comparative harmony with labor. If monopoly sector workers were compelled to contribute as much as they receive upon retirement, current money wages would have to be slashed sharply. But if retired workers received what they actually paid in, retirement benefits would be impossibly low. In either event, monopoly sector labor-management relations would be seriously impaired. Workers would bitterly resist technological and other changes that threatened their jobs, the ability of unions to maintain discipline would be undermined, and in most industries management would be faced with more uncertainty.[10]

Moreover, as rank-and-file workers have come to agitate for better pensions, labor leaders and corporate managements have moved

[9] Milton Friedman, "The Poor Man's Welfare Payment to the Middle Class," *The Washington Monthly* (May 1972): 16.
[10] O'Connor, pp. 139–40. Also see, "Congress Clears Social Security Tax Increase," *Congressional Quarterly*, December 17, 1977, pp. 2621–24.

to resolve their shared dilemma by pressuring the federal government for more liberalized social-insurance programs. The ritual pattern was set in 1949 when Walter Reuther, the president of the United Automobile Workers (UAW), successfully prodded the automobile companies to pressure for liberalized social security by negotiating a contract that included an expensive pension plan. "The effect of the 'Reuther system' is that corporations socialize . . . costs . . . and thus defend their profits, union leaders conserve their hegemony over the rank and file, and labor discipline and morale are maintained."[11]

SMALL CAPITAL AND THE WELFARE STATE

The relationship between small capital and the welfare state is quite different from that between the welfare state and corporate capital. First, although the small-capital sector is increasingly anachronistic, the federal government helps maintain the existence of "surplus capitalists" by providing them with a form of welfare in much the same way it provides foreign aid to "underdeveloped" countries. The cost of this support is billions of dollars in direct and indirect subsidies to farmers (under the direction of the Department of Agriculture) and small businesspeople (financed by the Small Business Administration).[12]

Workers in the small-capital sector tend to be lower paid, less unionized, and less economically secure than corporate-sector workers. They are more likely to be unemployed for longer periods. They are often excluded from social-insurance programs, and when included, receive smaller benefits. These sectoral imbalances, historian Eric Hobsbawm noted, constitute "the rhythm of social disruption" of industrial capitalism.[13] Industrial growth increases imbalances between regions of the country (the Southwest is booming, but the older urban cores are stagnating economically) and between different industries (plastics production has increased considerably, while the domestic shoe industry has declined).

[11] O'Connor, p. 141.
[12] C. Lowell Harriss, "Subsidies in the United States," *Public Finance* 16 (no. 4, 1961): 276.
[13] O'Connor, p. 159.

Whereas corporate workers share somewhat in the gains of corporate growth and technical progress, small-capital workers do not; on the contrary, the wage gap between the two sectors has widened considerably in the past quarter century.

As a result, an increasing proportion of the small-capital–sector population has become dependent on welfare programs for subsistence. With the continuing decline in the economic position of small-capital–sector workers, the traditional correlation between unemployment and AFDC welfare rates no longer held by the middle 1960s. Since the depression, the number of new welfare cases rose and fell with the monthly rise and fall of male unemployment. But "with the onset of the 1960s the relationship weakened abruptly, and by 1963 vanished altogether. Or rather, reversed itself. For the next five years the nonwhite male unemployment rate declined steadily and the number of AFDC cases rose steadily."[14]

This shift reflected the growing gap between corporate- and small-capital–sector wages. At the end of the Second World War, small-capital–sector workers earned roughly 75 percent of the wages of corporate-sector workers; in the 1960s, their relative earnings declined to 60 percent.[15] Thus even those in the small-capital sector who had jobs were increasingly unable to adequately support their families. Men deserted their wives and children either out of a sense of shame or because their families would be better off with AFDC payments. The welfare rolls skyrocketed as more and more families became dependent on the state. Low wages and underemployment, as well as unemployment, now contributed directly to the growth of the welfare state. Throughout the 1960s, the number of welfare recipients grew by almost 10 percent per year.[16]

In response to this trend, the federal government experimented with job-training schemes in an attempt "to transform social expense outlays (welfare) into social capital for the competitive sector."[17] The Manpower Development and Training Act of 1964 provides for on-the-job training that equips workers for small-capital, not corporate, sector jobs. After studying the program, economist Jerome Joffe concluded that it "has primarily

---

[14] Daniel P. Moynihan, *The Politics of a Guaranteed Income* (New York, 1973), p. 82.
[15] Barry Bluestone, "Economic Crisis and the Law of Uneven Development," *Politics and Society* 3 (Fall 1972): 68.
[16] *Wall Street Journal*, April 24, 1969.
[17] O'Connor, p. 166.

provided training for low-skill high-turnover jobs in both the rising sectors in the central city, e.g., nurse's aide, and the traditional low-wage industry occupations, e.g., sewing machine operator."[18]

Most importantly of all for the small-capital sector, the operations of the welfare state reinforce the harsh employment market. In periods when the social order is not under stress, the welfare system operates to compel people into low-paid, menial work by following the principle of "less eligibility" proclaimed in England in 1834, which declared that welfare payments should provide a standard of living less desirable than "the situation of the independent laborer of the lowest class." The traditional workhouses that underpinned this principle in England were

> designed to spur men to contrive ways of supporting themselves by their own industry, *to offer themselves to any employer on any terms*. It did this by making pariahs of those who could not support themselves; they served as an object lesson, a means of celebrating the virtues of work by the terrible example of their agony.[19]

This principle makes it possible to understand the ritual degradation of the welfare client, a degradation that is no accident. In contrast to the insurance programs O'Connor labelled social capital, one of the main functions of the social-expenses welfare system is to demarcate a boundary between the "deserving" and "undeserving" poor. The boundary is made clear as soon as a person applies for welfare. AFDC welfare centers are typically dingy, forbidding places; long waits for attention and a clinical atmosphere set a dehumanizing tone. Once applicants are called to meet a caseworker, their lives are probed in intimate, exhaustive detail—work, family, and finances are all grist for the welfare workers' mill. One prospective welfare recipient described an early experience with the system:

> At the Welfare they got this man they call him the Resources man and sometimes he is also a woman. Whenever you apply for welfare, you must be sent to him because he must ask you a lot of questions. All kinds of questions. Like he may ask you if you belong to a union or are in the Army. Then he will try to do something about that to keep you off welfare.

Finally, after being shunted between four caseworkers who re-

[18] Jerome Joffe, "The Limits of Urban Policy," *Review of Radical Political Economics* 4 (Summer 1972): 101.
[19] Piven and Cloward, pp. 34, 35.

fused to put him on the rolls, "I go away from the welfare center as rich as when I came there." He found a subsistence wage job, but the factory was unionized and the workers went out on strike.

> I have no savings yet, so I must go again to welfare, but this man wants to know when I got my last check. Then he says he can't help me because it is not so long ago that I shouldn't have some money. And he tells me to come back in another week if the strike isn't settled, but today when I went to see him he said, 'Look for work and come back again in another week.' I just don't think he wants to give me the welfare. So that's the way it is again. I have moved out of my room and I am staying with my uncle. . . . If the strike ends soon maybe I will save my money and go to another city. I have friends in Philadelphia. They say it is not so cruel about the welfare.[20]

Once they succeed in getting on the welfare rolls, recipients are subjected to further degradation. Routinely they are kept under surveillance, exhorted by welfare workers to "rehabilitate" themselves, and asked to prove that they are not welfare chiselers or frauds. They are underbudgeted by welfare workers who are given incentives to keep costs down. They are defined as useless in a society that values work and production; and from time to time, they are denounced as such by politicians in search of headlines. Most importantly, they are treated as, and become, functionally powerless, dependent on the decisions of others over whom they exercise virtually no control. They come to share the society's image of them as unworthy, and to collaborate in the system that perpetuates their subordination. There are almost no appeals made by welfare recipients on grounds of deprivation either of money or of civil liberties, which are their due under the Social Security Act.[21] This process of systematic degradation also works to discourage *potential* welfare clients, who will accept subsistence wages rather than suffer the consequences of being on welfare.

Active discouragement of qualified relief recipients increases as the threat of mass discontent ebbs. In the late 1960s, for example, after the wave of ghetto rebellions had passed, city after city moved to make it more difficult to get on the welfare rolls. In New York, the Bureau of the Budget recommended to the mayor that a case backlog be deliberately created by consolidating the welfare centers and by cutting welfare personnel. Consolidation of the

---

[20] Richard M. Elman, *The Poorhouse State* (New York, 1966), pp. 94–96.
[21] Piven and Cloward, p. 173.

centers began in 1970. Since then, the rise of the welfare rolls has dramatically stopped—at the cost of much human suffering.

Perhaps the dilemma is most acute in the case of the welfare mother who is given contradictory cues by society. She is told to stay at home with her children, on the one hand, but to work to support herself, on the other. The welfare system also makes it virtually impossible for her to better her situation.

> Mary Thomas' case was typical. She would like to quit her job as a saleswoman in a clothing store, in order to return to school and become a medical technician. Unfortunately, though welfare will subsidize the day care of her five children while she works at the store, it will not do so while she returns to school for four years. Nor will welfare pay her tuition. It is thus difficult, if not impossible, for her to work in anything except a low-paying, dead-end job. . . . The federal minimum wage of $1.60 an hour means that for all her hard labor, a woman who has several children will still be stuck in poverty. . . . there are ten million jobs that pay less than the minimum wage; if she is a woman, she has a good chance to get one of these. In fact, public officials such as Senator Long and Elliot Richardson have argued that welfare recipients ought to work for less than the minimum wage ($1.20 an hour) if private industry jobs are unavailable.[22]

Welfare thus perpetuates the dependency it claims to find distressing by using wretchedness to reinforce job-market exploitation.

At the extreme, welfare recipients are treated as nonpeople. In Aiken, South Carolina, County Hospital records show that thirteen of thirty-four welfare mothers whose children's births were paid for by government funds in 1972 were sterilized. The doctor who performed the hysterectomies received payments of $60,000 for his hospital work that year. The doctor "defended his policy in the local press and said that he required welfare mothers with three children to receive care. He said he was doing so because of the heavy tax burden they were causing."[23]

The economic benefits for the small-capital sector are obvious. But there are ideological payoffs as well. By segregating and stigmatizing the "productively useless," "the welfare state does not oppose but counterbalances the utilitarian assumptions of the middle class."[24] In terms of the dominant American ideology, the

[22] Lynne Iglitzin, "Women and Welfare," unpublished manuscript.
[23] *New York Times*, August 3, 1973.
[24] Alvin Gouldner, *The Coming Crisis of Western Sociology* (New York, 1971), pp. 81–82.

clients of the AFDC system are obvious failures and are punished as such.

TWO KINDS OF WELFARE STATE PROFESSIONALS

As the welfare state has grown since the mid-1930s, so have the numbers of professionals who plan and staff its operations. Since the Second World War, in particular, the rapid growth of the social-science field has provided the welfare state with a cadre of professional planners. Indeed, the expansion of the welfare state and of the social sciences has occurred in tandem. Thus, between 1962 and 1964, boom years for new welfare programs, federal expenditures on social-science research increased by 70 percent to $200,000,000 per year.

These monies were not simply intended to further knowledge in the abstract. As sociologist Alvin Gouldner pointed out, the government expected that "the social sciences will help solve ramifying practical problems. In particular, it is expected that the social sciences will help administrators to design and operate national policies, welfare apparatus, urban settlements, and even industrial establishments."[25] In response to these demands, the social sciences have developed new techniques—including decision-theory, cybernetics, and operations research—that provide policymakers with politically acceptable options.

But, as Gouldner also pointed out, social scientists not only provide the state with a refined capability in developing welfare programs but they also provide the appropriate reformist rhetoric

> to persuade resistant or undecided segments of the society that such problems do, indeed, exist and are of dangerous proportions. Once committed to such intervention, the state acquires a vested interest of its own in "advertising" the social problems for whose solution it seeks financing. In other words, the state requires social researches that can *expose* those social problems with which the state is ready to deal.[26]

A second group of professionals—social workers, nurses, nursery-school teachers—administer the programs directly, and

[25] *Ibid.*, p. 345.
[26] *Ibid.*, p. 35.

distribute welfare-state rewards, such as they are, to clients. But the interests of this group of professionals, as distributors of desired or necessary goods and services, often clash with the interests of the consumers of those services. These clashes, political scientist Deborah Stone observes, are of three kinds:

(1) The theory of professional work has a middle-class orientation. Service to a client is assumed to be discrete and temporary, on the assumption that all is basically well, but a transient "ailment" needs to be remedied. The result is that professionals "offer help with individual problems, while lower-class people face discrimination as a class." Regressive tax and credit laws, slums, and inadequate health care are not individual problems. Hence, professionals, "by treating their clients on an *ad hoc*, short-term, and symptomatic basis, can at the very best only restore them to the *status quo*, and at the worst make their lives more difficult."

(2) The reward structure of service professions, in general, discourages service to a lower-class clientele. New public health nurses, school teachers, social workers, police officers, and child guidance therapists are initially assigned to the poorest neighborhoods and, with time and experience, "promoted" to wealthier districts:

> This kind of reward structure means that the most needy . . . are served, if at all, by the least experienced and least competent members of the profession. It also serves to inculcate class prejudices into individual members of the profession. Thus, the status concerns of a profession lead the profession as a whole to provide its best services to higher-status groups, and lead individual professionals to eschew services to the poor.[27]

(3) Professionals seek to maintain freedom from outside control and an image of competence. One of the hallmarks of a profession is its autonomy—its freedom to set its own standards of behavior. As a result, professionals typically resist any moves toward community control that would jeopardize their authority. This resistance is justified by a claim of superior competence; hence, to safeguard this image, professionals protect even the most incompetent of their members.

Both groups of professionals, and their clients, have a vested interest in the expansion of welfare-state programs. Even more important is the manner in which these programs maintain the dual

[27] Deborah Stone, "Professionals and the Welfare State," unpublished manuscript.

economy. Together, these two sets of factors—pressures directed
through the democratic system and the requirements of an advanced capitalist economy—account for the steady growth of
social-welfare programs even during periods of relative social
peace. But such programs have not expanded at an even pace. The
first major period of social reform, we have seen, occurred during
the depression of the 1930s. The second major period of welfare-
state innovations was the 1960s.

SKIRMISHES AGAINST POVERTY:
A WAR ON DISORDER

At the end of the second period, in April 1969, President Nixon
proposed a Family Assistance Plan (FAP) that, if it had passed,
would have guaranteed a minimum income to every American
family with children, and would have supplemented the earnings of
the working poor. Every family of four, for instance, would have
received a minimum of $1600 per year and would have had its
income supplemented as long as family earnings were under $4000.
It was estimated that the plan would have cost $4 billion in its first
year of operation.

Coming from a conservative Republican president who had
campaigned against welfare, for the work ethic, for "law and
order," and who had been elected without direct black support,
this proposal to give federal funds directly to the poor seemed
remarkable. *Newsweek* called the proposal "so sweeping that even
some of his own Republican Cabinet Officers were left gasping for
conservative breath." The liberal Detroit *Free Press* found FAP
"more radical than anything done by the Johnson administration,"
whose actions had included the creation of an Office of Economic
Opportunity (OEO) to supervise a multimillion-dollar War on Poverty.[28]

Such comments stressed the apparently radical content of
FAP without adequately coming to terms with the program's intent, which was to stabilize the structure of society, not to change
it. From the perspective of those who governed the United States

[28] Moynihan, *The Politics of a Guaranteed Income*, pp. 252–53.

in the late 1960s, the social order gave every impression of crumbling. Daniel Moynihan, who served in subcabinet and cabinet-level positions under Presidents Kennedy, Johnson, and Nixon, and who was the architect of the welfare reform bill, captured the mood of near panic at the top:

> Nixon shared the anxiety . . . that the spiral of increasing urban racial violence . . . had not ceased. In 1965 there had been four major riots and civil disturbances in the country. In 1966 there were twenty-one major riots and civil disorders. In 1967 there were eighty-three major riots and civil disturbances. In the first seven months of 1968 there were fifty-seven major riots and disturbances. . . . In retrospect the domestic turbulence of the United States in the late 1960s may come to appear something less than cataclysmic. But this was not the view of the men then in office. Mayors, governors—presidents—took it as given that things were in a hell of a shape and that something had to be done.[29]

Moynihan rightly argued that Nixon's FAP proposal can only be understood as an attempt to deal with growing mass black discontent. Indeed, the leaders of the corporate community, who had the most to lose in the face of mass insurgency, largely favored the Nixon initiative. The specific features of the Family Assistance Plan were developed from proposals of a conference Governor Nelson Rockefeller of New York called in March 1967 "to help plan new approaches to public welfare in the United States." The steering committee consisted of some of the most successful members of the corporate complex, including Joseph Block (chairman of the executive committee of Inland Steel), Albert Nickerson (chief executive officer of Mobil Oil), Gustave Levy (head of the New York Stock Exchange), and Joseph Wilson (chairman of the board and chief executive officer of the Xerox corporation).

The conference collectively recommended that the present welfare system be replaced by a program of income maintenance. It argued for the acceptance of the objective that basic economic support at the federally defined poverty level be provided for all Americans. But any such system, the conference cautioned, "should contain strong incentives to work." Moynihan commented that the "governor's inspiration was to turn to the heads of the large capitalist enterprises of the nation, a community with few ties, certainly, to the Social Security system, having bitterly opposed its establishment, but now including among its members

[29] *Ibid.*, pp. 101–02.

men of generous disposition on social issues, *a tendency much accentuated by the onset of urban rioting.*[30] In other words, rather than the existence of poverty, what concerned many businesspeople was the disruption resulting from poverty.

President Nixon's proposal was not passed into law. Conservative members of Congress, especially those from the South, were adamantly opposed to any extension of welfare benefits. Many liberal Democratic members argued the legislation was not generous enough. But difficult as it might have been for Nixon to forge a majority coalition for the bill, most observers believe he could have had he not lost interest in the legislation. As the urban turmoil of the period receded, the president ceased to lobby for support of FAP. This turning away from his own bill makes sense when we understand that FAP was not meant in the first instance to change the welfare system for the better, but to restore social peace. With that goal accomplished by other means, welfare reform was set aside.

But if FAP was a clear response to riot and unrest, the main causes of the formulation of the social-welfare legislation of President Kennedy's New Frontier and the early proposals of President Johnson's Great Society have puzzled many observers. In 1961, when John F. Kennedy sponsored the appropriation of $10 million for grants to "youth development" under the Juvenile Delinquency and Youth Offenses Control Act; when, two years later, $150 million were authorized for community mental health centers; when, in 1964, Title Two of the Economic Opportunity Act (the antipoverty bill of the War on Poverty) allocated $350 million to community action programs that called for the "maximum feasible participation of residents of the areas and members of the groups served"; and when Congress passed a Model Citizens program to rehabilitate blighted neighborhoods in 1966, there was a marked *absence* of interest groups pressing for the legislation. At the initiative of the White House the bills all passed in an apparent political vacuum. How could this phenomenon be explained?

Moynihan developed a widely accepted explanation that he labeled "the professionalism of reform":

> Increasingly efforts to change the American social system for the better arose from initiatives undertaken by persons whose profession was to do just that. Whereas previously the role of organized society had been largely passive—the machinery would work if

[30] *Ibid.*, p. 56. Emphasis added.

someone made it work—now the process began to acquire a self-starting capacity of its own.[31]

Unlike the New Deal programs, he argued, which were generated by long sustained political pressure and discontent, and which in turn defused discontent, the early New Frontier and Great Society programs of Presidents Kennedy and Johnson originated in a period when "the American poor, black and white, were surprisingly inert. . . . The war on poverty was not declared at the behest of the poor: it was declared in their interest by persons confident of their own judgement in such matters."[32] The development of these programs thus reflected the rise of a technocratic professional elite and the growth of a knowledge industry based on universities and foundations.

While the professionalism of reform played an important part in the expansion of the welfare state in the 1960s, it is not the whole story. It does not account for the *political* appeals of the professionals' proposals and, hence, the reasons for their adoption by politicians, and it tells us little about the impact of the new programs in dealing with the unprecedented black discontent of the middle and late 1960s.

Kennedy's close election victory in 1960 revealed basic weaknesses in the Democratic coalition. The South in particular was no longer a secure party base. In the Northern cities, many Democratic voters were moving to the suburbs, where their political allegiances were more uncertain. In their place were millions of black migrants from the South—a large number of whom did not vote—who had few established links with urban party organizations.

It was this new constituency that the Kennedy and Johnson administrations needed. Hence they welcomed the programs proposed by the reform professionals:

> Each program singled out the 'inner city' as its main target; each provided a basketful of services; each channeled some portion of its funds more or less directly to new organizations in the 'inner city', circumventing the existing municipal agencies which traditionally controlled services. . . . it was ghetto neighborhoods that these programs were chiefly designed to reach, and by tactics reminiscent of the traditional political machine.[33]

[31] Daniel P. Moynihan, *Maximum Feasible Misunderstanding* (New York, 1969), p. 23.
[32] *Ibid.*, pp. 34–35.
[33] Piven and Cloward, pp. 260–61.

By creating a direct link between the federal government and the ghettos, the Democratic administrations not only bypassed existing service bureaucracies but also left the traditional white ethnic party organizations relatively undisturbed. In short, the new programs promised a high electoral payoff at relatively low risk. Blacks were to be integrated into the predominantly Democratic urban political system by way of social-welfare programs in traditional machine-like fashion.

However, this combination of professional proposals and electoral imperatives provided authorities with effective tools to defuse the black rebellions in the middle years of the decade in two respects. First, the programs created a vehicle for the political integration of the most talented, articulate, militant young blacks of the period. Militant action was now often directed at winning larger shares of urban patronage rather than at working for structural change. In Baltimore, political scientist Peter Bachrach noted that the federally funded programs "provided black groups with . . . decision-making arenas in which the struggle for power could be fought out in the open and within the confines of the political system." Similarly, urbanist John Strange noted that in Durham and other North Carolina cities, "community action, with special emphasis on participation and community organization, has . . . channeled dissatisfaction and unrest into forms and issues which can be dealt with."[34]

Secondly, the expansion of the government's welfare role helped defuse mass discontent by providing tangible, if limited, benefits, including easier access to AFDC welfare, higher welfare payments, and new job opportunities. In short, then, black discontent was not caused by the new programs (the causes were structural, not manufactured by government), nor were the programs originally aimed at defusing discontent (electoral considerations were of primary importance). Nevertheless, with the outbreak of massive civil disorder in the middle 1960s, the state used both traditional welfare programs like AFDC and the newly created programs like Community Action to absorb and canalize the discontent. In this respect, the expansion and operation of welfare-state programs in the 1960s bear a striking resemblance to the programs of the New Deal.

Whether or not they were proposed or passed as the result of

[34] Cited in *ibid.*, p. 274.

mass movements and pressures, all the welfare-state programs, from the Social Security Act of 1935 to the most recent, share one basic characteristic: *they are meant to stabilize the social order, not create structural change.* They do not challenge the existence of the corporate complex. Instead, they seek to alleviate—not correct—the basic structural inequalities that are part and parcel of the American corporate-capital system.

This point was stressed by the German sociologist Georg Simmel, who commented at the turn of the century on Bismarck's social-welfare program:

> If we take into consideration this meaning of assistance to the poor, it becomes clear that the fact of taking away from the rich to give to the poor does not aim at equalizing their individual positions, and is not, even in its orientation, directed at suppressing the social difference between the rich and the poor. On the contrary, assistance is based on the structure of society, whatever it may be. . . . The goal of assistance is precisely to mitigate certain extreme manifestations of social differentiation, so that the social structure may continue to be based on this differentiation.

This structure-protecting feature of welfare-state measures, he argued, is apparent because "if assistance were to be based on the interests of the poor person, there would, in principle, be no limit on the transmission of poverty in favor of the poor, a transmission that would lead to the equality of all." But structural transformation is what the dominant want to prevent; as a result, "there is no reason to aid the person more than is required by the maintenance of the *status quo*."[35]

THE FRAGMENTATION OF SUBORDINATES

Political scientist Alan Wolfe defined "alienated politics" as "the process through which people in similar positions are separated from each other, forced to compete instead of cooperate."[36] In this

---

[35] Georg Simmel, "The Poor," in Chaim I. Waxman, ed., *Poverty: Power and Politics* (New York, 1968), pp. 3–9.

[36] Alan Wolfe, "New Directions in the Marxist Theory of Politics," *Politics and Society* 4 (Winter 1974): 148.

fashion, the routine operation of the American welfare state divides different groups from each other along sectoral and ethnic lines. Consider the divide between the corporate- and small-capital–sector workers. As we noted, both sectors' workers are taxed at identical rates for social security, yet the better-paid corporate workers receive higher benefits on retirement. In complementary fashion, welfare programs for small-capital–sector workers are paid for in part by the taxes of corporate-sector workers. Thus, while the real income of corporate-sector workers is increased by social-insurance programs, it is reduced in turn by the taxes they must pay to finance a welfare population created as a consequence of corporate-sector growth. "In this sense," O'Connor concluded, "the state budget can be seen as a complex mechanism that redistributes income backward and forward within the working class—all to maintain industrial and social-political harmony, expand productivity, and accelerate accumulation and profits in the monopoly sector."[37] The divisions thus promoted between workers are further accentuated by a racial divide, since most white workers are in the corporate sector, but a majority of blacks are in the small-capital sector. Thus welfare-state programs exacerbate racial stereotypes and antagonisms by establishing pocketbook conflicts of interest.

In still another way, the Great Society programs of the 1960s, which undoubtedly did provide new resources to the poor, often divided the poor from each other. A study of a Community Action Program (CAP) in the Tremont section of the Bronx, New York, for example, found that three-quarters of the people in the area believed that the CAP had intensified antagonism between Puerto Ricans and blacks and had had little effect on the neighborhood's poverty. Black and Puerto Rican leaders focused their energies on relatively nonproductive programs and on fighting each other. For this reason, the study concluded, the program operated primarily as "a social control output, with the community action bureaucracy functioning as a social control agent and as another authority with which the poor must cope."[38]

This case is hardly unique.[39] Within the limits of Community

---

[37] O'Connor, p. 162.

[38] Kenneth J. Pollinger and Annette C. Pollinger, *Community Action and the Poor* (New York, 1972), pp. 201ff, 18.

[39] Peter Marris and Martin Rein, *Dilemmas of Social Reform* (Chicago, 1967); and Kenneth Clark and Jeanette Hopkins, *A Relevant War Against Poverty* (New York, 1970).

Action and Model Cities programs and other welfare-state activities that mandate participation by the poor, the following situations develop:

> Key processes and mechanisms 1) blunt and defuse demands; 2) coopt potential opposition; 3) create so *much* participation that effective policy making by representative groups is stalemated; 4) create so *much* representation that a classic veto-group situation is created which allows almost any group to block action, and 5) require so *much* consensus that decisions which challenge the vital interests of *any* group are impossible.[40]

The consequence is heightened frustration that further divides the victimized from each other.

THE WELFARE STATE AND STRUCTURAL CHANGE

Although the welfare state complements, and is in fact necessary for, the country's advanced capitalist economy, its logic of need is diametrically opposed to the economy's logic of profit. Welfare-state programs are publicly fought over, defended, and legitimized on the basis of the deprivation of one group or another. Carried to its conclusion, as Simmel argued, this logic of need would be satisfied only when structural inequalities are overcome.

Yet welfare-state programs and debates about them take place within a context of corporate capitalism, which is driven by goals of growth and profit. For this reason, French commentator André Gorz has argued that *logically* the welfare state is in "antagonism to the capitalist system. . . . Collective needs are . . . objectively in contradiction to the logic of capitalist development . . . since the welfare sector is necessarily outside of the criteria of profit."[41]

Even more importantly, the expansion of the welfare state requires a large surplus of capital for programs that, by themselves, do not turn over a profit and which are not directly productive. For this reason, German political sociologist Claus Offe has argued that "the political-administrative system of late capitalist societies, tailored to satisfy in concrete ways the requirements of

[40] Robert Alford, "Social Needs, Political Demands, and Administrative Responses," unpublished manuscript.
[41] André Gorz, *Strategy for Labor* (Boston, 1968), p. 98.

maintaining the capitalist order will reveal itself as an alien element."[42] However, where working class parties and movements have been relatively strong, as in Scandinavia, the expansion of the welfare state has made more likely the creation of a socialist alternative. In Sweden, for example, the expansion of the welfare state in the past half century, which occurred largely when Social Democratic governments were in power, has given political authorities considerably more control over the economy than is the case in the United States. Moreover, as recent survey research has found, the experience of an advanced welfare state has made socialism both plausible and desirable to Swedish workers.[43] Workers in the United States, who have not experienced a bountiful and democratic welfare state, are much more skeptical about the possibility of major structural change.

Where strong working-class socialist or social democratic parties compete for power, their very existence pushes the development of the welfare state forward at a pace more rapid than is required for the maintenance of their countries' economies. Even in routine periods of relative social peace, the very existence of a credible electoral alternative and an organized working class severely constrains the actions of government and the dominant classes. Thus, for example, the Conservative British governments of the 1950s had to maintain high employment policies despite the preferences of most businesspeople who wished to give priority to the problems of inflation and balance of payments deficits. The Labour party thus provided a brake on government activity that would be directed against the interests of workers by its very existence as a potential government.[44]

The United States is distinguished from other western capitalist democracies in that it lacks such a regular political instrument for securing progressive expansions in the welfare state that go beyond the minimum needed to keep the economy going and to preserve order. The American welfare state is a cluster of programs without a persistent, coherent organized popular movement that attempts to direct and improve the programs. As a result,

[42] Claus Offe, "The Abolition of Market Control and the Problem of Legitimacy," *Kapitalistate* 1 (1973): 112.

[43] M. Donald Hancock, "The Swedish Welfare State: Prospects and Contradictions," *The Wilson Quarterly* I (Autumn 1977); Richard Scase, *Social Democracy in Capitalist Society* (London, 1977).

[44] Andrew Martin, *The Politics of Economic Policy in the United States: A Tentative View from a Comparative Perspective* (Beverly Hills, Calif., 1973), p. 44.

the American welfare state has expanded in one of two ways: attempts by elites to solve what appear to be technical problems, and *ad hoc* social movements that in special periods compel concessions. Although major initiatives in social policy have been the product of such special times, *ad hoc* social movements are very short-lived. When they disappear from the scene, the more "normal" pattern of connections between the dual economy and the welfare state reasserts itself.

Indeed, the American pattern is strikingly similar to the dynamics of social policy innovation in England in the 1880s, when the resources of the new unionism were only beginning to be available to British workers and those of the Labour party were more than a decade away. The disruptive protests of London's casual workers were marked by the absence of a coherent movement ideology, and by the "co-existence of violence and reformism."[45] Writing in February 1886, George Bernard Shaw noted, "Angry as they are, they do not want revolution, they want a job. If they be left too long without it, they may turn out and run amuck through the streets until they are destroyed like so many mad dogs. But a job or even a meal will stop them any time."[46] This expressive radicalism nevertheless provoked panic among politicians and professional reformers. The predominant feeling was not one of guilt, but one of fear. The response to this social crisis did in fact produce advances for the poor, as the collective sphere of the state expanded. But, as historian Gareth Stedman Jones stresses, these new policies can only be understood as part of an effort to reassert order and social control. For every proposal to provide subsidized housing and meals, there were "parallel proposals to segregate the casual poor, to establish detention centers for 'loafers,' to separate pauper children from 'degenerate' parents or to ship the 'residuum' overseas."[47] In the context of the very limited political capacity of the disorganized, pre-social democratic English working class, repression and reform were joined by policymakers in an effort to find a formula for the protection of British capitalism.

This parallel, however, cannot be stretched too far. For the kind of welfare state that the United States has today is far more developed than the English situation of a century ago. And, even in the absence of working-class pressures organized in a political

[45] Gareth Stedman Jones, *Outcast London* (London, 1971), p. 345.
[46] *Pall Mall Gazette*, 11 February 1886, p. 4; cited in *ibid*.
[47] *Ibid.*, p. 314.

party demanding structural change, the American welfare state has continued to grow as a complement to the corporate and small-capital sectors of American capitalism.

But the compatibility of the welfare state and the operation of the economy is an uneasy one. The relationship is characterized by a number of tensions, the most important of which is a growing fiscal crisis.

The growth of the corporate sector and the maintenance of a small-capital sector, we have seen, require the continued expansion of welfare-state programs. This produces a massive increase in state expenditures, both in grants and in salaries to a growing number of employees. The programs, in routine periods, continue to expand at roughly the same rate in both Democratic and Republican administrations and under liberal and conservative presidents (their rhetoric notwithstanding). The annual wage bill at the federal, state, and local levels continues to rise because the number of workers has increased and their increased unionization in a period of high inflation has brought about accelerated wage demands.

An increase in costs affects the government very differently from the way it affects private industry. Corporations administer their prices to pass along costs to consumers. Government, by contrast, has three ways it can increase its revenues. First, it can try to step up the economy's rate of growth by deficit spending in order to generate more tax revenues. But this strategy is flawed on two counts—it is inflationary (and hence politically risky), and it often exacerbates inequalities between the corporate and small-capital sectors, thus necessitating the further expansion of welfare expenditures.

Secondly, the government can try to increase the productivity of state employees, but this is inherently difficult since, unlike the corporate sector, the government is a "labor intensive," not a "capital intensive" economic arena. Like most new government activities, new welfare programs require more people to a greater extent than they require or use more hardware.

Thirdly, the government can raise taxes. Politically, this solution is increasingly risky to attempt. Since most corporate taxes are passed on to consumers, and the tax structure as a whole is highly regressive, a disproportionate tax burden falls on corporate-sector workers, who find it difficult to shelter their income from taxation. They have come increasingly to understand, resent, and resist this pattern of disproportionate taxation and bitterly recognize that they are expected to foot the bill for the expansion of the welfare state. Thus, while tax issues have divided workers from each other, all workers are united in opposing higher taxes, thus making it increasingly difficult for the state to fund its programs.

Because of this tax revolt, and because the economic position of the United States is declining in the world market, and because the size of the state sector is growing faster than the corporate sector, the funds needed for welfare-state programs are not as readily available as in the past. In the 1950s and 1960s there were sufficient funds to provide both social capital (which made corporations more productive and profitable) and social expenses (which defused discontent). Today, more choices have to be made between these kinds of programs. Thus, programs of social expenses that are challenging the imperatives of growth and profit are being cut. The resolution of these tensions may be in doubt, but the antagonism between a logic of need and a logic of profit may be a promising basis on which to build movements for structural change.

8

corporate capitalism and government abroad: military and foreign policy

AMERICA AND THE WORLD

Some statistics provide the context for understanding American foreign policy: with less than 6 percent of the world's population, the United States accounts for the annual consumption of half the world's manufactured products, one-fifth of the world's steel and fertilizer, and one-quarter of the world's tin, tractors, rubber, and television sets. More than one-third of all telephones are in the United States. The United States consumes one-quarter the world's total energy; the average American uses five times the world average. One-half of all airline passengers each year are

American. Nearly half of all Americans between the ages of 20 and 24 are enrolled in an institution of higher education; the comparable proportion for Europe is one-quarter, for Latin America, Asia, and Africa, it does not exceed one-twentieth.[1] Overall, most Americans are wealthier, better-fed, and receive more education, material benefits, and services than most people in the world. Although these figures do not take note of the extensive inequalities *within* the United States, which are the subject of other chapters, they suggest that even greater inequalities exist between the United States (along with the capitalist countries of Western Europe and Japan, to a lesser extent) and the rest of the world. When American political leaders talk of the need to maintain world order and stability, they are referring to a world based on this inequality. Stability means the persistence of United States privilege.

However, a situation of inequality is not natural or inevitable. Just after the Second World War, the United States rapidly attained a position of unprecedented world power. American dominance has rested on two pillars, described by political scientist Samuel Huntington as "U.S. military superiority over the Communist world and U.S. political-economic hegemony in the noncommunist world."[2] To put it another way, American dominance has consisted of United States corporate penetration of other countries coupled with the use of the government's political and military power abroad. This chapter describes how American corporate capitalism and government function abroad and shape American foreign policy.

A common view holds that after the Second World War the United States did not deliberately seek to extend its power, but, "having many obligations and vast responsibilities in the world," was forced to "adopt a policy not dictated by any American material needs and certainly not in response to any American ambition or desire."[3] President Lyndon B. Johnson proudly stated, "History and our own achievements have thrust upon us the principal responsibility for the protection of freedom on Earth."[4] Writing in

[1] United Nations, *U.N. Statistical Yearbook, 1976*, pp. 2, 69; *New York Times*, October 2, 1972.
[2] Samuel P. Huntington, "After Containment: The Functions of the Military Establishment," *The Annals* 406 (March 1973): 4.
[3] Charles E. Bohlen, *The Transformation of American Foreign Policy* (New York, 1969), p. 124.
[4] Quoted in Richard J. Barnet, *Roots of War* (New York, 1972), p. 19.

the fiscal 1975 annual Defense Department report, the secretary of defense observed:

> The United States today, as opposed to the period before 1945, bears the principal burden of maintaining the worldwide military equilibrium which is the foundation for the security and the survival of the free world. This is not a role we have welcomed; it is a role that historical necessity has thrust upon us. . . . There is nobody else to pick up the torch.

Nonetheless, the facts remain that the United States has emerged as the foremost power in the world, that it has devoted many resources to maintaining dominance, and that it has derived rich benefits from its position. American military, diplomatic, and economic influence is visible in virtually every country. The United States leads all other countries in investments abroad and in military power. However, American dominance was challenged from the beginning and has proved extremely short-lived. In the words of a report by the Trilateral Commission, an influential organization to be discussed below, "The international system is undergoing a drastic transformation through a series of crises."[5] This is a result of declining United States political and economic power.

The most dramatic illustration of this decline was America's defeat in Vietnam. More broadly, "While American military power has declined relative to that of the Soviet Union, American economic strength has declined relative to that of Europe and Japan. . . . The United States remains the strongest power in the world. But the preeminent feature of international politics at the present time is the relative decline in American power."[6]

American Foreign Policy Before the Second World War

During the eighteenth and nineteenth centuries, the United States was far removed from world power struggles. In his farewell address, George Washington advised the country to profit from the good fortune that geographic accident provided and not to get involved in "entangling alliances." For more than a century, the

[5] Quoted in Laurence H. Shoup and William Minter, *Imperial Brain Trust: The Council on Foreign Relations and United States Foreign Policy* (New York, 1977), p. 267.
[6] Huntington, p. 5.

United States attempted to derive maximum benefit from isolation and refused to ally for long with any European power.

During the eighteenth and nineteenth centuries, United States expansion was toward the vast western frontier. Although this differed from the overseas expansion and the search for colonies of European powers during the same period, it represented imperialism none the less—and on a continental scale. Other elements in this expansion were the conquest and extermination of Indians, the enslavement of blacks as a source of cheap labor, and war with Mexico in 1846 (which resulted in the annexation of a substantial portion of that country, including the area that is now California, New Mexico, Utah, Arizona, and Nevada). Other examples of territorial expansion include the taking of Florida from Spain in 1819 and the annexation of Texas in 1845.

Furthermore, isolation from Europe did not mean abstaining from foreign intervention. Uninterested in Europe's struggles, the United States attempted to stake out its own sphere of influence close to home. In 1823, President Monroe issued a proclamation warning European powers not to intervene in Latin America. "But it is not the negatives [in the Monroe Doctrine] that really count. It is the hidden positive to the effect that the United States shall be the only colonizing power and the sole directing power in both North and South America."[7]

In the half century between the Spanish-American War in 1898 and the Second World War, the United States vacillated between a new expansionism overseas and an inward-looking isolationism. War with Spain resulted in United States control over the Philippines, Puerto Rico, and Guam. Gunboat diplomacy in Latin America insured that this area would remain a preserve for United States business interests. The navy and marines overthrew "uncooperative" governments and installed and kept in office puppet regimes. For example, American marines occupied and governed Nicaragua between 1926 and 1932. President Theodore Roosevelt maneuvered to build the Panama Canal by carving up Colombia and creating the client state of Panama, which quickly ceded to the United States sovereignty over the land for the canal.

United States influence was mostly confined to the Western Hemisphere until the two world wars made the United States a

[7] Richard W. Van Alstyne, *The Rising American Empire* (Chicago, 1965), p. 99.

global power, although American political leaders had a lively interest in Asia (for example, President McKinley dispatched five thousand troops to China to help crush the Boxer Rebellion in 1900). The wars resulted in a weakening of the leading European nations; the United States did not enter either war until years after it began, and it was an ocean away from the actual fighting. The Second World War was decisive, for it signified the irrevocable decline of Great Britain, the dominant capitalist power and the hub of world production, commerce, and banking.

The Soviet Union (USSR), Japan, Germany, and France—the other major industrialized countries—all suffered direct damage from the war. The United States was the only country to emerge unscathed. Indeed, in 1945 the United States was far stronger than before the war, partly because the government-sponsored technological innovation and wartime expansion of productive capacity were quickly converted to peacetime production and overseas expansion when the war ended.

After the Second World War, there was no question of returning to the isolation of the Western Hemisphere. Europe's decline, the existence of a political and ideological rival in the Communist regime of the Soviet Union, and the fear of American officials that a domestic depression would recur unless the United States expanded outward, resulted in the transformation of the United States from a powerful, but insular, country to the dominant force shaping the world political and economic system.

Cold War Rivalry

In 1945, United States officials hoped to create a peaceful, stable world free for international trade, where there would be formal equality among nations, and where American industry would have easy access to raw materials and markets throughout the world. Like Woodrow Wilson after the First World War, American leaders after the Second World War pressed the colonial powers (Great Britain, France, and the Netherlands) to dismantle their empires. Only one country threatened the vision of an integrated capitalist world order: the USSR.

The Soviet Union opposed a capitalist trading bloc and was perceived as a potential aggressor, bent on territorial conquest in Europe. American foreign policy since the Second World War, which has depended heavily on military power, has usually been interpreted as an attempt to counter the threat of Communist aggression around the world.

Although the Soviet Union played a crucial role in the allied coalition during the Second World War, it was prostrate after the war. "The moment of victory was to find the Soviet Union enfeebled and devastated on a scale unprecedented in the past by countries *defeated* in a major war."[8] Soviet losses far exceeded those of the other allied powers.

> For three years, from June of 1941 to June of 1944, the Soviet Union carried the main burden of the fight against Hitler. . . . Partly because of Russian military successes, the United States Army got through the war with less than half the number of divisions prewar plans had indicated would be necessary for victory. Casualty figures reflect with particular vividness the disproportionate amount of fighting which went on in the east. A conservative estimate places Soviet war deaths—civilian and military—at approximately 16 million. Total Anglo-American losses in all theaters came to less than a million.[9]

In 1945, Soviet industrial output was only 58 percent of the 1940 level, and the country faced famine because of drought and destruction of its agriculture.[10] This contrasted sharply with the United States, whose industrial base had expanded during the war and whose military strength was enhanced by exclusive possession of atomic weapons. Most historians "now generally agree on the limited nature of Stalin's [postwar] objectives."[11] Invaded twice from the West within a generation, Russia aimed to create a buffer zone under her control in Eastern Europe. Regardless of the ethics, legality, or wisdom of this goal, it was far from an attempt to foment global revolution. Indeed, Premier Joseph Stalin restrained Communists in Western Europe, Yugoslavia, and China from seeking power.

In part, American political leaders probably sincerely misjudged Soviet intentions after the Second World War when they continually alarmed Americans with the prospect of a Soviet inva-

[8] Adam Ulam, *The Rivals: America and Russia Since World War II* (New York, 1971), p. 11.
[9] John Lewis Gaddis, *The United States and the Origins of the Cold War, 1941–1947* (New York, 1972), pp. 79–80.
[10] Joyce Kolko and Gabriel Kolko, *The Limits of Power: The World and United States Foreign Policy, 1945–1954* (New York, 1972), p. 53.
[11] Gaddis, p. 355, fn 2.

sion of Western Europe.[12] In part, however, the Soviet threat was used to frighten Americans into supporting activist policies. "Scare hell out of the country," Senator Vandenberg advised President Truman. Truman heeded the advice and went to Congress in 1947 to advocate passage of his Truman Doctrine, which symbolized American expansionism. Just three years after the United States and the Soviet Union were wartime allies, the cleavage between the two hardened into what English leader Winston Churchill called the "iron curtain."

More important than the question of which country "started" the cold war is the ensuing and continuing destructive spiral of arms production, which has maintained world tensions at a dangerous pitch. The period soon after the war ended saw the emergence of a desperate arms race, for which the United States shares heavy responsibility.

Global Expansion and the Invisible Empire

Focusing on the US–USSR cold-war rivalry—important as the issue is—may obscure another development possibly of greater significance that occurred following the war. Joyce and Gabriel Kolko have suggested that the most important aspect of American foreign policy during the last thirty years has not been US–USSR hostility but the postwar quest of the United States for worldwide domination.[13] As restated by foreign-policy analyst Graham Allison, "Historians in the year 2000, looking back with detachment on the cold war, are apt to conclude that the main feature of international life in the period 1945–1970 was neither the expansion of the Soviet Union nor Communist China. Instead, it was the global expansion of American influence: military, economic, political and cultural."[14]

In the years after the Second World War, the United States sponsored the creation of a new integrated world order. Its chief elements included easy access for American capital to both the

[12] Many of those influential in shaping the containment policy have subsequently admitted their error in judgment. See, for example, Dean Acheson, *Present at the Creation* (New York, 1969), p. 753; George Kennan, "'X' plus 25: Interview with George F. Kennan," *Foreign Policy* no. 7 (Summer 1972): 14; and others cited in Ronald Steele, "The Power and the Glory," *New York Review of Books*, May 31, 1973, p. 30, fn 3.
[13] Kolko and Kolko, *passim*.
[14] Graham Allison, "Cool It: The Foreign Policy of Young America," *Foreign Policy* no. 1 (Winter 1970–71): 144–45.

markets of industrialized nations and the raw materials (notably petroleum) of nonindustrialized nations, as well as an American government guarantee of stable procapitalist governments throughout the world. (American-Soviet rivalry can be better understood when placed in this context, for the Soviet Union opposed both elements of American foreign policy and erected a rival noncapitalist military and trading bloc in opposition to the American world order.) American efforts were relatively successful and permitted a worldwide economic boom, sparked by American industrial expansion, during the postwar period.

However, the American "empire" was not a traditional form of imperialism or colonialism. With the exception of a few protectorates—Puerto Rico, the Virgin Islands, and some Pacific possessions—the United States did not establish legal custody over territory. Although American power is both more global in scope and more far-reaching within individual countries than past imperial situations, it is exercised through informal political, military, and economic influence rather than formal colonial arrangements. What must be examined, then, are the specific new features of American dominance, which are linked to corporate capitalism, rapid communications, and military technology.

Underlying the new expansionism—a process that was already underway when the United States began to pick up the slack left by England, France, and Germany after the First World War—was a fear shared by political officials and corporate leaders that the depression, which had sapped the United States economy in the 1930s and had ended only when war needs created new demand, would recur. "Fully aware that the New Deal had not solved the problem of unemployment in peacetime, Roosevelt and his associates hoped that foreign markets would help absorb the vast quantity of goods which would have to be produced if employment levels were to be maintained after the fighting had stopped."[15]

The search for foreign markets and spheres of influence took several forms.

Replacing Western Europe as a world power   Before the First World War the capitalist countries of England, France, Germany, Belgium, Italy, and the Netherlands were the leading world producers, traders, and colonial powers. All were severely

[15] Gaddis, p. 21.

Figure 8-1
Foreign investments of capital-exporting countries

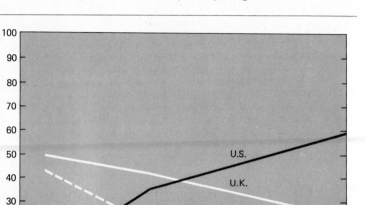

Source: Adapted from William Woodroof, *Impact of Western Man* (New York, 1966), p. 150.

weakened by the two world wars. Within a few years after the end
of the Second World War, the United States moved into the
vacuum thus created—and used economic aid and political pressure to hasten the process.

The United States set out to replace England, which had been
the keystone of the former international capitalist system and the
largest trader, banker, and colonial power. This was the price
England was forced to pay for American assistance in the desperate years after the Second World War. Historian John Gaddis notes
that "blunt pressure from the [American] negotiators eventually
forced London to accept most of Washington's plans. Dependent
on American aid for both its war effort and postwar reconstruction,
Great Britain was in no position to resist." [16] Within a few years, the
United States succeeded in supplanting England as international
trader and banker. By the Bretton Woods agreement of 1944, the
dollar replaced the British pound as the international currency,

[16] *Ibid.*, p. 22.

providing the United States with substantial benefits. For example, other countries must maintain reserves in dollars, which results in the equivalent of a several-billion-dollar low-interest loan to the United States each year. Through this means and recurrent United States balance of payments deficits, other countries have helped pay the costs of American takeovers of their economies and American foreign military intervention overseas. Soon the United States replaced European countries as the leading world investor.

The Third World   Since European countries needed all their available resources to rebuild their own economies after the Second World War, American business was uniquely situated to expand into other areas. American aims in the Third World were to open up these areas to investment by American corporations and to prevent local government control by regimes that might challenge foreign (particularly American) interests. (The Third World is usually defined as the rural, poor countries in Asia, Africa, and Latin America, which are aligned with neither the Communist nor Western capitalist bloc. Yet nearly all countries in the Third World are tied—by trade, investment, political, and military links—to the capitalist bloc under United States direction.)

With Latin America already to a large extent under informal American control, the United States expanded into other resource-rich areas. Particularly important was the Middle East, which contained vast petroleum deposits that American petroleum companies soon dominated, as well as countries in Africa and Asia with mineral deposits. In 1940, Great Britain controlled 72 percent of Middle East oil reserves; the United States, 10 percent; and other countries, the rest. By 1967, Great Britain controlled 29 percent; the United States, 59 percent; and other countries, the remainder.[17]

Containment   The new expansionism required checking potential challengers. Both because the Communist trading bloc represented an alternative to the Western capitalist trading bloc, and, from a fear of Soviet expansion, American policy aimed to confine Soviet influence to Eastern Europe, reserving the rest of the world for capitalist economic development and political control. The world was thus divided into two areas: the Communist countries of the Soviet Union, Eastern Europe, and (after 1948) China; and the capitalist areas (both industrialized and agricultural).

[17] Harry Magdoff, *The Age of Imperialism: The Economics of U.S. Foreign Policy* (New York, 1969), p. 43.

The United States gave first priority to rebuilding war-torn Europe, militarily, economically, and politically, in order to assure reliable and prosperous allies among the industrialized nations. In 1948, Secretary of State George Marshall proposed a program of American financial and technical aid to Europe. Marshall defended his plan to Congress on the humanitarian ground that famine was sweeping Europe. Moreover, he warned, unless the United States helped other countries to recover, "the cumulative loss of foreign markets and sources of supply would unquestionably have a depressing influence on our domestic economy."[18] The secretary of the interior also defended the plan as essential to America's continued productivity and prosperity.

The Marshall Plan was further justified as a way to prevent socialist regimes from taking power in Western Europe and to stop the spread of communism. Marshall Plan funds were provided to Germany, America's enemy in the war, but conditions imposed on funds offered to the Soviet Union, the wartime ally of the United States, virtually insured the USSR's refusal. At the same time that the Marshall Plan was launched, two military initiatives were also taken by the United States. The Truman Doctrine provided military aid to Greece and Turkey, and justified aid and intervention abroad on the grounds that they were necessary to bolster regimes against domestic challenge; the North Atlantic Treaty Organization (NATO) linked the United States and Western Europe in an anti-Soviet military alliance.

American expansion abroad has thus taken two major forms: economic penetration by multinational corporations, and political and military influence exercised by the American government. The two are intertwined and each has contributed to advancing the other. According to political economist Robert Gilpin, the income generated by American business investments abroad in the postwar period was used "to finance America's global political and military position. The income from foreign investments, in other words, had become an important factor in American global hegemony."[19] In the following section, we will discuss economic penetration and America's political and military influence in the world.

[18] William Appleman Williams, *The Tragedy of American Diplomacy* (Cleveland, 1959), p. 177.
[19] Robert Gilpin, *U.S. Power and the Multinational Corporation: The Political Economy of Direct Foreign Investment* (New York, 1975), p. 161.

ECONOMIC PENETRATION AND
MULTINATIONAL CORPORATIONS

American corporate capitalism has expanded outside the United States in response to three internal dilemmas. Each one has shaped a different form of American economic expansion.

Dependence on raw materials   The United States is among the countries best endowed with natural resources. It has some of the world's largest deposits of coal, copper, natural gas, iron, petroleum, and aluminum. The United States is also among the world's leading food producers; for example, it is the largest producer of corn, soybeans, cotton, and oranges, and the largest exporter of wheat and rice.[20] However, no country is fortunate enough to contain within its borders all the raw materials it needs for modern industrial production—and the United States is no exception. Moreover, the United States has begun to deplete many of the natural resources it once contained in abundance. Both factors produce a growing dependence on other countries for essential raw materials.

The speed with which the United States has come to rely on other countries for raw materials can be seen from the following figures: of the thirteen minerals considered essential for a modern industrial economy, the United States had to import more than half its supplies of only four in 1950; yet by 2000, estimates are that the number will have climbed to twelve. The United States already imports all its natural rubber, over 90 percent of its manganese, cobalt, and chromium, and over half its aluminum, platinum, tin, nickel, antimony, bismuth, mercury, and zinc.[21] Most of these raw materials come from less developed countries in Latin America, Asia, the Middle East, and Africa.

American corporations and government seek to assure a cheap and adequate supply of minerals and other natural resources flowing to the United States. The most effective way in the past has been for American corporations to invest in the Third World and to gain direct control over foreign raw materials. Thus, Kennecott and Anaconda control much of the world's copper deposits, located in Zambia, Chile, and elsewhere. And five American petro-

---

[20] *New York Times*, January 6, 1974; Emma Rothschild, "The Politics of Food," *New York Review of Books*, May 16, 1974, p. 17.
[21] *New York Times*, November 5, 1972; December 22, 1973.

leum corporations (and two foreign companies) control most of the world's petroleum supplies, located in the United States, the Middle East, and Venezuela.

Petroleum-exporting nations, organized in the Organization of Petroleum Exporting Countries (OPEC), have begun to demand more benefits for the use of their petroleum resources. In informal alliance with the major international petroleum companies, they tripled the price they charged for petroleum in 1973–74. Since that time, the United States has been paying a foreign energy bill of more than $25 billion annually; this sum has contributed to America's international trade deficit and its declining international economic position. (The rise in petroleum prices came at the expense of American and other consumers, not the petroleum companies, whose profits soared after the price rise.)

Foreign trade: export of manufactured products and food In 1973, American business exported $70 billion worth of goods produced in the United States, providing a profitable outlet for surplus agricultural and industrial capacity. Most foreign activity is organized within the sector of corporate capital. Encouraged by government help, including tax incentives, technical assistance, insurance against political difficulties, and, most important, a foreign policy that aims at creating conditions throughout the world favorable to American corporations, the expansion of America's foreign trade has been rapid.

Capital export: foreign investment In recent years, sagging demand in the United States has meant that American corporations now find it more profitable to invest capital in building new factories abroad rather than to expand manufacturing at home. Foreign investments give American corporations direct access to foreign markets and a hold over the economies of other countries. When manufactured products or food are exported, the transaction ends once they are purchased by foreign customers. However, when capital and technology are exported, and an American corporation creates a foreign manufacturing subsidiary, the transaction only *begins* with the initial investment: the foreign subsidiary remains year after year, continuing to produce and sell goods that make a profit for the American home company. American corporations began investing heavily in foreign manufacturing subsidiaries during the 1950s and a substantial investment has piled up abroad. Between 1950 and 1977, direct overseas investment by American corporations increased from $12 billion to $149, and foreign in-

Table 8-1
The growth of U.S. private investment abroad, 1950–1974

	Value of Direct Investment Assets (billions of dollars at end of year)	Direct Investment Flows (billions of dollars during year)		
Year	Total	Capital Outflow from U.S.	Total Inflow[1] to U.S.	Income from Investment Abroad
1950	11.8	0.6	1.5	1.3
1955	19.4	0.8	2.1	1.9
1960	31.9	1.7	2.9	2.4
1965	49.5	3.5	5.2	4.0
1970	75.5	4.3	7.9	6.0
1974	118.6	7.5	20.7	17.7

[1] Includes investment income plus royalties and fees.
Source: Richard C. Edwards, Michael Reich, and Thomas E. Weisskopf, eds., *The Capitalist System: A Radical Analysis of American Society*, 2nd ed., © 1978, p. 470. Reprinted by permission of Prentice-Hall, Inc., Englewood Cliffs, N.J. Sources listed in original.

vestment continues to rise at the rate of about $10 billion yearly. United States multinational corporations produce about four times more abroad than they export.

Profits on foreign investments represent a substantial and growing proportion of total American corporate profits. The share of after-tax corporate profits accounted for by foreign investment rose from 7 percent of all corporate profits in 1950 to 25 percent in 1974.[22] About one-third of foreign profits flowed back to the United States as corporate income. The rest remained abroad as new foreign investment. Thus, American corporations use the resources extracted from a foreign country to increase the profitability of the corporation and to enrich its American stockholders, as well as to strengthen American corporate control over that nation's economy.

The multinational corporation   The term *multinational corporations* has been coined to describe corporations heavily involved in foreign operations. Multinationals have reshaped the world political economy and are the new Goliaths of the present

[22] Table 13-B in Richard C. Edwards, Michael Reich, and Thomas E. Weisskopf, eds., *The Capitalist System: A Radical Analysis of American Society*, 2nd ed. (Englewood Cliffs, N.J., 1978), p. 477.

era. In 1970, 51 corporations ranked among the world's 100 largest economic units (measured by countries' GNP and corporate sales).[23] Multinational corporations straddle countries. They make decisions about research, investment, manufacturing, and sales without much regard for national boundaries: decisions are governed by profitability. In an exhaustive study of multinational investment abroad, economist Mira Wilkins concludes that, when a multinational shops around for a location for new foreign investment, the most important factor influencing its decision is the local political climate, that is, which government offers the corporation the biggest tax breaks, shows a willingness to crack down on workers, and the like.[24]

Economist Daniel R. Fusfeld explains that the multinational corporation

> was made possible by advances in the technology of transportation and communication after World War II (jet aircraft and automatic data communication, for example). U.S. corporations were able to take advantage of the new technology much more readily than foreign corporations, in part because much of that technology was developed here, but chiefly because of the predominance of the United States in world trade and international finance.[25]

Multinational corporations can integrate far-flung operations as a result of technological advances in communications and information-processing. A multinational corporation may carry out product research in one country, obtain raw materials from another, manufacture parts in a third country, assemble the product in a fourth, and market it in other countries.

Most huge American corporations are multinational and most American investments abroad are carried on by the largest corporations and financial institutions. Seventy-one of the top 100 American manufacturing corporations have over one-third of their payroll employed overseas. Some of the largest American corporations, including Exxon, Mobil Oil, Woolworth, National Cash Register, Burroughs, Colgate-Palmolive, and Singer have larger sales abroad than at home. By the late 1960s, nearly all the largest

---

[23] U.S. Congress, Senate, Select Committee on Small Business, Subcommittee on Monopoly, *The Role of Giant Corporations in the American and World Economies*, 92nd Cong. 1st sess., November 9 and 12, 1971, p. 1043.

[24] Mira Wilkins, *The Maturing of Multinational Enterprise: American Business Abroad from 1914 to 1970* (Cambridge, Mass., 1974), p. 458.

[25] Daniel R. Fusfeld, *The Rise of the Corporate State in America* (Andover, Mass., 1973), p. 3.

corporations had over one-quarter of their assets abroad. Foreign investments are heavily concentrated among these large corporations: the top 200 American corporations account for over three-quarters of all foreign investment.

The rapid growth of United States banks abroad has kept pace with corporate expansion. Deposits in foreign branches of American banks went from $9 billion in 1965 to $90 billion in 1972 to $181 billion in 1976.[26] The foreign operations of United States banks are highly concentrated: two-thirds of all overseas United States banking business is carried on by thirteen of the fifteen thousand American commercial banks. Between 1970 and 1976, American banks' profits stagnated in the United States but rose five times abroad. Foreign profits have quickly become an essential component of United States banking. In 1970, the ten largest American banks derived only one-fifth of their profits from overseas operations. By 1977, they earned more from foreign than domestic operations.[27]

Banks and multinational corporations remain national in their ownership and management: a majority of multinational corporations are based in the United States, and their stockholders and managers are mostly American. Some multinational corporations, including Nestlé, Phillips, Sony, and Royal Dutch Shell, are based in Europe and Japan. However, American corporations predominate: they are a majority among the 300 largest multinationals.[28]

This has important consequences both for the United States and the countries where multinationals invest. Professor Gilpin points out that "the essence of American direct [foreign] investment has been the shift of managerial control over substantial sectors of foreign economies to American nationals."[29] This shift in control has transformed the United States and other countries. The United States is becoming a headquarters economy: for many corporations, "the headquarters and staff operations remain in the United States, as directing and service facilities, while manufacturing operations are extended abroad."[30] When corporations create jobs abroad, there are fewer jobs in the corporate sector in the United States; and American workers are forced to take low paying

---

[26] Statistics based on Barnet, p. 230; Richard J. Barber, *The American Corporation: Its Power, Its Money, Its Politics* (New York, 1970), p. 251; *Business Week*, December 19, 1970, p. 58; and *Dollars & Sense* 31 (November 1977): 12.

[27] *New York Times*, December 21, 1977.

[28] Daniel Bell, *Toward a Post-Industrial Society* (New York, 1973), p. 484.

[29] Gilpin, p. 11.

[30] Bell, p. 485.

jobs in the service sector or in the spheres of small-scale capital or marginal labor, or remain unemployed.

Foreign profits get repatriated but not jobs. As a result, "Production of the traditional industrial goods that have been the mainstay of the U.S. economy is being transferred from $4-an-hour factories in New England to 30-cents-an-hour factories in the 'export platforms' of Hong Kong and Taiwan."[31] For this reason, American trade unions have begun to oppose foreign corporate expansion.

Trends in Corporate Trade and Investment Abroad

In the Third World   In the early years of United States foreign expansion, most investments were directed toward gaining control of the mineral resources of Third World countries. In recent years, however, corporations have also been investing in the manufacturing sector in these countries. Setting up a factory in Indonesia or Singapore (rather than Ohio, for example) provides attractive advantages, including lower wages paid to workers, low taxes, and few outlays for pollution control and safety devices.

At the extreme, one can speak of company countries, where foreign-owned (often United States) corporations monopolize the country's raw materials and manufacturing sector. An example is provided by Chile, where a few American mining companies (Anaconda and Kennecott) control half the country's extractive industries—on which Chile relies for nine-tenths of her exports. ITT owns the Chilean telephone and electric companies, two Sheraton hotels, and a radio station. Most Chilean shipping is controlled by W. R. Grace, an American shipper. Multinational corporations are among the best organized, wealthiest, and most powerful forces within many Third World countries. In addition, through the development of a local capitalist group and government whose interests are tied to the foreign corporate sector, political conditions favorable to multinational corporations are fostered.

Although Third World nations have increasingly challenged the situation, their economies have largely been shaped to serve the needs of multinational corporations. Their natural resources fall under foreign ownership and control; the multinationals locate

---

[31] Richard J. Barnet and Ronald E. Muller, *Global Reach: The Power of Multinational Corporations* (New York, 1974), p. 216.

low-paid manufacturing in the Third World but not technologically innovative research operations. Multinationals have the clout to obtain the resources from within these countries to finance expansion of their control. For example, in the 1960s, four-fifths of United States manufacturing operations in Latin America were financed by local capital, squeezing out entrepreneurs in these countries. At the same time, American firms in Latin America shipped home half their profits, further draining resources from the area.[32]

An examination of the sphere of agriculture, the largest sector in most Third World nations and the source of subsistence for their populations, provides an important example of how local needs are subordinated to multinational profits. The crisis of world food production is largely a by-product of the expansion of agribusiness.

Agribusiness transforms patterns of land use in ways that are the opposite of what is needed by the people of these areas. Rather than land being devoted to raising staple foods for local consumption, it is increasingly devoted to raising cash crops for export to the West, with agribusiness taking the profits. Throughout the Third World, local farmers have become hired help for United States and other Western nations' agribusiness or are thrown off the land altogether. In some Third World countries the rate of rural unemployment has reached 40 percent, and the vicious cycle continues when the surplus agricultural population migrates to cities to seek jobs, swelling the ranks of the urban unemployed.

Third World countries may achieve high rates of growth. But these figures are deceptive, for the growth is achieved by local subsidiaries of United States corporations, with profits sent out of the country. Often this is growth achieved at the expense of local living standards. For example, new foreign investment in Mexico between 1961 and 1970 amounted to $1.1 billion, while remittances and payments on interest, royalties, and patents was $1.8 billion. This represented resources "contributed" by Mexicans to the industrialized nations. Thus, Mexico supplied North American and West European stockholders with $700 million during this period.[33]

Third World countries also pile up heavy foreign debt as they

[32] *Ibid.*, p. 153.
[33] North American Congress on Latin America (NACLA), *Report on the Americas* 11 (September–October 1977): 15.

are forced to borrow to gain access to Western technology. The public-debt burden of Third World countries now equals one-fifth the value of their exports. The cost of servicing this debt was $14 billion in 1974; countries are thus forced to borrow merely in order to pay interest charges on past debts. When they borrow, they must agree to pursue conservative economic policies dictated by the foreign lending agency, whether this be a United States bank or international financial institution. The result is to integrate Third World countries into the world capitalist system on terms of dependency.

A few countries may be escaping the spiral of unemployment, foreign debt, and political and economic subordinacy. The major reason for this is the existence of vital raw materials (the petroleum-exporting countries are a good example). But for most countries, multinational penetration has brought not development but, in the words of economist André Gunder Frank, "the development of underdevelopment."[34] Although this pattern has been challenged, as countries resist being made into tributaries of the West, the trend will continue until the power of the multinationals is checked.

In industrialized nations   The small size of most Third World countries means that American investments have a heavy impact on their economies. But in the past several decades, most new American investments have gone to Europe and Canada rather than the Third World. Industrialized countries offer more attractive investment opportunities, higher consumer demand, and more stable political situations. American multinational corporations have gained an important role in these countries. Some of the most advanced industrial sectors in Western Europe are under American control, including 80 percent of the market for computers, 95 percent of integrated circuits, 50 percent of semiconductors, and an important share in automobiles, electronics, and home appliances. American corporations control 10 percent of England's total production. The most extreme case is Canada, where United States corporations control half of the country's manufacturing.[35]

Although far more is invested in industrial capitalist countries

[34] André Gunder Frank, "The Development of Underdevelopment," in James D. Cockcroft, André Gunder Frank, and Dale L. Johnson, *Dependence and Underdevelopment: Latin America's Political Economy* (Garden City, N.Y., 1972).

[35] Raymond Vernon, *Sovereignty at Bay: The Multinational Spread of U.S. Enterprises* (New York, 1971), p. 20.

than in the Third World, American firms derive nearly equal income from their investments in the two areas. And, since far more of the profits derived from industrialized countries are reinvested, more than three-quarters of the profits and royalties flowing back to the United States between 1965 and 1971 came from the Third World.[36] These regions thus pay tribute to the United States as surely as if they were outright colonies: in 1970, for example, three times more resources from the Third World flowed back to the United States than were newly invested in these areas from the United States.

In the Soviet Union, China, and Eastern Europe   The rapid

Table 8-2
The distribution of U.S. direct private investment assets abroad by area and sector: 1929–1974

	1929	1950	1959	1969	1974
ALL AREAS	$7.5 b.	$11.8 b.	$29.7 b.	$70.8 b.	$118.6 b.
Center	49%	52%	61%	72%	76%
Canada	27	31	34	30	24
Western Europe	18	15	18	31	37
Japan	*	*	1	2	3
Others[1]	4	6	8	9	12
Periphery	51%	48%	39%	28%	24%
Latin America	47	39	30	19	16
Middle East	*	1	2	3	2
Africa[2]	*	2	3	3	2
Asia[3]	4	6	4	3	4
Mining & smelting	16%	9%	10%	8%	5%
Petroleum	15	29	35	38	26
Manufacturing	24	33	32	42	43
Other sectors	45	29	33	22	26

*Denotes less than 0.5%.
[1] Includes South Africa, Australia, and New Zealand.
[2] Excluding South Africa.
[3] Excluding Japan and the Middle East.
Sources: Richard C. Edwards, Michael Reich, and Thomas E. Weisskopf, eds., *The Capitalist System: A Radical Analysis of American Society*, 2nd ed.,© 1978, p. 478. Reprinted by permission of Prentice-Hall, Inc., Englewood Cliffs, N.J. Sources listed in original.

[36] Fred L. Block, *The Origins of International Economic Disorder: A Study of United States International Monetary Policy from World War II to the Present* (Berkeley, Calif., 1977) , p. 153.

Table 8-3
Earnings on U.S. direct foreign private investment by area, 1959 and 1976

	Reported Earnings (millions of dollars during year)	Value of Investment (millions of dollars at year-end)	Rate of Earnings (%)
1959			
Underdeveloped countries	1,615	11,536	14.0
Developed countries	1,640	18,199	9.0
Total investment	**3,255**	**29,735**	**11.0**
1976			
Underdeveloped countries	5,763	22,925	25.2
Developed countries	5,217	43,838	11.9
Total investment	**10,980**	**76,245**	**14.4**

Source: 1976 figures calculated from United States Department of Commerce, *Survey of Current Business*, August 1977, pp. 39–40; 1959 figures from Thomas E. Weisskopf, "United States Foreign Private Investment," in Richard C. Edwards, Michael Reich, and Thomas E. Weisskopf, eds., *The Capitalist System: A Radical Analysis of American Society,* © 1972, p. 430. Reprinted by permission of Prentice-Hall, Inc., Englewood Cliffs, N.J.

economic growth of Western Europe and Japan has weakened the dominant position of American multinationals. In an attempt to find new outlets, American business has turned to Communist countries, with whom there were few economic ties before the 1970s. The decision to increase trade between the United States and Communist countries was part of a more general policy of détente, which signifies a decline of the virulent rhetoric of the cold war. East-West trade has boomed following a trade agreement between the United States and the USSR that was signed in 1972. American exports to the Soviet Union and Eastern Europe climbed from $400 million to nearly $2 billion yearly between 1971 and 1973. A recently opened branch office of the Chase Manhattan Bank (whose board chairman, David Rockefeller, comes from a family that epitomizes Western capitalism) is located at 1 Karl Marx Square, a block from the Kremlin. As reporter Harvey D. Shapiro put it, "Alexei Kosygin has a friend at Chase Manhattan."[37] International Harvester, G.E., and other large American corporations have opened offices in Moscow to facilitate the ex-

[37] Harvey D. Shapiro, "Alexei Kosygin has a friend at Chase Manhattan," *New York Times Magazine*, February 24, 1974.

port of goods and technology to the Soviet Union. Trade with the People's Republic of China is less extensive but also on the upswing, especially after the establishment of diplomatic relations in 1978.

The significance of American corporate expansion abroad cannot be overestimated. The prosperity of American corporate capitalism has become heavily dependent on overseas operations, whose expansion has been far more rapid than growth within the United States. Between 1957 and 1971, the overseas assets of American manufacturers increased more than 500 percent, compared to a 90 percent rise in domestic assets. Foreign investments are particularly attractive because their rate of profit is about double that on domestic investments.

Thanks to United States dominance after the Second World War and the American government's policy of maximizing worldwide access for multinational investments, the functioning of capitalism internationally has produced an integrated global system of production and consumption shaped by the needs of United States, West European, and Japanese corporations. Much of the multinational takeover has occurred through peaceful, legal means. Multinationals have, however, frequently used their vast resources in illegal ways to further their interests and corrupt the

Table 8-4

The relative size and profitability of U.S. direct private investment abroad: 1950–1972

Year	Total Investment (Domestic and Foreign)			Investment Abroad			Foreign/Total Ratios	
	After-tax Profits (billions of dollars)	Invested Capital (billions of dollars)	Profit Rate (%)	After-tax Profits (billions of dollars)	Invested Capital (billions of dollars)	Profit Rate (%)	After-tax Profits (%)	Invested Capital (%)
1950	24.9	223.6	11.1	1.8	11.2	16.3	7.3	5.0
1957	26.0	344.4	7.5	3.7	23.9	15.4	14.2	6.9
1960	26.7	409.0	6.5	3.9	30.8	12.7	14.6	7.5
1965	46.5	536.0	8.7	6.3	47.0	13.4	13.5	8.8
1970	39.3	752.0	5.2	10.2	73.2	13.9	26.0	9.7
1972	57.7	887.0	6.5	14.1	86.7	16.2	24.4	9.8

Source: Reprinted from Richard C. Edwards, Michael Reich, and Thomas E. Weisskopf, eds., *The Capitalist System: A Radical Analysis of American Society*, 2nd ed., © 1978, p. 477. Reprinted by permission of Prentice-Hall, Inc., Englewood Cliffs, N.J. Sources listed in original.

political process of other countries. Arms companies, notably Lockheed, Boeing, and Northrop, have bribed government officials in France, Germany, Japan, Indonesia, Italy, the Philippines, Saudi Arabia, and South Korea in an attempt to secure lucrative arms contracts. As part of its $20 million campaign of political and commercial corruption, Lockheed bribed Prince Bernhard of the Netherlands and the prime ministers of Italy and Japan. Petroleum companies have also bribed lavishly. Exxon, for example, contributed $50 million in secret payments to Italian politicians between 1963 and 1972. Fifty large American industrial corporations reported to the Securities and Exchange Commission in 1976 that they had made questionable payments abroad totalling $100 million over the preceding five years.

For multinational expansion to occur, friendly policies are necessary from the American as well as foreign governments. But the alliance between multinationals and the American government has come under strain as resistance to it grows both within the United States and overseas.

THE SEARCH FOR MILITARY
AND POLITICAL SUPREMACY

The United States has a vast military establishment, the largest and most powerful in the world. It maintains nearly four hundred major military bases around the globe as well as several thousand smaller ones. Over one-half million troops are stationed abroad; the navy has patrols in every ocean; reconnaissance satellites circle the world. American military missions are stationed in fifty foreign countries.[38] Military treaties link the United States to the regimes of over forty countries in Europe, Asia, and Latin America. Each year, more than $100 billion is spent to support the armed forces and purchase new weapons. (This constitutes half as much as the combined military expenditures of all other nations.)

The Arms Race with the Soviet Union

Much of the American military budget has gone to develop sophisticated thermonuclear weapons directed mainly against the Soviet

[38] Adam Yarmolinsky, *The Military Establishment* (New York, 1971), p. 115.

Union. Beginning with the cold war arms race in the 1950s, there has been a never-ending search by each country for military advantage. The result has been to create a world permanently poised for war and total devastation. Each country possesses a staggering "overkill" capacity: the United States possesses a stockpile of 9000 strategic nuclear warheads and 22,000 tactical nuclear weapons. For example, the multiple warhead MIRV missiles from one Poseidon submarine could destroy about one-quarter of Soviet industry; the United States possesses more than 30 Poseidon submarines equipped with MIRVs, along with sufficient long-range bombers and missiles to destroy the Soviet Union many times over. Although the United States and the Soviet Union appear to share responsibility for developing new weapons systems, military analyst Barry Blechman points out, "The United States has generally been the first to introduce new types of [weapons] systems—from the atomic bomb itself to MIRVs." [39]

One goal in the arms race is a *second*-strike capability: the development by a country of a strategic force sufficiently invulnerable and powerful that it could survive a nuclear attack and retaliate against the attacking country. Another goal is *first*-strike capability, enabling a country to launch a preemptive attack that could destroy the other country's second-strike force, and thus not incur a nuclear counterattack in return. Yet the cruel irony is that the *more* weapons produced, the *less* security exists because of the greater danger that (through accident or intention) the deadly weapons will be used by one side, inviting retaliation by the other and resulting in the destruction of both.

The arms race produces stalemate (what has been called the "balance of terror"), but it is not a static one. As each country develops more dangerous weapons, it drains productive resources for military purposes, without increasing security or effective power. As a result of popular and congressional pressure, attempts were initiated in the 1970s to limit new weaponry. Strategic arms limitation talks in 1972 (SALT I), extended by accords concluded in 1974, resulted in an agreement between the United States and the USSR to regulate arms buildups. The agreements provided for ceilings on the total number of intercontinental missiles allowed each side. However, the ceilings were high enough to allow substantial expansion of existing strategic weapons systems for both countries. SALT thus conveys a misleading impression: by

[39] Barry M. Blechman et al., "The Defense Budget," in Joseph A. Pechman, ed., *Setting National Priorities: The 1978 Budget* (Washington, D.C., 1977), p. 104.

placing limits in some areas (for example, the total number of missiles), it encourages a speedup in others (for example, the search for more sophisticated and deadly weaponry). One arms control expert has noted that "SALT may be a great boon for weapons procurement; a mechanism for generating and sustaining support for new weapons programs at a time when . . . they would otherwise be in jeopardy." Military analyst Fred Kaplan comments that this is "using arms control negotiations to propel the arms race."[40]

Many of the new United States weapons appear to be designed not to develop a better defensive force but to achieve a first-strike capability. The result may be to increase the risk of a desperate Soviet attack to prevent the United States from gaining a decisive advantage. Despite the SALT I agreement and the probability of a SALT II accord, new weapons systems—including the Cruise and the MX mobile missile, the neutron bomb, and the Trident submarine—are still in the process of development and production, and the number of United States strategic warheads continues to increase. The focus of the arms race has shifted from quantitative to qualitative factors, but its pace has now slowed. In fact, after a period of stabilization for military spending following the Vietnam war and public opposition to military costs, military expenditures have continued to climb. In 1978, military spending was up to $117 billion, about one-fifth of all federal expenditures.

Developing Compliant Regimes

American foreign policy has undergone many shifts since the Second World War. But its basic aim has remained the same: to use American political, military, and economic power to assure "friendly" foreign regimes. Whether a government is friendly or not depends on whether it permits American corporations to operate freely within its borders to obtain raw materials, trade, and investment opportunities; and whether it supports the United States position in the international arena. Note that Third World regimes friendly to the United States are likely to be reactionary and repressive: no democratic government could permit its country's resources to be developed on terms favorable to American corporate and governmental interests. It is no accident that

[40] Fred M. Kaplan, "SALT: The End of Arms Control," *The Progressive* 42 (January 1978): 22.

America's closest allies in the Third World are among the most authoritarian regimes: South Korea, South Africa, Indonesia, Brazil, and Taiwan. Conversely, countries struggling to overcome internal inequality and Western control (including Cuba and Chile, when it was under the Socialist regime of Salvador Allende Gossens) have become opponents of the United States.

In the strange logic of American foreign-policymakers, since the United States represents democracy and protects freedom in the world, nearly any actions are justified. The double standard has been described by historian Henry Steele Commager:

> When the Soviet Union intervenes in Czechoslovakia, that is naked aggression, but when we land 22,000 marines in Santo Domingo, that is peace keeping. When communist countries carry on clandestine activities abroad, that is part of an 'international conspiracy,' but when the CIA operates clandestinely in sixty foreign countries, that is a legitimate function of our foreign policy. When Russia establishes a missile base in Cuba (on the invitation of Cuba), that is an act of war which must be met with all the force at our command, but when we build the largest airbase in the world in Thailand, that is part of our ceaseless search for peace.[41]

Political Influence

The government attempts to influence other countries through a variety of institutional mechanisms. Financial agencies, including the Agency for International Development (AID), the Export-Import Bank, and the Overseas Private Investment Corporation, provide aid and loans to foreign governments and technical help and insurance to American businesses in an attempt to facilitate American business operations abroad. The United States uses its preponderant influence within international financial institutions, including the International Monetary Fund, the Organization for Economic Cooperation and Development, and the International Bank for Reconstruction and Development (also called the World Bank, whose current president is Robert S. McNamara, former United States secretary of defense), to regulate an international capitalist order within which American business can prosper. The United States exerts influence through its participation in NATO and other international organizations, including the Organization

---

[41] Henry Steele Commager, "The Defeat of America," *New York Review of Books*, October 5, 1972, p. 12.

of American States, the United Nations General Assembly, the Security Council, and UNESCO. More intensive means of influence include foreign aid and military intervention.

Foreign Aid

The foreign aid program of the United States has operated in over sixty countries of Africa, Asia, and Latin America. Since the Second World War, the United States has given $200 billion in grants and loans to foreign regimes. This figure includes Marshall Plan grants to Europe. The purpose is presumably to help poorer nations develop. But foreign aid is often a lever used to extract concessions from other countries to assure cooperation with American corporate and political interests.

Military assistance   This form of foreign aid is given not to help countries industrialize and achieve self-sufficiency, but to build foreign armies who protect multinational corporations and regimes favorable to the United States in these countries. Over one-fourth the $8 billion appropriated in foreign aid in 1977 went for military assistance.[42] Military aid goes to equip and train foreign military personnel each year. More than 250,000 foreign military officers were trained by the United States between 1950 and 1968.[43] Thus, when regimes friendly to the United States are threatened by internal challenge, foreign armies and police attempt to defend those in power.

Economic assistance   It is frequently assumed that foreign aid for economic development is evidence of American altruism. However, aid is often given in the form of loans, which must be repaid with interest. And the more loans given, the more interest charges pile up. In 1956, the underdeveloped countries used about 4 percent of their exports to repay past loans; this figure had risen to 20 percent in 1975. In 1970, repayment of past debts to the United States exceeded new aid by over $1 billion. One of the most important effects of foreign aid is to create dependence on the United States.[44]

[42] AID, *U.S. Overseas Loans and Grants, July 1, 1945–Sept. 30, 1977* (Washington, D.C., 1977), p. 4.
[43] Yarmolinsky, p. 146; Michael T. Klare, *War without End: American Planning for the Next Vietnams* (New York, 1972), p. 241.
[44] Gabriel Kolko, *The Roots of American Foreign Policy* (Boston, 1969), p. 72; Magdoff, p. 150; and Michael Hudson, *Super-Imperialism: The Economic Strategy of American Empire* (New York, 1972), pp. 118, 166.

In order to receive foreign aid from the United States, countries must agree to two conditions. First, they must agree to "buy American," that is, use American aid to buy American products wherever possible. As former AID administrator David Bell stated, "Aid has in fact been one of our best export promotion mechanisms." Foreign aid thus increases the demand for American products and represents a hidden subsidy to American producers. The second condition countries must accept to qualify for foreign aid is not to take over American companies operating in the country without generous compensation.

Much foreign aid has gone to shore up client states of the United States, like Taiwan and South Korea. In the late 1960s, the bulk of foreign aid went for military assistance to Vietnam. Opposition to foreign aid, as well as America's own domestic economic difficulties, led to a sharp reduction in recent years: whereas foreign aid represented nearly 3 percent of America's Gross National Product in 1949, it was down to .3 percent in the late 1970s.

Intervention: The CIA

The routine operation of United States influence can be considered a form of imperialism, in which countries remain legally sovereign in principle but dependent on the United States in fact. When cooperative foreign regimes are threatened or an unfriendly regime takes power, the United States may intervene more actively. United States forces invaded Lebanon in 1958, the Dominican Republic in 1965, and Laos, Cambodia, and Vietnam for fifteen years after the mid-1950s. American-financed forces intervened against civilian regimes in Iran in 1953, Cuba in 1961, the Dominican Republic in 1965, and Indonesia in 1966. In many of these countries, United States intervention subverted democratic processes when democratically chosen governments pursued policies opposed by the American government. Thus, American policymakers (and, as we saw earlier in the chapter, American corporate officials as well) consider procedural democracy in other nations to be less important than pro-capitalist policies.

In addition, the Central Intelligence Agency (CIA) operates in more than sixty countries, using bribery, subversion, espionage, and "dirty tricks" to influence politics in these countries. The CIA has supported pro-American political parties, labor unions, and media in foreign countries. It carried on its own secret war in Laos, subverted the government of Guatemala (1954), helped plan the 1961 Bay of Pigs invasion of Cuba, and organized the capture and murder of Ernesto "Ché" Guevara in Bolivia (1967).[45]

The CIA organized an overseas propaganda and intelligence network that integrated United States corporate executives and journalists located abroad to aid the CIA. At the peak of the cold war, the CIA paid 100 American journalists working abroad as well as 800 foreign journalists. The CIA secretly subsidized periodicals, had several hundred books published reflecting its views, and fabricated news when it served its purposes. Although the CIA's charter prohibits it from operating within the United States, it continues to carry on domestic surveillance and other activities.[46] For example, the CIA has developed a network of professors at American colleges and universities who secretly provide the agency with useful information, including conditions in foreign countries and the names of foreign and American students at these universities who might be likely candidates for the CIA to recruit. When Harvard University adopted guidelines in 1977 prohibiting Harvard professors from engaging in this and other undercover intelligence activities, the CIA announced that it would violate Harvard's guidelines if it could find cooperative collaborators among the Harvard faculty.[47]

Intervention: Chile and Vietnam

Two recent examples illustrate the "soft" and the "hard" types of United States intervention.

Chile   Although the United States did not send troops to invade Chile in the early 1970s, the intertwining of American government and corporate activity in Chile illustrates the soft face of foreign intervention by the corporate complex.[48]

In July 1970, Harold S. Geneen, board chairman of ITT, secretly offered the CIA $1 million to bribe Chilean politicians and

[45] Richard J. Barnet, *Intervention and Revolution: The United States in the Third World* (New York, 1968); and two books by Daniel Wise and Thomas B. Ross: *The Invisible Government* (New York, 1964), and *The Espionage Establishment* (New York, 1967).
[46] *New York Times*, December 25–27, 1977.
[47] Morton H. Halperin, "CIA's Campus Recruitment: Secrets From Whom?," *Washington Post*, September 6, 1978.
[48] This account is based on Jeffrey L. Kessler, "The Relationship of U.S. Multinational Corporations with Chile during the Allende Years," unpublished paper; *New York Times*, April 1, 1973; April 3, 1973; September 24, 1974; and *Wall Street Journal*, October 23, 1978.

sabotage Allende's election in Chile's presidential elections the following November. ITT made the offer because it feared its Chilean investments would be endangered by a victory for Allende, whose program included the expropriation of foreign companies. In seeking CIA help to prevent free elections in a foreign country, ITT had excellent access to the CIA: ITT's offer was personally delivered to Richard Helms, CIA director, by John A. McCone, a member of ITT's board of directors and Helms's predecessor as director of the CIA. The CIA turned down the offer, although it did spend $400,000 in the election campaign to buy newspaper advertising in an unsuccessful attempt to defeat Allende. However, after the election, the CIA approached ITT with a plan of its own: ITT and other American corporations with investments in Chile should delay deliveries of spare parts to Chile, withdraw credit, and bring home American technical personnel. An ITT vice president later expanded the plan in an attempt to insure, in his words, "that Allende does not get through the next six months."

Under ITT's leadership, American banks and multinationals slowed down their operations in Chile, stopped all further investments there, withdrew technical aid and personnel, and reduced United States trade with Chile. Among United States government actions were the cutting off of all loans to Chile by the government and international financial agencies.

The result was a veritable economic blockade of Chile. The actions of the United States government and multinational corporations helped produce severe economic dislocations, difficulties in production, inflation, a shortage of international credit, and a lack of spare parts and technical personnel for Chilean industry. The only United States government aid that did not cease was to the Chilean military. (In fact, military aid doubled.) Allende was overthrown by a military coup in September 1973. The military junta, which continues to carry out torture and political repression, immediately invited back American multinational corporations. It was rewarded with loans by American banks (amounting to $2 billion by 1976) and government agencies and with new investment in Chile by American companies.

Although American government officials repeatedly denied any direct United States government intervention in Chilean domestic affairs and any responsibility for Allende's downfall, a more accurate picture was provided by the disclosure in 1974 of secret congressional testimony by CIA Director William Colby.

Beginning prior to Allende's election and accelerating in 1972 and 1973, the CIA (at the direction of Secretary of State Henry Kissinger) spent $8 million for espionage, subversion, and other efforts aimed at overthrowing the Allende regime. Most of the money was spent to bribe Chilean politicians and newspapers and to encourage strikes by truckers and shopkeepers. The result of the CIA's activities was to disrupt the Chilean economy and thus increase the likelihood that Allende would be driven from office. The combination of United States multinational corporation efforts, withdrawal of United States government economic assistance, CIA subversion, and increased government aid to the Chilean military was instrumental in leading to the bloody suppression of Chile's experiment in democratic socialism. The full story of the CIA and ITT collaboration to subvert Chilean democracy is still not known. Despite several investigations by the Justice Department and various congressional committees, the CIA and ITT have engaged in a coverup to suppress information about their activities. Several criminal indictments have resulted for alleged perjury by ITT officials to federal investigators.

When President Gerald Ford was asked at a press conference about the CIA's illegal activities, he replied that the CIA had acted "in the best interest of the people in Chile, and certainly in our best interest." A clue to the motivations of American policymakers was provided by investigative reporter Seymour Hersh. In an analysis appearing in the *New York Times* of September 24, 1974, Hersh described American officials as "concerned that if the United States continued to appear 'soft' toward underdeveloped countries that expropriated American assets, a rush of similar actions would be precipitated [in other countries]."

Vietnam   The Vietnam war, the longest war in American history, began as a conflict no different than many others in which small numbers of American military advisers attempted to prop up weak, undemocratic, and corrupt regimes. American involvement in the war began long before the first American combat soldier ever set foot in Indochina—the area that is presently Vietnam, Laos, and Cambodia. In 1950, the United States began to supply military aid to France, who was fighting in Indochina to reestablish the colonial control that she lost during the Second World War. By the time the French admitted defeat in 1954 and withdrew, unable to overcome the Viet Minh insurgent forces led by Ho Chi Minh, the United States was paying most of the costs of the French colonial war.

For the next several years, a civil war was fought in Vietnam between insurgent forces in the South and an American-supported-and-financed puppet regime. As this government crumbled, American intervention was stepped up. What makes Vietnam unusual, however, is not that the United States intervened—this happened in a variety of ways in a number of other countries. The difference is that, after the Vietnam conflict erupted into a war, the United States was unable to crush insurgent forces, either through backing a pro-American repressive government or through direct military involvement.

During the height of the American invasion in 1968, more than 500,000 American troops fought in South Vietnam. Perhaps even more devastating than the killing and damage resulting from ground combat was the destruction caused by the American aerial bombardment, the most massive in history. From air bases in Vietnam, Thailand, and Guam, the United States dropped over seven million tons of bombs in Indochina—the equivalent tonnage of 350 Hiroshima blasts and more than three times the tonnage of all bombing in the Second World War.[49] In order to destroy the rural strongholds of the Vietcong insurgent forces, the Vietnamese countryside was ravaged: between 1961 and 1970, the United States applied twenty-seven pounds of herbicides, defoliants, and poisons per acre in South Vietnam. Defoliation destroyed 15 percent of South Vietnam's forests and 7 percent of its arable land, as well as over one-third the forests and arable land of North Vietnam.[50]

An even greater cost was paid in human life. One million people were killed in Vietnam, several million were injured, and ten million were made homeless. While several massacres of villages by American troops were publicly reported, including My Lai and Song My, American forces engaged daily in aerial bombardment, search-and-destroy missions, and "interrogations" that maimed and killed far more people with no more legality or military justification.

Despite overwhelming military superiority and the prolongation and brutality of the war, the United States was unable to crush the Vietcong or the Democratic Republic of Vietnam. Continued defeat in Vietnam and opposition within the United States to American involvement forced Lyndon Johnson to renounce his candi-

---

[49] *New York Times*, December 26, 1972.
[50] Barry Weisberg, *Beyond Repair: The Ecology of Capitalism* (Boston, 1971), pp. 88–90.

dacy for reelection in 1968 and call for peace negotiations, and led Richard Nixon, his successor, to announce the phased withdrawal of American combat troops. In 1973, the United States signed an armistice agreement and withdrew from Vietnam; and in 1975 the puppet regime backed by the United States fell.

While American influence over regimes around the globe continues, America's defeat marks a turning point: it demonstrated that the United States could not impose its will on small nations throughout the world. American policymakers are now seeking to limit direct United States intervention, relying instead on collective efforts with other industrialized capitalist nations as well as the efforts of local regimes themselves to control domestic opposition.

THE MILITARY-INDUSTRIAL COMPLEX

The growth of a powerful domestic military sector is quite recent. Throughout most of American history, the military has been viewed with suspicion. Except during wartime, the armed forces were small and few resources were devoted to their maintenance. Planning and preparation for war were relatively easy because military technology was simple, and a wartime economy was quickly demobilized when peace arrived. As recently as the period just before the Second World War, the economy was on a peacetime basis, with little military production. In 1918, it took only several months to mobilize and retool civilian industry for the production of war matériel. And several months after the war ended, the economy returned to peacetime patterns.

The Second World War represented a transition in the history of warfare. Military technology advanced enormously, with such innovations as radar, missiles, mechanized warfare, and, perhaps the greatest advance in the science of destruction, atomic weapons. General Dwight D. Eisenhower, the top-ranking Army officer after the Second World War, understood the fundamental implications of the change in military technology that had occurred as a result of the war. In a memorandum entitled "Scientific and Technological Resources as Military Assets," he wrote:

> The recent conflict has demonstrated more convincingly than ever before the strength our nation can best derive from the integration of

all of our national resources in time of war. It is of the utmost importance that the lessons of this experience be not forgotten in the peacetime planning and training of the Army. The future security of the nation demands that all those civilian resources which by conversion or redirection constitute our main support in time of emergency be associated closely with the activities of the Army in time of peace. . . .

This pattern of integration must be translated into a peacetime counterpart which will . . . draw into our planning for national security all the civilian resources which can contribute to the defense of the country.[51]

The peacetime cooperation among the armed forces, business, and science advocated by General Eisenhower began soon after the Second World War. In the decades since then, the new partnership has become a permanent part of the American political and economic system.

Fifteen years after he had written his memorandum, General Eisenhower returned to the subject. Yet this time, in his farewell address after eight years as president, he expressed alarm about the new trend:

Our military organization today bears little relation to that known by any of my predecessors in peacetime, or indeed by the fighting men of World War II and Korea.

Until the latest of world conflicts, the United States had no armaments industry. American makers of plowshares could, with time and as required, make swords as well. But now we can no longer risk emergency improvisation of national defense; we have been compelled to create a permanent armaments industry of vast proportions. . . .

The conjunction of an immense Military Establishment and large arms industry is new in the American experience. . . . In the councils of government we must guard against the acquisition of unwarranted influence whether sought or unsought, by the military-industrial complex. The potential for the disastrous rise of misplaced power exists and will persist.

The term *military-industrial complex* refers to the alliance of government, business, and science devoted to war preparation. It is a mighty alliance: the annual budget of the Department of Defense (DOD) exceeds $100 billion.

[51] As noted in Seymour Melman, *Pentagon Capitalism* (New York, 1970), pp. 231–32.

Business: Military Production and Profits

Sociologist Daniel Bell lists the development of a mobilized war economy as one of the three major changes in American society in the past thirty years.[52] (The other two are a managed, planned economy described in Chapter 4, and the welfare state, described in Chapter 7.) Producing for war is the biggest industry in the United States: over 5 percent of the labor force is engaged in military activity. More than two million Americans serve in the armed forces, another million civilians work for the Pentagon (the Department of Defense), and another two million civilian workers are engaged in military production.

The military sector has close links with corporate capitalism and reaches throughout American society. The Department of Defense is the single largest customer in the world: it purchases 15 percent of American manufactured goods.[53] The Pentagon is the nation's largest landlord, owning $40 billion in property. Through the post-exchange (PX) system, it is the third largest retail distributor, after A&P and Sears, Roebuck.

A war economy differs from civilian manufacturing in important respects. What is produced for military purposes cannot be eaten, worn, lived in, or used in the manufacture of other products. Since the end of the Second World War, $2 trillion have been spent for missiles, nuclear warheads, radar, submarines, tanks, and military personnel.[54] The magnitude of such an amount is hard to grasp. Written out, it looks like this: $2,000,000,000,000 and represents the value of all homes and business structures in the United States.

Although the $40 billion of military weapons and equipment purchased annually by the Pentagon is distributed throughout the economy, military spending is particularly concentrated in the most technologically advanced sectors. Three-quarters of defense spending in the civilian sector is located in three industries: aircraft and missiles, electronics and communications, and shipbuilding and repairing. The military purchases 60 percent of the output of the shipbuilding industry, 87 percent of aircraft, 41 percent of

[52] Bell, pp. 360–61.
[53] Tom Christoffel, David Finklehor, and Dan Gilbarg, "Corporations and Government," in *Up Against the American Myth* (New York, 1970), p. 101.
[54] James L. Clayton, "The Fiscal Cost of the Cold War to the United States: The First 25 Years, 1947–1971," *Western Political Quarterly* 25 (September 1972): 375–94.

Figure 8-2
U.S. military expenditures, 1800–1970

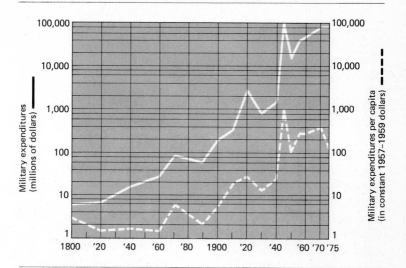

Source: Adapted from James L. Clayton, "The Fiscal Cost of the Cold War to the United States: The First 25 Years, 1947–1971," *Western Political Quarterly* 25 (September 1972): 380; and James L. Clayton, "The Fiscal Limits of the Warfare-Welfare State: Defense and Welfare Spending in the U.S. Since 1900," *Western Political Quarterly* 29 (September 1976): 371.

communications equipment, 39 percent of electronics, and 30 percent of scientific and control instruments.[55]

Many large corporations benefit heavily from military contracts. Among the 100 largest corporations in the country, 65 are significantly involved in military production. Among the 25 largest corporations, all but 5 were on the list of the top 100 firms receiving DOD contracts. Thus, there is extensive overlap between the largest military firms and the largest firms in the country.

The military industry is concentrated. Most military purchasing occurs through the Defense Department awarding prime contracts for large weapons systems—nuclear-powered submarines, missile launchers, radar equipment, and space stations—to a single firm. The firm receiving the prime contract is responsible for

[55] Paul M. Sweezy and Harry Magdoff, *The Dynamics of U.S. Capitalism: Corporate Structure, Inflation, Credit, Gold and the Dollar* (New York, 1972), p. 11; Seymour Melman, *Our Depleted Society* (New York, 1965), p. 225.

the overall work. Prime contracts involve hundreds of millions of dollars. For example, two aircraft carriers (the *Nimitz* and the *Eisenhower*) cost $1 billion apiece. And most prime contracts go to a handful of firms.

A company with over $2 billion in annual sales is immense: that is the amount Lockheed Aircraft Corporation received in Pentagon procurement awards in 1977. Lockheed is not alone in obtaining lavish military contracts: six other companies each won over $1 billion in Pentagon awards. These seven firms, with nearly $10 billion in military contracts, received one-quarter of the total military procurement in 1972. The top 100 companies received more than four-fifths of the $47 billion in prime contracts in 1977 and virtually all the military grants to industry for research and development. However, from another perspective, only a few among the top corporations produce exclusively for the military. Among the 100 largest corporations in 1968, 5 sold over half their total output to the Defense Department, 47 sold between 5 and 50 percent, and the remaining 48 sold less than 5 percent of their output to the military.[56]

Although the largest firms derive greatest profit from military production, small companies throughout the United States also benefit, since giant firms subcontract out much of the actual work on prime contracts. Twenty thousand firms throughout the country are engaged in production for the military, integrating communities and small business into the war economy.

Military spending is high in part because it is popular. Military dollars provide business to corporations and communities all over the country. Military spending represents subsidies to diverse elements in large- and small-scale capital as well as to corporate labor. Thus, there is a built-in lobby for militarism that comes from labor unions, local businesspeople, congressional and other local political officials, as well as from the Pentagon and the large military firms who benefit most.

Military production is a lucrative business. One study found that the profits of military contractors are 18 percent compared to 11 percent for large firms producing civilian goods.[57] This is primarily the result of government generosity. (It is also an extreme instance of how corporate costs are socialized while profits

[56] Stanley Lieberson, "An Empirical Study of Military-Industrial Linkages," *American Journal of Sociology* 76 (January 1971): 568.

[57] Murray Weidenbaum, *The Modern Public Sector* (New York, 1969), p. 56.

remain private.) Payments for cost overruns, which in recent years have amounted to $31 billion on forty-five major new weapons systems, are the most dramatic instance of government generosity to military contractors. For example, the C-5A transport plane produced by Lockheed cost the government $2 billion more than the original estimate.

The government also loans factories, equipment, and capital to military contractors. In 1971, Lockheed and the General Dynamics Corporation were each using over $200 million worth of government plants and equipment—one-quarter of each firm's total manufacturing assets.

Focusing on costs, however, misses the major point. Neither the Pentagon nor military producers have an incentive to keep costs low. Quite the contrary. The Pentagon is mainly interested in insuring a steady flow of funds to military producers. These payments can be considered a subsidy to support a constituency for militarism. Both the Pentagon and military contractors share an interest in maximizing the threat of war—which in turn generates support for more military spending.[58]

Military Sales Abroad

Sales of military equipment abroad have climbed sharply in the 1970s. Thanks to government sponsorship of arms sales, the means of destruction have become one of America's major exports. The United States is by far the world's largest arms exporter. In 1978, total military sales abroad were $13 billion. Sales to the nonindustrialized countries exceed $6 billion annually and these countries spend more on arms than on health and education together. Whenever there is an armed conflict anywhere in the world, it is a safe bet that American-made arms will be used— often by both sides. United States military sales have contributed to militarizing the entire world, fuelling regional arms races, increasing the risks of war, and tying up resources that might go for productive purposes. (Arms sales by the Soviet Union are a fraction of American arms sales.) Despite President Carter's campaign pledge to limit arms exports, the level did not decline in the late 1970s.

[58] Melman, *Pentagon Capitalism, passim*; and *The Permanent War Economy* (New York, 1974).

Science: The Knowledge Industry

As superiority in the science of weaponry has become the criterion of military power, the arms race has become largely a scramble to develop ever more technologically advanced weapons. Scientists, engineers, and other technical personnel are crucial to the design and production of missiles, sensor devices, unmanned bombers, electronic homing devices, reconnaissance satellites, and antipersonnel weapons.

Social scientists also have an important role in the military-industrial complex. They are called upon to find ways to secure reliable allies among foreign countries by gathering information, analyzing problems, and suggesting alternatives. Anthropologists have developed ways to penetrate Third World cultures and mobilize groups against insurgent movements. Political scientists have elaborated strategic doctrines, such as first-strike capabilities and flexible response. And experts in propaganda, linguistics, psychological warfare, cartology, cryptology, and geographic regions have contributed their skills.

The federal government provides about $30 billion annually for research and development (R and D), which goes for military and aerospace research. The intellectuals and scientists who are the major beneficiaries of these funds move back and forth between universities and private industries, think tanks and government. Some statistics suggest the interlocking relationship between science, industry, government, and war. Over half the 250,000 scientists in the United States and a higher proportion of engineers work on projects supported with federal funds. Two-thirds of all university research funds are provided by the Defense Department, Atomic Energy Commission, and National Aeronautics and Space Agency. Four-fifths of federal funds for research and development are spent for military-related research.[59]

The United States spends more on research and development than any other country in the world. However, Western Europe and Japan spend about twice as much per capita as the United States on civilian research and development and half as much per capita on the military. Among the reasons why Japan and West Europe are able to devote more effort to civilian production is because the United States acts as their army. America's scientific resources are thus geared primarily to nonessential military pro-

[59] Melman, *Pentagon Capitalism*, p. 97; Barber, p. 137; and Bell, p. 253.

duction. American industry has been steadily deteriorating and growing less competitive than foreign industry partly because American scientists devote their talents to improving weapons rather than improving the production of peacetime goods.

Government: The Foreign-Policy Establishment

The men who shape American foreign policy have close links with big business, finance, and law. Many of them come from upper-class social backgrounds. They circulate among the different sectors of industry, government, education, and foundations. The prominent business connections of America's foreign-policymakers can be seen from the fact that seventy of the ninety-one men who were secretaries and undersecretaries of state and defense, secretaries of the three armed services, chairmen of the AEC, and directors of the CIA between 1940 and 1967 came from big business and finance.[60]

The cold war foreign-policy establishment is bipartisan: its members held high office under both Democratic and Republican administrations in the period since the Second World War, developing a new view of America's role abroad. The policy they formulated advocated active American military, political, and economic intervention overseas, on the grounds that American dominance was in the interests of all. An activist role for the United States would promote a healthy domestic economy as well as bring economic growth and political democracy to regimes throughout the world. The crumbling of the foreign-policy consensus beginning in the 1960s has occurred in large part because these optimistic premises have failed in practice. Unprecedented intervention abroad has not prevented America's economic decline nor has the result been economic and political progress in other nations.

The American foreign-policy establishment was informally organized in the Council on Foreign Relations, a private organization dating back to the First World War. The council provided a setting for government officials, corporate and banking executives, and academics to meet. The policies worked out by the council frequently were adopted as official United States policy, often by the very council members who served in government.

[60] Richard J. Barnet, "The National Security Managers and the National Interest," *Politics and Society* 1 (February 1971): 257–68.

(About half of the top government foreign-policymakers since the Second World War were members of the council.) President Carter's national security adviser, secretary of state, secretary of the treasury, and head of the Arms Control and Disarmament Agency were all members of the Council on Foreign Relations.[61]

In an attempt to develop a foreign-policy consensus throughout the industrialized capitalist world in the face of declining United States power and increasing competition among capitalist nations, David Rockefeller, chairman of both the Chase Manhattan Bank and the Council on Foreign Relations, sponsored a new organization in 1973. The Trilateral Commission consists of a small number of influential government officials, business executives, and academics from North America, Western Europe, and Japan who are trying to hammer out a common approach and minimize economic competition among the capitalist nations. Another goal of the Trilateral Commission is to create shared responsibility among the major capitalist powers for stabilizing the world and containing the Soviet and Third World challenge.

A shared responsibility is necessary because American power is no longer adequate for the purpose; and part of the threat to American dominance comes from within the capitalist world itself. The Trilateral Commission emphasizes limits: limits to what the United States can and should try to accomplish on its own, limits to the value of democratic decision making (which, in the commission's view, encourages citizens to make unreasonable demands), and limits to what the Third World can expect. The Trilateral Commission is attempting to create a new international framework in which the industrialized capitalist nations will cooperate more and compete less, minimal concessions to the Third World will assure guaranteed access by the West to raw materials and markets, and even the Communist nations will become integrated into a worldwide capitalist economic system.

CHALLENGES TO AMERICAN DOMINANCE

American policies after the Second World War attempted to create a stable international order in which American corporate and political interests would flourish. In the first years, there was little

---

[61] Shoup and Mintern, *passim.*

conflict between the goal of safeguarding the overall framework as well as American interests. Given its predominance after the war, American corporate and political interests were served by whatever contributed to achieving a stable and prosperous world order. For example, American capitalism benefited when Japan and West Europe recovered from the war. But the costs to the United States of supporting the international framework have proved to be a heavy burden, and the United States has begun to fall behind in competition with other industrialized capitalist nations. Because they are not saddled with heavy arms budgets and can devote their resources to economically productive purposes, Japan and West Europe have drawn near the United States in the economic realm. For thirty years, American dominance rested on the head start that the United States enjoyed after the Second World War both as a result of the war itself and other advantages the United States possessed: a vast market, a skilled labor force, and abundant natural resources. The United States remains today the most powerful nation in the world. However, the 1970s have witnessed a relative decline of American military and economic supremacy. The gap between the United States and other industrialized capitalist nations has shrunk, and American dominance has become increasingly more costly and difficult to maintain.

Militarily, the USSR has drawn closer to the United States in recent years. "There was only one global power in 1947; today there are two."[62] In 1964, the United States had five times more intercontinental missiles than the USSR. Today it has fewer than the Soviet Union. The SALT I agreement symbolizes United States acceptance of the narrowing military gap with the USSR rather than superiority.

The United States has experienced intense economic competition from other major capitalist countries. In 1959, the combined production of the five other major capitalist countries was less than half that of United States production; by 1977 their production exceeded that of the United States. The American rate of growth, both per capita and total growth, lags behind most other Western capitalist countries. Worker productivity in other capitalist countries as well as in the USSR has risen faster than in the United States. Japan has grown at an especially rapid pace and may achieve economic parity with the United States within several decades.

[62] Raymond Aron, *The Imperial Republic: The United States and the World, 1945–1973* (Englewood Cliffs, N.J., 1974), p. 149.

These overall figures are reflected in the changing pattern of multinational corporate competition and in particular industrial sectors. Whereas in 1969, only 2 of the world's 20 largest corporations were non-American, by 1976 there were 8 non-American firms among the top 20. Between 1950 and 1970, America's share of world steel production fell from 55 percent to 20 percent, its share of world automobile production from 82 percent to 29 percent. In 1948, the United States exported twice as much as the original six countries of the European Economic Community; in 1972, these countries exported two and one-half times more than the United States.[63]

The declining productive capacity of the United States is reflected in the reduced value of the dollar. Whereas one dollar was worth four German marks in 1965, it was worth only about two marks in 1978. The Japanese yen and Swiss franc showed a comparable rise against the dollar. Economic analysts David Calleo and Benjamin Rowland comment that "the dollar gap [of the 1940s and 1950s] became a dollar glut."[64] Nonetheless, a weaker dollar—and the correspondingly lower price of United States exports—did not reverse a trade deficit that began in 1971 and has continued nearly

Table 8-5
Gross domestic product (GDP) as percentage of U.S. GDP

	1950	1960	1969	1972	1977
France	9.7	12.0	15.1	16.5	20.1
West Germany	8.1	14.1	16.5	22.2	27.2
Italy	4.9	6.8	8.8	10.1	10.1
Japan	3.8	8.5	18.0	23.9	36.2
United Kingdom	12.6	14.0	11.7	13.6	13.0
All Five	**39.1**	**55.4**	**70.1**	**86.3**	**106.6**

Source: Agency for International Development, *Economic Growth of OECD Countries, 1976–77* (Washington, D.C., 1978); and Albert Szymanski, "The Decline and Fall of the U.S. Eagle," *Social Policy* (March–April 1974): 6. *Social Policy* published by Social Policy Corporation, New York, New York 10036. Copyright 1974 by Social Policy Corporation.

[63] Albert Szymanski, "The Decline and Fall of the U.S. Eagle," *Social Policy* (March–April 1974): 7–8.
[64] David P. Calleo and Benjamin M. Rowland, *America and the World Political Economy: Atlantic Dreams and National Realities* (Bloomington, Ind., 1973), p. 88.

Table 8-6

The economics of developed capitalist economies

Country	GNP per capita U.S. $ 1974	Growth of GNP per capita per annum 1970–74	GNP growth per annum 1970–74
U.S.A.	6051	2.1	3.0
Japan	3697	4.7	6.0
W. Germany	5615	2.3	3.0
France	5002	4.1	5.2
U.K.	3112	2.5	2.7
Italy	2582	2.7	3.5
Canada	5487	4.1	5.5
Australia	4185	3.0	4.6
Spain	1802	5.6	6.7
Netherlands	4495	2.7	3.7
Sweden	6379	2.2	2.6

Source: Agency for International Development (AID), *Gross National Product: Trends by Region and Country, 1950–1974* (Washington, D.C., 1977).

every year since. (In 1977, it exceeded $30 billion.) Thus, American industry has proved less competitive than foreign industry.

Another illustration of the growing economic power of Europe and Japan is that their multinational corporations are beginning to penetrate the American market. Sony (a Japanese producer of television receivers) and Michelin (a French tire company) are among the foreign corporations who have recently built large factories in the United States. In 1977, foreign investment in the United States increased by $3.5 billion. In the pharmaceutical sector, foreign companies now control over one-third of the United States industry.

The growing weakness of the United States has generated resistance by the industrialized capitalist nations to American dominance. Other nations are less inclined to allow the United States to write the rules of the international monetary system — and to break them when it serves its purpose. (This occurred, for example, in 1971 when President Nixon broke the American pledge to redeem dollars held abroad in gold.) International monetary and economic disorder are in large part a reflection of the breakdown of the system dominated by the United States. Because of the key role the United States occupies, the crisis of American capitalism has been exported to other countries and has become the crisis of world capitalism.

United States power, however, is not at an end. For example, the energy crisis of 1974 helped reestablish American hegemony, since Japan and West Europe are more dependent than the United States on petroleum imports.[65] But the era of continued economic expansion by Western capitalism has slowed considerably and American economic power has come to damage other capitalist nations rather than help them.

There is also growing resistance to multinational economic control in the Third World. Countries exporting petroleum, bauxite, copper, tin, and other commodities have begun organizing to resist American and European control of their resources. The three major techniques they use all strike at multinational corporations: raising the price of raw materials charged to foreign firms, requiring that raw materials be processed locally rather than exported for processing elsewhere, and gaining national control over their resources rather than allowing multinational companies to exercise control.[66]

One example of the growing Third World resistance is the United Nations Conferences on Trade and Development—UNCTAD, which have been held periodically since 1964. At the conferences Third World nations have pressed for higher and more stable prices for the raw materials they export to Western nations as well as for easier access to Western technology and a reduction in the debt they owe the West. For several years, in the middle 1970s, there was a slight shift in power toward Third World nations, symbolized by a rise in the prices they received for their commodity exports. During this period, there was much discussion about restructuring the world economic system dominated by the United States and, to a lesser extent, the other industrialized capitalist nations. The New International Economic Order was to assign a more equitable share of world resources to the nonindustrialized nations. However, the international economic crisis provoked by America's economic decline has had the paradoxical effect of weakening Third World nations. The fall in world production has

[65] James Petras and Robert Rhodes, "The Reconstitution of U.S. Hegemony," *New Left Review* 97 (July–August 1976): 37–53.
[66] Bill Warren, "Imperialism and Capitalist Industrialization," *New Left Review* no. 81 (September–October 1973): 3–44, has analyzed the new trends.

diminished the demand for their commodities, and the prices of their commodity exports have resumed a downward drift. Third World nations have been further weakened by dissension among them on how to confront the United States and other capitalist powers.

Thus, the present unstable world economic situation does not necessarily spell an end to capitalism, nor even to inequalities within or among countries. What often occurs is local capitalist development in the Third World and the creation of locally powerful capitalist classes. A multinational corporation may continue to prosper after its production facilities or raw materials are taken over by a Third World nation. Lucrative management contracts, continued control by the multinational of processing and marketing, joint development agreements, and royalties from patents on technological processes can provide steady sources of profit.

Among nations, the gap between wealthy capitalist countries and many poor countries is increasing. Some Third World countries are displaying patterns of rapid economic growth. During the decade from 1960 to 1970, for example, the following countries achieved higher per capita growth rates than the United States: Taiwan, South Korea, Thailand, the Ivory Coast, Tanzania, and the petroleum-exporting countries of the Middle East. However, other countries, including India, Indonesia, Nigeria, and Morocco, barely grew at all during this period if population increases are taken into account. There is thus increasing inequality *among* nonindustrialized countries and the development of a Fourth World of impoverished nations.

There are many future alternatives. Third World nations may use the profits from the sale of commodities to hasten the development of their own manufacturing and high-technology sectors, thus shutting out multinational corporations. Or multinational corporations may succeed in allying with Third World commodity producers *against* the rest of the world to the benefit of capitalist groups both in the Third World and the West. (This is largely the present outcome in the case of petroleum.) A third possibility is that insurgent forces may wrest control over their country away from local capitalist groups and multinational corporations.

Much will depend on political struggles within the United States and other industrialized capitalist nations. Domestic political struggles within the United States will probably increase for reasons made clear by Professor Gilpin: "Having already lost much of its technological superiority and technological rents [profits], the United States will have to finance its economic and military position abroad at an even higher cost to the American economy. That is to say, the cost of political and economic hegemony will now descend on the American people themselves."[67]

While the future is not certain, what is apparent at the present time is that American efforts have failed to fashion a stable, integrated capitalist world order with the United States in the commanding position. Whatever else the future holds, it will doubtless witness further challenges to American power.

[67] Gilpin, p. 258.

institutional
patterns

9

the president as manager of corporate america

When delegates to the Constitutional Convention were meeting in Philadelphia in 1787 to consider ways to revise the Articles of Confederation, Alexander Hamilton, a thirty-year-old delegate from New York, shocked the gathering by praising the British monarchy—against whom the colonies had revolted a mere decade before—as "the best in the world." Recognizing that hereditary monarchy would never be accepted in America, Hamilton suggested that the new federal government should be directed by an elected monarch, holding office for life. Hamilton later returned to this idea in *The Federalist* No. 70, one of a series of papers written by Hamilton, James Madison, and John Jay to persuade voters to ratify the proposed Constitution.

Hamilton's proposal was ignored by the Convention and it occupies barely a footnote in histories of the founding period. Instead, the Constitutional Convention proposed a government of separated institutions, embodying the delegates' belief in the necessity for a system of checks and balances to prevent any one branch from overpowering the others and gaining the chance to exercise tyranny.

Yet, aside from the fact that the president is elected every four years, rather than holding office for life as Hamilton favored, the term *elected monarch* is as accurate as any to describe the contemporary presidency. Senator Jacob Javits has observed that the United States had lodged "more power in a single individual than any other system of government that functions today," a strange irony in a country that once prided itself on limited government and that regarded "the accumulation of all powers, legislative, executive, and judiciary in the same hands," according to James Madison's formulation in *The Federalist* No. 47, as "the very definition of tyranny."[1] Contrary to the intention of the framers—who attempted to distribute the legislative (policy making), executive, and judicial functions of government among separate branches of government, with the three responsive to different constituencies but sharing the functions of government—the contemporary presidency has substantially absorbed many of the powers of government.[2]

The modern presidency is at the center of the executive branch of government, which numbers two million civil servants. The presidency has taken over much of the function of policy initiation—although Congress may amend or reject presidential proposals, the president largely determines the legislative agenda. In recent years, the courts have curbed presidential power only in extreme instances, such as Watergate. Nor have the sovereign people posed major obstacles to presidential power. In all but two of the twelve cases in the twentieth century where incumbent presidents have sought reelection, they have been successful. (This does not include 1976, when incumbent president Gerald Ford reached office through appointment.) But in recent years, public opposition has played a major role in the downfall of two presidents: Lyndon Johnson's decision not to seek reelection in 1968 was the result of deep division over his conduct of the Vietnam war; and Richard Nixon's resignation was brought about by public indignation over Watergate.

Since the 1960s, the lot of presidents has not been easy. Every

---

[1] *New York Times*, April 28, 1974.
[2] This is one of the themes in James MacGregor Burns, *Presidential Government* (Boston, 1965), pp. 124–54.

president since John Kennedy has encountered severe difficulty while in office, and no president since Dwight D. Eisenhower in the 1950s has served two complete terms. The Watergate affair, in particular, fed public suspicion of government and damaged the presidency. It somewhat reversed the trend toward an all-powerful presidency, in part through public opposition and in part through Congress reasserting its powers. Yet even in weakened form, the presidency remains the single most powerful office in the world.

The presidency did not assume its present character overnight nor was the development inevitable. In constitutional doctrine and in political practice through much of American history, the three branches of government have been relatively coequal. Prior to the twentieth century, most presidents exercised few powers, and the entire national government had a limited influence. Bold innovators like Andrew Jackson, Abraham Lincoln, Theodore Roosevelt, and Woodrow Wilson were isolated exceptions, not the rule.

As late as the end of the nineteenth century, the presidency was viewed by many scholars as a weak branch of government. In 1885, a young Princeton professor published an influential study of American politics, entitled *Congressional Government*, in which he asserted that Congress was the foremost policy-making institution of American government. Indeed, the president was powerful only to the extent that he participated, by his limited veto power over bills passed by Congress, in the legislative domain. Twenty-three years later, the author changed his view and, in *Constitutional Government in the United States*, developed a far more expansive theory of the presidency. Soon after, by his actions as president, Woodrow Wilson, the former Princeton professor, contributed even more directly to the creation of a powerful presidency.

Through much of the nineteenth and early twentieth century, there were swings between strong and weak presidents, between presidential and congressional supremacy, and between an interventionist and a restrained federal government. Underlying the particular changes, however, was the slow but steady growth in size and power of the federal government. A decisive shift occurred in the early twentieth century. The development of the modern presidency has accompanied the growth of big government, which, we saw in previous chapters, was a product of the rise of corporate capitalism within the United States and its penetration abroad. Particularly since Franklin D. Roosevelt, the balance of power among the three branches of government has tilted toward the president.

The rapid growth in size and power of the presidency can be illustrated by one statistic. When Herbert Hoover served as president from 1928 to 1932, he was aided by a personal secretary and two assistants. Less than half a century later, the Executive Office of the President (EOP) exceeds five thousand staff members, including six hundred members of the White House staff.[3]

Every president for nearly half a century has probably been more powerful than even the most powerful presidents of the nineteenth century. The bold innovations of one president have come to be accepted as a normal feature of presidential rule by the next. "In instance after instance," Richard Neustadt, a student of the presidency, has observed, "the exceptional behavior of our earlier 'strong' Presidents has now been set by statute as a regular requirement."[4] As political scientist Robert Gilmour describes it, "At least in part, routinization of the presidency represents a formalization of presidential actions that were once thought to be extraordinary."[5] Gilmour cites both Grover Cleveland's and Theodore Roosevelt's interventions to end strikes—actions that became institutionalized in later congressional legislation empowering the president to submit strikes to arbitration or to prohibit them.

Until the Watergate scandal, it was fashionable for presidents unabashedly to proclaim the need for wide-ranging power. The president, stated John F. Kennedy during the 1960 presidential campaign

> must be prepared to exercise the fullest powers of his office—all that are specified and some that are not. . . . For only the president represents the national interest. And upon him alone converge all the needs and aspirations of all parts of the country, all departments of the government, all nations of the world.[6]

---

[3] Arthur M. Schlesinger, Jr., *The Imperial Presidency* (Boston, 1973), p. 221.

[4] Richard E. Neustadt, *Presidential Power: The Politics of Leadership* (New York, 1963), p. 5.

[5] Robert S. Gilmour, "The Institutionalized Presidency: A Conceptual Clarification," in Norman C. Thomas, ed., *The Presidency in Contemporary Context* (New York, 1975), p. 155.

[6] Campaign speech by John Kennedy, quoted in Robert S. Hirschfield, ed., *The Power of the Presidency: Concepts and Controversy*, 2nd ed. (Chicago, 1973), pp. 130, 133.

During a television interview in 1964, Lyndon Johnson asserted:

> The office of the Presidency is the only office in this land of all the
> people. . . . At no time and in no way and for no reason can a
> President allow the integrity or the responsibility or the freedom of
> the office ever to be compromised or diluted or destroyed, because
> when you destroy it, you destroy yourselves.[7]

In a 1968 election campaign address, Richard Nixon stated:

> The days of a passive Presidency belong to a simpler past. Let me be
> very clear about this. The next President must take an activist view
> of his office. He must articulate the nation's values, define its goals
> and marshal its will. Under a Nixon Administration, the Presidency
> will be deeply involved in the entire sweep of American public
> opinion.[8]

On another occasion, Nixon suggested, "Only the President can
hold out a vision of the future and rally the people behind it."[9]

However, it was partly Richard Nixon's excesses and the
resulting public disgust surrounding his resignation following the
Watergate affair that led his successors to display a more modest
approach to presidential activism. Perhaps even more important to
this trend was that when the political and economic crisis emerged
in the 1970s, presidents sought to lower popular expectations, not
raise them.

It is a measure of the current crisis that presidents have begun
to claim that government cannot cope with the many problems
facing the United States. Nonetheless, the tradition of bombastic
claims by the president has not completely ended. When running
for president, Jimmy Carter declared, "The Congress is inherently
incapable of leadership. There's only one place that leadership can
be derived, and that's in the White House." Later in the campaign
he said, "I see an American President who does not govern with
vetoes and negativism but with vigor and vision and affirmative
leadership."[10]

All modern presidents aim to be remembered as innovators. It
has become standard practice to group an assortment of policy
recommendations and present the package as an original program

[7] *Ibid.*, p. 150.
[8] *New York Times*, March 4, 1973.
[9] Hirschfield, p. 165.
[10] *New York Times*, May 21, 1978.

of the president. The precedent was set by Theodore Roosevelt's Square Deal, followed by Woodrow Wilson's New Freedom, Franklin Roosevelt's New Deal, Truman's Fair Deal, Kennedy's New Frontier, and Johnson's Great Society. Richard Nixon continued this tradition when he proclaimed, "This will be known as an Administration which advocated . . . more significant reforms than any Administration since Franklin Roosevelt in 1932."[11]

Yet, however powerful the president, there are limits as well. Presidents Johnson and Nixon could order aerial bombardments of Indochina, but this did not assure victory. Presidents can prepare economic plans, but this may not prevent inflation. They can submit legislation to Congress, but they cannot compel congressional consent. And, as Nixon discovered, although a president can pursue his goals by a variety of means, he violates the standards of procedural democracy at his peril.

A good way to understand the political significance of the presidency is to study the various areas in which the president exercises power. Different scholars have suggested alternative classifications. Clinton Rossiter, a student of the presidency, identifies various "hats" or roles of the president, including (following Rossiter's terminology) chief of state, chief executive, commander in chief of the armed forces, chief diplomat, chief legislator, chief of party, voice of the people, protector of the peace, manager of prosperity, and world leader.[12] Political scientist Thomas Cronin describes four spheres, or subpresidencies: foreign policy, aggregate economic functions, domestic-policy functions, and symbolic and moral leadership.[13] Aaron Wildavsky, a specialist in public policy, has pointed to two presidencies, one for foreign and the other for domestic affairs.[14]

Adapting these classifications, we suggest three broad purposes on behalf of which contemporary presidents exercise power: to assist corporate production at home, defend corporate capitalism abroad, and maintain social control. The three represent major founts of modern presidential power, resulting from the growth of corporate production, corporate and government ex-

---

[11] *New York Times*, November 10, 1972.
[12] Clinton Rossiter, *The American Presidency,* revised ed. (New York, 1960), chapter 1.
[13] Thomas E. Cronin, "Presidents as Chief Executives," in Rexford G. Tugwell and Thomas E. Cronin, eds., *The Presidency Reappraised* (New York, 1974), p. 235.
[14] Aaron Wildavsky, "The Two Presidencies," *Trans-action* (December 1966): 7–14.

pansion abroad, and the nationalization of American political and cultural life through the mass media. Each sphere can be identified with particular constitutional grants of authority and particular agencies within the Executive Office of the President. Before examining each of these areas, however, a warning is in order. Richard Neustadt has questioned the validity of dividing the presidency into separate roles. In his view, the classification of presidential activity into various functions or powers conveys the misleading impression that the spheres exist in isolation from one another. Neustadt emphasizes that the various presidential functions are woven together into an indistinguishable whole. The common ingredient that gives presidential actions their coherence is the exercise of presidential power. Presidential activity can be understood better as the attempt to exert influence rather than the mechanical performance of separate roles.[15]

In our view, Neustadt is correct in stressing the need to understand the overall coherence of presidential activity. Yet he does not specify what ends are served by the successful exercise of presidential power. Unless one can supply an answer, the exercise of presidential power appears meaningless, like a dog chasing its tail. Our interpretation is that presidential power can best be understood as an attempt to reconcile the conflict between the need to aid corporate capital at home and overseas (the goal of fostering capital accumulation) and the need to gain the assent of the broad majority (the goal of maintaining social control). The two goals would dictate very different policies: one serving the corporate sector, the other serving the broad majority. Presidents generally try to obscure the conflict between the two under the cloak of the common interests of the whole society. In the absence of government policies aimed at abolishing inequality, the result is to favor continued dominance by private capital at the expense of the majority. Note how, during a television interview, President Lyndon Johnson links government to corporate production and foreign involvement in a paean to the United States, thus weaving together what we identify as the three major presidential functions:

> I am so proud of our system of government, of our free enterprise, where our incentive system and our men who head our big industries are willing to get up at daylight and get to bed at midnight to offer employment and create new jobs for people, where our men work-

[15] Neustadt, chapter 3.

ing there will try to get decent wages but will sit across the table and not act like cannibals, but will negotiate and reason things out together. . . . We have one thing they [the USSR] don't have and that is our system of private enterprise, free enterprise, where the employer, hoping to make a little profit, the laborer, hoping to justify his wages, can get together and make a better mousetrap. They have developed this into the most powerful and leading nation in the world, and I want to see it preserved.[16]

This chapter examines how the president carries out the three broad functions of defending the corporate complex abroad, assisting corporate capitalism at home, and maintaining social control.

THE IMPERIAL PRESIDENT
AND THE IMPERIAL REPUBLIC

The rise of the modern presidency has been inseparable from the rise of the United States as an imperial power. Presidential power has thrived on foreign involvement, crisis, and war. The titles of two books published a few months apart—*The Imperial Presidency* by historian Arthur Schlesinger, Jr., and *The Imperial Republic* by French scholar Raymond Aron—evoke the parallel expansion of the presidency within the government and the United States in the world.[17] Presidential power has taken a quantum leap each time the United States has expanded abroad or been involved in a military, diplomatic, or commercial crisis.

One of the chief pegs on which increased presidential prerogative has been hung is the president's role in foreign affairs, including the constitutional power to negotiate treaties, receive ambassadors from foreign countries (which implies the right to recognize or refuse to recognize the regime of a particular country), and, above all, command the armed forces. The framers intended the president's power as commander in chief to be confined to the limited authority of a military leader to issue orders once hostilities exist. The Constitution granted Congress, not the president, the power to declare war and appropriate funds for military expenditures.

Early presidents soon expanded their power as commander in

---

16 Hirschfield, pp. 147–48.
17 Schlesinger, *The Imperial Presidency*; Raymond Aron, *The Imperial Republic* (Englewood Cliffs, N.J., 1974), first published in France in 1973.

chief—and thereby the power of the presidency as a whole—by deploying American troops in pursuance of their foreign policies. James K. Polk, for example, provoked war with Mexico in 1846 by sending American troops into disputed land between Texas and Mexico. When the troops were fired upon by Mexican forces, Polk quickly extracted from Congress a declaration of war. Polk's actions brought forth an angry reaction from a young Illinois congressman, "Allow the President to invade a neighboring nation, whenever *he* shall deem it necessary to repel an invasion . . . and you allow him to make war at pleasure. Study to see if you can fix *any limit* to his power in this respect."[18]

Abraham Lincoln's words proved prescient. The scenario was repeated over a century later when, in 1964, President Johnson ordered naval destroyers deployed close to the coast of North Vietnam, in the Gulf of Tonkin, and provoked an encounter with North Vietnamese forces. The incident was quickly used to obtain from Congress a resolution drafted by the executive (ostensibly in the heat of the crisis—it was later revealed that the resolution had been prepared long in advance) authorizing the president "to take all necessary measures" to pursue the war. The Gulf of Tonkin resolution paved the way to American aerial bombardment of North Vietnam the following year.

Lincoln himself, when president, used presidential war powers during the Civil War in a drastically expanded manner. During the first months after the war broke out, Lincoln refused to call Congress into special session. Among the unauthorized measures he took were the blockading of Southern ports, suspending constitutional rights in judicial proceedings, expanding the armed forces beyond their congressionally prescribed size, and spending money for purposes not approved by Congress. During the course of the war, Lincoln took additional measures without congressional approval: he proclaimed martial law behind the lines, arrested people without following judicial procedures, seized property, suppressed newspapers, and laid out a plan for reconstruction.[19] Edward Corwin, a scholar of constitutional law, notes that Lincoln's actions "assert for the President for the first time in our history, an initiative of indefinite scope . . . in meeting the domestic aspects of a war emergency."[20]

---

[18] Schlesinger, p. 42, italics in original.
[19] *Ibid.*, p. 58.
[20] Edward S. Corwin, *The President: Office and Powers, 1787–1957* (New York, 1957), p. 232.

Woodrow Wilson was prophetic when, as a professor, he wrote of the president's new position arising from American power internationally:

> The President can never again be the mere domestic figure he has been throughout so large a part of our history. The nation has risen to the first rank in power and resources. . . . Our President must always, henceforth, be one of the great powers of the world, whether he act greatly and wisely or not. . . . We can never hide our President again as a mere domestic officer. . . . He must stand always at the front of our affairs, and the office will be as big and as influential as the man who occupies it.[21]

Chapter 8 described how presidents in the twentieth century have promoted expansion of American power abroad. Following a policy of "gunboat diplomacy" in the early part of the century, presidents ordered American forces to Latin America to "collect debts for American banks and enforce the will of American sugar, fruit, and other interests."[22] President Wilson during the First World War and President Roosevelt during the Second World War exercised wide-ranging powers as military leaders. Through the destroyer deal with Great Britain, in which (by executive agreement) Roosevelt exchanged United States destroyers for the use of British naval bases, the president circumvented Congress to accelerate military preparations. During the war he relocated the entire Japanese-American population (70,000 people) living on the West Coast to makeshift-intern camps in California and elsewhere; he created wartime agencies on his authority to regulate prices, rents, and raw materials; and he seized sixty strike-bound plants to force workers to return to their jobs. After the Second World War, President Truman enunciated the Truman Doctrine on his own authority; its pledge to intervene militarily anywhere in the world represented a basic shift in American foreign policy.

Presidents nowadays justify their increased power by reference to the litany of the cold war, the threat of nuclear destruction, the requirements of national security, and the need for speed and secrecy. In Neustadt's words, "Technology has modified the Constitution. The President . . . becomes the only . . . man in the

[21] Woodrow Wilson, *Constitutional Government in the United States* (New York, 1908), pp. 78–79.
[22] I. F. Stone, "Can Congress Stop the President?" *New York Review of Books*, April 19, 1973, p. 23.

system capable of exercising judgment under the extraordinary limits now imposed by secrecy, complexity, and time." [23]

Presidents frequently defend their actions on the basis of their unique access to secret information. "If you knew what I know," asserted Lyndon Johnson, "then you would be acting in the same way." [24] Yet "backstage" glimpses of workings of the presidency, such as those provided by the Pentagon Papers and the transcription of the White House tapes in the Watergate affair, reveal the limited role of superior information. Moreover, Johnson's argument has a suspiciously self-serving ring. First, presidents do their utmost to withhold information (the top-heavy security-classification system is an example)—and thus try to prevent citizens from knowing what presidents know. Further, the quality of this inside information can be questioned: "I used to imagine when the government took actions I found inexplicable that it had information I didn't have," relates Charles Frankel, who served as an assistant secretary of state under President Johnson. "But after I had served in the government for some months, I found that the information was often false!" [25] George Reedy, press secretary to President Johnson, notes, "The most easily observable fact about 'secret diplomacy' is that it has not worked very well." [26]

The major consequence of the presumed need for secrecy and the secret information presidents possess is to shield presidential activity from public scrutiny. An extreme illustration is the secret air wars President Nixon conducted in Cambodia during 1969–70 and 1973. (When announcing an American ground invasion of Cambodia in April 1970, Nixon stated that until then the United States had "scrupulously respect[ed] the neutrality of the Cambodian people," and had done nothing "to violate the territory of a neutral nation.") So expansive had the president's war power become that the House Judiciary Committee investigating possible grounds for presidential impeachment in 1974 decided that Nixon's actions and duplicity regarding Cambodia did not constitute grounds for impeachment.

[23] Richard Neustadt, "Testimony of Richard Neustadt Before the Senate Subcommittee on National Security Staffing and Operations," in Aaron Wildavsky, ed., *The Presidency* (Boston, 1969), p. 516.
[24] Robert T. Nakamura, "Congress Confronts the Presidency," in Robert Paul Wolff, ed., *1984 Revisited: Prospects for American Politics* (New York, 1973), p. 82.
[25] Charles Frankel, *High on Foggy Bottom* (New York, 1969), p. 78.
[26] George E. Reedy, "On the Isolation of Presidents," in Tugwell and Cronin, p.130.

The need for speed as a justification for presidential power is also open to doubt. Presidential decisions rarely need to be made in a hurry. The usual process is policymaking by accretion, in the words of former Senator William Fulbright. Foreign engagements such as Vietnam occur through a slow process of escalation, not as the result of a crisis demanding a rapid decision. The image of the finger on the nuclear button has been unjustifiably extended to the entire range of presidential activity. The president's expanded powers in the exceptional conditions of wartime have become standard in an era where the economy is permanently mobilized, American corporations routinely operate throughout the world, and the armed forces are stationed in every continent and are on the brink of war twenty-four hours a day. Presidential power is given an awesome boost by the fact that the United States is a militarized economy.

As commander in chief and chief of the executive branch, the president is in overall control of the military-industrial complex; he can be considered board chairman of the military establishment. His reach is extended through staff members in the Executive Office of the President, notably the National Security Council, whose members include the secretaries of state and defense, the director of the CIA, and the president's personal national security adviser. The president must contend with conflicting interests among the army, navy, and air force as well as the entrenched power of the service chiefs, key members of Congress, and corporate military producers, and he must bargain and compromise to develop policies. Nonetheless, the president is at the apex of the most powerful military machine in history.

Although national security is usually invoked to justify this vast enterprise, the heavy dependence of American corporations on foreign operations means that presidential policies are formulated with an eye to the overseas interests of corporate capitalism. Foreign-investment policies, tariffs, and decisions about currency and other economic matters aim to strengthen American multinational corporations in their worldwide activities. The previous chapter reviewed how anticommunism and foreign economic penetration were intertwined as twin justifications for international expansion. The president manages the vast foreign policy and military establishment that has been developed to achieve these goals.

Acting as protector of America's national security strengthens the president at home. "Don't bother the president," presidential adviser Sherman Adams was fond of telling visitors who wanted to see Eisenhower. "He's busy trying to keep us out of war." But national security and international tensions may be invoked for reasons having more to do with presidential interests than with the survival of the United States. The Watergate affair provides a good illustration. In a speech in May 1973 minimizing the gravity of the events, President Nixon mentioned national security thirty-one times.[27]

Even when a president does not consciously exaggerate the danger of war and the need for a free hand abroad, his power is greater in foreign affairs, where there are fewer internal obstacles, than in domestic affairs. Aaron Wildavsky suggests that the president's "scoreboard" of success with Congress in foreign affairs is nearly twice as high as in domestic affairs.[28] Congress is more fearful of questioning the president on foreign policy, where the danger seems greater and congressional expertise less sure. As the automobile industry thrives on traffic accidents and the FBI on crime, so the president is a principal beneficiary within the government of the growth of the military-industrial complex, the cold-war crisis, and America's expanded role abroad.

Limited recognition of the need to restrict presidential freedom in foreign affairs was demonstrated when Congress passed the War Powers Act over President Nixon's veto in 1973. The law requires congressional approval of the use of American forces in hostilities beyond a certain period. Although the law signifies some shifting back of the balance of power between Congress and the president, the reaction against presidential abuse of authority in foreign affairs is limited for three reasons. First, a president can evade a congressional injunction by invoking a crisis or an emergency. Congress would not dare question a president's judgment during the heat of a crisis. Second, the most significant feature of presidential power in foreign affairs is not the sudden and dramatic resort to military force. Instead, presidential activity is part of an institutionalized process directed to the defense of corporate and governmental interests abroad. There are few dramatic acts in this vast domain comparable to the escalation of the Vietnam war. Third, debates about whether Congress or the pres-

[27] Charles M. Hardin, *Presidential Power and Accountability: Toward a New Constitution* (Chicago, 1974), p. 24.
[28] Wildavsky, "The Two Presidencies."

ident should exercise greater power in foreign affairs overlook the substantial measure of agreement between the two branches of government on the aims of America's actions abroad. Despite some confrontations between Congress and the president on foreign and military policy, the usual situation is the predominance of a "hard line" in both branches and agreement on the desirability of corporate expansion abroad.

MANAGING THE MANAGED ECONOMY: DEFENDING CORPORATE CAPITALISM AT HOME

The modern presidency has been pictured as a series of concentric circles, with the president himself at the center. Surrounding the president are his most trusted personal advisers in the presidential agency—the White House staff. Close to these personal advisers are agencies in the Executive Office of the President. The contemporary presidency is not one person but the several thousand who make up the EOP. Another ring is constituted by the cabinet: the secretaries of the twelve executive departments. They are followed by the "permanent government": the over two million civil servants who work in the bureaus and other agencies within the executive departments.

The sprawling, diverse bureaucracies in the executive give to the government its proverbial character of being slow to act, internally divided, and formless. Yet one agency within the executive does represent the interest of the whole system of established arrangements and attempts to safeguard these arrangements: the presidency.

Whereas the agencies comprising the executive branch carry out government programs, overall planning is mostly centered in the institutionalized presidency. Sociologist Daniel Bell notes, "In the long run, it is not the growth of personal powers and prestige of the President that is important, but the institutionalization of such crucial control and directing functions—as are now carried out by the Budget Bureau and the Council of Economic Advisers—in the executive."[29]

The Constitution provides ample latitude for the expansive

[29] Daniel Bell, *Toward a Post-Industrial Society* (New York, 1973), p. 312.

Figure 9-1
Executive Office of the President

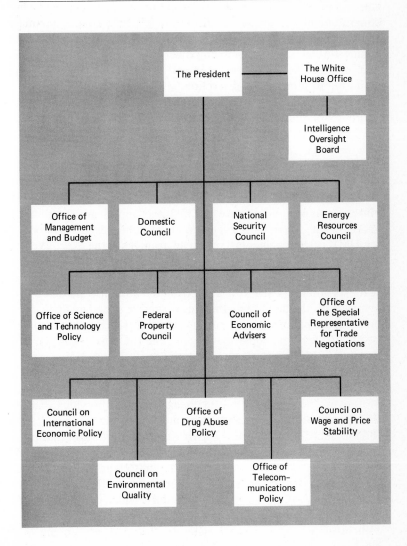

Source: *United States Government Manual, 1977–78* (Washington, D.C., 1978), p. 90.

exercise of presidential power. Executive power is vested in the president as well as the power to nominate high officials in the executive and judiciary. The president is instructed to deliver an annual state-of-the-union address and is given a qualified veto over congressional legislation. (For a bill to pass over a presidential veto, a two-thirds vote is required by both the House and the Senate.) An elastic provision empowers the president to take care that laws are faithfully executed and represents an open-ended invitation to presidential discretion.

Congress has played an important role in expanding presidential policy planning and management of the economy. Numerous laws make the president responsible for wide-ranging planning functions. The Budget and Accounting Act of 1921 instructs the president to prepare the annual budget and created the Bureau of the Budget (since renamed the Office of Management and Budget—OMB) to assist him in its preparation. Preparing the budget is important because the budget signifies government in action: what government will do. With six hundred staff members, the OMB is among the most powerful agencies in the executive. It exercises surveillance and control over the entire federal establishment. Working closely with the president, it reviews budgetary requests and proposed legislation from the administrative departments, with the aim of trimming government spending and coordinating the policies of the various agencies. OMB control is limited by the fact that departments can "end run" their proposals to Congress, thus by-passing presidential control. In addition, presidential and OMB control over the bureaucracy is limited by clientelism and lobbying, to be described later in this chapter. Moreover, there is usually little change from the previous year in the amount of money requested by most government agencies.[30] But the fact that the OMB prepares the federal budget and preclears proposed legislation considerably increases presidential control over the executive, Congress, and (given the mammoth size of the federal budget: 20 percent of the GNP) the whole economy as well. In the "new economics," which calls for federal expenditures to be used to regulate overall economic conditions, control of the budget and legislative clearance are among the most important tools of presidential power.

Another landmark piece of legislation contributing to the

[30] Aaron Wildavsky, *The Politics of the Budgetary Process* (Boston, 1964), pp. 13–16.

transformation of the presidency into an agency responsible for overall direction of the economy is the Employment Act of 1946, which instructs the president to take steps to maintain high employment and production, combat inflation, and satisfy economic needs. The act created the Council of Economic Advisers (CEA), a group of three professional economists with staff assistance, within the Executive Office of the President. Other congressional legislation that delegates responsibility for economic planning includes the Trade Expansion Act of 1962, which empowers the president to negotiate tariffs with other nations, and the Economic Stabilization Act of 1970, which grants the president broad authority to "issue rules and regulations as he may deem appropriate to stabilize prices, rents, wages, and salaries."

Presidential planning has become an essential feature of corporate capitalism. It functions routinely and during crises. Annual presidential messages concerning the state of the union, the budget, and the economy provide an opportunity for the president to present a coherent program. The result of these developments is that the presidency has become the nerve center of corporate capitalism. Through law and custom, it is widely accepted that the president will be in overall charge of coordinating the corporate economy.

Outside the EOP, but partially subject to control by the president and agencies within the EOP, is the group of department heads collectively known as the cabinet. Most departments represented in the cabinet are concerned with aspects of the economy: agriculture, energy, commerce, labor, housing and urban development, treasury, transportation, and so on. Partial exceptions are the departments of state and defense, whose bailiwick is American interests abroad.

Cabinet members are appointed by the president and can be removed by him. Although the departments are formally equal, there is an informal division between the most powerful cabinet departments—state, defense, treasury, and justice—and the rest. A few powerful department heads consult with the president quite frequently and advise him on broad political issues. Most cabinet heads, however, rarely see the president, and they have separate interests that derive from their administrative positions as heads of large departments. A cabinet secretary's day-to-day work consists of supervising the thousands of civil servants within his or her department. Presidential control and planning may be diluted by the fact that cabinet secretaries (and bureau chiefs and others within the bureaucracy) may oppose presidential directives. If the president can issue directives to cabinet members, they may find ways to evade presidential instructions. Commands issuing from the top levels of the bureaucracy have a curious way of being distorted or ignored at the bottom. So powerful is the bureaucracy that it has been called the "fourth branch of government."

The enormous size, diversity, and fragmentation of the federal executive means that the bureaucracy is a lumbering giant. A major aim of the president and his advisers in the Executive Office of the President is to subdue and rationalize the bureaucracy to make it a more efficient instrument to assist capital accumulation. But the attempt runs up against deep-rooted tendencies in American politics and administration.

Rationalizing the Bureaucracy

The federal bureaucracy is a patchwork of agencies, commissions, and departments that reflect, in imperfect form, the varied interests of American society. Thousands of groups have achieved special protection and help from government through "their" particular government agency. Often this is under the guise of government regulation, as with the railroads and truckers, who fall under the jurisdiction of the Interstate Commerce Commission. The linkage between a government agency and its constituency is called clientelism. Clientelism enables groups to make their voice heard within the corridors of power and to gain special help from government, such as tax breaks, subsidies, and protection from competition. A consequence of this relationship is to farm government out to those groups powerful enough to appropriate a government agency for themselves. A further consequence is that the bureaucracy resists presidential efforts to use the executive on behalf of the whole system of corporate capitalism rather than individual parts. Political sociologist Claus Offe points out that "too much responsiveness towards [their] clientele would almost necessarily push administrations beyond the limits of what they can do and are required to do within the framework of a capitalist organization of the economy."[31]

---

[31] Claus Offe, "The Theory of the Capitalist State and the Problem of Policy Formation," in Leon N. Lindberg et al., eds., *Stress and Contradictions in Modern Capitalism: Public Policy and the Theory of the State* (Lexington, Mass., 1975), p. 140.

Lobbying is similar to clientelism in that it enables some groups to gain informal access to government. Clientelism links an interest to a specific agency; in lobbying, an interest aims to find help throughout government either to press for governmental action or to prevent action from being taken. Lobbyists rarely concentrate on broad issues; rather, they aim to get a bureaucratic regulation rewritten or a bill modified or withdrawn. Given the enormous power of government, a slight rewording of a clause of a bill or administrative regulation can spell prosperity for a corporate producer or a whole industry.

Lobbying has increased enormously in the past decade: one estimate is that the number of lobbyists doubled to 15,000 in the past five years. For example, the Ford Motor Company had a Washington staff of three in the 1960s, it now has forty lobbyists. The reason for the increase in lobbying is partly the growth in power and complexity of governmental regulation. Additionally, in the aftermath of Watergate, there is more possibility of lobbying due to a weakened presidency and a more powerful Congress. Presidential coordination on behalf of corporate capitalism is hindered by lobbyists who can persuade administrative officials and members of Congress to favor their cause.

Lobbying and clientelism are ways for groups to filter their views to government. But the filter is imperfect: some groups are especially well represented while others are ignored. Corporate capital has many government agencies safeguarding its interests, including the most powerful, such as the Department of the Treasury, Council of Economic Advisers, Federal Reserve Board, and Department of Commerce. Large corporations are well organized to defend their interests. Each one constitutes a lobby of its own, and there are thousands of trade associations as well as umbrella organizations like the Chamber of Commerce and the Business Roundtable. When corporations wish a hearing from government, they go right to a department secretary, presidential adviser, or the president himself. Few other interests have comparable power.

Within a given industry, large producers are better organized and represented than small ones. For example, large farmers dominate the American Farm Bureau Federation, and the Department of Agriculture is more responsive to agribusiness than to small family farmers. One-fifth of all farmers receive over three-fifths of all federal farm subsidies.

From the standpoint of the president and his advisers, the major drawback with the present bureaucratic arrangements and the process of lobbying and clientelism is not that they underrepresent some groups but that they overrepresent too many groups. By providing access to so many interests, clientelism makes the bureaucracy resistant to presidential coordination and direction. Clientelism immobilizes the bureaucracy, as when different agencies conflict over "turf" or jurisdiction. For example, in 1978, the departments of Commerce and Housing and Urban Development fought over which one would administer programs for economic development in cities. Different interests are favored or harmed by the outcome of such a conflict. "Economic development run by H.U.D. would be particularly sensitive to the interests of big city mayors, while that run by Commerce would respond primarily to businessmen."[32]

Since the bureaucracy is responsive to so many specific interests, this hinders it from acting cohesively on behalf of the whole system of corporate capitalism. When the bureaucracy serves the function of social control and legitimation, by providing specific benefits to various groups, this hinders its function of assisting capital accumulation.

Most recent presidents have attempted to reorganize the executive to increase their hold over it and thus make it serve better the overall goal of assisting corporate capitalism. Administrative reorganization, streamlining, and eliminating "red tape" are not neutral: they serve some interests and harm others. Presidents attempt to rationalize the bureaucracy, redirecting its goals away from clientelism toward capital accumulation.

SOCIAL CONTROL: MANAGING DISCONTENT
AND PACKAGING THE PRESIDENT

Because of the fundamental conflict of interest between capital and labor, and the necessity for presidents to foster corporate success to insure their own success, a third arena of presidential activity consists of containing the discontents generated by capitalist production. Thomas Cronin suggests that "calibration and man-

[32] *New York Times*, January 23, 1978.

agement of conflict is the core of presidential leadership."[33] The president's concern in this arena is to keep conflict from threatening structural stability and is centered on those who do not control corporate capital: small-capital business, wage earners, racial minorities, the unemployed, and consumers.

Although the president is responsive above all to corporate capital, he is limited in his attempt to please this sector by the necessity to gain popular support for his policies. The legitimacy of American corporate capitalism depends on the periodic ratification of existing arrangements by popular majorities. A tendency toward conflict is thus inherent in the American political process. Attempting to anticipate and resolve conflicts, what Claus Offe has called preventive crisis management, is the third arena of presidential action.

When discontented groups express grievances, the president often takes to the media. In a public address, sympathetic symbolic gestures are made on behalf of the aggrieved group. Persistent opposition may be met by more tangible measures: the president may develop new policies, programs, and institutions to deal with the crisis. Illustrations are provided by presidential reactions to the urban crisis, poverty, and civil rights.

When groups are strong, angry, and determined, they may succeed in wresting real benefits from government. Often, however, they can be subdued by symbolic means or repression. Consider, as an illustration of presidential approach to crisis, the issue of black insurgency in Northern cities during the 1960s. The "urban crisis" was viewed by several presidents less as the impoverished and disadvantaged conditions in which a large proportion of blacks lived than as the political challenge posed by black militancy. By a combination of government aid, institutional innovation, and police repression, presidents Kennedy, Johnson, and Nixon managed to get confrontation out of the streets without substantially altering the conditions that caused the challenge. In 1972, President Nixon declared that the "urban crisis has passed" and that the "ship of state is no longer in danger." Given the fact that the social, economic, and political situation of black and Spanish-speaking urban groups had declined, not improved, since the late 1960s, the president's declaration represented an exercise

---

[33] Thomas E. Cronin, " 'Everybody Believes in Democracy Until He Gets to the White House . . .': An Examination of White House-Departmental Relations," *Law and Contemporary Problems* 35 (Summer 1970): 575.

in public relations. But the kernel of truth contained in his statement—that black insurgency had been overcome—is revealing of how presidents define crisis.

The president attempts to reassure Americans (and the world) that established arrangements are basically sound—and whatever problems do exist will be solved if his proposals are accepted. Whether he claims that America's invasion of Vietnam has ended in "peace with honor," or that government-imposed wage and price controls further a free economy, or that the national interest requires reducing federal subsidies to the poor, the president's aim is to legitimize and preserve established arrangements—in other words, to defend the interests of corporate capitalism. When the president calls on all Americans to work together to support the country, he is in fact asking them to support the capitalist system despite the conflicts of interest that divide Americans. The president has unique opportunities to provide an authoritative interpretation of the political and economic situation through his reports and recommendations to Congress, his ceremonial role as chief of state, and his instant access to the media.

A president's staff contains specialists in legitimizing established arrangements and packaging the president. Speechwriters, press secretaries, and media consultants strive to present the president and his policies in a favorable light. The methods used to sell the president are not fundamentally different from those used to sell toothpaste. At the extreme, as in the Watergate affair, they may include outright deceit, the suppression of damaging information, and the stretching of truth to suit the president's interests. But the routine activity is more significant than the extreme case. Much presidential action represents an exercise in public relations. Presidential use of the media, especially television, is particularly important. In the electronic age, presidents can reach out to millions of homes to present the presidential message. No other person in the world can command comparable access to the media. Prime-time speeches, presidential press conferences, and other public appearances all provide occasions for packaging the president.

An illustration of packaging techniques was the manner in which Richard Nixon nominated Gerald Ford to succeed Spiro Agnew as vice president in October 1973. During the speech announcing his choice of Ford, carried live by the three major television networks, Nixon never mentioned that Agnew was the first vice president in American history to resign from office because of criminal misconduct. (Agnew pleaded no contest to a criminal charge involving nonpayment of income taxes, amid extensive evidence of accepting bribes.) Instead, the president turned the occasion into a celebration—a "fiesta" in the words of a television correspondent.

The president can draw upon the salience and pomp of the presidential office and thereby link up with the secular rituals of patriotic America. He issues a national proclamation on Thanksgiving, the Fourth of July, and New Year's Day. In a country without a state religion, patriotism has taken its place—with the president as high priest.[34] Another analogy, with which we opened the chapter, is to an elected monarch. One account of White House personnel enumerates

> seventy-five retainers, including forty-two mechanical and maintenance workers, thirty domestic employes, and three civil servants on loan from other Federal agencies. Among the seventy-five are: a head butler and four butlers; a chief floral designer; four doormen; a foreman of housemen and six housemen; six maids, a pantryman and a pantrywoman; a *maitre d'hôtel*; a chef, an assistant chef, a second cook, a pastry chef, and two kitchen stewards; a head laundress, an assistant laundress, and a combined porter and laundryman. There are also a transportation specialist, a film projectionist, three operating engineers, and someone with the title of "principal foreman operating engineer."
>
> Not included are extra waiters and other help recruited for special events, U.S. military personnel assigned to the White House, Secret Service agents, Navy cooks for the White House staff mess, fifteen gardeners, Executive Protection Service officers, General Service Administration employes who handle the West Wing business office area, and the President's executive staff.[35]

Scholarly writing on the president from Franklin D. Roosevelt until the early 1970s was close to unanimous in its celebration of strong presidents. For a generation, political scientists equated strong presidents with good and wise presidents. Theodore Sorenson, staff aide to Presidents Kennedy and Johnson, notes, "A president cannot afford to be modest. No one else sits where he sits

[34] Henry Fairlie develops the point in *The Kennedy Promise: The Politics of Expectation* (New York, 1973).
[35] Dom Bonafede, "The Keeping of the President," *The Progressive*, February 1974, p. 45.

or knows all that he knows. No one else has the power to lead, to inspire, or to restrain the Congress and country. If he fails to lead, no one leads."[36] According to Richard Neustadt:

> The more determinedly a president seeks power, the more he will be likely to bring vigor to his clerkship. As he does so he contributes to the energy of government. . . . The contributions that a President can make to government are indispensable. . . . In a relative but real sense one can say of a President what Eisenhower's first Secretary of Defense once said of General Motors: what is good for the country is good for the President, and vice versa."[37]

Clinton Rossiter marvels that the presidency is "one of the few truly successful institutions created by men in their endless quest for the blessing of free government."[38] One scholar laments that the American president's power "is seldom fully available or appropriate for the worst problems he must cope with."[39] Another declares, "Measured against the opportunities, the responsibilities, and the resources of others in our political system and in other nations, the powers of the Presidency are enormous. It is only when we measure these same powers against the problems of our age that they seem puny and inadequate."[40]

Thomas Cronin has questioned the picture of the president presented in most textbook accounts. He finds that textbooks present

> inflated and unrealistic interpretations of presidential competence and beneficence. . . . What is needed, most texts imply, is a man of foresight to anticipate the future and the personal strength to unite us, to steel our moral will, to move the country forward and to make this country governable. The vision, and perhaps the illusion, is that if only we can identify and elect the *right* man—our loftiest aspirations can and will be accomplished.[41]

One reason many textbooks present the president in such a light, according to Cronin, is that political science courses train citizens as well as communicate truth. In unvarnished language, this

[36] Theodore E. Sorenson, *Decision-Making in the White House* (New York, 1963), p. 83.
[37] Neustadt, *Presidential Power*, p. 185.
[38] Rossiter, p. 13.
[39] Louis W. Koenig, *The Chief Executive* (New York, 1968), p. 1.
[40] Nelson Polsby, *Congress and the President* (Englewood Cliffs, N.J., 1964), p. 30.
[41] Thomas E. Cronin, "The Textbook Presidency and Political Science," *Congressional Record*, October 5, 1970, S17102-03.

amounts to deceiving students by exaggerating the merits of presidents and concealing the deficiencies of American politics.

Thanks to his vast powers and the attention lavished on him by the media, a president quickly becomes a mythical figure. Nearly any personal qualities can be made the stuff of myth. For example, it would be hard to exaggerate the contrast between John Kennedy and Jimmy Carter. Yet each was mythologized after his election: Kennedy on the basis of his aristocratic manner, his dash and sparkle, and his glamorous wife; Carter because of his homely virtues. Much of the mythology surrounding presidents is humbug, and there is no particular reason to exaggerate the importance of the qualities presidents actually do possess. Save for the exceptional Lincoln or Franklin Roosevelt, most presidents are quite ordinary men.

Yet the result of this mythology is that the president usually occupies a position at the top of the pantheon of American heroes. Nearly every year the president emerges as "most admired man of the year" in the annual Gallup poll survey. However, several events in the 1970s, notably the Vietnam war, inflation, and Watergate, heavily tarnished the myth of presidential perfection. Several studies have recently been published challenging the dominant view. Among those who now stress the need for limits to presidential power are historians Henry Steele Commager and Arthur Schlesinger, Jr., both of whom were among the champions of a "strong president."[42]

WATERGATE

Major shocks to the American political system, from which it has not yet recovered, occurred as a result of the bitter divisions over the Vietnam war, the emergence of the economic crisis of the 1970s, and the Watergate affair, when tensions reached a fever pitch. Political analyst Jonathan Schell suggests, "In the years of the Vietnam War, the United States experienced a systemic crisis, which reached its final stages when, under the Nixon Administration, the American Constitutional democracy was almost destroyed by its President."[43]

On the one hand, Watergate was an isolated scandal, the result of blunders, misconduct, and treachery of a president. Yet on the other hand, Watergate cannot be isolated from the context of the increasing centralization of power in the presidency, the arbitrary power exercised by recent presidents, and, above all, the deep divisions engendered by war, economic crisis, and political conflict.

Background, Break-in, and Cover-up

On the evening of June 17, 1972, a security guard noticed a door suspiciously taped open in the luxurious Washington office building where he worked. When police responded to his telephone call, they spotted lights in an eighth-floor office, where they surprised and arrested five burglars. America's greatest political scandal began with an incident outwardly no different from thousands that occur in any city every year. Except that the office was the headquarters of the Democratic National Committee, the burglars were directed by close associates of the president, and the president himself soon helped to direct a criminal conspiracy to obstruct justice and cover up responsibility for the burglary.

The series of events that came to be known as the Watergate affair (the name of the building where the break-in occurred) stretched over years. Indeed, its roots were so deep and its consequences so wide that it is hard to distinguish Watergate from the administration of Richard Nixon. During the course of the investigations, massive evidence accumulated of the abuse of federal agencies for partisan purposes, sale of political favors, use of government and campaign funds for private gain, bribery, campaign finance violations, burglary, forgery, perjury, wiretapping, and obstruction of justice; more than a dozen of the president's closest advisers (including the highest members of the White House staff, cabinet officers, and presidential campaign officials) as well as a score of lesser officials were convicted of criminal acts; and—as a result of his own personal misconduct in office—

---

[43] Jonathan Schell, *The Time of Illusion* (New York, 1976), p. 337.

Richard Nixon became the first American president ever to be forced from office before his term expired.

The break-in at the Watergate was only one of many illegal and unethical activities sponsored by the White House, including burglaries, wiretapping for partisan political purposes, and sabotage against the Democratic party. National security and partisan politics became intertwined for the president and his advisers. Although the links between their actions and national security seem obscure, those in the White House (from the president down) appear to have sincerely believed that they were up against a subversive plot of massive proportions, which justified illegal retaliation. What distinguished the Watergate break-in from other illegal activities was that the Watergate burglars were caught and eventually traced to the White House, and the president subsequently attempted to cover up high-level involvement in the event. According to Jeb Magruder, chief of staff of the Committee for the Reelection of the President (CRP), the decision to conceal the break-in was "immediate and automatic; no one ever considered that there would *not* be a cover-up." [44] Starting immediately after the arrest of the Watergate burglars, leading government officials destroyed incriminating evidence and committed perjury in interviews with FBI investigators in an attempt to conceal the origins of the break-in. An order went out from the White House to the FBI to limit its investigation. After several years, as evidence implicated ever more influential public officials, it was demonstrated that the man who ultimately directed the cover-up attempt was the president of the United States.

At first, however, the cover-up succeeded, in part because a several-hundred-thousand-dollar CRP "slush fund" was given to Watergate defendants to pay their legal costs and buy their silence. The presidential press secretary's initial characterization of the incident as a "third-rate burglary attempt" was nearly universally believed. Watergate was regarded as a "caper" by most Americans, and it failed to mar Richard Nixon's triumphal reelection in November 1972.

Nonetheless, from the beginning, evidence began to accumulate that Watergate was far more than a harmless prank: it was revealed that the CRP security director was among the burglars; the electronic gear they installed suggested skilled help and ample

---

[44] Jeb Stuart Magruder, "Means," *New York Times Magazine*, May 19, 1974, pp. 104, 108.

funds; one of the burglars carried an address book containing a White House office address; and the bail money paid to free the defendants after their arrest was traced to CRP.

In March 1973, two major breakthroughs occurred that led to a veritable explosion of Watergate into public consciousness. As the result of pressure by John J. Sirica, the federal judge presiding at the trial of the Watergate burglars, one of the defendants finally admitted CRP involvement in the planning and cover-up of the Watergate affair. Attention was directed even higher—to the White House itself—by the admission of L. Patrick Gray, III, Nixon's nominee as director of the FBI, that presidential counsel John W. Dean, III, had "probably lied" to FBI agents during the post-Watergate FBI investigation. (Gray himself admitted to destroying incriminating evidence in the Watergate affair at the direction of White House aides, a criminal offense, and he withdrew from consideration as FBI director.)

Two official investigations were initiated in 1973, one by the Senate Select Committee on Presidential Campaign Activities (the Watergate Committee), the other by a special prosecutor for Watergate-related crimes. In the course of these investigations, it was learned that Nixon had initiated a taping system to record all presidential conversations. With these tapes, allegations of presidential involvement by White House counsel John Dean could be laid to rest. The president, however, refused to release the Watergate tapes, arguing that they contained sensitive material bearing on national security and that the separation of powers, executive privilege, and the need for confidentiality of presidential conversations justified withholding the tapes.

When the president did voluntarily release an edited version of some of the tapes, the reasons why he had resisted were obvious. They contained shocking revelations of presidential misconduct. Regarding the payment of hush money to Howard Hunt, who directed the break-in, the following discussion between the president and Dean occurred on March 21, 1973:

P. How much money do you need?
D. I would say these people are going to cost a million dollars over the next two years.
P. We could get that. On the money, if you need the money you could get that. You could get a million dollars. You could get it in cash. I know where it could be gotten. It is not easy, but it could

be done. But the question is who the hell would handle it? Any ideas on that?

*   *   *

P. Just looking at the immediate problem, don't you think you have to handle Hunt's financial situation damn soon? . . . It seems to me we have to keep the cap on the bottle that much, or we don't have any options.

*   *   *

P. That's why for your immediate things you have no choice but to come up with the $120,000, or whatever it is. Right?
D. That's right.
P. Would you agree that that's the prime thing that you damn well better get that done?
D. Obviously he [Hunt] ought to be given some signal anyway.
P. (Expletive deleted), get it. [When the actual tapes were eventually made available, Nixon's complete statement was: "You better damn well get that done but fast. . . . For Christ's sake, get it."]

Even the mutilated version released by the White House contained enough evidence of presidential misconduct to add fuel to the impeachment flames. The tapes reveal that Nixon worked ceaselessly to suppress the true story. He invented pretexts for concealing evidence, counseled how to evade investigators' questions, and fabricated a story that would cast him in the best light. (At one point he asked Ehrlichman and Haldeman: "How has the scenario worked out? . . . How do I get credit for getting Magruder to the [witness] stand?" In fact, Nixon had no part in Magruder's decision to testify.)

But Nixon refused to release some of the key tapes, including one from a conversation he had with advisers several days after the break-in. After a bitter series of confrontations with officials conducting the investigations, the Supreme Court unanimously ordered the president to release the tapes. When he did so, it became clear why he had fought so hard to keep them secret. Yet even before this point was reached, the president was well on the way to being impeached as a result of hearings by the House Judiciary Committee—the first time such a procedure had been initiated in over a century.

After examining the mountain of evidence gathered from the various investigations, the House Judiciary Committee voted three articles of impeachment charging the president with violating his oath to defend the Constitution and his constitutional duty to take care that the laws are faithfully executed. The first article charged the president with participating in a cover-up plan to obstruct the government's investigation of the Watergate break-in. Included in the charge were allegations of false or misleading statements, withholding evidence, counseling perjury, interfering with government investigative agencies, and approving the payments of money to buy the silence of witnesses. The second article accused the president of using the Internal Revenue Service to violate the constitutional rights of citizens, ordering the FBI to carry out electronic surveillance unrelated to national security or law enforcement, suppressing incriminating evidence, and interfering with the lawful operation of executive agencies. The third article of impeachment charged the president with failing to provide evidence subpoenaed by the House Judiciary Committee in the course of its impeachment inquiry. The articles were voted by bipartisan majorities of representatives from all sections of the country, with the vote reaching twenty-eight to ten on the second article, alleging abuse of presidential power (all twenty-one Democrats combining with seven of the seventeen Republicans). The final report of the Judiciary Committee unanimously charged that Mr. Nixon was responsible for "deliberate, contrived, continued deception of the American people." Obstruction of justice, abuse of power, and withholding evidence: these were weighty charges to be brought against a president by moderate representatives, including members of his own party.

Yet, for some people, lingering doubt remained of the president's personal responsibility for the illegal actions committed by his associates. However imprudent or mistaken the president had been, did this justify impeachment and removal from office? Diehard opponents of impeachment insisted on the necessity of incontrovertible evidence—the "smoking pistol." Then, days after the Judiciary Committee vote, it was found—thanks to the Supreme Court's decision that Nixon release the disputed tapes.

Nixon's determined, year-long resistance to making the tapes available became understandable when a transcript was released of a conversation between Nixon and Haldeman on June 23, 1972, only days after the Watergate break-in. Despite Nixon's attempt to explain away the evidence on this tape by invoking faulty recollection, even he was forced to admit that it contradicted his repeated public statements. Here is a portion of the conversation:

> H. You know the Democratic break-in thing. We're back in the problem area because the FBI is not under control. . . . . The way to handle this now is to have [deputy CIA director] Walters call [acting FBI director] Gray and just say, "Stay to hell out of this—this is, ah, business here we don't want you to go any further on it."
>
> P. What about Pat Gray? You mean Pat Gray doesn't want to?
>
> H. Pat does want to. He doesn't know how to, and he doesn't have any basis for doing it.

*   *   *

> H. And you seem to think the thing to do is get them [the FBI] to stop?
>
> P. Right, fine.

The tape gave the lie to Nixon's many assertions that he had not learned of the cover-up until nine months after it occurred and that his main aim had always been to make sure the truth came out. Nixon admitted that the tapes proved his deception when he repeatedly denied any involvement in the cover-up. But he argued that this did not justify his removal from office.

Few agreed with his position. The president's support, even among his attorneys and staunch defenders, melted away. The Republicans on the House Judiciary Committee who had voted against impeachment announced they would support Nixon's impeachment in the full House deliberations. Delegations of senior White House officials and influential Republican members of Congress reported to Nixon that his impeachment and removal from office were now a certainty. Rather than suffer the disgrace of being the first American president convicted of impeachment charges, Nixon became the first American president to resign from office.

The transition occurred smoothly. Vice President Gerald Ford, the man Nixon had picked to replace Spiro Agnew (who had been forced to resign as vice president because of his criminal misconduct) took office on August 9, 1974. Ford was the first president not to be elected by the people. Just as the furor over Watergate was diminishing, he provoked it anew by granting Nixon a full pardon for all federal criminal offenses Nixon might have committed while in office. Thus, although all other leading officials in the Watergate affair, including presidential advisers in the White House, cabinet officers, and high administrative officials, have served prison sentences for their criminal activities, the chief architect of the cover-up did not stand trial.

The Significance of Watergate

Many argued that the Watergate affair served to purify American politics and demonstrated that even the highest political officials cannot transgress the law with impunity. In the words of a *New York Times* editorial of July 28, 1974, Watergate showed that elected representatives could insure "the restoration of lawfulness and moral responsibility in the highest office in the land." Henry Steele Commager declared that the affair

> demonstrated to the world and, let us hope, to future generations that the Constitution is alive and well, that it can be adapted to the exigencies of governance, and that in an emergency an enlightened and determined democracy can protect and defend its principles, its honor, and its heritage.[45]

In his inaugural address, President Ford echoed the prevailing mood when he proudly stated, "Our Constitution works, our great Republic is a Government of laws and not of men."

Watergate may have slowed the drift of power to the presidency, narrowed the use of executive privilege, limited the use of federal agencies for partisan purposes, updated procedures for dealing with abuses of power by elected officials, and strengthened confidence in the legitimacy, responsiveness, and efficacy of American democracy.

Yet there was something bizarre in regarding Watergate as "a triumph for the system."[46] *New York Times* columnist Russell Baker was among those who replied, "It really didn't work."

> The outcome produced by the system is a political absurdity in a nation boastful of its democracy. What do we have as the logical, legal product of the system's working? A President who has never run for national office and who, when his party last worried about going to the people, was not even considered a useful candidate for the dim office of vice-president.

[45] Henry Steele Commager, "The Constitution is Alive and Well," *New York Times*, August 11, 1974.
[46] *Time*, August 19, 1974, p. 3.

The system left the choosing of this new president to his predecessor, a man driven from office by bipartisan suspicion of felonious conduct, a man whose previous selection at the vice-president shop had earlier been driven from office for taking cash under the desk and cheating on his income tax. . . .

Under the system, we have been cheated in a presidential election, submitted to nearly two years of government by men of criminal productivity and encouraged to feel delighted with the prospect of two more years of government by men we have not elected.

If your car worked as well as the system, you would have had it in the shop ages ago, if not on the used car lot.[47]

THE CRISIS CONTINUES

For two years, Gerald Ford led a caretaker administration. Economic crisis continued, and the scars of Watergate persisted. What was surprising about the 1976 presidential election, then, was not that Ford lost but that a Republican administration heavily associated with Watergate and the persistent economic crisis should have come so close to winning.

Jimmy Carter's presidential campaign avoided addressing political issues in an attempt not to alienate any group; he sought to obscure the past in the morally elevating rhetoric of populism and religious rebirth. (One journalist described Carter's presidential race as "a campaign of good intentions."[48]) Carter portrayed himself as a simple citizen and political outsider. He promised to gain control over the government and bring it closer to the people. Yet his personal qualities were no substitute for a political program, and the crisis of Watergate and economic decline could not be wished away by informal dress and appearances at New England town meetings.

Once in office, Carter revealed a different side of his personality from the engaging Southern farmer: the hard-nosed technocratic manager. His nuclear engineering training as a naval officer at Annapolis seems to have predisposed him to reduce broad political

[47] Russell Baker, "It Really Didn't Work," *New York Times*, August 19, 1974.
[48] Marshall Frady, "Why He's Not the Best," *New York Review of Books*, May 18, 1978, p. 22.

problems to narrow technical ones. He instituted new budgetary procedures and emphasized administrative reorganization. James Schlesinger, Energy Department secretary under Carter, commented, "He looks upon government as machinery to be improved, to be lubricated."[49]

Despite an overwhelming Democratic majority in Congress, Carter's initiatives as president fell far short of a fundamental reform effort. Political commentators soon began speculating on Carter's personal inadequacies and the possibility that he would be a one-term president. In part, Carter fostered the impression himself that there was little that he could do. From the outsider railing against government's limitations and calling for a new beginning, he soon became a weary realist, urging Americans to lower their expectations. In his 1978 State of the Union address, he declared

> There is a limit to the role and function of Government. Government cannot solve all our problems, set all our goals, or define our vision. Government cannot eliminate poverty, provide a bountiful economy, reduce inflation, save our cities, cure illiteracy, provide energy or mandate goodness.

The new beginning Carter promised thus quickly petered out in the tired warning that things are not likely to change. Despite the difficulties of blacks, workers, and urban dwellers (the core of the Democratic constituency that elected Carter), there were cutbacks in government benefits for these groups from the meager level of the past two Republican administrations. In the absence of a social movement energizing change, the downward spiral will probably persist.

Yet, whatever his personal and political limitations, President Carter cannot be held solely responsible for the fact that the aftermath of Watergate has not been a new beginning but, instead, a continued economic and political crisis. To do so would help perpetuate the myth of the benevolent president who is all-powerful and all-responsible.

In every one of the areas that form the president's policy agenda—stimulating domestic and overseas prosperity by American corporate capitalism as well as restoring public legitimacy to the present political and economic regime—there has been a pervasive and widening crisis in the past decade. Political tinkering

[49] Hedrick Smith, "Problems of a Problem Solver," *New York Times Magazine*, January 8, 1978, p. 30.

and managerial reforms are insufficient. The president represents the focal point where these crises meet, and this in part accounts for the unhappy fate that every president since John Kennedy has met, ranging from an assassin's bullet to various forms of public repudiation. But the presidency cannot be separated from wider political struggles. The emergent crisis of the 1970s is not primarily a crisis of presidential leadership but of American corporate capitalism—which cannot be resolved by a fireside chat from the Oval Office.

10
formal representation: congress

Because the United States is a sprawling, complex society, it is not possible for all citizens to participate directly in political decision making. Instead, political democracy depends on representative institutions. The House of Representatives and the Senate are the basic formal representative links between the American people and the national government. Congress makes laws, shapes and constrains the actions of the president and the federal bureaucracy, conducts investigations, certifies appointments, and can remove officials from office.

Utilizing the standard of representative democracy discussed in Chapter 1, this chapter examines congressional representation. The place of the Congress in the political system has changed in this century in ways more complex than such phrases as "the decline of Congress" can capture. The causes, features, and implications of these changes are terribly important, not only because they are crucial to the state of American democracy but because Congress is the institution that most directly legitimizes the political system as an open, responsive democracy.

THE PLACE OF CONGRESS

Even before the Watergate events put Congress in the national limelight, increasing numbers of Americans had begun to lament the decay of Congress as a representative institution. "That branch of government," one press account noted, "that most closely represents the people is not yet broken, but it is bent and in danger of snapping."[1] Although Congress exercised its constitutional responsibilities in the Watergate affair by holding investigative hearings and conducting the impeachment process until Richard Nixon resigned, the pattern of decline has not been reversed. This decline has been occurring for a long time. The story of the changing place of Congress in the American political landscape, we shall see, is to a large extent a tale of the contradictions between the imperatives of corporate capitalism and those of substantive, representative democracy.

The Constitutional Convention of 1787 raised and resolved basic institutional questions of representation. It was widely assumed at the Convention, political scientist Robert Dahl has written, that a popularly elected House of Representatives "would be the driving force in the system; that the people's representatives would be turbulent and insistent; that they would represent majorities and would be indifferent to the rights of [elite] minorities; that the people would be the winds driving the ship of state and their representatives would be the sails, swelling with every gust."[2]

The delegates were divided on the questions of whether, and how, this popular force should be modified and checked. James Madison, in particular, pointed to the dangers of class conflict and popular sovereignty in a strikingly modern statement that put issues of social control on the delegates' agenda:

> In all civilized Countries the people fall into different classes having a real or supposed difference of interests. There will be creditors and debtors, farmers, merchants, and manufacturers. There will be particularly the distinction of rich and poor. . . . An increase in population will of necessity increase the proportion of those who

[1] *Time*, January 15, 1973, p. 12.
[2] Robert Dahl, *Democracy in the United States: Promise and Performance*, 2nd ed. (Chicago, 1972), p. 151.

labour under all the hardships of life and secretly sigh for a more equal distribution of its blessings. These may in time outnumber those who are placed above the feelings of indigence. According to the equal laws of suffrage, the power will slide into the hands of the former. . . . How is the danger in all cases of interested coalitions to oppress the minority to be guarded against?[3]

The Convention's answer was a Senate whose principle of representation was very different from that of the House. There were to be two senators from each state, irrespective of its size, and they were to be chosen by the state legislatures, which were presumed to be more favorable to mercantile, financial, and business interests than the electorate as a whole.[4]

Together, the House and the Senate were given substantial responsibilities by the Constitution. Article I, section 8 enumerates Congress' power to levy taxes, borrow and spend money, regulate interstate and foreign commerce, declare war, support the armed forces, create courts inferior to the Supreme Court, and, most generally, "to make all laws which shall be necessary and proper for carrying into execution the foregoing powers, and all other powers vested by this Constitution in the government of the United States, or in any department or officer thereof." In addition, the House of Representatives was granted the power to impeach—that is, to bring charges against—members of the executive and judiciary branches; and the Senate, the power to try all impeachments (conviction requires a two-thirds majority of those voting).

In the early nineteenth century, the Convention's conception of the House as the popular driving force of government was borne out. Indeed, under the leadership of Henry Clay, the House of Representatives dominated the government. When President Madison called for a declaration of war in 1812 (which was approved by both houses), he was largely bowing to pressure from the House. Supreme Court Justice Joseph Storey aptly remarked in 1818, "The House of Representatives has absorbed all the popular feelings and all the effective power of the country."

A transition that heralded future changes in the position of Congress was the presidency of Andrew Jackson (1828 to 1836)

---

[3] Charles Tansill, ed., *Documents Illustrative of the Formation of the Union of the American States* (Washington, 1927), pp. 180–81.
[4] Senators were not popularly elected until the passage of the 17th Amendment to the Constitution in 1912.

who claimed to represent *all* the people—an assertion echoed by most twentieth-century presidents—and attempted to place the presidency at the center of national decision making. In spite of his success in augmenting the power of the Executive Branch, Congress remained preeminent. Even the nineteenth century's most domineering president, Abraham Lincoln, conceded that "Congress should originate as well as perfect its measures without external bias." If anything, the position of Congress was strengthened after the Civil War. In the late nineteenth century, the House, in particular, increased its power under the leadership of strong Speakers who centralized the powers of the chamber in their hands.

Congress reached the height of its powers in the early years of this century. In the opinion of some observers at the time, the Speaker of the House from 1903 to 1911, Joe Cannon, was even more powerful than the president. Like other strong Speakers before him, Cannon made skillful use of his wide congressional powers as presiding member: to make committee assignments; to control floor debates by recognizing only those members he wished to allow to speak; and to chair the Rules Committee, which determined which legislation would be allowed to come up for debate on the House floor. In the utilization of these powers, Cannon and his late nineteenth-century predecessors functioned much like a British prime minister; they led the party caucuses that adopted formal legislative agendas, which were passed by disciplined party majorities.

Under Cannon, the power of the Speaker and the House grew tremendously, but the power of the individual representative was reduced to near impotence. In 1910, the rank and file of the House rebelled. Cannon was disqualified from serving on the Rules Committee; he lost his absolute power to make committee appointments and his arbitrary authority to decide who should speak. No subsequent Speaker has regained these powers.

Paradoxically, the strengthening of the individual representative's hand vis-à-vis the Speaker weakened the power of the House and made it easier for the president to exercise legislative authority. After his election in 1912, Woodrow Wilson fundamentally transformed the president's legislative role. The shift in the congressional-presidential balance in his administration "was to alter permanently the relationship between Congress and the President." Whereas formerly, strong Speakers like Joe Cannon had been able to function like a British prime minister, now it was the president who assumed the role of party leader and legislative initiator:

> Wilson laid out to Congress a fully formulated legislative program and then used the full powers of his office to induce Congress to enact it. He signalled this major political alteration of the President's role in American politics by dramatically going before Congress in person to address the members. It was the first such appearance of a President before Congress since Jefferson gave up the practice in 1801.[5]

With ups and downs to be sure, the relationship between Congress and the executive has remained much the same since Wilson's presidency. And the most basic changes and crises in twentieth-century American society have further widened the gap in power between these two branches of government. During the depression, Franklin Roosevelt called Congress into special session, presented a presidential program to meet the crisis, and virtually ran over Congress as the Senate and House passed legislation they barely had time to read. In his administrations, the leaders of both houses became the president's men on Capitol Hill. And when Congress balked at presidential legislation, Roosevelt went over the head of Congress and appealed directly to the general public through press conferences and radio "fireside chats." Much of the legislation he proposed, and many bills proposed since then by presidents Truman, Eisenhower, Kennedy, Johnson, Nixon, Ford, and Carter, have been rejected by Congress. Yet the shift in the initiation of domestic legislation to the executive has gone unchallenged. The president proposes, Congress disposes.

The decline in the ability of Congress to initiate major new policies is shared by other legislative bodies in the West. As a French journalist recently noted, "Representative democracy in every industrially advanced country is in a state of profound crisis." But, he added, "we have been accustomed for so long to accept democracy in the form of its outward appearances and parliamentary institutions that its decay often does not become apparent to us until those institutions have either been brushed aside or reduced to a purely descriptive role."[6]

[5] Neil MacNeil, *Forge of Democracy* (New York, 1963), p. 32.
[6] André Gorz, *Socialism and Revolution* (New York, 1973), p. 73.

The Congress, we shall see, has not yet become merely decorative; among the national legislatures of the capitalist democracies it remains the most important. Yet the fundamental reason for the decline in its ability to initiate policy can be traced to a development common to advanced capitalism in the United States and other Western democracies: the growth of a vast corporate complex, in which a powerful executive government and powerful economic interests act in concert. The turning point in the history of the policy-making relationship between Congress and the executive branch took place at the end of the formative period of the corporate complex, when President Wilson assumed the role of party leader and legislative initiator. Political scientist Lawrence Chamberlain has noted that between 1882 and 1909 Congress was responsible for initially drafting 55 percent of the major laws passed in that period. After 1910, that percentage declined to a low of 8 percent during the New Deal years (between 1933 and 1940).[7]

The new political and economic configurations of the corporate complex required long-term investment planning, political and administrative stability, and the rationalization of bureaucratic administration. From the vantage point of those who directed the complex, congressional initiative and intervention in these matters were potentially threatening. A far safer solution was provided by the creation of a bureaucracy of regulatory agencies. These agencies, not Congress, set the ground rules for future interactions between corporate capitalism and government, and in so doing, they also presaged and contributed to the changing place of Congress.

The alterations in the position of the Congress have not all pointed in the direction of a decline in importance. The *constitutional* autonomy of Congress is unique in the West, and it guarantees that Congress will remain more capable of independent action than Parliament in England or even in France. This capacity, however, rarely takes the form of the initiation of new public policies, though there are uncommon instances, as in the Clean Air Act of 1970, of congressional initiative. More often it takes the form of saying "no"—no to a program, no to appropriations and spending, no to excessive presidential behavior. Precisely because of the vast growth of government and the corporate complex—the

[7] Lawrence Chamberlain, *The President, Congress, and Legislation* (New York, 1946), pp. 450–52.

very cause of Congress' loss of ability to initiate policy—Congress has more opportunities to say "no," and in this way its veto has become more important. Indeed, before the late nineteenth century, when Congress was relatively important within the national government, it was less significant a body than most state legislatures, since the federal government itself was relatively weak. The decline of the Congress is thus not absolute, but rather a relative decline within a growing government in Washington.

This growth has given members of Congress more to do. As more and more legislation has been proposed by the president who sets the basic policy agenda, more and more legislation must be disposed of by Congress. Such headlines as "A Coming Logjam for Congress," "Time Pressures on the Senate," and the like have become increasingly common. In part, this development reflects the emergence of new issues, such as energy matters, but it also is the result of the fact that the United States has yet to deal with many social-policy questions, such as national health insurance and welfare reform, which have already been resolved in the other capitalist democracies.

Members of Congress have more to do, too, because the growth of the corporate complex has made their activities as providers of access to the bureaucracy and of tangible services to constituents more important. As political scientist Morris Fiorina notes, "the growth of an activist federal government has stimulated a change in the mix of congressional activities. Specifically, a lesser proportion of congressional effort is now going into programmatic activities and a growing proportion into pork-barrel and casework activities."[8]

How Congress carries out these functions depends in large measure on the nature of congressional representation. Given the enhanced and changing scope of congressional action (in volume if not in importance), one might ask *whose* legislature is the Congress of the United States. The answer can be approached best by applying the four criteria of representation discussed in Chapter 1. There, we distinguished between procedures, especially elections, by which representatives are selected; personnel, or the social-background characteristics of representatives; consciousness, their substantive orientations; and effectiveness, the ability of representatives to produce the results they desire. Let us examine each in turn.

[8] Morris Fiorina, *Congress: Keystone of the Washington Establishment* (New Haven, Conn., 1977), p. 46.

THE NATURE OF CONGRESSIONAL
REPRESENTATION

Elections: Who Cares? Who Wins?

Elections are the centerpiece of procedural democracy. They forge the link between representatives and their constituents. They provide a mechanism not only for choosing between candidates (and between different public policies) but also for keeping elected representatives attentive to the needs and demands of the represented. The Constitution requires the election of the entire House of Representatives and one-third of the Senate every two years. This is intended to insure that the members of Congress will be strongly influenced by the wishes of their constituents as a whole. To the extent that this pattern of influence is attenuated, Congress' claim to be a substantively representative institution diminishes.

But this ability of voters to influence representatives is predicated on an electorate that is politically interested, informed, and involved, and the evidence is increasingly to the contrary. In a classic article on constituents' awareness of congressional candidates, political scientists Donald Stokes and Warren Miller found that the public's knowledge about those competing for office was meager: "Of the people who lived in districts where the House seat was contested in 1958, 59 percent—well over half—said they had neither read nor heard anything about either candidate for Congress, and less than 1 in 5 felt they knew something about both candidates."[9]

More recent findings not only confirm the general lack of public awareness but also indicate that the indifference of constituents to their representatives is on the increase. A Gallup poll conducted in 1970 found that 53 percent of Americans did not know their representative's name; 75 percent had no idea how he or she had voted on even one bill in the past year; 76 percent admitted knowing nothing about the activities of their representative on behalf of the district; 67 percent had given little or no thought to the coming congressional elections; 38 percent did not even know whether their representative was a Republican or Democrat.[10]

As a result, in spite of the need for representatives and

[9] Donald Stokes and Warren Miller, "Party Government and the Saliency of Congress," in Theodore Lowi and Randall Ripley, eds., *Legislative Politics USA* (Boston, 1973), p. 170.
[10] *Gallup Opinion Index* 64 (October 1970): 9–14.

senators to renew their electoral mandate with regularity (every two and six years, respectively), the typical member of Congress is remarkably free on most matters from broad constituency pressures, or even from constituency knowledge. This near absence of a give-and-take relationship between members of Congress and the public may be thought somewhat surprising since enormous sums are spent on election campaigns, and a very large proportion of a member's time is spent on cultivating ties to constituents. It is often said—especially about members of the House—that they must begin to run for reelection the day they are elected. What accounts for the failure of congressional elections to develop a reciprocal interchange between representatives and represented?

One part of the explanation has to do with the changing role of the member of Congress within his or her district. As one student of politics has argued:

> Fifty years ago, in his district or state, the campaigning Congressman did not have to compete in a world of synthetic celebrities with the mass means of entertainment and distraction. The politician making a speech was looked to for an hour's talk about what was going on in a larger world, and in debates he had neither occasion nor opportunity to consult a ghost writer. He was, after all, one of the best paid men in his locality, and a big man there.[11]

Today, by contrast, there are a multitude of diversions competing for the public's attention, the television set has supplanted the public meeting as a means of campaigning, and the congressman or woman is no longer a leading celebrity in the community.

Nevertheless, the job is a desirable one. Other occupations, such as corporate management and the practice of law in national law firms, offer talented local figures high remuneration and prestige. But the perquisites of office continue to attract the ambitious. In addition to their annual salary of $57,000, members of the House and Senate receive generous pensions (if they last at least five years in office), inexpensive life insurance, tax breaks if they own two homes, a stationery allowance, a large telephone allowance, almost unlimited mailing privileges, nearly free medical care, free underground parking, and command over a large staff. Each year many members of Congress travel abroad at government expense, sometimes with little apparent government purpose. Congress also functions as a full-service club for its members. The Senate alone

---

[11] C. Wright Mills, *The Power Elite* (New York, 1959), p. 250.

has a dozen restaurants and a barbershop where the senators may get their hair cut for nothing. There are two swimming pools, steam baths, and a shop that sells stationery supplies at discount prices. The total package of salary, benefits, and services has been estimated to be worth from $100,000 to $250,000 a year. All this is joined to the more intangible importance of ease of contact with the powerful both in and out of government, access to a hectic social life, and continual deference. The "most seductive part of it," a congressman from the Midwest observed, "is the deference. My God, it's amazing how many people can never seem to do enough for you, here or when you go home. . . . Maybe I could and maybe I couldn't make more money in private business, but I do know this: I'd never have my ego fed half so grandly."[12]

Not surprisingly, most members of Congress spend a great deal of time getting reelected. Indeed, some political scientists argue that most of the behavior of members of Congress follows from their principal goal—the desire for reelection. By getting favorable publicity, by claiming credit for government actions, by delivering benefits to specific constituents, and by taking broad policy positions calculated not to offend too many people, they work hard to please their constituents.[13] "This is a business, and like any business you have to make time and motion studies," one member told Richard Fenno when he studied the activities of representatives in their constituencies. Since the first order of business is to stay in business by getting votes, representatives develop what Fenno calls a "home style" calculated to make the member appear qualified, as a person who identifies with constituents, and as a person who empathizes with their feelings and needs.[14] This need to construct such a relationship inevitably makes Congress the most representative of our national institutions.

But, increasingly, the electoral connection builds ties between members of Congress and those they represent that are based more on the delivery, or claim of delivery of specific services (getting a dam built, finding a lost social security check), and on matters of style (appearing to be above politics or to be trustworthy) than on

---

[12] James Wooten, "Washington Journal: A 'Mighty Nice' Life," *New York Times*, May 30, 1978.

[13] David Mayhew, *Congress: The Electoral Connection* (New Haven, Conn., 1974).

[14] Richard Fenno, "U.S. House Members in Their Constituencies," *The American Political Science Review* LXX (September 1977): 883–917.

coherent and consistent positions on political issues. Indeed, Fiorina argues that there is a connection between how safe a representative is and how openly he or she talks about issues. So long as districts

> are represented by congressmen who function as national policymakers, . . . reasonably close congressional elections will naturally result. For every voter a congressman pleases by a policy stand he will displease someone else. The consequence is a marginal district. But if we have incumbents who deemphasize controversial policy positions and instead place heavy emphasis on nonpartisan, nonprogrammatic constituency service (for which demand grows as government expands), the resulting blurring of political friends and enemies is sufficient to shift the district out of the marginal camp.

More and more members of Congress have come to understand this reality, and come to prefer to be "reelected as an errand boy than not be reelected at all."[15]

As all candidates, but especially those running without the advantages of incumbency, find it harder to command public attention, they must spend more in an effort to get it. Some of the expenditures are staggering. When Abraham Lincoln ran for Congress in 1846, he had one campaign expense—a barrel of cider. Today, a typical House race will cost more than $100,000. In the thirty-two Senate races of 1976, the candidates spent over $38 million. Most expenditures are for media time.[16]

Funds to finance congressional campaigns can be raised from three sources: the candidate's personal wealth, local economic interests, and national economic interests. Personal wealth may be especially important in Senate races. Fifteen candidates for the Senate gave their campaigns at least $50,000 in the form of personal contributions or loans in 1976. In one spectacular example, John Heinz personally contributed nearly $2.5 million of the $3 million spent on his successful campaign in Pennsylvania. But of course not all successful candidates are personally wealthy. As discussed in Chapter 6, most campaign funds come from business interests and, secondarily, from trade unions. The leading congressional contributors in 1976 were the American Medical Association; dairy committees; the AFL-CIO; maritime unions; the United Automobile Workers (UAW); coal, oil, and natural gas interests; the National Education Association; the National Associations of

[15] Fiorina, pp. 36–37.
[16] *Congressional Quarterly*, June 25, 1977, p. 1291.

Realtors; and financial institutions.[17] And one analyst has estimated that in some metropolitan areas, from 10 to 15 percent of
Democratic campaign funds came from gangsters and rac-
keteers.[18]

Elections are meant to be the mechanism for insuring the
substantive representativeness of the Congress. In 1787, George
Washington endorsed the two-year term for congressmen. Power,
he wrote, "is entrusted for certain defined purposes, and for a
certain limited period . . . and, whenever it is executed contrary to
[the public] interest, or not agreeable to their wishes, their servants
can and undoubtably will be recalled." The House would rapidly
turn over in membership, it was expected, thereby giving the
people a hold on the actions of their representatives.

This expectation has not been borne out. In the nineteenth
century, congressional turnover was very high; in 1870, more than
half of the representatives sent to the House were newly elected.
By 1900, fewer than one-third; and in 1978, over 85 percent of the
members of the House of Representatives had been elected to
office more than once. The average representative in 1978 had
served for over seven two-year terms; the average senator for over
10 years.[19]

No district is ever completely safe. In their careers, about one
in three members is eventually thrown out of office by voters either
in a primary or in a general election.[20] Yet fewer and fewer seats
today can be classified as "marginal," where winning percentages
are from 50 to 55 percent. Once a person is elected there is an
excellent chance that he or she will stay in the seat for a long time.

This change reflects the decline in the number of marginal
seats. Political scientist David Mayhew has found that fewer and
fewer districts are competitive. More and more are safe for incumbents. The vast majority of incumbents win by securing more than
60 percent of the vote.[21] Elections, as a consequence, have come

[17] *Congressional Quarterly*, April 16, 1977, p. 710.
[18] G. William Domhoff, *Fat Cats and Democrats: The Role of the Big Rich in the Party of the Common Man* (Englewood Cliffs, N.J., 1972).
[19] Samuel Huntington, "Congressional Reponses to the Twentieth Century," in David Truman, ed., *The Congress and America's Future* (Englewood Cliffs, N.J., 1965), pp. 8–9; Mark Green, James Fallows, and David Zwick, *Who Runs Congress?* (New York, 1972), pp. 226–27.
[20] Robert S. Erikson, "Is There Such a Thing as a Safe Seat?," *Polity* 8 (Summer 1976): 623ff.
[21] David Mayhew, "The Case of the Declining Marginals," *Polity* 6 (Winter 1973): 295–317.

to have less and less of a capacity to keep Congress representative. Rather, Fiorina argues, as marginal districts disappear, and therefore as dissatisfied voters have increasingly limited chances to defeat incumbents, "we face the possibility of a Congress composed of professional officeholders oblivious to the changing political sentiments of the country."[22] Who are these representatives?

The Representatives

In the representative ideal, a representative body mirrors the population as a whole. But no legislature in the world measures up to this standard. It can be argued, moreover, that not only is perfect symmetry between representatives and represented unlikely but that even without it the interests of the population as a whole can be substantively represented. Fair enough—but a disproportionately unrepresentative legislature on the other hand is likely to leave many members of the population without representatives who even minimally comprehend their life situations and needs; while others, who are overrepresented, are likely to have their views taken into account as a matter of course, sometimes without the representatives even being aware of their own predispositions.

These considerations are important in the case of Congress, since the average social background of representatives differs so strikingly from the population as a whole. In the words of a recent comprehensive study:

> Against the background of the great cultural, religious and ethnic diversity that is America, a close focus upon the Congress reveals it as predominantly an elite club for aging, white Protestant men from the upper levels of the income ladder. Those who represent America in its national legislative bodies are, as a group, a narrow slice of the American pie. Large segments of the population—especially women, working people, and non-whites—are minimally, if at all, represented in Congress.[23]

More than half of Americans are female. In 1978, of the 435 House members, 17 were women (up from 9 in 1942); and of 100 senators, none were women. One in nine Americans is black. One member of the Senate and 16 members of the House were black. In the United

---

[22] Fiorina, p. 14.
[23] Richard Zweigenhaft, "Who Represents America?," *The Insurgent Sociologist* V (Spring 1975): 121.

States, 58 percent of the people are Protestant, 37 percent Catholic, and 5 percent Jewish. In the Congress, 69 percent are Protestants, 25 percent Catholics, and 6 percent Jewish.[24]

Class patterns of representation are even more skewed. A student of Congress, Richard Zweigenhaft, found that "the fathers of Congressmen are likely to be businessmen or professionals as are the fathers of corporate executives, corporate lawyers, or Ivy League college professors. Apparently the 10 percent of the male population engaged in business or professional careers are highly overrepresented in the number of sons they have who assume leadership in several arenas of American society," including the Congress.[25] Just over half of House members, and two-thirds of senators have been trained as lawyers. Other frequent occupations are business, teaching, banking, and farming. One American in three thousand is a millionaire; at least one in five senators is a millionaire. A few members of Congress come from working-class backgrounds. Senator Daniel Moynihan's father was a bartender. Edmund Muskie's father is a tailor. But in 1978 there were *no* former manual workers in the Senate, and only three former union officials in the House.

Members of Congress are unrepresentative in terms of geography as well. Although more and more Americans have come to live in urban and suburban areas, well over half of all senators and representatives are from rural areas or small towns. Less than one-tenth of American families live on the farm, yet almost one-third of all senators come from farm families. A study in 1959 found that 41 percent of senators still lived in their hometowns, and a striking 77 percent of congressional leaders were still living in the state of their birth.[26]

The average member of Congress is very much a local notable:

> The typical Congressman may have gone away to college, but he then returned to his home state to pursue an electoral career, working his way up through local office, the state legislature, and eventually to Congress. The typical political executive in the executive branch on the other hand, like the typical corporation executive, went away to college and then did not return home but instead

[24] *Congressional Quarterly*, January 1, 1977, pp. 19–27.
[25] Zweigenhaft, p. 122.
[26] Huntington, p. 13.

pursued a career in a metropolitan center or worked in one or more
national organizations with frequent changes of residence. . . .
    Among the sixty-six lawyers in the Senate in 1963, for instance,
only two . . . had been "prominent" corporation counsels before
going into politics. Administration leaders, in contrast, are far
more likely to be affiliated with large national and industrial corporations, with Wall Street or State Street law firms, and with New
York banks.[27]

Thus most members of Congress come from and represent an
overwhelmingly white, male, Protestant, small-town elite that is
distinct from the more cosmopolitan (but not more representative)
dominant national elite. Big-city representatives are more likely to
be nonwhite, female, Catholic, or Jewish. But like their small-town
counterparts, their orientation is predominantly local (urban representatives with seniority are likely to be local party-machine
stalwarts), and their campaigns are largely financed by local capital
(especially the real estate, banking, and insurance firms in the
district). Both rural and urban representatives tend to be "parts of
a local consensus of local politicians, local businessmen, local
bankers, local trade union leaders, and local newspaper editors
who constitute the opinion-making elite of their districts."[28] They
are likely to be part of the group at the weekly lunchtime Rotary
Club meeting.

Representation on Whose Behalf?

As representatives, members of Congress deliberate about public
policy. They are influenced in part by the desire to be reelected as
well as by their own backgrounds and experiences. The dimension
of representation we have called "consciousness" (which is concerned with how representatives see the interests they represent
and how they act on behalf of those interests) is also shaped by the
opportunities different individuals and groups have to influence
legislation, the norms guiding behavior in the Congress, and the
rules and dynamics of the legislative process itself.
    Discussions of substantive representation in Congress do well
to distinguish between policies that affect small, local capital and
its political allies, and those that directly concern the corporate
complex of large capital and the federal government. In the latter

[27] *Ibid.*, pp. 14, 15.
[28] *Ibid.*, also see Fenno, p. 889.

case, the Congress' principal role is that of nay-sayer to initiatives taken by others. But in the former case, the Congress is a principal spokesperson for the constituency-based business and political elites—the people who support congressional campaigns, make party nominations, and join the representative at the local Rotary Club.

Support for programs that advance the interests of small capital, including agricultural interests, is the price the corporate complex must pay for the continued lack of congressional interference in its basic affairs. As economist James O'Connor has noted:

> Corporate capital must forge alliances with traditional agricultural interests (especially those of the southern oligarchy) and small scale capital. The votes of southern and midwestern farm congressmen and other representatives bound to local and regional economic interests (e.g., shipping, soft coal mining, fishing) are indispensible for the legislative victories of corporate . . . policies.[29]

The cost of this support has been high. The loan program of the Small Business Administration, which includes the underwriting of small banks, capital grants to the fishing industry for new boats; stockpiling of textiles by the government at favorable prices; and other subsidy programs to local builders and developers, is an example of the effective representation of these interests by representatives and senators. No local or regional group has used the mechanism of congressional representation more effectively than America's farmers. The following is a typical example.

In the spring of 1974, the federal government ordered the destruction of millions of chickens on Mississippi farms because the chickens had eaten feed that contained traces of a powerful pesticide that has been linked to cancer. Rather than accept the loss or sue the companies that produced the feed, a delegation of farmers and processors from Scott County visited Washington to convince the Department of Agriculture to allow the contaminated chickens to be marketed. Rebuffed there, they sought to get Congress to agree to have their loss covered by the government.

A few days after their arrival, Senator Eastland of Mississippi introduced a bill to pay "a fair value" for the chickens and the cost of destroying them, estimated at $10 million, or about a dollar a

---

[29] James O'Connor, *The Fiscal Crisis of the State* (New York, 1973), p. 168.

chicken. The bill passed through the Senate Agriculture Committee in one day without any public hearings and passed the Senate by a 2 to 1 margin.

Scott County, Mississippi, is overwhelmingly rural. Many of its farmers are black and poor. They are politically unorganized and have little bargaining power, since they must sell their chickens to one of five county processors, who pay the farmers about two cents a pound. The processors, who owned the nine million chickens, are the dominant economic force in the county and the largest source of political campaign financing. The bill Eastland directed through the Senate was heavily weighted in their favor. "Out of a total of the $10 million indemnification, 785 farmers will divide about $585,000; 1100 workers will divide about $450,000. Five integrated processors will divide nine million dollars, which covers not only their total investment and the cost of killing the birds, but their profits!" [30]

In the past century, Congress has consistently been the most effective spokesperson for local farming interests in Washington. As the corporate complex developed, small farmers found themselves out of step with economic developments and at the mercy of the new large corporations and banks for machinery, financing, and transportation. Farmers used their democratic access to Congress as a counterweight. Since the 1930s, farmers have captured control of federal agricultural programs and have successfully used Congress to defend their position.

Large farmers who control agricultural policymaking in Congress often pass legislation that works in their own interests. In the 1960s, the chairman of the House Agriculture Committee pushed a controversial tobacco subsidy through Congress; he owned two vast tobacco farms. Two members of the Senate Agriculture Committee, Senators Talmadge and Byrd, Jr., were huge landholders; Byrd was the owner of the most extensive apple orchards in the world. When Byrd, Sr., served in the Senate he pushed through a subsidy to an unprofitable shipping line that carried his apples to Europe. Columnists Drew Pearson and Jack Anderson argue:

> The farmer legislators . . . pretend to protect the farmer through legislation that actually increases their own profits and gouges the consumers. Their legislative efforts have produced little to improve

[30] James Hightower, "Mississippi Saga of the Chicken-Fried Taxpayer," *The New Republic*, May 4, 1974, p. 13.

the lot of the impoverished farm worker or to aid the small farmer. In a very real sense, their Congressional power enables them to wage class warfare upon the poor.[31]

Potentially, the electorate has a check on congressional behavior of this sort. But in practice, the six-year and two-year terms have become a device to hold members of Congress accountable to the wealthier segment of the small-capital sector that finances elections and that, unlike many voters, not only knows the representative's name but how he or she acts in minute detail. A reciprocal relationship has developed between powerful local interests and members of Congress, who shape policies that are essential for small capital.

By contrast, senators and representatives do not make the fundamental decisions about the organization or running of the corporate complex. They are, however, in a position to delay, block, or veto policies the corporate complex wishes to implement. As a result, corporate capital attempts to establish working relationships with those members of Congress who occupy strategic locations in the congressional hierarchy. As a representative or senator gets reelected, he or she becomes less dependent on local capital for campaign financing and more able to hinder or facilitate the passage of legislation favored by national corporate interests. The most obvious of these strategic locations that members of Congress with seniority come to occupy "include elective leadership posts, memberships on party policy (agenda) and steering (committee assignment) committees, committee chairmanships (or in the case of the minority, 'shadow' chairmanships), chairmanships of subcommittees, membership on more than two regular legislative committees, and membership on the Appropriations Committee."[32]

The relationship between corporate capital and influential members of Congress is reflected in campaign contributions. Committee chairmen in particular often attract money from those whose profits their committee's legislation might affect. Thus, for example, Congressman Wayne Aspinall, who was chairman of the House Interior Committee in 1970, received 79 percent of his $50,000 reelection campaign fund from outside his district. His

[31] Drew Pearson and Jack Anderson, *The Case Against Congress* (New York, 1968), p. 162.

[32] Nelson Polsby, *Congress and the Presidency* (Englewood Cliffs, N.J., 1964), pp. 38–39.

committee's actions significantly affect profit rates in the oil, mining, and timber industries.

> Aware of this, Kennecott Copper sent Aspinall nine separate checks in 1970; Humble Oil mailed seven checks from Texas; and Shell Oil, Martin Marietta, and American Metal Climax and Oil Shale Corporation also chipped in. From Washington, D.C., help came from lobbyists and executives of Union Oil, Atlantic Richfield, Dow Chemical, Burlington Northern Railroad, and the Southern tobacco industry. . . . The Southwest Forest Industries of Phoenix and the Western Wood Products Association of Portland, Oregon also sent funds.[33]

As a trucking lobbyist put it, after the industry had spent $30,000 to support campaigns of members of the Public Works and Rules committees who had jurisdiction over a pending bill to permit bigger trucks on interstate highways, "We do what we can for those on the committees who might help us. It's as simple as that."[34]

Perhaps the close connection between corporate interests and members of Congress in strategic locations, and the narrow nature of the substantive representation members provide, are most apparent in the area of military spending. The Pentagon budget is regularly approved with relatively little examination. Given the lack of pressure from the electorate in general, the most tangible publicly-funded project a representative can get for his or her district is a military installation or a defense contract for local firms. Hence the defense budget is characterized by a great deal of logrolling; it is implicitly understood that Representative A will not question defense spending in Representative B's district so long as the favor is reciprocated. Not surprisingly, the most vigorous advocates of military retrenchment come from areas with no military installations or defense contractors. Congressman Jamie Whitten, a Mississippi Democrat who chairs the House Appropriations Committee, Subcommittee on Defense, was candid on this point:

> I am convinced that defense is only one of the factors that enter into our determinations for defense spending. The others are pump priming, spreading the immediate benefits of defense spending, taking care of all services, giving military bases to include all sections. . . . There is no state in the Union, and hardly a district in a

[33] Green et al., p. 21.
[34] *Ibid.*, p. 231.

state which doesn't have defense spending, contracting, or a defense establishment.[35]

Quite often, members who occupy strategic positions engage in business activities in industries that benefit from their institutional position. One of the most important committees in the House is the Committee on Ways and Means. Its tax-writing powers include granting oil depletion allowances, drafting laws setting net income taxes paid by banks, and writing tax rules to help favored corporations. In 1975, ten of its thirty-seven members either owned bank stock or served as bank officers, and thirteen members owned holdings in energy-related industries, ranging from a few shares in Texaco stock to an oil well. Members of the House Armed Services Committee own stock in companies that are leading defense contractors. The chairman of the House Agriculture Committee earned over $17,000 in 1977 in honorariums from agricultural or food-processing organizations.[36] Many of the senators and representatives who are lawyers are attached to firms that represent clients in litigation before federal agencies.[37] During George Smathers' service in the Senate, clients of his law practice included Pan American Airlines, Standard Oil, and the Home Insurance Agency, a combination that aptly coincided with Smathers' membership on such committees as Finance, Small Business, Judiciary, and Joint Internal Revenue Taxation.[38]

Given the shift in the locus of national political power in this century from the Congress to the executive branch, most of the efforts of corporate interests to influence Congress are essentially *defensive*. As David Truman, a leading analyst of Congress, has noted, organized interest group activity does not seek to convince members of Congress to initiate new policies. Rather, most such activity, especially that of lobbyists in the corporate sector, is "dedicated to preventing any change in the existing order of things. Where there are groups whose claims involve a change, there are as likely to be others . . . vigorously defending the *status quo*."[39] After studying the relative success or failure of congressional

[35] Testimony before the Joint Economic Committee's Defense Procurement Sub-committee, January 29, 1960.
[36] *Chicago Tribune*, March 9, 1975, section 2, p. 8.
[37] The law stipulates that members of Congress may not collect legal fees in federal cases; their firms typically find legal dodges, such as creating two juridically separate firms, one listing the member, the other omitting his or her name from the roster of partners.
[38] Martin Tolchin and Susan Tolchin, *To the Victor* (New York, 1971), pp. 242–43.
[39] David Truman, *The Governmental Process* (New York, 1951), p. 353.

interest-group activity, he concluded that "the business corporation has been such a favored group in the United States . . . it
normally enjoys defensive advantages."

An important factor in accounting for corporate "veto power"
in Congress is the corporate lobby. The most influential corporate
lobbies—including those of the oil, armaments, tobacco, sugar,
and automobile industries—are well financed and staffed, often by
former members of Congress or members of the executive branch
who had worked with members of Congress. The American Petroleum Institute, the most powerful—but not the only—trade association, has an annual budget of more than $10 million and a
permanent Washington staff of over 200. Its Washington office has
been directed in the past decade by Frank Ikard, a Texas congressman from 1952 to 1961. This is a common pattern. Former
Senator Earle Clements of Kentucky was an influential tobacco
lobbyist in the 1960s; Harold Cooley, a former House Agriculture
Committee chairman, has served recently as a lobbyist for sugar
interests in Liberia and Thailand; and at least five active members
of the banking lobby in 1970 had served on the staff of the Senate
Banking and Currency Committee and a subcommittee on housing
and urban affairs.[40]

An atmosphere of easy, comradely interchange is developed
by lobbyists with members of Congress. Senators, representatives, and members of their staffs are routinely treated to favors by
lobbyists who have lavish expense accounts. A committee aide
said, "You begin to look forward to those three or four good
lunches a week with the lobbyists at the good restaurants, to the
$25 bottles of scotch, the football tickets, the occasional junkets,
and if you don't watch out, you get pulled into the lobbyist's frame
of reference." A former senator has explained the experience:

> The enticer does not generally pay money directly to the public
> representative. He tries instead, by a series of favors, to put the
> public official under such a feeling of personal obligation that the
> latter gradually loses his sense of mission to the public and comes to
> feel that his first loyalties are to his private benefactors and pat-
> rons.[41]

The effect of lobbying on a member of Congress is thus a subtle
and gradual process, with the result that the typical member is
often sincerely convinced that there is no direct causal connection
between these favors and his or her legislative actions.

[40] Green et al., pp. 44–45.
[41] *Ibid.*, p. 41.

Indeed, most members of Congress believe that lobbyists are indispensable to the legislative process. A Brookings Institution study argued that "because of the publicity given to early, blatantly improper attempts to influence legislators, the general public views with suspicion anyone classified as a lobbyist. The constructive services that are provided by today's professionals are often little known." A representative whose views were typical had this to say:

> A lot of people seem to think that lobbying is a bad thing. I think that is one misconception which still needs to be corrected as far as the general public is concerned. Lobbying is an essential part of representative government, and it needs to be encouraged and appreciated. Lobbyists are frequently a source of information. If they come to your offices and explain a program or factors contributing to the need for legislation, you get a better understanding of the problems and answers to them. If you have your independence, and I think we all do, they can teach you what an issue is all about, and you can make your own decision.[42]

But what this perspective fails to see is that lobbying activity systematically injects a powerful bias into the legislative system on behalf of those who command specialized information (such information is never neutral), staff, and money, and who ensnare representatives in a web of favors ranging from an early evening drink to substantial campaign contributions.

But the success of the corporate sector in developing a built-in veto over congressional action is not merely the result of weak constituency pressures, campaign contributions, or effective lobbying. Congress is not merely a sounding board or "passive registering device . . . for the demands of organized political interest groups."[43] As an institution, Congress has an autonomy and life of its own. Hence we turn to an examination of Congress as an institution and of the ways in which its institutional life affects the character of congressional representation.

Limitations and Controls on Effective Action

The last criterion of representation is effectiveness, a measure of how the procedures and institutional life of representative bodies affect both the orientations of the representatives and their capacity to achieve their aims. Four features of the institutional life of

---

[42] Charles Clapp, *The Congressman* (New York, 1964), pp. 183, 184.
[43] Truman, p. 350.

Congress are especially important: its clublike atmosphere, the norm of professionalism, the committee structure, and the nature of the legislative hurdles a bill must leap before it can become a law.

We have seen earlier how the social backgrounds of members of Congress separate them from direct contact with and understanding of the relatively subordinate and how the general disinterest of constituents creates a vacuum that is filled by the member's own predispositions, reelection needs, and an elaborate network of favored relationships with powerful interests. Congress as an institution further isolates representatives from the general public by providing a comfortable clublike setting for the interaction of members with each other and with noncongressional political participants.

Like most clubs, Congress has an elaborate set of norms to regulate the interpersonal behavior of its members. Collectively, these norms dampen conflict among members, restrict their scope of action, and reinforce their general parochialism.

In December 1956, newly elected Senator Joseph Clark of Pennsylvania had lunch with an old friend, Senator Hubert Humphrey. Clark reports that he asked Humphrey, "Tell me how to behave when I get to the Senate."

> He did—for an hour and a half. I left the luncheon I hope a wiser man, as well briefed as a neophyte seeking admission to a new order can be. In essence he said, "Keep your mouth shut and your eyes open. It's a friendly, courteous place. You will have no trouble getting along. . . . You will clash on the filibuster rule with Dick Russell and the Southerners as soon as you take the oath of office. Don't let your ideology embitter your personal relationships. It won't if you behave with maturity. . . . And above all keep your mouth shut for awhile." [44]

This advice, given a quarter century ago, summarized some of the most important unwritten rules of the Senate at that time: members were expected to work at their legislative tasks, to concentrate attention on a specialized set of matters connected to his or her constituency or committee assignment, to be courteous and avoid personal conflicts, to help colleagues when possible and to keep bargains, and to serve a period of apprenticeship. [45] All but the last of these norms still operate today (although the norm of

---

[44] Joseph Clark, *Congress: The Sapless Branch* (New York, 1964), p. 2.
[45] Donald Matthews, *U.S. Senators and Their World* (New York, 1960).

specialization has less of a hold on members than in the past). At present, "not only do junior members not want or feel the need of an apprenticeship, but also the senior members do not expect them to do so."[46] With this exception, Senator Humphrey's advice to Senator Clark would still hold.

In addition, members of Congress take pride in their institution and are expected to defend it against detractors. Members often feel that whatever differences they have are largely internal matters; to the outside world they present a largely united front. In this enclosed world, those who raise nettlesome issues do so at the cost of influence, friendship, and esteem. When Congressman Michael Harrington revealed CIA activity in Chile in 1974, for example, many members thought "he had acted inappropriately in violating committee's rules in making the information public."[47]

Institutional arrangements are not neutral. As political scientists Wallace Sayre and Herbert Kaufman indicated, procedural matters "are not merely abstract exercises in political architecture and processes. The kinds of decisions that emerge are directly related to the participants favored or disadvantaged by such rules."[48]

The most important congressional procedures are committee organization and seniority. Almost a century ago, Woodrow Wilson observed that "Congress, in its Committee rooms, is Congress at work."[49] The same observation could be made today. Although there were only 36 House, 29 Senate, and 4 joint committees in 1977–78, there were 263 subcommittees, a number that indicates the extent to which congressional work is specialized and decentralized.[50]

Each party handles its members' assignments to committees. The Republicans in the Senate and the House have a Committee on Committees, with an elected chairman. Senate Democrats use a nineteen-member Steering Committee, chaired by the majority leader. House Democrats' assignments are made by the members

[46] Norman J. Ornstein, Robert L. Peabody, and David Rohde, "The Changing Senate, From the 1950's to the 1970's," in Lawrence C. Dodd and Bruce I. Oppenheimer, eds., *Congress Reconsidered* (New York, 1977), p. 8.

[47] Philip Brenner, "Notes," Workshop on 'Congress and U.S. Foreign Policy,' Conference on the United States, U.S. Foreign Policy, and Latin American and Caribbean Regimes, March 1978.

[48] Wallace Sayre and Herbert Kaufman, *Governing New York City* (New York, 1965), p. 106.

[49] Woodrow Wilson, *Congressional Government* (New York, 1956), p. 83.

[50] *Congressional Quarterly*, April 30, 1977, pp. 4–50.

of the Democratic Steering Committee. The committee assignments made by these bodies are critical to their colleagues'
careers. If they are to make a substantive impact or "deliver the
goods" in their districts, it is likely to be through their committee
work. Although junior members are given important assignments
more frequently today than in the past, they still must compete
with more senior members for the choice assignments. As a result,
in spite of the fact that the waiting period to join the leading
committees has been reduced, it is unusual for freshmen to get
placed on them (the three most significant are the House Ways and
Means Committee and the Senate Finance Committee, which have
jurisdiction over the country's tax structure, and the House Appropriations Committee, which oversees the federal budget and is
more important than its Senate counterpart). As an experienced
representative put it, "It would be too risky to put on a person
whose views and nature the leadership has no opportunity to
assess."[51] Those who show themselves to be nonconformists are
screened out in favor of members who have proved that they will
act in accordance with prevailing standards of behavior.

Committees are the places where legislation is shaped, promoted, or buried. In his study of the Senate, Donald Matthews
found that if a proposal was supported by over 80 percent of the
members of the relevant committee, it passed on the floor every
time; if from 60 to 79 percent supported the bill in committee, it
passed 90 percent of the time. In accordance with the norms of
reciprocity and courtesy, most legislators will follow the decision
of the committees unless they have a basic reason to doubt it. For
almost all legislation, the committee actions are the decisive factor.

Congressional committees work on specialized subject areas,
such as labor, education, defense, and agriculture. In theory, they
are major battlegrounds where different interests compete in the
making of public policy. Individuals and groups who are affected
by proposed legislation are usually granted the chance in public
hearings to argue their positions, transmit information, and attempt to generate congressional and public support for their point
of view. In practice, the routine operation of congressional committees *limits* controversy and buttresses prevailing patterns of
dominance in the following ways.[52]

[51] Green et al., p. 55.
[52] Philip Brenner, "Committee Conflict in the Congressional Arena," *The Annals*
411 (January 1974): 98–100.

Limited participation and close interaction   The number of people who work on bills in congressional committees is small. Much of the day-to-day work is accomplished in subcommittees of about five legislators. The largest committees are those dealing with appropriations. Yet even their membership totals only 13 percent of the House and 26 percent of the Senate. "Limited participation in a conflict," political scientist Philip Brenner observes, "engenders quick resolution because there are fewer positions to reconcile." Further limiting the range of options explored is the fact that small committees engender close interaction and friendships.

> Over many years members do come to see each other as friends with common problems, rather than as representatives of a position. . . . Close interaction thus encourages members to avoid intense conflict in order to maintain cordial relations with their "friends." It further discourages the congressman who might fight for a position which is antagonistic to prevailing interests from continuing his fight, because in doing so he tends to alienate himself from the people with whom he works closely.[53]

Thus, committees duplicate the clublike atmosphere of Congress as a whole and take on an integrated life of their own that often cuts across party lines. Richard Fenno's study of the House Appropriations Committee, for example, found a deeply rooted committee consensus on goals. Members were recruited to produce "a group of individuals with an orientation especially conducive to Committee integration. . . . Key selectors speak of wanting, for the Appropriations Committee, 'the kind of man you can deal with,' or 'a fellow who is well-balanced and won't go off half-cocked on things.' "[54]

Secrecy   Given the wide range of specialization and the sheer number of subcommittees, they cannot adequately be covered by the press. Moreover, much committee work is held in secret. In the Senate in 1968, according to the *Congressional Quarterly Almanac*, 93 percent of the hearings of the Rules and Administration Committee were held behind closed doors; 46 percent of the Foreign Relations Committee meetings; 30 percent of the Public Works Committee sessions; 67 percent of the Armed Services Committee hearings; and 47 percent of the hearings of the Labor

[53] *Ibid.*, p. 99.
[54] Richard Fenno, Jr., "The Appropriations Committee as a Political System," in Robert Peabody and Nelson Polsby, eds., *New Perspectives on the House of Representatives* (Chicago, 1963), p. 85.

and Public Welfare Committee. In the House, *all* of the Appropriations Committee hearings were conducted in secret. The overall figure for committee hearings held in secret was 43 percent.[55] Although the 1970 Legislative Reorganization Act required that all committee sessions be opened to the public unless a majority of the committee voted for a closed session, approximately 30 percent are still secret. As a consequence, not only is the general public excluded, but most members of Congress must depend on the judgment of the members of the relevant committee. When a bill reaches the Senate and the House for debate, only the committee members have a detailed acquaintance with the legislation, and they usually remain in control of the floor debate.

Seniority   Power within the committee system is determined by seniority. The chairmanship of a committee is allocated traditionally, though no longer automatically, to the member of the majority party who has served longest on the committee, thereby preventing a potential cause of conflict. Further, as Philip Brenner notes, seniority procedures "take away a focal point for outsiders [who] . . . would be encouraged to pressure members, and for candidates [who] might be 'encouraged' to campaign on the basis of their positions on upcoming issues."[56]

The seniority system puts a premium on specialization. It is widely agreed that effective legislators are those who focus their energy only on matters that either affect their districts directly or come before their committees. The most senior people on the committees have been there a long time. They have been enmeshed in a mutually beneficial relationship with special-interest groups for decades; and they tend to identify with and share the defensive interests of the most powerful lobbies. As a result, the committee structure based on seniority is substantively biased for the status quo and against fundamental change.

The committee-agency nexus   We saw earlier in this volume how corporate capitalism and the executive branch of the federal government have formed the relationship we call the corporate complex. Congress is at the periphery of this complex. Congressional committees, however, pose the key legislative hurdle for corporate-complex policies. Committees can oversee the practices of government agencies and regulatory commissions, fail to pass

[55] *Congressional Quarterly Almanac* (Washington, 1968), pp. 798–99.
[56] Brenner, p. 100.

legislation initiated by the executive branch, and modify the president's proposed budget.

These checks are not routinely applied. Individual standing committees have fashioned close and stable relationships with their companion executive agencies. The Department of Agriculture and the agriculture committees, the Pentagon and armed services committees, and the Department of Labor and the education and labor committees have become mutually supportive. The agencies are attentive to the wishes of the committees that formally supervise them, and within Congress the agencies are regarded as the substantive property of the relevant committees.

The support of powerful corporate-sector interest groups for members of Congress in strategic locations and the close interaction, secrecy, and seniority system of the committees facilitate the development of an enduring committee-agency nexus that functions in the interests of the corporate complex. Most issues "tend to be decided in accord with agreements reached in close cooperation between key members of Congress (usually senior committee and subcommittee members), key representatives of interest groups, and key bureaucrats."[57] In this way, Congress, though not an integral part of the corporate complex, becomes its predictable ally.

Consider the operation of what political scientist Gordon Adams calls "the military subgovernment," consisting of the Pentagon, defense contractors, and the military committees in Congress. "The natural congressional inclination to delegate authority for expenditure review to subunits," he writes, "created a powerful committee that came to consider the military as its client. Committee hearings provided a forum insulated from outside criticism of military assumptions about foreign policy and from competing social programs." As a result, Congress has largely abdicated its responsibility to review the Pentagon budget. Only very rarely do executive-branch defense recommendations get cut.[58]

The committee-agency nexus has been mitigated to a minor degree by the Budget and Impoundment Control Act of 1974, which established new Budget Committees in each chamber. These new committees specify target ceilings for fourteen categories of federal spending by May 15 of each year. All spending

[57] Lowi and Ripley, p. 161.
[58] Gordon M. Adams, "Disarming the Military Subgovernment," *Harvard Journal on Legislation* 14 (April 1977): 461.

bills must be approved by the appropriations committees by Labor Day, and both houses must reconcile their spending differences by September 25. Programs authorized by the Senate and House in specific appropriations bills are considered in relationship to each other, thus giving the Congress the means to shape priorities as a whole. Although this new procedure has imposed some discipline on spending, and in isolated instances has forced a rollback of recommendations by appropriations committees, it is important to realize that the new procedure was overlaid on the old, more entrenched committee system. The Budget Committees, as general committees, usually are no match for the specialized substantive committees and their staffs.[59]

For a bill to become a law, it must pass through a labyrinth of procedural hurdles. The nature of this legislative course reinforces the status-quo orientation of most representatives.

Although a bill must be formally introduced by a representative or senator, major legislation is rarely the work of an individual or even initiated in the Congress. Proposals that lack presidential support usually are doomed. Most major bills are drafted in the executive agencies and are put on the president's legislative program, which becomes the basic legislative agenda. Major legislation is almost always introduced by a leading member, often the chairman, of the standing committee to which the bill is referred. Once the bill is introduced, its fate is largely in the hands of senior committee members, who guard their committee's prerogatives.

Committee procedures in the Senate and the House are essentially similar. Most of the bills referred to committees are never taken up. After they have been introduced on the floor—often by representatives seeking to build political capital with their constituency—they die a quick death. Public hearings are held on the majority of bills that survive. At their conclusion, the real legislative work begins. The committee goes into closed executive session, where the bill is read line by line. This is called the mark-up stage. At this critical point, the bill is amended, rewritten, or, if no version can be worked out that is acceptable to the majority of the committee, the legislative process ends and the proposal dies. The relatively few bills that emerge successfully from this procedure have the support of a large majority of committee members and are the product of the closed committee process that puts a premium on interpersonal relationships and a broad

[59] Louis Fisher, "Congressional Budget Reform," in *ibid.*; John Ellwood and James Thurber, "The New Congressional Budget Process," in Dodd and Oppenheimer.

substantive consensus. Thus, controversial proposals rarely survive.

Once a bill is passed by the relevant committee in the House or the Senate, it is placed on the chamber's calendar. In the Senate, major bills are usually taken up for consideration from the calendar by the majority leader. In the House, bills must be reported out by the Rules Committee, which schedules House business, before they can reach the floor. As one of the more traditionally conservative committees, the Rules Committee has been a major barrier to the consideration of legislation that challenges patterns of dominance.

By now, before the legislation is debated on the Senate and House floors, the bill's substance and possibilities for passage have largely been determined. Though the floor debates seem to the observer to be the most important phase of the legislative process, in fact, the debates rarely influence any votes.

When the House Rules Committee schedules debate on legislation, the representatives meet as a Committee of the Whole House (identical to the membership of the House of Representatives) to consider the bill and proposed amendments. At this stage, no recorded votes are taken, debating procedures are relaxed, and a quorum of only 100, instead of the usual 218, is required for business. Like the mark-up, this procedure takes place behind closed doors. The Committee of the Whole then reports the bill to the House with any new amendments that have been added. These changes may be voted on again. Then the entire bill as amended is put to a vote.

By contrast to the House, where the Rules Committee usually sets time limits to the floor discussion, debate in the Senate is unlimited. More frequently than not, the majority leader, in agreement with the minority leader, fixes time limits for debate. But this schedule requires unanimous consent. Should one senator object, debate continues.

The Senate provision for unlimited debate can lead to a filibuster, in which one or a group of senators attempt to defeat a measure by holding the floor for hours, or even days, and thus preventing the bill from coming to a vote. If they succeed in holding up Senate business for a long period, the bill is usually dropped. This tactic has been used successfully in the past, principally by Southerners opposed to civil rights legislation. Cloture, a vote to limit debate, needs support by three-fifths of those voting, not just a majority. Many senators who support a bill are reluctant to vote for cloture for fear of weakening a device that they might wish to use in the future. Like the House Rules Committee barrier, the filibuster is another device used to quash controversial legislation.

If a bill is one of the lucky few to be approved by both the House and Senate, it has still not become law. If, as in most cases, there are differences between the versions passed by the House and the Senate, the bills are sent to a conference committee charged to iron out the discrepancies. Usually composed of five or six members from each house, these *ad hoc* bodies may alter provisions, insert new amendments, or even write a whole new bill.

The members, or managers, of these committees are not selected at random from the House and Senate. Rather, the conference committee's membership is chosen on the recommendation of the chairman of the standing committee that had jurisdiction over the bill in the first place. Normally, the chairman proposes senior members from his or her own committee. In this way, the legislative process comes full circle, as the same senior committee specialists who marked-up the bill in private once again have a critical private task—producing the final legislation.

Conference committee reports are the privileged business of each house, since other floor business must be put aside to consider the reports. They may be approved, voted down, or returned to the conference committee. Typically, they are approved, and the bill, now passed in identical form by the Senate and House of Representatives, goes to the president for his approval or veto. Should he sign the bill, it becomes law; should he veto, a vote of two-thirds of the House and Senate is needed to override the president's action and pass the bill into law.

Trends and Prospects

No institution is a "constant." Buffeted by internal and external pressures, institutions change, often in incoherent and partially contradictory ways. Such has been the case for Congress in the 1970s. This period has been one of major alterations in the way Congress conducts its business. These shifts, however, do not all point in one direction; yet, overall, a general trend may be discerned.

Some reforms have made Congress more of a centralized legislature and have highlighted the role of the two political parties.

During the Nixon presidency, Democrats in Congress sought to develop the means to assert their influence against the Republican administration. Moves to increase the power of the Speaker of the House was one result. In 1973, the Speaker was placed on the Committee on Committees, thus giving him a major role in the selection of committee members and chairmen. In the same year, a new Steering and Policy Committee was founded. Its members included the Speaker, the chairman of the party caucus, the majority whip, the chief deputy whip, the three deputy whips, four members selected by the Speaker, and twelve representatives elected by regional party caucuses. This committee became the principal instrument of shaping party policy. Since it was chaired by the Speaker and its membership was determined principally by him, it augmented his abilities to shape the activities of Democrats in important ways. Further, in 1974, this committee was given the responsibilities of the Committee on Committees. And in that year, the Speaker was given new control over the scheduling of legislative business by the power to appoint the chair and the Democratic members of the House Rules Committee, which oversees such scheduling. Finally, the prerogatives of the Speaker were increased by more staff being added to the office of the whip, whose job it is to try to impose party discipline on members. In the Senate, under majority leaders Mansfield and Byrd, the Democratic Conference has become a significant forum for Democrats, and the place where many reforms concerning the filibuster (reducing the number required to break one from two-thirds to three-fifths of voting members), open committee hearings, and staffing have been initiated.

But these centralizing trends concerning the leadership and party life of each house have been crosscut by even more powerful trends of decentralization. The most important of these developments has been the dramatic increase in the size of congressional staffs and in the number and scope of subcommittees. The Senate authorizes each member to hire an aide to work full time on each committee assignment held by that senator. In the House, the majority- and minority-party staffs on each committee serve all the committee members from their party. In 1972 the Senate had 3,339 staff committee aides working for it; in the House, there were 6,063. By 1976, the 1972 total of 9,402 had grown to 13,272 staff members.[60] This growth in numbers has allowed each member of

[60] *Time*, January 23, 1978, pp. 14–15.

the Senate and House to be more autonomous, as he or she develops sources of expertise and service independently of the parties, the leadership, and the institution as a whole.

This autonomy has been augmented by the growth of the subcommittee structure. The number of subcommittees has nearly doubled in the past quarter century. In 1971 a committee of the Democratic Caucus on reform, chaired by Representative Julia Butler Hansen, limited subcommittee chairs to one per member and specified that each subcommittee chair could select a staff member for the group. These changes not only made more chairs available to more representatives, but they added to subcommittee activity. "It provided sixteen members with new policy forums" and "it recognized that subcommittees would remain ineffective without minimal staff support."[61]

The next round of reform of the Hansen Committee, in 1973, was even more important. The "Subcommittee Bill of Rights" gave subcommittees a budget, an enlarged staff, clear jurisdiction over specific areas of legislation, and other incentives for subcommittee chairs to be active in this role. Subsequent Hansen reforms reinforced this "Bill of Rights" by requiring all committees with more than fifteen members to have at least four subcommittees. The main concomitant of this rise in the importance of subcommittees and their chairs has been a matching decline in the power of committee chairmen. These fragmenting trends have been accompanied by provisions to make the legislative process more open by requiring roll-call votes in committee in many cases, by making committee hearings—and even conference committee sessions—open to the press and public, and by modifying the previously automatic operation of seniority.

On balance, these recent changes have had the following principal effects. They have made the job of a member of Congress—even a junior member—more desirable. They have given members a larger "piece of the action." They have allowed members to allocate more staff to district offices and to service constituents from Washington. They have made it more likely that a member will serve on a committee or a subcommittee that relates to constituency interests directly. And they have provided more forums for the construction of cooperative ties between agencies, relevant industries, and congressional committees and subcom-

---

[61] Dodd and Oppenheimer, p. 35. Also see, Philip Brenner, "Congressional Reform," *Harvard Journal of Legislation* 14 (April 1977).

mittees. Overall, they have reinforced localism and nonprogrammatic activities, and have provided for a plurality of access points by organized interests, including bureaucrats, to the Congress. The outcome is a legislature of individual "political businesspeople" better informed and more capable in many ways than members in the past, but less concerned with coherent policy formulations and less disciplined by party organizations and programs. Speaker "Tip" O'Neill summarized the new world of the Congress this way:

> Congressmen were much different fifteen to twenty years ago. . . . [Today] they're *reformers* who demand openness and everything out there glaring in the sun. The new Republicans are the same as the Democrats on this. A few years back, any new congressman who got a phone call from the president just couldn't believe it. Now it means nothing anymore. Years back a congressman had to make an appointment to see Speaker Sam Rayburn. Now he sticks his head in my door and says, 'You got a minute, Tip?' I try to help them all, see all the hometown delegations they bring through and then when I ask them to give me a vote on the consumer protection bill, they say, 'Gee, Tip, I can't now. But if you need a vote at the end, I'll be there.' But you can't find them at the end. They're all independent now. . . . The organizations have fallen apart.[62]

---

[62] Nick Thimmesch, "Portrait of the Speaker as a Party Man," *New York*, February 20, 1978, p. 10.

11

the quality of justice

The American justice system of the police, prisons, and courts is the largest in the world. Federal spending on criminal justice alone increased seven times between 1967 and 1977. All levels of government spend approximately $20 billion each year on police, courts, and prisons. Well over 1 million Americans are employed by the justice system. Jails run by local governments alone confine at least 1.5 million Americans each year. Roughly one of every two hundred citizens in the country's largest cities is a police officer or court officer. More than 450,000 Americans are lawyers.[1] Each state has dozens of different kinds of courts that conduct trials, hear lawsuits, and provide chances to appeal decisions. Federal courts also hear both criminal and civil cases. What tasks does this immense justice system perform? How does it manage these activities? On behalf of which interests?

THE DEVELOPMENT OF FORMAL LEGALISM

Formally, the justice system is a nonpolitical system of written laws, legal procedures, and institutions that are the means of

[1] National Criminal Justice Information and Statistics Service, *Expenditure and Employment Data for the Criminal Justice System* (Washington, D.C., 1976); *Time*, April 10, 1978, pp. 56–76.

securing justice for all Americans. In appearances, trappings, and stated principles and procedures, the justice system is committed to upholding the equality of all citizens before the law. Police officers wear uniforms and judges robes to signify that they are performing their duties in the interest of justice, not for their personal gain. Police officers are protected from partisan political pressures by civil service regulations; judges, by long tenures of office. And all participants in the courtroom process are bound by deference to the authority of the law.

The development of a formally nonpolitical legal system was intimately bound up with the development of capitalism in Western Europe. The assertion of parliamentary prerogatives in England after 1688 and the toppling of the Old Regime by the French Revolution of 1789 paved the way for the elaboration of modern legal codes and institutions that adhered to predictable, publicly articulated sets of regulations and procedures. The new capitalist enterprises in these countries were not based on the traditional authority of the lord-serf relationship, and they needed the new legal systems to legitimize their existence and to provide a calculable context within which capitalists could make contracts and exchange goods for money. The law thus provided capitalist enterprises with the legal stability and security they required.

America's legal system, from the colonial period to the present, has had its roots in British law. After the American Revolution, however, key legal questions remained unresolved, the most important being the relationship between the individual states and the national government. The Articles of Confederation, the country's first constitution that went into effect in 1781, allowed each state to retain "its sovereignty, freedom and independence" and declared that every power not "expressly delegated" to the national government was reserved to the states. In the national Congress, each state had one vote.

The new national government could neither tax nor regulate commerce. As a result, it failed to prevent costly economic disputes between states and provide the kind of stable climate necessary for economic development. The Constitutional Convention of 1787 was largely the result of the dissatisfaction of financial and commercial groups with existing legal arrangements.

The Founding Fathers drafted a Constitution that provided for truly revolutionary democratic procedures and liberties. But they also acted to protect their economic interests. Many provisions of the Constitution were drafted to protect property rights. By creating a national government that had powers of taxation, sole control over a national monetary system, and the right to regulate interstate and foreign commerce, the Constitution provided an overarching legal framework that facilitated the growth of American capitalism in the nineteenth and twentieth centuries.

American law was transformed in the period from the Revolution to the Civil War. The law became increasingly formal in appearance as it simultaneously facilitated economic growth and development. The most basic change was what legal scholar Morton Horwitz calls "the emergence of an instrumental conception of law." In the late eighteenth-century republic, law was still conceived of as a set of principles that were eternal, "expressed in custom and derived from natural law." The law was primarily a guide to achieve justice in individual cases. By the Civil War, this conception had been eroded. Instead, the law came to be seen as an instrument to promote desirable policies and social ends, most notably those of the growth of the market and rapid industrial development.[2]

These changes, Horwitz shows, entailed basic alterations in conceptions of property and contract. Before the nineteenth century, the law recognized a static, basically rural, understanding of property that entitled its owner to undisturbed enjoyment. As the tempo of economic growth altered after the turn of the century, property came to be seen in more instrumental terms that stressed the virtues of productive use and development. In the case of *Palmer* v. *Mulligan* (1805), the New York State Supreme Court reversed traditional common-law understandings by holding that a landowner could obstruct the flow of water downstream in the interest of supplying a mill on his property. This obstruction, of course, hurt others downstream, but in this case and in subsequent cases the courts held that the possession of property implies above all the right to develop it for business purposes. Indeed, throughout the period of early industrialization, the common law was often used to give property-owners protection from legal liabilities when they undertook programs of economic development.[3]

The early nineteenth century also witnessed basic changes in the law of contracts, changes that were basic to the development of

---

[2] Morton J. Horwitz, *The Transformation of American Law, 1780–1860* (Cambridge, Mass., 1977), chapter 1.
[3] *Ibid.*, chapter 2.

a modern capitalist economy. Before this period, judges had regularly held that the inherent fairness, or justice, of a contract determined its legality. Contracts were void when they were substantively inequitable. This traditional practice was replaced by the "will theory of contract," which held that the validity of contracts depended not on their equity but on the willingness of the parties to make the contract.[4]

This shift prepared the way for the coexistence of formal justice and substantive inequalities. Unlike feudal relationships, which tied serfs to particular fiefs, capitalist relationships are contractual. Workers sell their labor for a wage to those who contract to buy it. This exchange relationship is an exchange among legal equals: wages for work. Yet, of course, these legal equals are not substantively equal. But the premise of a contract now was that of equal bargaining power among the parties. Since the only measure of justice was the contractual agreement between the parties—between unequals assumed to be equal—"the law had come simply to ratify those forms of inequality that the market system produced. . . . Law, once conceived of as protective, regulative, paternalistic, and, above all, a paramount expression of the moral sense of the community, had come to be thought of as facilitative of individual desires and as simply reflective of the existing organization of economic and political power."[5]

Ever since the mid-nineteenth century, the contrast between formal legal equality and substantive inequality has been mirrored in the routine operation of the American justice system. The law is formal and technical. It has no official political or economic ends or goals. Once understandings of property and contract had been "modernized" to function in harmony with the new market economy, the law certified as "legal," and by implication just and fair, the rules and patterns of the new industrial capitalism. While serving these interests, the justice system acts in a way that is based on an objective, apolitical, and professional conception of the law. The distributive and political functions of law are thus masked.

Legal formalism, however, is not simply a hidden system of domination. For formal legal equality has also considerably widened the average citizen's freedom by granting and protecting basic rights, including free speech, freedom from unreasonable search

---

[4] *Ibid.*, chapter 6.
[5] *Ibid.*, pp. 209–10.

and seizure, and religious choice. Even political elites may be penalized for violating the norms and procedures of the justice system—at least, as in the case of Watergate, when the violations are so flagrant as to arouse public indignation. Thus the justice system does not simply protect the social order; it also sets a formal framework of rights and procedures that gives citizens tangible resources and acts to restrain the power of dominant authorities. The justice system routinely upholds the equality and rights of citizens as it perpetuates inequalities. It enlarges and protects freedom at the same time that it acts as an instrument of social control.

THE ROLE AND POWERS OF THE SUPREME COURT

The United States Supreme Court bestrides the entire justice system. It is the court of last resort; there is none higher. Indeed it is the only court mentioned in the Constitution: "The Judicial power of the United States shall be vested in one Supreme Court, and in such inferior courts as the Congress may from time to time ordain and establish."

Historically, the Supreme Court has performed four basic functions:

First, with the exception of transitional periods like the mid-nineteenth century and the 1930s, the Court almost without fail has supported the policies of the dominant national, as opposed to regional, interests of the time.

Second, the Court has provided an arena where conflicts can be settled between those in positions of economic and political power: between unions and corporations, state and federal governments, Congress and the executive branch. The Court thus provides an extrapolitical means of resolving intraelite conflicts.

The third function of the Supreme Court has been to issue decisions that may be too difficult or unpopular for the president or Congress to take. The May 1954 *Brown* v. *Board of Education* decision, which held segregation in public schools unconstitutional, was fundamental in challenging the quasi-feudal, pre-capitalist pattern of social relations in the South. But at the time, neither the president nor Congress would have been prepared to take this step because of the electoral perils involved. Thus, through the Court, elites can satisfy some of the needs and demands of subordinates without taking responsibility for these actions.

Fourth, the Court, more than any other part of the justice system, has acted to protect and extend the system's formal legal protections. Hence the Supreme Court has been the pivotal arena for the expansion of the rights of criminal defendants and the protection of civil liberties and civil rights. In this respect, the Court has at least partial institutional autonomy, since it makes these decisions according to the logic of formal legal justice, often over the opposition of important members of the corporate and political elite. Let us examine how the Court has carried out these four functions.

The United States has a dual court system. Both the states and the federal government maintain trial courts. State courts far outnumber federal courts: there are only eighty-nine federal district courts for the entire country (with 333 federal district court judges in all), but there are thousands of state courts, reaching into every governmental jurisdiction. Federal courts hear criminal matters that concern federal law; they hear noncriminal, or civil, matters that involve either citizens of more than one state or complaints filed by the federal government. State courts hear the rest.

Today, both state and federal courts have their own appeals procedures. Decisions of city, county, and state trial courts may be appealed to state appellate courts; decisions of United States district courts may be appealed to one of eleven federal courts of appeal, and then to the Supreme Court. In a few cases, decisions of district courts may be appealed directly to the Supreme Court.

This dual structure dates only from 1891. For the first century of American independence, the basic structure of the federal courts was a subject of struggle between competing regional and national interests. By mentioning only the Supreme Court, the Constitution left two basic issues unresolved: "(1) Should lower federal courts be created at all, or should adjudication of claims of a federal nature be adjudicated in the first instance by state courts? and (2) if lower federal courts were created, what limitations should Congress place over their jurisdiction?"[6]

The Judiciary Act of 1789 represented a compromise between

[6] Richard Richardson and Kenneth Vines, *The Politics of Federal Courts* (Boston, 1970), p. 19.

those who saw federal courts as a threat to state interests and those who viewed a system of state courts as inevitably parochial, and thus unable to dispense justice fairly to out-of-state citizens. The act established lower federal courts, but limited them to a state focus: their jurisdictions were drawn along state lines, the federal district judge was required to be a resident of his district, and the major task of the new lower federal courts was the preparation of materials for Supreme Court justices who traveled to the localities to hear cases.

Institutional federal supremacy was finally established with the creation of a federal court of appeals in 1891. The new court detached the appeals procedure from the pressures of the states and districts, diminished the possibilities of interpretations of the law varying too widely from area to area, and freed the Supreme Court from routine duties so that it could concentrate on more substantive matters.

The Supreme Court caps the dual court system, whose basic organization has remained virtually unchanged since 1891. The Court receives the vast majority of its cases from the federal district and appellate courts and from the state courts. Whereas review of lower federal court decisions has been widely accepted as logical and necessary, the Court's power to review state court decisions, as we shall see, has been the source of much dispute.

In addition, in a very small number of cases involving foreign diplomats or a state as a party, the Court has original jurisdiction and gets the cases directly. Though often ignored by students of the Supreme Court, these cases are usually extremely important and politically controversial. Recent examples have included disputes between the federal government and California, Louisiana, Texas, and Florida concerning title to rich oil deposits just off the coast; and *South Carolina* v. *Katzenbach* (1966), in which the Court sustained the constitutionality of the 1965 Voting Rights Act, whose purpose was to guarantee Southern blacks the right to vote in the face of restrictive state practices.

Many more cases are filed with the Court each year than it has time or inclination to hear. Hence the Court carefully chooses which cases to hear, following principles expressed by Justice Fred Vinson in 1949:

> The Supreme Court is not, and never has been, primarily concerned with the correction of errors in lower court decisions. In almost all cases within the Court's appellate jurisdiction, the petitioner has

already received an appellate review of his case. . . . The function of the Supreme Court is, therefore, to resolve conflicts of opinion on federal questions that have arisen among lower courts, to pass upon questions of wide import under the Constitution, laws and treaties of the United States, and to exercise supervisory power over lower federal courts. If we took every case in which an interesting legal question is raised, or our *prima facie* impression is that the decision below is erroneous, we could not fill the Constitutional and statutory responsibilities placed upon the Court. To remain effective, *the Supreme Court must continue to decide only those cases which present questions whose resolution will have immediate importance far beyond the particular facts and parties involved.*[7]

Supreme Court decisions have frequently been the result of legal battles that mirrored the basic cleavages between different economic and political interests expressed in different periods of American history. Broadly, the Court has passed through three ideological periods: until the Civil War it was preeminently concerned with protecting national economic and political interests at the expense of state and regional interests (there were important countercurrents within the Court to be sure). It advanced the legal doctrines of national supremacy, judicial power, and the protection of an emerging market system. After a period of decline, before and after the Civil War, the Court, in the late nineteenth century to the New Deal of the 1930s promoted the interests of industrial capitalism, and validated the largely, but not exclusively, laissez-faire economic programs of the Republican party, which governed for all but eight of these years. From the New Deal, especially after 1937, to the present, the Court has lent support and legitimacy to the corporate complex, and has taken decisions in the areas of civil rights and liberties that could not have been taken easily by the president or Congress.

The Marshall Court: Two Landmark Decisions

Up to the Civil War, the basic issues to confront the Court concerned the scope of national, as opposed to state, powers. The earliest broad cleavage in the country was that between the largely Southern and Western agrarian, planter, and small landowning interests in the Republican party led by Thomas Jefferson; and the

---

[7] Fred Vinson, "Work of the Federal Courts," *Supreme Court Reporter*, 1949, cited in Emmette S. Redford et al., *Politics and Government in the United States* (New York, 1968), p. 474. Emphasis added.

largely Northern manufacturing, finance, and mercantile interests who dominated the Federalist party led by Alexander Hamilton. Two key decisions taken by the Supreme Court in this period under the leadership of Chief Justice John Marshall (who served from 1801 to 1835) established the national supremacy of the federal government and the principle of judicial review by the Supreme Court of acts of Congress. Each marked the triumph of national, industrial interests over agrarian, local interests.

In 1791, the Congress established a United States Bank. The issue found Hamilton and Jefferson sharply divided. Hamilton argued that the bank was necessary for the national fiscal well-being of the country and that the authorization of the bank was constitutional because Congress had the power "to make all laws necessary and proper for carrying into execution" the powers of the national government (Article I, Section 8). Jefferson, who hoped America's future would be one of a small landowning agrarian democracy, opposed the bank. He argued that Congress did not have the power to establish a national bank: Congress had the right to pass only those laws that were *indispensably* necessary to carry out governmental powers. By passing the bank bill, the Federalist-dominated Congress opted for the more liberal interpretation of its powers.

The issue came to the Supreme Court in 1819, after the state of Maryland had taxed the bank and the bank had refused to pay. In a far-reaching decision in the case of *McCulloch* v. *Maryland*, the Court supported the bank. "Let the end be legitimate, let it be within the scope of the Constitution," Marshall wrote, "and all means which are appropriate, which are plainly adapted to that end, which are not prohibited, but consist within the letter and spirit of the Constitution, are Constitutional."

The decision not only supported Hamilton's broad reading of the "implied powers" clause of the Constitution but it made clear that where state and national laws conflicted, the state law would be declared unconstitutional by the Court. The Court has never wavered from this principle since, but it has been a recurring point of controversy as many state regulations and programs, including provisions for racial segregation, have been struck down.

Earlier, in the case of *Marbury* v. *Madison* (1803), the Marshall Court first asserted the Supreme Court's right to declare acts of Congress or the president unconstitutional. This power, called *judicial review*, authorizes the Court "to hold unconstitutional and hence unenforceable any law, any official action based upon it, and any illegal action by a public official that it deems to be in conflict with the Basic Law, in the United States its Constitution."[8]

The case itself is fascinating. Thomas Jefferson defeated President John Adams' reelection bid in 1800. Adams feared for the survival of his Federalist party and decided before leaving office to pack the federal judiciary with as many Federalists as possible. Early in 1801, at Adams' suggestion, the outgoing Federalist-dominated Congress passed two court acts providing for the appointment of forty-eight new federal judges. Adams also appointed his secretary of state, John Marshall, chief justice of the Supreme Court.

As secretary of state, Marshall was given the task of delivering the commissions to the new judges. But on the eve of the inauguration of Thomas Jefferson, and of his own assumption of the duties of chief justice, Marshall ran out of time and was unable to deliver seventeen of the commissions. He left them to be delivered by his successor as secretary of state, James Madison.

Jefferson and Madison decided not to carry out Adams' appointments. A number of the disappointed prospective judges hired Adams' former attorney general, Charles Lee, to seek redress in the courts. Lee petitioned to the Supreme Court on behalf of William Marbury, basing his case on an article of the Judiciary Act of 1789 that gave the Supreme Court the power to issue a writ (called a *writ of mandamus*) ordering public officials to perform their official duties.

It was probably expected that Marshall would rule on behalf of Marbury in order to get more Federalists on the bench and to use the full powers granted to the Court by Congress. Indeed, in his opinion, Marshall stated that he thought Marbury had a just complaint based on the law. But instead of upholding Marbury's case, he used the opportunity to make a landmark decision that widened the power of the Court more than any other before or since.

He argued that the article of the Judiciary Act of 1789 was *unconstitutional* because Congress had by law added to the original constitutional jurisdiction of the Supreme Court, something that the Constitution does not permit. By rejecting the claims of a Federalist petitioner and overturning a law passed by a Federalist Congress, Marshall succeeded in securing a basic Federalist

---

[8] Henry J. Abraham, *The Judicial Process* (New York, 1965), p. 251.

objective—the doctrine of judicial review, which at the time was seen as a protection to the propertied against the dangers of congressional democracy.[9] He wrote, echoing almost exactly Alexander Hamilton's arguments in *The Federalist* No. 78: "It is emphatically the province and duty of the judicial department to say what the law is. . . . A law repugnant to the Constitution is void; . . . courts as well as other departments are bound by that instrument." As a result of this decision, Federalist principles triumphed, even though the Federalist party soon disintegrated. The Supreme Court had asserted the right of judicial review and had strongly reinforced the Constitution's declaration that it is the supreme law of the land.

After Marshall's death in 1835, President Andrew Jackson appointed Roger Taney, a Maryland Democrat, to the post of chief justice. In contrast to the Marshall Court, and in the context of growing threats to the integrity of the Union, Taney and his court tended to look more favorably on states' rights and landed interests. As one scholar notes, "Taney, and with him the great majority of his court, demonstrated a faithful attachment to the economic interests of the South and the rapidly developing frontier of the West."[10] Nevertheless, it is possible to overstate the contrast between the Marshall and Taney Courts. In the noted case of *Charles River Bridge* v. *Warren Bridge Co.* (1837), the court ruled on the claim by the owners of a toll bridge in Massachusetts who argued that their state-granted charter implied a promise that the legislature would not authorize a competing bridge; by implication, the owner said the state had granted them a constitutionally guaranteed monopoly. The Court disagreed with the company, holding that the charter did not confer such exclusive rights and that public grants should be interpreted narrowly and strictly. At the time, many thought the Taney Court had reversed Marshall's concern for the sanctity of contracts; but in retrospect it is clear that this was not the case. Rather, as one legal historian has put it, the decision presented "no challenge to the basic principles of Marshall's contract-clause doctrine—that a charter is a contract that binds the state—nor is there evidence in later contract-clause cases that the Taney Court was reckless of property rights."[11] The

[9] Wallace Mendelson, *Capitalism, Democracy and the Supreme Court* (New York, 1960), p. 20.
[10] Abraham, p. 303.
[11] Robert G. McCloskey, *The American Supreme Court* (Chicago, 1960), pp. 88–89.

Court, instead, found a middle way, by giving the states some say in commercial affairs but by also insisting that the state keep the actual promises it contracted for.

The Taney Court might better be seen not as the antithesis of the Marshall Court but as the Court that had to struggle with the tensions between an industrializing North and a slave-owning agrarian South. The Court's balancing act stumbled in its decisions on slavery, presenting judgments that cost the Court both its prestige and its ability to act for some time to come.

In the Taney Court's best-known decision, *Dred Scott* v. *Sanford* (1857), by a 7 to 2 vote, the Court decided that no black could be an American citizen; that a black was "a person of an inferior order"; that no individual of African descent was "a portion of this American people"; and that blacks were slaves and possessions of their owners no matter whether they were in a slave or a free area of the country. This decision, historians agree, hastened the onset of the Civil War.

It also speeded the demise of the Taney Court. Taney continued to serve until 1864, but he was stripped of effective power by the outbreak of the Civil War; during the Civil War (1861 to 1865), President Lincoln acted as a near-dictator, ignoring constitutional niceties where he thought appropriate, and in 1863 Congress increased the size of the court from nine to ten.[12] By 1864, with the appointment of Salmon Chase as chief justice, the Court was securely in the hands of Northern Republicans, who were chiefly concerned with safeguarding property and providing a legal climate for the development of competitive industrial capitalism.

The Court as Protector of Corporate Capitalism

The Marshall Court in two landmark cases—*Gibbons* v. *Ogden* (1824) and *Dartmouth College* v. *Woodward* (1819)—had provided the legal framework for the protection of incipient industrialization by ruling in favor of federal control of interstate commerce (thus laying the groundwork for national capitalism) and by declaring that contracts were inviolable. The predominantly Republican-dominated Courts of the late nineteenth and early twentieth century further extended the legal infrastructure of capitalism. Most notably, corporations were given legal status as persons in 1888; they now had a charter of civil liberties, which would be used to

[12] Congress altered the size of the Court two more times in this decade; from ten to seven in 1866, and from seven to nine in 1869.

declare unconstitutional state and federal laws that restricted their operations as well as labor-union activities of organizing and strikes. In 1895 alone, other Court decisions dismissed prosecutions against the sugar trust, declared the income tax unconstitutional, and upheld the contempt conviction of Eugene Debs, a socialist who was president of the American Railway Union.

After the turn of the century, with the development of an increasingly dominant corporate sector, the Court's continued probusiness orientation was no longer as clear-cut. In attempting to curb attacks on the unbridled power of business by labor unions and Progressive reformers, the Court often struck down or delayed measures that the immense new corporations either wanted or did not oppose. For example, workmen's compensation bills, which the corporations wanted to limit their liability for workers' accidents, were declared unconstitutional by the Supreme Court in 1920 and 1924; it struck down child-labor legislation from 1916 to the late 1930s (unlike small-capital farms and family farms, the larger corporations did not need to employ children).

Yet, on balance, the zealous protection of property, the shackling of unions, and the limitations on corporate legal vulnerability won for the Supreme Court the enthusiastic support of America's capitalists. In 1895, a New York bank president told an audience of businessmen: "I give you, gentlemen, the Supreme Court of the United States—guardian of the dollar, defender of private property, enemy of spoliation, sheet anchor of the Republic!" Sixteen years later, a Standard Oil executive praised a Court decision limiting the scope of the Sherman Antitrust Act: "I am for the Supreme Court every time. For more than a hundred years it has been at work and it has never made a mistake." [13]

This kind of direct, often blatant defense of the capitalist order that the Supreme Court provided, however, stood in the way of the New Deal effort to save corporate capitalism during the depression of the 1930s. The Court continued to rule narrowly on behalf of laissez faire by striking down legislation regulating agriculture, the railroads, and setting minimum wages. In 1937, President Roosevelt sought to smash this roadblock to modernized capitalism by proposing "whenever a Judge or Justice of any Federal Court has reached the age of seventy and does not avail himself of the opportunity to retire on a pension, a new member

[13] Cited in Redford et al., pp. 498–99.

shall be appointed by the President then in office, and with the approval, as required by the Constitution, of the Senate of the United States."[14] Since six of the nine justices then serving were over seventy, Roosevelt was in effect proposing to add up to six new members to give the New Deal a majority.

Though Congress refused to go along (an alliance of those opposed to the New Deal and those who favored the change but thought it should be done by constitutional amendment, rather than legislation, prevented the bill's passage), two of the justices now began to vote with the New Deal. By 1941, the turnabout was complete. Roosevelt was able to make four new appointments in four years, cementing his majority.

The Warren and Burger Courts

From the late 1930s to the present, the relationship between the Court and the corporate complex has generally been much more indirect than it was before and during the New Deal. Since 1937, the justices have consistently held themselves aloof from the management of the economy. Instead, they have let the corporate complex manage and regulate the economy without Court interference. In this respect, the Court has served the interests of corporate capital, since its hands-off policy has made it possible for the elaborate interpenetration of government and corporate capitalism to continue to develop.

Thus, while almost all of the Court's pre-1937 rulings were in the field of property controls, including taxation, regulation of commerce, antitrust cases, and labor relations, today the Supreme Court's economy-related rulings are largely confined to settling conflicts between authorities: they turn largely on interpretations of actions by federal regulatory commissions, of tax laws, and of the federal regulation of labor relations. In all these areas of decision, however contentious they may be at times, the existence of corporate capitalism is never questioned.

The Court increasingly came to spend the bulk of its time on cases dealing with criminal procedures, civil liberties, and civil rights, especially under Chief Justice Earl Warren, who was appointed by President Eisenhower in 1953 and served through the Eisenhower, Kennedy, and Johnson administrations. The Warren

---

[14] Theodore Becker and Malcolm Feeley, eds., *The Impact of Supreme Court Decisions* (New York, 1973), p. 41.

Court consistently acted to protect and extend the legal system's commitment to formal equality. Among its landmark decisions were *Baker* v. *Carr* (1962), in which the Court held that the federal courts could act to ensure that the drawing of election district lines by state legislatures give each vote equal meaning (thus each district had to have roughly the same population); *Miranda* v. *Arizona* (1966), which stated that confessions obtained under interrogation from criminal suspects were not admissable as courtroom evidence unless the accused person had been informed of his or her rights to remain silent and be represented by a lawyer; and *Harper* v. *Virginia State Board of Elections* (1966), in which the Court determined that requiring voters to pay a poll tax (a device to keep blacks from voting) violated the guarantees of equal protection of the Fourteenth Amendment. Desegregation and voting rights have consistently been upheld, defendants' pretrial rights have been made more explicit, and one man, one vote has become the national standard.

It is striking that none of these landmark decisions were in the area of economic relations. When the University of Michigan *Law Review* devoted a special issue to a critical analysis of the Warren Court, its articles focused on desegregation, reapportionment, criminal procedure, religious liberty, and the press. Minor emphasis was paid to labor and antitrust decisions.[15] In these areas, most of the Court's activity reaffirmed pre-existing doctrines. The Warren Court was thus devoted, with a passion, to legal equality. Its decisions widened the political community and made more and more citizens legal equals. But issues of substantive economic equality were beyond the purview of the Court.

Like almost every other president before him, Richard Nixon made appointments to the Court (Chief Justice Burger as well as justices Blackmun, Powell, and Rehnquist) to change its ideological complexion. As a candidate in 1968, Nixon attacked the libertarian decisions of the Warren Court and pledged to rectify the Court's shortcomings by appointing conservative justices. His four appointments in his first term were calculated to win the votes of "middle America" to the Republican party.

The Burger Court has behaved as President Nixon expected only in some respects. It reversed some of the protections the Warren Court extended to criminal defendants, and it ruled in

[15] Richard Sayler, Barry Boyer, and Robert Gooding, Jr., *The Warren Court: A Critical Analysis* (New York, 1969).

favor of allowing communities to decide their own standards of obscenity (subject to Supreme Court review). The Court also supported the Nixon administration's stand against busing to achieve racial integration of the schools. In July 1974, the Court overturned a lower court ruling that had mandated busing across city lines in the Detroit metropolitan area to integrate the region's public schools. All of Nixon's appointees voted with the majority, and all of the dissenters had served on the Warren Court.

Ironically, the Burger Court played a major role in bringing down the Nixon presidency. Like its predecessors, this Court refused to yield to the president its role as the protector of the legal process. When President Nixon sought to withhold tape-recorded conversations on the grounds of executive privilege that the special prosecutor had requested as evidence for the Watergate trials of the president's closest political allies, the Court ruled unanimously that the tapes had to be turned over. In this case, *United States* v. *Nixon* (1974), the Court reaffirmed the principle laid down by the Marshall Court in the early nineteenth century that the Supreme Court is the ultimate arbiter of the Constitution.

During the Ford and Carter administrations, the Burger Court has not been as conservative as conservatives had hoped or as liberals had feared. By and large it has avoided judicial activism. Rather than overturning most of the egalitarian and libertarian gains of the Warren years, the Court has refused to extend them. In decision after decision it has told would-be litigants to turn to lawmakers or regulatory agencies to solve their problems. "The justices made it clear," *Business Week* observed, "that they will narrowly read the statutes they are being asked to interpret and will defer to decisions made by administrative agencies." [16] The Nixon appointees have voted together less and less often. In 1976, these four justices voted together 73 percent of the time, but only 36 percent in 1978. Overall, law professor A. E. Dick Howard remarked that the Burger Court has "no overarching doctrine. They're taking cases as they come in pragmatic fashion." [17]

This pragmatism was the Court's most obvious feature in the most dramatic case it has ruled on to date, *Regents of the University of California* v. *Bakke* (1978). After earning a Masters Degree in engineering, Allan Bakke applied to a number of medical schools, none of which accepted him. One of the schools to which

[16] *Business Week*, July 10, 1978, p. 23.
[17] *Time*, July 17, 1978, p. 44.

he applied, the University of California at Davis, reserved 16 out of
100 places for disadvantaged minority students. Arguing that this
affirmative-action program discriminated against himself, Bakke
sued and won on appeal in the California Supreme Court. The
California Regents appealed. The United States Supreme Court
was asked to rule if Bakke should have been admitted, and, therefore, if it was legal for admissions programs to give some preference to blacks over whites in order to remedy the effects of past
racial discrimination.

The Court, dividing 5 to 4 each time (with Nixon appointee
Justice Powell providing the swing vote), affirmed the lower-court
order admitting Bakke to medical school, and ruled that the
special-admissions program at the University of California, Davis,
violated the Civil Rights Act of 1964. Numerical quotas based
entirely on race, where no previous pattern of discrimination was
found, were illegal. In the second decision, however, the Court
upheld affirmative-action programs, declaring that a university
could take race into consideration in admissions, along with other
criteria. Universities were thus left with a good deal of discretion;
how they will use it is entirely up to them. The largest question left
open by this decision, which was won in some respects by both
sides, "is how far a remedy may go if an institution or industry is
found to have excluded minorities itself." [18]

The divisions and fragmentation of the Burger Court on this
and other issues yield to a more consistent philosophy in business
and labor affairs. Here, unlike the Warren Court on these matters,
and unlike its judicial reserve on other questions, the Burger Court
has consistently supported business in antitrust, regulatory, and
labor questions. Since 1969, the *Wall Street Journal* has noted,
"the court has made it easier for employers to halt strikes that
violate no-strike pledges, harder for unions to win employer recognition on the basis of employee-signed cards, and easier for management to press antitrust damage suits against building-trades
unions." In other areas too, as those affecting the environment,
mergers, the stock market, and pricing, the "imprint is generally
pro-business." [19] More often than not, this orientation takes the
form not of making law by explicit decisions but by making it more
difficult for anticorporate groups to bring cases to court.

[18] Anthony Lewis, " 'Bakke' May Change a Lot While Changing No Law," *New York Times*, July 2, 1978, section 4, p. 1.
[19] Wayne E. Green, "Supreme Court Shows a Pro-Business Tilt in a Series of Rulings," *Wall Street Journal*, July 1, 1975, pp. 1, 11.

The Court as Policymaker

More than two decades ago, political scientist Robert Dahl argued perceptively that the Supreme Court is involved in the making of public policy. It is called upon to select between competing policies in areas of wide disagreement. Who benefits, he asked, from this role of the Court? He concluded, after an examination of cases where federal legislation was found unconstitutional by the Court, that "the main task of the Court is to confer legitimacy on the fundamental policies" of the dominant coalition of groups and interests in control of the national regime:

> Except for short-lived transitional periods when the old alliance is disintegrating and the new one is struggling to take control of political institutions, the Supreme Court is inevitably a part of the dominant national alliance. As an element in the political leadership of the dominant alliance, the Court, of course, supports the major policies of the alliance. By itself, the Court is almost powerless to affect the course of national policy.[20]

In the few instances, such as *Dred Scott* and attempts to reject New Deal legislation, when the Court sought to make policy against the wishes of the dominant governing classes, it paid a heavy price in terms of its autonomy and prestige.

A recent empirical test by political scientist Richard Funston bears out these claims. Examining the 168 laws found to be unconstitutional by the Court within four years of their passage by the Congress in the period from 1801, when Chief Justice Marshall was appointed, to 1969, when Chief Justice Warren retired, he found that the Court's pattern of rejecting legislation was not random. Rather, "over long periods of time, the Supreme Court reflects the will of the dominant political forces." In stable periods of electoral alignments, the Court strikes down national legislation far less frequently than it does during periods of partisan upheaval and electoral realignment, periods which are usually also marked by major social and economic changes in the society. During realignment periods, the Court is about three times as likely to strike down federal legislation; and more of the legislation that it does find unconstitutional had been passed in the four preceding years.[21]

---

[20] Robert Dahl, "Decision-Making in a Democracy: The Supreme Court as a National Policy-Maker," *Journal of Public Law* 6 (Fall 1957): 293.

[21] Richard Funston, "The Supreme Court and Critical Elections," *The American Political Science Review* LXIX (September 1975): 796, 806.

One lesson of this finding is that it is a mistake to equate an activist Court with a liberal Court, and a restrained Court with a conservative one. Rather, as law professor Philip Kurland has suggested, "An 'activist' court is essentially one that is out of step with the legislative or executive branches of the government. It will thus be 'liberal' or 'conservative' depending upon which role its prime antagonist has adopted." [22]

Even in the long periods when the Court is in tune with the policy orientations of the president and the Congress, however, it still helps shape public policy. Above all, it stamps its label of constitutional legitimacy on controversial legislation. The Voting Rights Act of 1965, for example, which struck down barriers to black voting in the South, was quickly brought to the Court for a constitutional test; the Court upheld the act. In economic matters, the Court has provided ''nonpolitical'' approval and indispensable support for such basic features of the economy as private property, contracts, and the regulatory activities of government. It follows, Dahl wrote,

> that within the somewhat narrow limits set by the basic policy goals of the dominant alliance, the Court *can* make national policy. Its discretion, then, is not unlike that of a powerful committee chairman in Congress who cannot, generally speaking, nullify the basic policies substantively agreed on by the rest of the leadership, but who can, within these limits, often determine important questions of timing, effectiveness, and subordinate policy. Thus the Court is least effective against a current lawmaking majority—and evidently least inclined to act. It is most effective when it sets the bounds of policy for officials, agencies, and state governments or even regions, a task that has come to occupy a very large part of the Court's business. [23]

By constitutionally standing apart from the elected branches, the Supreme Court is cast in the role of the protector of minority rights and opinions in the face of popular pressures. But here, we shall see in the next section, the Court's record is mixed, as is that of the justice system more generally.

---

[22] Philip B. Kurland, *Politics, the Constitution, and the Warren Court* (Chicago, 1970), pp. 17–18.
[23] Dahl, p. 294.

LEGAL REPRESSION AND THE POLITICAL TRIAL

The myth that the judicial system is nonpolitical is clearly punctured when we examine the ways in which its institutions have been used to quash articulate, organized political opposition that has operated *outside* of the limits of party politics, elections, and interest-group competition. When challenges have been mounted against the prevailing social order, especially from the left, authorities have moved to use the formal justice system to eliminate foes from political competition and to establish the outer limits of safe, acceptable dissent.

The most important legal basis for recent political prosecutions is conspiracy. Conspiracy laws make it a crime to conspire to commit certain acts, whether or not the acts are carried out. Conspiracy, legal scholar Herbert Packer has noted, is the "shabbiest weapon in the prosecutor's arsenal" because "it is what is referred to as an 'inchoate crime.' It does not require proof that anyone did anything illegal, but only that he intended to commit a crime, or . . . that he 'agreed' to commit a crime."[24]

Throughout the nineteenth century, conspiracy laws were routinely used to prevent workers from organizing unions. In the landmark cases of the *Boot and Shoemakers of Philadelphia* in 1806 and the *Journeymen Cordwainers of New York* in 1811, workers were convicted of the charge of criminal conspiracy for trying to organize a union. Today, union activity is seen as basically supportive of the corporate complex and is protected by law. But conspiracy laws are still being used. In the late 1960s and early 1970s especially, when social unrest was high, antiwar activists and black militants were prosecuted by the government for conspiracy.

To name only some of the more celebrated cases: In 1968, five well-known antiwar spokesmen, including Dr. Benjamin Spock and the Reverend William Sloane Coffin, were tried for conspiracy to counsel, aid, and abet violations of the Selective Service law and to hinder administration of the draft. Only one defendant (Marcus Raskin) was acquitted. In 1969, eight radical activists were tried for conspiracy under an amendment to the Civil Rights Act of 1968

[24] Noam Chomsky et al., eds., *Trials of the Resistance* (New York, 1970), p. 173.

that made it a crime to cross state lines with the *intent* to incite a riot. They were charged with conspiring to create disorder at the 1968 Democratic party convention in Chicago. Six (including Black Panther Bobby Seale, Tom Hayden, and Abbie Hoffman) were convicted. And in 1970, Manhattan's district attorney charged twenty-one members of the Panthers with conspiracy to blow up department stores, the Statue of Liberty, and other public targets. They were acquitted; eventually the convictions of the draft and Chicago cases were reversed on appeal.

The Justice Department knew that most of its cases were weak. In this respect, the 1973 trial, held in Gainesville, Florida, of seven antiwar veterans (and an eighth supporter) on charges of having conspired to assault the 1972 Republican national convention with automatic weapons, slingshots, and crossbows was typical. After a month-long trial, the jury took only three hours to bring in its verdict of not guilty. "They had nothing on those boys," a juror remarked afterwards.[25] The prosecution of this conspiracy case and others was not aimed primarily at conviction, but at disrupting and harassing radical activity. Conspiracy trials take a long time; they keep radicals away from their activities; they cost a good deal of money; and they provide others with a symbolic warning of what might be in store for them. The cases were brought not to uphold the conspiracy laws, but to crush opposition through legal means.

In virtually all of these trials, moreover, evidence revealed how thoroughly the government had sought to use its police powers to infiltrate radical organizations. The Gainesville veterans' group had been infiltrated by undercover police officers; in one case, where five priests were accused of raiding the offices of a New Jersey draft board, the judge told the jury it could acquit because "of overreaching participation by government agents or informers."[26]

Conspiracy laws and trials, of course, are not the only means of overt political repression. Some laws are explicitly directed at political opposition.[27] In 1940, Congress passed the Alien Registration Act (Smith Act), which made it illegal to teach or advocate the overthrow of the government of the United States by force, or to organize groups or publish materials for that purpose. Conspiring

---

[25] *New York Times*, September 9, 1973.
[26] *Ibid*.
[27] Much of the following discussion is drawn from Alan Wolfe, *The Seamy Side of Democracy: Repression in America* (New York, 1973).

to commit these acts was also made a crime. A decade later, the Internal Security Act (McCarran Act) was passed. This act established a Subversive Activities Control Board that was to hold hearings to determine whether certain organizations were "Communist." If they were found to be, they were required to register with the attorney general, disclose their sources of funding and expenditures, and give the names and addresses of their officers. Members of organizations identified by the board as Communist were forbidden to work in defense plants, apply for or use a passport, or hold nonelective federal jobs. These acts and numerous others passed by the federal and state governments were aimed to suppress not the actions of individuals or groups, but the expression of their opinions and their ability to organize.

These laws were passed in the heyday of the cold war. Up to the early 1960s, the Supreme Court consistently held that the anti-Communist legislation was constitutional; in 1961, for example, the Court found in favor of the government, which had prosecuted individuals under the Smith Act for "knowing membership" in the Communist party. But as the cold war began to ease, as the Kennedy, Johnson, and Nixon administrations pursued a policy of détente with the Soviet Union, the Supreme Court began to find many aspects of these laws unconstitutional. As one judicial scholar noted, "The dominant lesson of our history in the relation of the judiciary to repression is that courts love liberty most when it is under pressure least." [28]

Very few laws are overtly repressive. But a great many can be used for repressive purposes. For example, immigration and deportation laws, which define the attributes of citizenship, were often used in the past to exclude and deport political activists. In the case of *Fong Yue Ting* v. *The United States* (1893), the Supreme Court found that the federal government's right to expel foreigners who had not become naturalized citizens "is as absolute and unqualified as the right to prohibit their entrance into the country." Leaders of the radical trade union, Industrial Workers of the World, were deported in the early 1920s as undesirables. Deportation has since been used retroactively; people who had joined the Communist party when membership was legal were deported after passage of the Smith Act in 1950.

Indeed, virtually any law, however innocuous, can provide the basis for the repression of political opposition. In the late

[28] John P. Frank, cited in Redford et al., p. 554.

1960s, the police in Oakland, California, enforced traffic regulations much more strictly against members of the Black Panthers, a
radical nationalist organization, than the general public in order to
keep Panthers off the streets and to make them conscious that they
were likely to be stopped and searched regularly. A fund-raising
party for the Marxist W. E. B. DuBois Club held in Manhattan in
1966 was raided by narcotics police who claimed to be searching
for drugs:

> All the young people were held for fifteen hours by the police, then
> charged and cleared for arraignment. As there were no narcotics
> present (the DuBois Club, the group's infiltrator must have in-
> formed the police, was opposed to the use of drugs), the charges
> were eventually dismissed. No convictions were seriously
> entertained. The purpose of the raid was just one of nuisance.[29]

The existence of many laws prohibiting certain forms of conduct,
in short, makes it possible for police and prosecutors to use their
wide enforcement discretion to establish limits of legitimate political action. As an analysis of legal repression concluded, "Laws
exist in a political context. . . . The existence of a government of
laws and not men is sometimes praised, but when the laws are used
by the men to preserve their own power, the law itself becomes the
problem."[30]

The leading law enforcement agency in the United States, the
Federal Bureau of Investigation (FBI), became the problem when
it undertook a campaign of harassment and unrelenting surveillance of civil rights leader Martin Luther King, Jr. One month
before King was assassinated, a memo from FBI headquarters to
field offices on March 4, 1968, expressed the fear that King might
become a "black messiah." Stating that one of the goals of its
counterintelligence operation was to prevent the rise of such a
"messiah," the memo went on to say that "King could be a very
real contender for this position should he abandon his supposed
'obedience' to 'white, liberal doctrines' (nonviolence) and embrace black nationalism."[31]

The FBI had been watching King since the late 1950s. A few
years later, after FBI Director J. Edgar Hoover wrongly informed
President John Kennedy and Attorney General Robert Kennedy

[29] Wolfe, p. 96.
[30] *Ibid.*, pp. 101–02.
[31] David Wise, "The Campaign to Destroy Martin Luther King," *The New York
Review of Books*, November 11, 1976, p. 38.

that King's Southern Christian Leadership Conference had many communists in its leadership, the attorney general authorized the bureau to wiretap King's phone conversations. Taps were installed on King's phones at home, in sixteen hotel rooms where King stayed, and in SCLC headquarters in Atlanta and New York. In fall 1964 the FBI told reporters that it had uncovered evidence that King had had extramarital affairs; the FBI coupled these unsupported claims with the old, equally unsupported, claims that King was under communist control. When this campaign failed to discredit King, Hoover told the press in November 1974 that King is "the most notorious liar in the country." Three days after this attack, the FBI mailed an anonymous letter and a tape of the alleged hotel room bugs to King and to his wife Coretta. The letter read:

> King, there is only one thing left for you to do. You know what it is. You have just 34 days in which to do it. This exact number has been selected for a specific reason. It has definite practical significance. You are done.

The letter was mailed three weeks before King was scheduled to receive the Nobel Peace Prize in Norway. As journalist David Wise observes, "Since it was accompanied by a tape which the FBI considered compromising, the letter could be interpreted as an invitation for King to kill himself." [32] More petty harassment continued until King's assassination.

CRIMINAL JUSTICE

Almost all of us are criminals at one time or another. In 1965, the President's Crime Commission found that 91 percent of all adult Americans "had committed acts for which they might have received jail or prison sentences." Since most Americans do not go to jail, it is obvious that the criminal justice system pays *selective* attention to crime, concentrating on the crimes of homicide, rape, assault, robbery, and burglary. Former Attorney General Ramsey Clark noted that almost all of these crimes are committed for the purpose of obtaining money or property; fully seven-eighths of the FBI-Index crimes are crimes against property.

[32] *Ibid.*, pp. 39–42.

THE QUALITY OF JUSTICE

There is a great deal of crime committed in the United States. In 1975, according to official statistics, 20,500 Americans were murdered, 56,000 raped, 465,000 robbed, 3,252,000 burglarized. In addition, there were almost 6 million cases of larceny, and 1 million cars were stolen.[33] These are only the reported offenses. White-collar crimes like tax evasion, embezzlement, price-fixing, and consumer-fraud are less visible and often overlooked, but they are much more profitable than crimes that command most police and media attention.

> Illicit gains from white-collar crime far exceed those of all other crime combined. . . . One corporate price-fixing conspiracy criminally converted more money each year than all of the hundreds of thousands of burglaries, larcenies, or thefts in the entire nation during those same years. Reported bank embezzlements cost ten times more than bank robberies each year.[34]

The crimes committed by those who work in the small-capital sector of the economy, which includes the majority of blacks and other minorities, are the chief business of the criminal justice complex, while, more often than not, white-collar criminals are dealt with by private auspices—"private psychiatric and counselling assistance often supplant prosecution."[35] Even in the "classes of offenses committed by rich and poor equally, it is rarely the rich who end up behind bars."[36]

It is important to recognize that conditions in contemporary America make crime particularly attractive and accessible. Poor blacks confined to the small-capital sector of the economy often find that crime brings higher financial rewards and higher group status than they could ever hope to achieve otherwise and even, as in numbers-running, carries relatively low risks of apprehension and conviction. Many illegal activities run by organized crime— drug traffic, gambling, prostitution—are "consensual crimes . . . desired by the consuming public."[37] The goods and services provided by organized crime are not only desired, they are in great demand; and profits are high. And corporate white-collar crime is consistent with the logic of profit of corporate capitalism.

The basic difference between the kinds of crime people com-

[33] *Crime in the United States, 1975* (Washington, D.C., 1976), p. 11.
[34] Ramsey Clark, *Crime in America* (New York, 1970), p. 38.
[35] David Gordon, "Class and the Economics of Crime," *Review of Radical Political Economics* 3 (Summer 1971): 54.
[36] Ronald Goldfarb, "Prison: The National Poorhouse," *The New Republic* (November 1969), p. 312.
[37] Clark, p. 68.

mit is largely due to the opportunities presented them. Ghetto residents do not have easy access to jobs in large corporations, to relatively unobtrusive patterns of communication, or to paper transactions involving large sums of money. Moreover, poor-people's crimes, economist David Gordon notes, are much more apt to be violent because of the selectivity of the criminal justice complex. He notes that it is only natural

> that those who run the highest risks of arrest and conviction may have to rely on the threat or commission of violence in order to protect themselves. . . . Completely in contrast, corporate crime does not require violence because it is ignored by the police; corporate criminals can safely assume that they do not face the threat of jail, and do not therefore have to cover their tracks with the threat of harming those who betray them.[38]

Of course not all white-collar crime is ignored: when the criminal practices of the relatively well-to-do become egregiously offensive in their violation of the law, they must be punished in order to protect the ideological claim that all are equal under the law. But for the most part, the justice system disregards white-collar crime. In the past, much violent and working-class crime was also ignored by the justice system, since those "crimes rarely impinged on the lives of the more affluent. Gambling, prostitution, dope and robbery seemed to flourish in the slums of the early twentieth century, and the police rarely moved to intervene."[39] As crime has burst out of its traditional slum boundaries, it has become a "crisis." The justice system's concern with crime by subordinates has thus been directly related to the class status of the victims (most crimes, however, are still committed by the poor against the poor).

Indeed, crime and the creation of means to control it have traditionally been problems of boundaries and social control. The origins of modern police forces provide a case in point.

The Police

Modern police forces are only a century and a half old. They were created quite consciously to protect existing structural arrangements. London's police force, which was the model for American urban police, was the first to be established. Its founding in

[38] Gordon, p. 61.
[39] *Ibid.*, p. 62.

1829 was not a response, as sociologist Allan Silver notes, to criminality as such, but to the growth of a destitute underclass in early industrial England that was thought to threaten the social order.

> It was more than a question of annoyance, indignation, or personal insecurity; the social order itself was threatened by an entity whose characteristic name reflects the fears of the time—the "dangerous classes". . . . But even where the term is not explicitly invoked, the image persists—one of an unmanageable, volatile, and convulsively criminal class at the base of society.[40]

Before the creation of the professional, bureaucratic police force, police functions in England were carried out by local property owners who acted as constables. However, as the size of the underclass grew under the impact of industrialization, most large property owners became increasingly vulnerable as direct targets of popular abuse. The agrarian rich responded by attempting to strengthen the private constabulary, but most of the new manufacturers "turned towards a bureaucratic police system that insulated them from popular violence, drew attack and animosity upon itself, and seemed to separate the assertion of 'constitutional' authority from that of social and economic dominance." From the moment of their creation, modern police forces were the officially sanctioned legal enforcers of the prevailing structural arrangements. By their regular presence among all classes, especially the new industrial proletariat, the police permeated society in a way that traditional landed constabularies could not. As one authority noted, "the police penetration of civil society lay not only in its narrow application to crime and violence. In a broader sense, it represented the penetration and continual presence of central political authority throughout daily life."[41]

Individually, the police officer maintains order and tranquility on the beat; collectively, the police act as guardians of the social order as a whole. This structural role is fraught with tension, since, often, the police must *police* a hostile public, and their definition of order and appropriate public behavior may clash with the perspectives of the community. A reporter who spent two years with the Philadelphia police force found that the police interpenetrated poor

---

[40] Allan Silver, "The Demand for Order in Civil Society: A Review of Some Themes in the History of Urban Crime, Police, and Riot," in David Bordua, ed., *The Police: Six Sociological Essays* (New York, 1967), p. 3.
[41] *Ibid.*, pp. 12–13.

neighborhoods so completely that they often produced heightened tension, anxiety, and the disruption of neighborhood life:

> The neighborhoods seem to be overflowing with police cars, which give the police an enlarged presence as they pass. Cars are frequently seen whizzing down the street, their sirens blaring and their emergency lights flashing. It is common to see police cars streak down intersections, breaking red lights, running over sidewalks and into alleys. Every day, many times on some days, people walking on the sidewalk see the police converge, jump from their cars with guns drawn, abandoning their cars in the middle of the street, doors open.[42]

In this context, police develop what sociologist Jerome Skolnick calls a working personality. They use a perceptual shorthand of characteristics such as race, dress, language, and gestures to identify in advance those people likely to pose a threat to order on their beat. Thus police often come to see the world as divided between "us" and "them"; anyone identified as one of "them" is likely to be the target of harassment that goes beyond the law. The result is a significant number of what have been called police abuses, a term that is misleading since these "abuses" are an integral part of routine policing.

Police act to preserve their authority even if their actions violate the formal rules under which they operate. After conducting an extensive study into abuses by the New York City police, attorney Paul Chevigny concluded that challenges to police authority are consistently met by "anger and one or more weapons out of the arsenal of legal sanctions from a summons up through summary corporal punishment. Criminal charges, beginning with disorderly conduct and ranging up to felonious assault, are commonly laid to cover the actions of the policeman and to punish the offender." Chevigny found that for most police officers, arrest was equivalent to guilt; hence many arrests are followed by false or misleading testimony by officers in court. "Distortion of the facts becomes the most pervasive and the most significant of abuses. The police ethic justifies any action which is intended to maintain order or to convict any wrongdoer (i.e., anyone actually or potentially guilty of a crime)."[43]

This pattern of routine illegal policing to protect police authority is made possible by the extraordinary discretion police

---

[42] Jonathan Rubenstein, *City Police* (New York, 1973), p. 351.
[43] Paul Chevigny, *Police Power* (New York, 1969), pp. 276–77.

have on the job, by the presumption of innocence their actions
carry, and by the protective solidarity of police bureaucracies. The
officer on the beat, despite the hierarchical proto-military characteristics of police organization, operates virtually without supervision. Police selectively enforce the law by deciding which people
to suspect and which laws to enforce (white-collar crimes, as we
have seen, and the wealthy are rarely police targets).

In a police officer's world of "us" and "them," the only completely trustworthy people are fellow officers. Socially and organi-
zationally isolated from the communities in which they work, the
police develop a sense of solidarity and exclusiveness. Thus corrupt officers as well as those who violate the legal rights of citizens
are usually protected by their colleagues. The overworked, haras-
sed, possibly authoritarian and racist officer may use unnecessary
violence, make illegal arrests, lie in court, and be on the take, but is
more likely than not to escape detection outside the precinct work
group.

Criminal Courts

Once arrested, a defendant becomes enmeshed in the other two
institutions of the formal justice complex—criminal courts and
prisons. Bail is the first step in the process beyond arrest, and bail
practices weigh heavily on the poor. Early Anglo-Saxon law provided for bail because the wait between arrest and trial was often
lengthy, and the cost of detention to the sheriff was high. When
defendants posted collateral security, they were free pending trial.
Virtually the same system operates today, at least in theory.

The Constitution prohibits "excessive bail," yet does not give
defendants an absolute right to bail. But it is widely agreed among
jurists that since those arrested are formally presumed innocent
until proven guilty, defendants should ordinarily be allowed freedom until they are tried. In practice, however, bail is often set at
levels higher than defendants can afford. A study in New York
found that of all defendants charged with criminal assault,
burglary, forgery, larceny, narcotics possession, robbery, and sex
crimes, 29 percent were denied bail, and fewer than one-third were
granted bail under $1,000.[44] Of those whose bail exceeded $1,000,
only about half were able to post bond. As a result of such prac-

[44] Charles Ares et al.,"The Manhattan Bail Project: An Interim Report on the Use of
Pre-Trail Parole," in James Klonoski et al., eds., *The Politics of Local Justice*
(Boston, 1970), pp. 79, 80, 86.

tices, of the prisoners in local and county jails in the United States in 1970, *fully 52 percent had not been convicted of a crime.* Most of these were poor and black.[45] The wide discretion available to judges in setting bail is thus routinely used to segregate and punish those whom the police identified as guilty and who are too poor to raise bail.

Those who are put in jail because they are unable to make bail are treated exactly like convicted prisoners and for no inconsiderable period of time: a wait of up to six months is common. Perhaps most importantly, they are placed at a great disadvantage in terms of their defense, as it is much more difficult to prepare a defense in jail than out. As political scientist Herbert Jacob notes, "Even if one receives assigned counsel or is defended by a public defender, one cannot personally round up witnesses and assist the attorney in interviewing them."[46] As the classic study on bail in New York City revealed, there is a demonstrable relationship between being detained in jail awaiting trial and the likelihood of having to go to prison after the trial. Almost half of those freed pending trial were either found innocent or spared prison sentences, while over 90 percent of those detained while awaiting trial were found guilty and sentenced to prison. The latter group not only were more likely to be convicted but they automatically forfeited their chance of probation after conviction. One of the basic conditions of probation is that the individual be employed; but it was hardly likely that those imprisoned pending trial could have kept their jobs. The class bias of policing procedures is thus reinforced by the administration of bail and parole.

The vast majority of criminal cases never come to trial. A thorough analysis of the disposition of felony cases averaged the available figures for 1965 to 1969 to give a rough indication of how cases are settled in a typical year in different cities. Of 22,000 felony arrests made in Chicago, only 900 came to trial with the defendant entering a not-guilty plea; in Houston, only 360 of 16,000 arrests; in Detroit, 900 of 20,000 arrests; in Brooklyn, New York, 300 of 15,000; and in Los Angeles, 10,400 of 69,000.[47] Most of the other cases are resolved by the defendant pleading guilty, often as the outcome of a process known as plea bargaining.

[45] Herbert Jacob, *Urban Justice* (Englewood Cliffs, N.J., 1973), p. 103.
[46] Herbert Jacob, *Justice in America* (Boston, 1972), p. 170.
[47] Donald McIntyre and David Lippman, "Prosecutors and Early Disposition of Felony Cases," *American Bar Association Journal* 56 (1970): 1156–57; also see Lewis M. Steel, "The Losers in Plea-Bargaining," *New York Times*, February 24, 1975.

Defendants are often charged with multiple crimes, some involving much more serious penalties than others. As a result, prosecutors have the leeway to negotiate with defendants: in exchange for a plea of guilty on the lesser charge, the others are dropped. Where there is only one charge against the defendant, the prosecutor offers to argue for a reduced sentence in exchange for a guilty plea. The extent of discretion available to prosecutors is not specified by law; hence they are free to act as *de facto* judges who make the critical decisions about innocence, guilt, and length of sentences.

One spectacular case of plea bargaining involved former Vice President Spiro Agnew. In October 1973, Agnew resigned his office and, in a Baltimore courtroom, pleaded "no contest" to a government charge of income-tax evasion. This plea was the outcome of elaborate bargaining between the vice president and the Justice Department, which had uncovered evidence that Agnew, a former Baltimore County executive and Maryland governor, had extorted bribes from state contractors for almost a decade. Had he been charged and convicted of all the crimes the prosecutors alleged he committed (Agnew has consistently maintained his innocence) he might have gone to prison for many years; instead, in exchange for his plea, the government settled for a sentence of three years of unsupervised probation and a $10,000 fine.

Most defendants are not nearly as well known, of course, and plea bargaining for them is much more routine. Generally, the formal adversary confrontation between prosecutor and the defendant's lawyer is a meeting of unequals. Most defendants in urban criminal courts are represented by court-employed public defenders or lawyers from private agencies like the Legal Aid Society. Many of these lawyers are well intentioned but have little experience in criminal law. They are usually just out of law school and have had virtually no courtroom experience. They lack funds to investigate the police-prosecutor version of events; since most cases do not even get to court, it is this version that serves as the basis for the terms of the bargain. Counsel may be assigned to the defendant many days after the arrest and pretrial imprisonment; by then, the defendant may have made an incriminating statement to the police or prosecutor that may be inadmissible as courtroom evidence but is damaging in the plea-bargaining process. And the public defender's or Legal Aid lawyer's caseload may be so heavy that there is almost no time to prepare for the confrontation with the prosecutor.

Plea bargaining has considerable advantages for the permanent members of the criminal justice system. It permits an extraordinarily high rate of conviction (sometimes even in cases where the evidence would be insufficient for a jury-trial conviction), which enhances prosecutors' law-and-order reelection appeals and helps police officers win promotions. It relieves prosecutors from having to prepare cases for trial, and it lightens and simplifies the judges' workload, since all they need do is ratify decisions reached by prosecutors and defendants' lawyers. In short, although some defendants may gain lighter sentences from the plea-bargaining process, the arrangement is much more likely to benefit the justice establishment.

Without the cooperation of criminal-court judges, plea bargaining could not exist. Judges who are supposed to be neutral arbiters of courtroom proceedings become accomplices in the inequitable dispensation of justice by permitting their courtrooms to be used at critical junctures. They "cooperate by imposing harsher sentences on defendants convicted after a trial than on those who plead guilty, by maintaining predictable decision patterns according to which defense and prosecutor can calculate their own actions, and by supporting requests for delay, plea and sentence made by prosecutors."[48]

It is often rightly observed that the behavior of criminal-court judges is limited by the actions of police, the size of their caseloads, deals worked out between prosecutors and defense lawyers, and administrative procedures beyond their control. Nevertheless, judges are the gatekeepers of the system of formal criminal justice. They not only legitimate plea bargaining but they also have the power to schedule cases, set bail, dismiss charges, admit evidence, influence juries (in the small proportion of cases that come to trial), and sentence with wide discretion.

Criminal-court judges are selected by a wide array of differing procedures. These include a "merit" procedure by which a governor appoints from a list of nominees compiled by a nonpartisan committee and selection by either the state legislature or local city councils. In most states, however, judges are chosen either through judicial elections or by governors and mayors. In both cases, public information is limited, and devotion to a political party is a more important test than legal competence.

Judicial elections rarely evoke much public controversy or

[48] Jacob, *Justice in America*, p. 104.

attention. Since it is against judicial ethics to campaign with great vigor, the candidates' campaigns usually lack issues or colorful personalities. As a result, the candidate nominated by the area's majority party is overwhelmingly likely to win. Securing the party's nomination is tantamount to election.

Appointment to the bench, likewise, is a procedure that is hardly subject to much popular control. Because the population processed by the courts is relatively powerless, and because they are often nonparticipants in the electoral system and thus do not threaten local politicians in any way, criminal-court judgeships give decaying party organizations the opportunity to reward loyal lawyers at almost no political cost. And in return for appointing friends to the bench, local politicians gain privileged access to the courts, opportunities to make more patronage appointments in auxiliary court personnel, and significant sums of money. (Political scientists Wallace Sayre and Herbert Kaufman estimated in 1960 that the typical judicial candidate in New York City contributed $20,000 to the Democratic party.)

For these reasons, undistinguished local lawyers who have been active in party affairs and who have sufficient funds to buy their judgeships are given preference. When the New York State legislature authorized twenty new criminal-court judgeships in 1968, party leaders broke their agreement to have their nominees cleared by the presiding justice for Manhattan and the Bronx and nominated people who could not have possibly secured approval. One, who was filling an interim appointment, routinely called defendants "idiots." A second was sixty-four years old and had little litigation experience. A third had admitted under oath that he had failed to report a $100,000 narcotics bribe attempt that involved a fellow state legislator.[49] As a result of such nominations, a New York district attorney has noted, the bench is full of lazy judges who keep bankers' hours and a funeral director's pace. "Bestowed as a reward for loyal party service, a place on the bench is seen as the most honorable sort of quasi-retirement."[50]

Appointments of judges like these are not to be deplored merely because they are political—any appointment procedure is political—but because of the way they affect those who are processed through the formal system of criminal justice. The interests

---

[49] Martin Tolchin and Susan Tolchin, *To the Victor: Political Patronage From the Clubhouse to the White House* (New York, 1971), p. 133.
[50] Richard Kuh, *New Leader*, January 8, 1973.

of *both* defendants *and* victims of crime (most of whom are poor) are hurt by the charade of most criminal courts.

Thus the criminal courts, through the *form* of legal institutions and assumptions, legitimize the control of the most subordinate. Hence the following description of the criminal courts by a journalist who has been investigating corruption is, on one level, a story of irrational inconsistencies, but, on another, is a description of how one critical institution deals with and controls those without power:

> The problem with the courts is more widespread than just the mere extremities of scandal—it is also the general lack of fairness, reason. and dignity for the mass of defendants . . . in the lower criminal courts . . . the average defendant confronts the average judge. Just sit there any morning and you will see judges who regularly remand 16-year old addicts to jail instead of paroling them to narcotics treatment programs. . . . You will see judges who don't listen, judges who insult lawyers and defendants, judges who are not intelligent enough to follow a complex or subtle argument. judges who are blatantly biased against blacks and Puerto Ricans. judges who call defendants names like "scum" and "animals."
>
> You will see inexperienced Legal Aid Lawyers represent 50 poor defendants in a day, and not have time to ask more than their names beforehand. You will see defendants who have been in jail for nine months without seeing a judge, and who could have been paroled months earlier. You will see pleas and sentences delayed because probation reports are lost in a maze of bureaucracy. You will see heroin dealers in red jump suits post $25,000 bail in cash and addicts locked up for a year because they don't have $50. And a cop convicted of selling heroin be given a suspended sentence.
>
> I have seen judges fine landlords $15 for 200 violations of the housing code, including failure to provide heat and hot water, and then have lunch with the landlord's lawyer. I have seen one judge sentence a Puerto Rican junkie to three years in prison for shoplifting some clothes and another judge give probation to a white defendant who wore a suit. and had a private lawyer, and had been convicted of embezzling $150,000 from a bank.[51]

Jury trials, as we have seen, are rare. But they are important in sustaining the public view that the judicial system is just. But even these most visible, and thus most just, exercises of the formal justice complex are biased in two ways.

[51] Jack Newfield, "Mindlessly, Randomly, Hurriedly, Blindly," *The Village Voice*, February 1973, pp. 8, 24.

The jury   The size of juries differs from state to state. In some, only six people serve in minor cases and twelve in major cases; in other states, twelve jurors are required in all cases. But everywhere, the composition of juries is likely to be unrepresentative. Businessmen and professionals tend to be much overrepresented, workers and minority groups much underrepresented. In Baltimore, for example, a study found that "professionals, managers and proprietors constituted only 18.7 percent of the population but contributed 40.2 percent of the jurors. . . . At the same time 41.4 percent of the population were working-class people but only 13.4 percent of the jurors were blue-collared."[52]

Procedures for the selection of juries make equal representation nearly impossible. In almost all cases, jurors are selected from lists of registered voters; but the poorer a person is, the less likely he or she is to register to vote. Many states excuse women from jury duty. Since jurors get paid for service, commissioners in small localities often use jury duty as a focus of patronage and choose friends and acquaintances to serve. On the other hand, a juror's pay is usually lower than a typical worker can earn in a day's work; hence many blue-collar workers who would lose wages ask to be excused on grounds of financial hardship. White-collar workers, by contrast, often continue to be paid while they serve. Class bias is thus built into the jury system. Finally, those previously convicted of a crime are ineligible for jury duty.

Sentencing   Conviction by a jury may result in vastly different consequences for different defendants, depending on the sentence handed out by the presiding judge. Here too the most subordinate are likely to fare least well. Numerous investigations have documented that blacks in both the North and South receive significantly longer prison sentences than whites convicted in the same jurisdiction for the same crime.[53] Small drug users of heroin and cocaine are often given long prison terms, but large drug dealers often go free; a state senate committee in New York found that of all those "*convicted* (not arrested) for possession of more than one pound of heroin or cocaine between January 1969 and

[52] Edwin S. Mills, "Statistical Study of Occupations of Jurors in a U.S. District Court," *Maryland Law Review* XXII (1962): 205–16, cited in Jacob, *Justice in America*, p. 124.

[53] Henry Bullock, "Significance of the Racial Factor in the Length of Prison Sentences," *Journal of Criminal Law, Criminology, and Police Science* 52 (1961): 411–17; United States Commission on Civil Rights, *Report Number Five: Justice* (Washington, D.C., 1961); and Martin A. Levin, *Urban Politics and the Criminal Courts* (Chicago, 1977), pp. 251–55.

October 1971, 40 percent received no jail sentence at all, and 26 percent received less than one year in jail."[54] Yet the crime of possession of more than one pound of hard drugs in New York carried a maximum penalty of *life imprisonment*. Not surprisingly, many observers have concluded that the temptations open to criminal-court judges because of the discretion they have in sentencing leads some to corruption.

Judges also look out for the interests of other members of the formal justice complex. Of the 80 police officers convicted for corruption in New York City between 1968 and July 1972, "49 were either set free or given suspended sentences, and 31 received jail terms, 14 for less than one year."[55]

Prisons

In 1970, there were 4,037 local and county jails in the United States holding a population of 160,000 on an average day; state and federal prisons hold 200,000 Americans. But since there is a continuous turnover, the number of Americans who are imprisoned each year is far greater: at least 1.5 million—and some estimates put the figure as high as 5.5 million.[56] The cost of running this incarceration system is staggering: in 1970, a total of $324,278,000 was spent on American jails, or about $2,000 per inmate per year.

These jails and prisons house America's most graphic losers, the most subordinate in a system of corporate capitalism. They are dependent on the decisions of others for the basic amenities of their lives and if convicted of a crime, stripped of political rights to vote and hold office. Most have not been convicted of a crime. Many are mentally ill, alcoholic, or addicted to hard drugs. Virtually all are poor, unemployed, ill-educated, and either black or Hispanic. About two-thirds have been in jail before. They are often despised by their fellow citizens.

Their condition of social, economic, and political subordination is reflected in the custodial brutality of American jails. Most rural jails hold inmates convicted of misdemeanors, transients awaiting transfer to other facilities, and people being detained before trial who cannot raise bail. These prisons are usually governed by local county boards and directly controlled by locally

[54] Newfield, p. 25.
[55] *Ibid*.
[56] Edith Elizabeth Flynn, "Jails and Criminal Justice," in Lloyd Ohlin, ed., *Prisoners in America* (New York, 1973), p. 55.

elected sheriffs who are also principally responsible for police duties. "The majority of county jails suffer from a perennial lack of funding, from physical neglect, from the absence of any kind of program. Frequently, they fail to meet even the most rudimentary safety and health standards."[57]

At a polar extreme is the large urban jail, such as Rikers Island in New York, Los Angeles' massive jail system, and Chicago's notorious Cook County Jail. More than half of the country's prisoners are held in jails of this type. Most often they are under the control of the chief of police; in some cities they are run by autonomous departments of correction. The overwhelming number of inmates in these jails are pretrial prisoners; 80 percent of the prisoners in Philadelphia have not been convicted of a crime. Without exception, these jails are characterized by overcrowding, brutality, and dehumanizing conditions.

Most jails as well as state and federal prisons in which most convicted felons are housed cage their prisoners in cells. Conditions are unsanitary: many cells lack toilets and sinks and most prisons smell of human excrement. These institutions are understaffed and fail to provide even minimal supervision to guarantee the safety of inmates. Indeed, dormitory conditions in most prisons, overcrowding, and the lack of useful activities and recreational facilities turn prisoners against each other, and inmates develop their own means of control. Robbery, homosexual rape, extortion, and other physical violence are not only tolerated but they are made inevitable by the institution's physical and human organization. For these reasons, when subordinates leave the prisons, they are even more ill-prepared than when they entered to challenge and overcome their subordination effectively. Hence most remain or become criminals. Once arrested, they enter the system of formal criminal justice again, and the cycle comes full circle.

CONTRADICTIONS

Legally, every American citizen is entitled to equal protection under the law. In actuality, only a small minority receive it. Within the bounds of present arrangements, the contradiction between

[57] *Ibid.*, p. 59.

formal equality and substantive inequality cannot be overcome. As political scientist Isaac Balbus has noted, at the core of the legal system are "the umbilical connections between formal legal rationality and capitalism; indeed . . . it is precisely the combination of formal legal equality and extreme economic inequality which is the distinctive character of the liberal state."[58]

Although the contradiction cannot be overcome within corporate capitalist America, it has been managed differently in different contexts. One set of circumstances may require the legal system to uphold formal equality even in an area where it does not usually intervene. Conversely, in a different situation, the justice system may abandon the principle of legal equality altogether. Consider the response of the criminal courts to the ghetto rebellions of the 1960s as a case in point.

The rebellions were seen at the time as profoundly threatening to authorities, since their targets of white-owned property and the police were the most visible symbols of economic legitimacy and public authority. It thus appeared that a *structural* challenge was being mounted against existing patterns of dominance. The justice system reacted by defending those arrangements *at the expense of formal legal protections*.

The police acted to contain and subdue the disorders, often quite ruthlessly and with unnecessary brutality. In New Jersey, the Governor's Select Commission on Civil Disorder, for example, concluded that "the amount of ammunition expended by police forces was out of all proportion to the mission assigned them . . . this reflects a pattern of police action for which there is no possible justification."[59] This behavior was quite consistent with the more routine pattern of police abuses, which, as we have seen, usually stem from what police see as direct threats to their authority. The greater the threat, the greater the likelihood that the police will act without reference to formal legal restraints.

The same proved true of the criminal courts, whose behavior unmistakably betrayed a commitment to civil order first and to formal standards of legality only secondarily.

Jerome Skolnick studied the judicial response to racial vi-

[58] Isaac Balbus, *The Dialectics of Legal Repression: Black Rebels Before the American Criminal Courts* (New York, 1973), p. 5.
[59] Governor's Select Commission on Civil Disorder of New Jersey, *Report for Action*, in Theodore Becker and Vernon Murray, eds., *Government Lawlessness in America* (New York, 1971), p. 4.

olence in Detroit, Newark, Washington, D.C., Baltimore, and Chicago. In all these cities, the "constitutional right to bail was almost invariably replaced by what in effect was a policy of preventive detention." In Detroit, the twelve judges who heard the rebellion cases agreed at a meeting on the second day of the violence to set bonds averaging $10,000, a sum very much higher than most of the defendants could afford. In violation of routine legal procedure, the high bail policy in all of the cities was "applied uniformly—ignoring the nature of the charge, family and job status of those arrested, the prior record, and all other factors usually considered in the setting of bail."[60]

The judges thus deliberately put aside the canons of formal legality to keep their prisoners incarcerated until structural stability was restored. The imperatives of social control overrode their commitment to legality and justice. In reply to a reporter who questioned the constitutionality of high bail, Chicago's chief judge said, "What do you want me to do—cry crocodile tears for people who take advantage of their city?" In Detroit, a criminal-court judge justified his actions by arguing, "We had no way of knowing whether there was a revolution in progress or whether the city was going to be burned down or what."[61]

But if the justice system is used both routinely and in "emergencies" to maintain social order, the contradiction between formal justice and substantive injustice provides possibilities—as the decisions of the Warren Court indicated—for enlarging the range of choice available to subordinates. Whether or not these opportunities will be taken up largely depends on the actions of movements for basic change, which can force the courts to rule on major issues in accordance with the principles of formal justice. Without the National Association for the Advancement of Colored People, there would have been no *Brown* v. *Board of Education*; and without the women's movement, there would have been no *Roe* v. *Wade* (1973) and *Doe* v. *Bolton* (1973), which upheld a woman's right to abortion. The formal legality that the justice system cannot do without can thus be turned back on substantive inequities.

[60] Jerome Skolnick, "Judicial Response in Crisis," in *ibid.*, pp. 161–62.
[61] *Ibid.*, pp. 164, 162.

conclusion

12

capitalism, socialism, and democracy

Travelers to the United States have often remarked on the extraordinary diversity and pace of life. In contrast to other industrialized capitalist countries, the most constant feature of American society is change. One American family in four moves every year. One out of every three couples taking out a marriage license today will divorce. Automobile styles change annually. Technological innovations from Teflon pans to precision laser-guided bombs are produced—and discarded—at a rate unmatched by any other nation.

Political change also appears amazingly rapid and widespread. Roughly four-fifths of American workers voted for the presidential candidate of the Democratic party in 1964; over half voted for the Republican candidate in 1972, and nearly half in 1976. Until the passage of the Voting Rights Act of 1965, blacks in most Southern states, indeed a majority of blacks in the United States, were denied the right to vote. Today, some Northern and Southern cities have black mayors. Even strongly held and expressed personal opinions shift dramatically. Some of the chief architects of the Vietnam war were expert witnesses for the defense at the 1971 trial of Daniel Ellsberg, who was accused by the government of damaging national security by leaking the Pentagon Papers to the press.

Yet an undifferentiated focus on change is misleading for two reasons. First, it obscures deep continuities in the American experience. The commitment to capitalism and democracy, and to the management of the tensions between the two, has been a constant, at least in the past century and a half. Unlike most other nations in the West, in the United States there have been virtually no direct mass assaults on democracy or capitalism as principles of social organization. As a result, in this century, the corporate complex of large capital and the executive branch of the national government have had the capacity to shape the character of American politics as well as to define its limits and policy choices. Second, an undifferentiated focus on change, by failing to distinguish which changes are significant, conveys the impression that no change is important or that every change is important.

American history is in fact littered with the passion of a great many lost and successful movements for change. Most aimed for change within the framework of a capitalist democracy, but some tested and sought to move beyond these limits, either, as in the case of the anticommunist agitation of the late 1940s and early 1950s, to a more authoritarian capitalism, or, as in the case of the political campaigns of Eugene Debs and Norman Thomas, to a socialist democracy.

The mere fact of change poses potential challenges to prevailing social and political patterns, often in unexpected ways. The mechanization and concentration of farming in the South, for example, increased output and profits for white Southern landowners. At the same time, these changes in production impelled five million blacks to migrate to northern and western cities in the last thirty years. This basic demographic change has "Southernized" Northern politics. A different kind of change involved the invention of long-playing phonograph records in the 1940s, which made it possible for musical traditions to develop among a vast young audience. Records are, of course, predominantly a form of entertainment. But in the 1960s, a number of folk singers, including Bob Dylan, Joan Baez, and Phil Ochs, used recordings both to reflect and create cultural change and political protest.

These examples suggest the unexpected ways that apparently nonpolitical changes may produce challenges that potentially threaten basic arrangements. Potential threats cannot entirely be eliminated unless change itself is totally suppressed—clearly an impossibility. A priority task for political and corporate authorities is to sort out and deal with those changes that are potentially threatening. Conversely, those who oppose patterns of dominance must utilize changes in order to focus political energies on strategies for promoting alternatives.

The framework for American politics as well as possibilities for basic and enduring alterations in the society are furnished by the contradictions between capitalism and democracy discussed throughout this volume. Such contradictions are characteristic of all the developed societies in the West; but more than in any other of these countries, everyday political reality in the United States does not appear to correspond directly to the clash of contradictory structural interests. The ideological and institutional mechanisms of American society—such as patterns of congressional representation, the functioning of the justice system, dominant and accommodative systems of ideas, and the institutionalized relationships between unions and the corporate complex—direct conflict away from basic structural questions.

At any given historical moment, in the United States as elsewhere in the West, there is no automatic, predetermined outcome to structural contradictions and political conflicts. Especially is this the case at times like the present, when traditional political loyalties and understandings are losing their capacity to give meaning to daily life. "Outraged. Apprehensive. Resigned. Angry. Frustrated. Turned Off. Cynical. Bitter. These are the adjectives," the *Wall Street Journal* noted in 1978, "that leading pollsters and public-opinion analysts use to describe the mood of America this summer. While the adjectives aren't quite synonymous, they all point to an unhappy and troubled nation."[1] Political parties have come to command the loyalties of followers less and less, Congress is viewed with increasing cynicism by Americans and has become an institution in search of a purpose, the presidency is losing its sacred aura, and the dominant ideology is losing its hold over public consciousness. As a result, people are becoming less attached to established political institutions and are potentially more available for new modes of action. Many have devel-

[1] *Wall Street Journal*, August 4, 1978, p. 1.

oped accommodative and even radical ideologies that call for change.

In periods when mechanisms of social control are strong, stability prevails despite structural contradictions. When mechanisms of control decay, however, citizens *may* see their interests more clearly, act on them, and begin to make history. This does not mean that structural change will necessarily occur: rulers may develop new mechanisms of control to manage new challenges. On the other hand, rulers may fail to contain the challenge. In a period of decaying ideology and institutions, contradictions sharpen and the future is more open.

But, to cite an old homily, people do not make history just as they please. Inherited patterns of politics and society shape understandings in the present and limit possible choices even as existing arrangements fail to make sense to more and more people. To assess possibilities for basic changes in American society, we first examine closely recent struggles in the country's oldest cities, for it is here that the contradictions between capitalism and democracy have been most acute. After this exploration, we focus on the future. Without trying to make precise predictions of what the future may hold, we will distinguish among three contrasting possible outcomes, which are based on the dominant, accommodative, and radical ideologies described in Chapter 2.

URBANISM AND CAPITALISM

Newark, New Jersey, is a city of 400,000 people. It does not have a single first-run movie theater. In the 1960s, half of its doctors moved out of the city to practice in the suburbs. Since 1940, the city's largest impoverished black population has quadrupled and is now a majority. For the most part they live in substandard homes, many beyond repair. One in five of Newark's houses has no central heating; 8,000 have no toilets. The decay and abandonment of old housing is proceeding at a much faster rate than new construction. Yet, downtown, two new office towers of eighteen and thirty floors have been built with urban renewal funds as headquarters for locally based corporations. Newark's former mayor is in prison for extortion. In the summer of 1967, racial violence rocked the city; as a result, twenty-three people were killed, and $10,500,000 worth of property was destroyed.

Newark is not a typical American city. Many cities, especially in parts of the South, Southwest, and West, whose economies are based on corporate expansion and new technology industries, such as aerospace, are prospering. But Newark, at the other extreme, as one observer has noted, is "a foretaste of things to come . . . the probable future that faces many of our older cities."[2] These older cities include the country's largest cities, which have been the focal point of American economic growth and international trade since the Civil War. Virtually all the major corporations are headquartered there. These cities are also home to most of the country's poor, and to a great variety of small-capital businesses. They are cultural and ideological centers.

An examination of the nature of politics in the major, older cities allows us to explore basic social and economic processes of American life. Thus, on his visit to the United States in 1904, the German sociologist Max Weber noted that America's cities resemble a "man whose skin has been peeled off and whose entrails one sees at work."[3] Moreover, since the politics of these cities involves increasingly harsh competition for scarce resources, their study concretely illustrates the contradictory relationship of capitalism and democracy. In these cities the tensions caused by class and racial inequalities have pressed these contradictions to the fore; at the same time, urban political elites have attempted to manage them successfully. Such tensions characterize American politics as a whole. But their expression is perhaps most apparent in cities like Boston, Chicago, New York, Philadelphia, and Detroit.

These older cities are caught up in a complex web of political and economic relationships with the wider society. They are not autonomous entities, not even legally. Changes in municipal tax laws, forms of government, jurisdictional boundaries, and local civil-service regulations usually require approval by state governments.

This juridical dependency is symptomatic of the broader substantive dependency of most cities. Their significant problems of

---

[2] George Sternlieb, "The City as Sandbox," *The Public Interest* 25 (Fall 1971): 14.
[3] Hans Gerth and C. Wright Mills, eds., *From Max Weber* (New York, 1958), p. 15.

housing, crime, transportation, welfare, and finance—commonly lumped together as "the urban crisis"—are generated by causes relating to class and race that are inherent in the society, and over which cities have little control.

Poverty is an example of this. The conditions that lead to widespread poverty are not "caused" by the cities, nor can they be significantly affected at that level. An individual's earning power and employability are dependent on many factors. These factors include characteristics of the local labor market, such as its rate of growth and the nature of the demand for labor; characteristics of the industry in which the individual is employed, such as profit rates, technology, unionization, and the industry's relationship to government; and individual characteristics, such as age, sex, and race.

The poverty in a given city also reflects migration patterns over which the receiving city has virtually no control. The increasing concentration of Southern agriculture, for example, has resulted in fewer jobs and has driven blacks off the land. Similarly, high unemployment rates in Puerto Rico and other Caribbean economies have impelled people to look for economic opportunities in the major urban centers of the United States. Like welfare, other poverty-related problems such as crime, drug abuse, ineffective schools, and severe health problems—all of which have to be dealt with by city governments—are caused by factors external to the cities where their impact is ultimately felt.

The cities' lack of control over the origins of the basic problems that beset them has been complemented by the changing economic functions of cities, growing class and racial divisions between cities and suburbs, and an increasing dependence of cities on external resources.

From the outset, the growth of industrial capitalism depended on the massive growth of cities. Factories demanded an available work force, detached from the land. Industries needed to be spatially concentrated to facilitate the exchange of goods and to insure the ready availability of banking and legal services. Not surprisingly, therefore, America's older cities grew most rapidly in the last third of the nineteenth and first third of the twentieth centuries. (Chicago's population doubled between 1900 and 1930; New York's almost quadrupled between 1890 and 1930, only partially as a result of the extension of the city's boundaries.) In these decades, the United States was transformed from a largely agrarian, land-holding society into an increasingly urbanized corporate capitalist society. The burgeoning cities were the repository of cheap unskilled labor, largely immigrant, that filled the menial positions at the lower levels of the expanding corporate economy. Hence, by the middle of this century, the following description of the urban economy was appropriate:

> The urban areas of this nation are the setting for the most powerful and complex industrialization in the world. Cities are the center of commerce and of the transportation and communications infrastructure which underpins the economy. Modern cities are central administration points for large corporations and the financial centers of America. They are also the central marketplaces for every conceivable kind of commercial good and service. The urban economy contains not only most of the productive capacity of the nation, but also most of its capacity to consume.[4]

The cities still maintain a strategic economic position today. Virtually all the headquarters of America's one hundred largest industrial corporations are in the large cities. The central business districts of these cities have continued to grow (often with the help of urban renewal funds) because corporate offices need to be in a location that maximizes their access to branch managers, sales executives, and buyers; because they need a large number of clerical workers to staff their headquarters; and because they need to be near the "business services which the corporation cannot internally provide. These often include: financing agents for investment and stock transfer, banks to service operating capital needs, advertising, printing, data processing, consulting firms in various managerial and technical areas, etc."[5] In the past two decades, most new private-sector urban jobs have been created by corporate headquarters expansion.

But this trend has been offset by the loss of jobs in corporate manufacturing, which is expanding in the suburbs and has declined sharply in almost every major city. New York City alone has lost almost 400,000 such jobs in the 1970s. In some cities they hardly exist any longer. As a result, the growth of the older cities has stopped. Major cities today are *losing* population, and a growing

---

[4] Roger Friedland, "Corporations and Urban Renewal," unpublished manuscript.
[5] *Ibid.*

proportion of wages and subsistence payments are being provided
by jobs in small-capital businesses, government employment, and
welfare.

Although the older city business centers remain important to
large industrial and financial corporations, increasing numbers of
their employees—from top-level executives to shopfloor
workers—have moved to the suburbs. The majority of small-
capital workers, by contrast, have been left behind in the inner
cities. Most are black and many poor. High rent and property value
levels and exclusionary zoning laws make it very difficult for these
workers to leave the cities. As a result, the relationship between
city and suburb largely reflects the relationship between the
small-capital and corporate sectors of American capitalism.

This division between cities and suburbs is a relatively new
development. Class, ethnic, and racial distinctions, of course,
historically have been expressed within American cities. The
largest cities in particular have long been divided into relatively
homogeneous neighborhoods. But since the Second World War,
these traditional urban divisions have been jumbled and reorganized under the impact of massive suburban growth.

Much like the dynamic discussed in Chapter 4 that insures that
the corporate sector grows and profits at the expense of small
capital, the suburbs have prospered at the expense of the cities.
Relatively affluent, largely white, suburban residents come into
the cities in the morning to work, utilize the cities' resources and
services during the day, and go home at night without paying city
taxes. They are thus subsidized by the taxes relatively poorer city
residents pay to maintain police, traffic, and other vital services;
and they take back to the suburbs a considerable portion of their
incomes and wealth, thus reducing the cities' resources even
further.

Urban politicians and officials must govern in this situation.
Since the cities are recipients of problems they do not generate or
control; since American society's basic inequalities of class and
race are expressed and experienced directly in the major cities; and
since those who rule the cities lack the resources to solve problems
of housing, poverty, education, and transportation (yet their constituencies widely expect them to be able to do so), their aim
becomes *the management of the consequences of their inability to
solve urban problems.*

URBAN DISCONTENT AND CHALLENGES TO AUTHORITY

The more people who accept the social structure as just, who consent to their relative subordination, the more secure authorities can be. As urban problems have increased and urban officials have not been able to deal with them successfully, growing numbers of people who live in the cities have come to be discontented not only in an imprecise, accommodationist way, but have developed what we called a radical perspective in Chapter 2.

In urban America in the 1960s, there was a marked decline in support for prevailing structures of political authority. The most prominent development was the ferment that took place in the urban black communities. The racial violence in New York in 1964, Watts in 1965, Newark and Detroit in 1967, and in hundreds of other cities during the decade, was profoundly political. The targets of attack by blacks, including the police and white-owned property, were visible symbols of public order and a capitalist social structure.

These rebellions reflected the particularly harsh impact the cities' plight has had on ghetto residents. Sociologist Robert Blauner argued that the riots were mass rebellions against a colonial-like status:

> The thrust of the action has been to clear out an alien presence, white men and officials, rather than a drive to kill whites as in a conventional race riot. . . . More accurately the revolts pointed to alienation from this system on the part of many poor and also not so poor blacks. The sacredness of private property, that unconsciously accepted bulwark of our social arrangements, was rejected. . . . Obviously the society's bases of legitimacy and authority have been attacked.[6]

Another analyst saw the riots as an amalgam of reformist and potentially revolutionary tendencies. In identifying the riots as reform movements, he said that the violence "may perhaps be best understood as a kind of wildcat strike" that represented a revolt "of the ghetto rank and file against an established black leadership which . . . has failed to deliver the goods, and a form of direct action intended to communicate grievances and apply pressure on the white 'managers' of the ghetto." The second and more radical

---

[6] Robert Blauner, "Internal Colonialism and Ghetto Revolt," *Social Problems* 16 (Spring 1969): 399.

aspect of the riots as a potentially revolutionary rebellion "consists of an impulsive, large-scale effort to break the control of the white authorities over the ghetto, to seize territory and property by force, and to replace white authority with indigenous control."[7]

Widespread black rejection of prevailing authority patterns has been expressed not only in these bloody rebellions. Movements for community control of school systems and the police emerged in most American cities. Protests and demonstrations became almost daily events, as tenants' organizations and welfare-rights groups developed in nearly every major city. Assaults on visible structures of authority became commonplace. School vandalism increased markedly. Police became the targets of verbal and, occasionally, fatal physical abuse. Street crime moved out of the ghettos into all-white areas that had largely been crime-free. Social analysts Frances Piven and Richard Cloward noted, "The main conclusion to be drawn from an appraisal of the disorder of the 1960s is that the old pattern of servile conformity was shattered: the trauma and anger of an oppressed people not only had been released, but had been turned against the social structure."[8]

Although the apparent rejection of the prevailing order was most dramatic in the urban black community, there were signs of parallel developments among other urban groups. The political behavior of white ethnic (largely Catholic) workers was in flux. As immigrants, and later as native-born citizens, they had been linked to the political system through three separate, yet related, institutions: the Democratic party urban political machines, the Catholic Church, and the trade unions of the AFL and CIO. Each of these institutions has undergone considerable change in the past three decades.

The Democratic party organizations have declined in power in almost every major city (Chicago is the leading exception), and in some have completely disappeared. In the Church, the ecumenicism of Pope John XXIII, the civil disobedience activities of radical priests like Philip and Daniel Berrigan and other members of the Catholic left, and the closing down of many parochial schools are

---

[7] David Boesel, "An Analysis of the Ghetto Riots," in David Boesel and Peter Rossi, eds., *Cities Under Siege: An Anatomy of the Ghetto Riots* (New York, 1971), p. 333.

[8] Frances Piven and Richard Cloward, *Regulating the Poor* (New York, 1971), p. 227.

just three of many signs of significant change. And, while party organizations have decayed and the Church has been in ferment, the unions have settled down to routine collective bargaining—hardly as exhilarating as the economic struggles of the 1930s. Thus, by the beginning of the 1970s, none of these three institutions commanded the legitimacy and emotional support among white ethnic workers that they had previously.

As a result, the high level of discontent that invariably pervades working-class life (the product of such factors as job insecurity, monotonous work, modest wages, and lack of control over the work process) not only appeared to increase but also was no longer necessarily channeled into institutional activities that lent direct support to the status quo. More and more workers appeared to echo the sentiments of the ironworker who told journalist Pete Hamill:

> I'm going out of my mind. I average about $8,500 a year, pretty good money. I work my ass off. But I can't make it. I come home at the end of the week, I start paying the bills, I give my wife some money for food. And there's nothing left. Maybe if I work overtime I get $15 or $20 to spend on myself. But most of the time, there's nothing.[9]

As traditional outlets for the increasing discontent of workers gave way, they vented their anger both at those beneath and above them in the social structure. Workers' behavior suddenly appeared as a jumble of contradictions: plant sabotage and attacks on welfare; support for quasi-populist candidates of the left and right and a majority vote for Richard Nixon; an assembly-line turnover at automobile factories that approaches 100 percent annually; and participation in drug and crime subcultures whose victims are often other workers.

In addition to blacks and workers, others joined in activities that at least potentially challenged urban structures of authority. Among university students and relatively well-off professionals, anti-Vietnam war protests became vehicles for a wider rejection of the prevailing pattern of structure and choice. In professions like medicine, social work, and education, radical professional groups were founded, and some, such as The Union of Radical Political Economics, flourished. And a burgeoning cultural revolution among young people, who rejected society's dominant sexual and

---

[9] Pete Hamill, "The Revolt of the White Lower-Middle-Class," in Louise Kapp Howe, ed., *The White Majority* (New York, 1970), p. 11.

work ethics, also contained the seeds of even more basic transfor-
mations.

For political activists committed to radical change, the 1960s
were times of heightened sensibilities, intoxicating alternatives,
and the erosion of boundaries between the political and the
private, the expected and unexpected, the routine and the irregular. The bursting of bounds—of segregation, deference, city
space, and on and on it seemed—in the main urban centers produced the spirit of a liberating party.

ORDER RESTORED

This party is over. From today's vantage point it is clear that this
particular era of urban crisis has come to a close. Neither the fears
nor the promises of radical or fundamental change have been
redeemed. A striking indicator is that of political language. In the
middle and late 1960s people spoke dramatically of participatory
democracy and community control. For a fleeting period such
things seemed to be real political alternatives. Yet only a decade
later the language of urban politics is very different. It is concerned
mainly with fiscal and managerial matters. The talk is of balancing
budgets, bondholder confidence, service cutbacks, wage freezes,
making do with less. The social needs of the 1960s have not been
overcome; but the social movements that demanded change then
no longer have the capacity to determine the political agenda.

What happened? An answer is important if we are to understand the obstacles that face mass movements—even those that
call for changes well short of socialism in the United States. Part of
the answer is the capacity of authorities to convert demands for
redistribution into policies that treat these demands for changes in
accommodationist terms. Another aspect is the absence of a
socialist tradition that sees work and community conflicts as essentially common struggles about capitalism, socialism, and democracy; without this tradition, urban conflicts were understood
as local conflicts rather than as broader questions concerning the
economic place of cities in the national political economy. As a
consequence of these two aspects, urban authorities were able to
alter local institutions in response to the social movements of the

1960s in minor ways, without addressing the most fundamental issues about race and class.

These alterations took a number of forms. Some were explicitly repressive. Local police forces were strengthened substantially in many cities after the ghetto revolts of the mid-1960s, and new police intelligence units were established. A second kind of response entailed the expansion of social service bureaucracies, which provided short-term limited gains to many disaffected urban residents.

Consider again the case of welfare. Between 1960 and 1970, the percentage of poor families in the major metropolitan areas remained roughly the same (although their composition changed—43 percent of poor families in New York City were black or Hispanic in 1960; 70 percent in 1970), as did the percentage of people eligible for welfare who claimed their benefits—yet welfare rolls more than doubled. Although the root cause of the welfare "crisis" was poverty, that alone cannot explain what happened in New York and other cities in that decade. A critical factor was the change in eligibility standards. Between January 1964 and November 1968, because of a liberalization of grant standards, the number of people eligible for welfare increased by about 170 percent. The implications, economist David Gordon wrote, are clear. "If New York State had not decided to offer people an income at least equal to what the federal government calls the poverty line, there would be no welfare crisis at all. We would, in its place, have a far greater amount of poverty." [10]

Thus the critical issue is why did New York and other states in this period opt, quite consciously, for a welfare "crisis" by lowering eligibility standards rather than maintain a continuation of the old levels that kept more people at depressed income levels? Altruism, perhaps?

Hardly likely, especially since elected officials had a great deal to lose by becoming publicly identified as supporters of expanded welfare programs. Piven and Cloward suggested the most persuasive answer. The rise in welfare rolls was directly related to the rise in black discontent, which was expressed most dramatically in the violent ghetto rebellions:

If the relief rise in the early 1960s coincided with the rise in disorder,

[10] David Gordon, "Income and Welfare in New York City," *The Public Interest* 16 (Summer 1969): 86.

this relationship was even more striking after 1964. As protests, demonstrations, riots, and other forms of disorder reached unprecedented heights between 1965 and 1968, the relief rolls climbed 58 percent, having already risen 31 percent in the preceding four years. The 121 urban counties showed an increase of 80 percent after 1964; in the "big five" urban counties, the rolls more than doubled (up to 105 percent).[11]

Historically, they argued, drawing on the English and American experience, there is a cycle of welfare relief: massive dislocations (early industrialization in England, the depression and mass black migration to the North in the United States) produce massive discontents. One response by authorities is to liberalize welfare requirements—a relatively simple, direct way of "buying off" discontent. As overt discontent ebbs, welfare eligibility standards are raised once more, thus channeling more people into low-paid menial work. Although a causal relationship is very difficult to prove, Piven and Cloward's approach to welfare could have been used to accurately predict the welfare contraction of the early 1970s. In almost every American state after 1972, welfare rolls dropped; not coincidentally, by 1972 the period of massive ghetto rebellions had passed—at least for the time being.

This case of an attempt at social control by bureaucratic rewards was not unique. The New York City municipal payroll expanded from 240,000 to 380,000 jobs in the 1960s. School expenditures in Boston rose from $35 million in 1961 to $96 million in 1971. "As the turmoil of the 1960s rose," Piven pointed out, "so did city costs. . . . New York [in 1973] spends half again as much per capita as other cities over a million, and three times as much as the other 288 cities."[12] In Chicago, by contrast, where machine-style politics have survived, garbage collection costs and per-pupil school expenditures are roughly *one-half* of New York's. Thus where party-control mechanisms that organize participation in politics continue to operate, the need for bureaucratic rewards to maintain control is much lower.

Urban authorities in cities marked by the advanced atrophy of party organizations also augmented the available bureaucratic tools of social control by creating new urban institutions designed to perform the buffer role once played so effectively by machines. This program of building "new machines" was sponsored by both

[11] Piven and Cloward, p. 245.
[12] Frances Piven, "The Urban Crisis: Who Got What and Why," in Robert Paul Wolff, ed., *1984 Revisited* (New York, 1973), pp. 184–85.

national and local political elites. In cities like New York and Boston, reform mayors, who had been elected in spite of the absence of effective party organizations to work on their behalf, developed a new type of urban political organization. This included neighborhood city halls, urban action task forces, and pilot programs for neighborhood government. Like similar federal programs (such as the community action programs discussed in Chapter 7), the city organizations sought to structure the political participation of angry people and to establish administrative mechanisms that would reach neighborhoods (without disturbing the existing structure of power and resources).

The case of New York is instructive. Mayor Lindsay, in June 1970, proposed the establishment of sixty-two "neighborhood government" offices, each serving a population of approximately 130,000. The stated aims of the program included the improvement of city services "by making [city] agencies more responsive and accountable at the neighborhood level"; the reduction of "the distance that citizens feel exists between themselves and city government"; and the creation of the "basis for a single coordinated governmental presence in each neighborhood, recognized and supported by the community, the municipal government, and all elected officials."[13]

This statement of goals indicated the "new machine" quality of the proposal. The program's organizational roots of neighborhood government (which, since its inception in 1970, has undergone significant changes in the pilot areas) further reveal the relationship of this kind of program to the urban political crisis of control. Running as the Republican-Liberal candidate in 1965, Lindsay lacked even the inadequate organizational support the Democratic party then was capable of providing its candidate. To compensate, his campaign manager organized storefront headquarters in the city's neighborhoods to duplicate the functions of the machines in getting out the vote. After Lindsay's election, these storefronts, in spite of the opposition from the Democratic city council, developed into neighborhood city halls, which served as grievance centers and dispensed services. Writing about one such neighborhood office, Lindsay noted that

> the hall was staffed by three professionals supplemented by volunteers who . . . both as residents and 'ombudsmen' . . . could channel complaints and intelligence directly into the machinery of the

[13] Ira Katznelson, "Urban Counterrevolution," in *ibid.*, p. 150.

city administration. The results were impressive. The number of cases handled jumped from 2,200 in 1967 to more than 8,000 in the first nine months of 1968. More important, however, was the fact that local residents realized that their neighborhood city hall was an effective mechanism for getting grievances resolved.[14]

From his perspective, Lindsay noted, the most pressing racial problem when he assumed office was not primarily one of racism or objective exploitation, but one of black alienation and discontent:

> What we saw in early 1966 was that within the ghetto, discontent and alienation were at the breaking point. We saw that a basic commitment to ending that alienation through greater contact was essential. And we knew that words alone would not do the job. . . . Thus, through the fall of 1966 and into the spring of 1967 *we made plans for a structured, formal link between the neighborhoods and the city*.[15]

The program for neighborhood government thus explicitly sought to create new links between citizens and government to maintain order.

These local institutional reforms were paralleled by others initiated by national authorities, who were concerned by the rising tide of urban discontent. The hallmark of the Great Society programs of Lyndon Johnson's presidency was "the direct relationship between the national government and the ghettos, a relationship in which both the state and local governments were undercut." It became apparent to some of the more sophisticated members of the national government that at least one cause of the massive discontent of the 1960s was the shift in the locus of political power from the machines to the bureaucracies. Hence an attempt was made to bypass the usual political arrangements that quite clearly were not adequately performing the function of social control. According to Piven and Cloward, the new federally sponsored "machines"

> became the base for new black political organizations whose rhetoric may have been thunderous, but whose activities came to consist mainly of vying for position and patronage within the urban political system. . . . Over a period of time, in other words, federal intervention had the effect of absorbing and directing many of the

[14] John V. Lindsay, *The City* (New York, 1970), p. 118.
[15] *Ibid.*, pp. 87, 95. Emphasis added.

agitational elements in the black population. . . . Those who regard these federal actions as unintended, as a mistake, will have to account for the reason the mistake was repeated and enlarged from one legislative program to another as the decade wore on.[16]

These new institutional forms, both locally and nationally sponsored, are appropriate buffers for large, heterogeneous (racially and ethnically) cities with atrophied party organizations. In other locales, urban politicians have responded to their political crisis of control by utilizing similar techniques. In Chicago, the one case where a strong Democratic party machine survives, with only minor signs of diminishing success, black and white workers are linked to the political system on traditional machine terms.

In cities with majority, or near majority, black populations (most notably, Cleveland, Gary, Newark, and Atlanta), black mayors were elected, usually with the financial support of both national and local corporations and foundations. Once in office, irrespective of the degree of their support for fundamental structural change, black mayors usually found it impossible to transform their cities' condition. Like other big-city mayors, they lacked political resources and power to solve their cities' most pressing problems.

The experience of Newark's Mayor Gibson, who was elected in 1970, indicates the limits within which even honest men of good will must operate in governing American cities. "I have promised to work toward that great day in 1970 when we shall have elected a talented, progressive and imaginative black mayor who will be able to give Newark an honest, moral and people-oriented government," a leading supporter of Gibson's proclaimed before his election.[17] In his terms of office, Gibson has largely lived up to this advance notice. Yet the city remains plagued by all of the substantive problems he inherited—a changing population base, loss of jobs, abandoned and decaying housing, a troubled educational system, a worsening fiscal crisis, and bureaucracies that remain independent and unresponsive—even to the Mayor. The police, in particular, the most autonomous of the city agencies, have resisted mayoral interventions. Their relationship is symbolized by what happened one night in 1971 when Gibson chose to tour the city's

---

[16] Piven and Cloward, pp. 274–77.
[17] Robert Curvin, "Black Power in Newark: Kenneth Gibson's First Year," unpublished manuscript.

hospitals. When his car broke down, he radioed for police assistance. The reply: "Let the son of a bitch walk."[18]

ACCOMMODATIONIST OUTCOME:
PIECEMEAL CHALLENGE AND RESPONSE

The piecemeal character of the challenges to the social order in the cities in the 1960s and the limited responses by authorities, which aimed more at restoring order than altering substantive arrangements, are typical of the mode of politics we have called accommodationist. Looking to the future, this kind of politics, which exemplifies American politics in the past, is more likely to persist in the near future than either of the other two main options—the dominant and radical outcomes.

In the accommodationist outcome, the corporate complex will remain in control but will face increasing problems and challenges to its power. Small businesspeople and farmers, burdened by higher taxes and the administered prices of the corporate sector, will use their available resources (control of local and state governments, the illusion of free enterprise, and access to Congress and parts of the executive branch) to resist further corporate expansion and state interference. The state will attempt to extend its area of control over other productive sectors both in order to carry out the function of rationalization and coordination more efficiently and to increase the power of state officials. State regulations will proliferate, and state capital will be used to extend the reach of the corporate complex. Small businesses and farmers will become dependent on state largesse (small business loans, agricultural subsidies).

A host of new groups will clamor for help from the government. Corporate capitalists will need massive inputs of state capital for advanced technological projects. Small capital will need government in order to defend itself from corporate encroachment. The state sector will flourish as government activities expand. Corporate-sector workers will seek help from the state in order to obtain higher wages, better social security programs, and

---

[18] *Ibid.*

better working conditions. Surplus labor and workers in the small-capital sector will become more vulnerable and hence come to depend on government even for basic amenities. As more and more Americans come to be consumers of vital government services and depend on government bureaucracies, citizens will feel powerless, resentful, and angry.

The growing contradictions in the economy will be expressed in a turbulent, issue-oriented ad hoc politics of increasing fragmentation and bitterness. On the one hand, many Americans will be increasingly discontent with the hand they are dealt and increasingly prone to challenge authorities. Within the productive sphere, workers' discontents will burst the bounds of institutionalized class politics. Workers will demonstrate anger toward corporate authorities by high turnover rates, absenteeism, wildcat strikes, and plant sabotage; toward union leaders by challenging them in union elections. Many state and professional employees will use the strike weapon as they never have before. Blacks will use expressive violence, guerrilla tactics, and sustained militant organization to challenge internal colonialism. Tenant associations, welfare-rights groups, and environmental-protection organizations will mount political campaigns. In the electoral sphere, voters will be increasingly frustrated in their efforts to utilize traditional channels of representation. The result may be either a further decline in voting turnout (thus discrediting the idea that the system is democratically chosen) or the emergence of new political movements seeking change.

Throughout the society, then, there will be pressure points where particular groups will strain against the bounds of established arrangements. Yet this protest activity, informed by an accommodative ideology, will direct its anger to particular authorities within particular spheres. It will not add up to a structural critique or structural challenge. Protest will remain fragmented, uncoordinated, and ephemeral, and it will often be directed at other subordinates (for example, white ethnic workers in the corporate sector against small-capital–sector blacks).

In face of these variegated challenges, authorities will improvise tactical and institutional responses. A rent strike may be met by a combination of court-ordered convictions, police harassment, and apparently conciliatory gestures—an offer to negotiate, appointment of a study commission, and a soothing pronouncement by a local city official. Authorities will constantly use the arsenal of

repressive techniques available to them and devise new responses to fit particular challenges. The effect will be one resembling the frenetic activity of a fire department—each day brings new crises. The resulting stalemate will add up neither to a secure victory for the dominant nor to structural change.

Evidence for the ascendancy of the accommodationist outcome begins with the fact that it is happening already. Merely open any daily newspaper for confirmation. Within recent years, the following series of crises have been solemnly proclaimed by political leaders, only to disappear from sight once the challenging group was disarmed: urban crisis, environment crisis, welfare crisis, energy crisis, moral crisis, law-and-order crisis, balance-of-payments crisis, and racial crisis. These crises are definitions by authorities of the ad hoc politics we described. They are crises for two reasons: they are manifestations of contradictions rooted in the social structure; and, from the vantage point of those on top, they potentially threaten existing patterns of dominance.

The emergence of new bases of inequality increases the probability of the accommodationist outcome. Welfare programs, for example, create two antagonistic groups—recipients and welfare bureaucrats. Similarly, the integration of universities into the corporate complex sets students and junior faculty against senior faculty and the administration. But each conflict is relatively self-contained, with its own autonomous set of issues, actors, institutions, and dynamics.

Although in the long run the accommodationist approach only patches up holes temporarily, in the short run it is likely to persist. Once the dynamic of ad hoc politics is set into motion, it tends to reproduce itself as more and more people become involved in "irregular politics," develop an accommodationist ideology, and discover their ability to challenge authorities. Demands achieved or denied generate new demands; awareness of grievances in one area may make individuals more aware of discontents in others. The result is a whirligig of action and reaction, challenge and repression.

Finally, the accommodationist alternative has been buttressed by the development of a problems-oriented social science. Prompted in large part by the need of authorities for solutions to particular challenges, economists, sociologists, political scientists, systems analysts, social planners, and policy analysts have churned out studies and technical solutions for each "crisis." Typically, they analyze the problem from authorities' points of view and adopt an apparently neutral, clinical perspective that in fact blurs fundamental structural conflicts.

However, the accommodationist alternative is inherently unstable, both for dominants and subordinates. At multiple pressure points in the system, authorities find themselves challenged by increasingly militant and irate subordinates. They are constantly tempted to abandon democratic procedures, escalate repression, and choose the dominant outcome in an attempt to eliminate challenge once and for all. For subordinates, a contrary dynamic is set in motion: demands and grievances pile up. As they are met by institutional and symbolic repression, authorities become increasingly unmasked. Thus, what begins as fragmented, accommodationist protest can escalate into coherent, broad-based opposition.

As a result, the accommodationist outcome, although a strong possibility in the near future, is not likely to be permanent. The fragile equilibrium of the accommodationist outcome may collapse as a result either of authorities trying to intensify control through the dominant outcome or of a radical movement gaining the strength to achieve structural change.

DOMINANT OUTCOME: SUCCESSFUL REPRESSION

If the dominant ideology prevails and the dominant outcome occurs in the future, the corporate complex will expand its control even further over other sectors of the economy, particularly small business, industry, and agriculture. The top few hundred corporations will control virtually the entire productive apparatus. The interpenetration of corporate capitalism and the state will become even closer. This economic Goliath will be capped by an enormous planning apparatus to coordinate manpower, raw materials, capital, and demand in the interests of the minority controlling the complex. More and more, costs will be socialized (borne by the whole community in terms of taxes, destruction of the environment, and cost of public education to train the work force), while profits will remain in private hands. Within the state, the executive branch will grow larger and more powerful.

The majority of the population will come to depend either on jobs in the corporate sector or on welfare payments from the state. The first group will be a skilled proletariat—engineers, statisticians, professors, electricians, computer programmers, and welfare workers—that will receive benefits and status from the corporate complex without having authority on the job or significant political power. The second group will consist of the productively useless. They will be dependent for their subsistence on government programs: medical aid, food allowances, cash transfer payments, rent subsidies. They will thus represent a politically impotent clientele of the corporate complex. Alongside the large productive sector, therefore, will be a growing social-welfare complex consisting of welfare bureaucrats who dispense government largesse and exercise social control over much of the population. The state will contract out many welfare activities to the corporate sector. As with the lucrative military procurement policies of the government, the corporate sector will benefit lavishly. Thus, this new arrangement will provide a guaranteed demand for corporate output and an additional outlet for the investment of surplus capital.

To replace the decaying instruments of control of the past, rulers will develop forms of repression adapted to a monolithic, rationalized, centralized social structure. Broadly, these will be of two kinds: hard and soft. Physical repression—surveillance techniques, "crowd control," police and military weapons—will become more technologically sophisticated and efficient. Police and military personnel will interpenetrate society, and the distinction between military and police forces will fade. Hints of dissent will be rooted out and crushed. The population, if unruly, will be treated like captives of a conquered province.

Soft measures of institutional repression will consist of increased inauthentic participation and symbolic control. The population will be manipulated to join organizations that will give them the illusion of power without the reality. Rigged by the dominant, these organizations will utilize the paraphernalia of democracy—debate, elections, investigations, petitions, and resolutions—to convince the majority that they are participating in an open, legitimate, democratic, political and economic system. These organizations may include neighborhood councils, professional associations, university senates, welfare clients' consultative committees, and shopfloor workers' committees. Despite the appearance, the result will be a further decline of democracy in America.

The corporate complex will become more adept at shaping values that sustain structural arrangements. Schools and media will more loudly proclaim the democratic virtues and material benefits of the corporate order. Culture will increasingly be controlled by the powerful and directed at maintaining happy political conformity. Entertainment and news will be almost indistinguishable, as news becomes mythologized and entertainment holds forth an idealized, perverted picture of reality. The outward forms of civil liberties may remain—free speech, free press, and rights of assembly—but the substance will be eroded. Dominant values will crowd out accommodative and radical ideologies. Those on top will seek to direct the resentments, frustrations, and grievances inevitably generated by this system of privilege not against the system as a whole or against those in authority but against fellow subordinates: blacks versus whites; welfare recipients versus skilled workers; neighborhoods versus impotent city governments.

A number of factors point to the likelihood of this outcome. The most persuasive piece of evidence is that much of what has been described already exists, and if some present trends continue uninterrupted, the dominant outcome might be the result. In previous chapters, we have described the increase in corporate concentration and control in past decades and the rise of the state in this century as a central economic participant. The presidency has become much more centralized and the executive branch of government increasingly influential. The state-welfare sector is the fastest growing segment of the economy. Police repression is an increasingly familiar feature of American life. New mechanisms of social control have been developed. Political trials and government intimidation of the media have partially succeeded in stifling the emergence of alternative ideologies.

Since the dominant outcome is obviously in the interests of those on top, and given the increasing challenges and the decay of existing mediations, it is not unthinkable that the dominant will try to protect their interests even at the expense of democracy. Moreover, the ability of most Americans to resist the dominant outcome will be limited. There is a continuing wide disparity in institutional and ideological resources available to the dominant and potential challengers. The institutions that remain powerful as mechanisms of social control—the media, the police, the courts—are largely in the hands of those on top. Most Americans will lack sufficient wealth, organizational resources, and influence to prevent a complete takeover by the dominant.

In the absence of countertrends our analysis could stop here. Fortunately, though, this is not the case. The record of the past few years is by no means simply one of increasing control by the powerful. Alongside the trends discussed above, there is evidence of increasing anger, resistance, and opposition by a growing number of Americans. Important new countermovements have emerged: union insurgencies against both corporate and established union leaders, black movements, and consumer organizations, to name only a few.

Corporate and state officials are not all-powerful, as witnessed by the decaying of traditional institutional and ideological controls. Moreover, the new mechanisms that rulers have devised to replace decaying institutions of the past have thus far proven less successful in manipulating the population. Professional bureaucracies at the city level are adept at disbursing state benefits, and professional campaign agencies can package candidates efficiently—but neither is as effective as the former party machine in organizing participation. Thus, the new institutional means of control may not be able to contain the structural contradictions of capitalism and democracy.

We have argued that democratic procedures alone are insufficient to assure substantive democracy. But procedural democracy does set limits that, if adhered to, would retard the emergence of the dominant outcome. Watergate and Richard Nixon's forced resignation indicate that public and corporate officials at the highest levels may suffer the consequences of gross violations of the law. The press may reveal details of surveillance, corruption, and physical abuse by those in authority. However limited the choices, elections do provide a chance for challenging those in control. Guarantees of free speech and press as well as the justice system provide the potential for the development of alternatives for seeing and understanding reality. In short, the tensions inherent in the relationship of capitalism and democracy constrain authorities and decrease the possibility of the dominant outcome.

RADICAL OUTCOME:
SOCIALISM AND DEMOCRACY

Both the dominant and the accommodationist outcomes are based on the *preservation* of the structural inequalities rooted in American capitalism. By contrast, the radical outcome would represent an elimination of structural inequalities and a qualitative change in both the social structure and political processes. It would consist of substantive as well as procedural democracy. It would democratize decisions not only in the sphere of government but in the spheres of the economy and society.

As we have suggested in this book, the key place to begin an analysis of structural transformation is the country's productive apparatus. The way a society produces its goods and the choice of goods it produces fundamentally shape the social and political life of the society.

At present, basic decisions for the whole American economy regarding what will be produced, the conditions of production, wages, and the setting of prices are largely controlled by a group no larger than the population of a small town. These people, as we have seen, are unrepresentative both of the American population generally and of workers within the productive sector. The direction of movement, then, from present arrangements to the radical outcome is clear: toward democratization of control over production, distribution, and consumption. The shift from present arrangements to the radical outcome represents a shift from corporate capitalism to democratic socialism. What might this mean?

Among the critical points at which democratization is necessary in order to overcome present structural contradictions and achieve socialism are the overall allocation of resources to the production of goods and services; the work place of production of goods (for example, factories) and services (universities, hospitals, welfare agencies, banks); the point of consumption of goods and services; and the realm of culture and values.

Presently, the corporate complex—executives of the top corporations, the very wealthy, and top officials of the executive branch of the federal government—decide how resources are allocated. Decisions are made not on the basis of the greatest social needs but on the basis of highest profits. Although all Americans are affected, those who have the greatest needs participate least in decisions and benefits. The radical outcome (or socialism) would reverse these priorities by democratizing decisions regarding America's productive capacity. In the present arrangement, although the costs of production are socialized, major benefits are appropriated by a minority. In the radical outcome, costs would be borne more equitably by the whole community and benefits would be socialized—shared by members of the community on the basis of their needs.

Once America's productive capacity is democratized and no longer controlled by the corporate complex, the uses made of that capacity will also be transformed. Full importance would be given to the social consequences of production. Instead of the principal criterion being production for profit and the maintenance of inequality between those who own and control capital and those who work for a wage, the principal criterion in the radical outcome would be production for the purpose of diminishing human misery and serving human need. Scarce resources would be directed where social need—not private profit—is greatest. For example, socialism would radically alter the balance between individual and collective transport. A system of transportation built almost exclusively around the automobile is more wasteful, costly, and dangerous than public transport by train, bus, or (for short distances) bicycle or walking. If the tight grip of the automobile lobby were broken, cities could be wrested away from automobiles and returned to people, and the resources presently squandered on automobiles, highways, and gasoline could be used to maintain a high-quality system of low-cost (or possibly even free) public transport. (The total cost to the community of transporting people by public transport is a small fraction of present transportation costs built around the automobile.)

What would be the concrete mechanism for making decisions under socialism? While the precise shape of such arrangements must be developed in practice—socialism is not a ready-made blueprint to be mechanically applied, nor do we want to impose our own view—some guidelines are possible. Various groups whose needs are not presently considered—workers, consumers, women, ethnic minorities—would be represented in democratic decision making. Machinery could be developed at all levels—community, state, and national—to represent groups in the decision-making process. One example is the French planning process.[19] Planning commissions are organized on the basis of the whole nation, of specialized sectors (particular industries, scientific research, and so on), and by regions. The commissions bring together representatives of producers, consumers, workers, and government to recommend goals and suggest how to allocate resources for the French economy.

The shift in procedures for making basic decisions over the allocation of productive resources involves a changed view of government. Presently, many of the most important decisions shaping the society are not regarded as political. Judged by the extent to which their decisions affect our lives, the top management of United States Steel and Minnesota Mining and Manufacturing are no less powerful than the mayor of Atlanta or the governor of Arizona. Yet what the latter do is considered political and what the former do is considered outside the public domain. The radical outcome would reflect a more accurate view of what is political. Moreover, it would recognize that even what is presently considered public—the activities of government—serve private interests by strengthening corporate capitalism and reproducing structural inequalities. Democratizing decisions over the use of productive resources reflects the recognition of the widened sphere of politics in an advanced industrial age.

The socialist outcome would democratize the work place of production. Presently, control over those who work to produce goods and services is from the top down: managers receive their authority from those who own and control the means of production and exercise that authority in undemocratic fashion over workers. The clearest example is in factories, where workers are rigidly controlled and continuously overseen by foremen. But by and large, all workers, including white-collar and professional workers, are in basically the same powerless situation. Although their situation may be obscured by higher status, higher pay, and more routine discretion on the job, they do not participate in basic management decisions any more than manual workers.

Socialism would reverse this situation by replacing the top-down principle with the principle of collective democratic decision

---

[19] Stephen S. Cohen, *Modern Capitalist Planning: The French Model* (Cambridge, Mass., 1969). The example is limited by the fact that France remains a capitalist society; private business interests remain powerful and often ally with government representatives on the planning commissions to dominate the planning process.

making by the workers. Such a principle is already in operation in factories in many countries—including Sweden, China, Cuba, and Yugoslavia. For example, in a Volvo automobile plant in Sweden (a country whose political system contains features of both capitalism and socialism), the traditional assembly line is a thing of the past. Labor unions helped develop the overall organization of the factory, and workers helped plan the assembly process. Instead of a worker having to repeat mindlessly the same operation for months, teams of workers, responsible for specified quotas, are free to divide up tasks and determine the pace of work. As a result, workers can vary tasks, exercise ingenuity in the work process, mingle with their coworkers on the job, and alternate work and rest. Each team of workers, numbering from fifteen to twenty-five, has a comfortably furnished lounge, equipped with refrigerator and sauna. The result of the radically transformed work process is that workers are relaxed and cheerful at the end of the working day. Yet the cost of the factory is only 10 percent more than the traditional automobile assembly plant, and even this extra investment is offset by low absenteeism and high output.[20] The Volvo example demonstrates that it is not technological obstacles that prevent worker control on the job but resistance by owners and managers in a capitalist economy.

Under existing arrangements, control over consumption is from the top down: regulations regarding eligibility for welfare, the choice of what goods shall be produced and how they shall be advertised, price-setting, tax policies to pay for government services, and the allocation of resources within the society as a whole to various uses—all these decisions are made by those who control the production of goods and services rather than by those who use them. With the exception of the wealthy and powerful, the customer is rarely king. In the socialist outcome, consumers would share in the process of controlling production and distribution. Thus, hospital patients, university students, and shoppers would not be treated as passive recipients but would have the opportunity to participate in decisions regarding the goods and services that these institutions dispense. For example, within the university, students would share responsibility for planning the curriculum, and for hiring and promoting staff members. This system of authentic participation contrasts with the present system of inau-

---

[20] *Le Monde*, June 11, 1974; Tom Wicker, "A Plant Built for Workers," *New York Times*, May 21, 1974, and Tom Wicker, "People vs. Production," *New York Times*, May 24, 1974.

thentic student participation in such forums as student government, whose powers are miniscule, or university senates, where students are in a tiny minority.

Democratizing consumption also means demystifying specialization. Much of what passes for specialized knowledge is in fact the jealously guarded preserve of "professionals" who privatize knowledge for profit and status. In the radical outcome, the unnecessary gap between "professionals" and "laymen" would narrow, and consumers would become less dependent on specialists to whom they now look for a host of goods and services. Automobile repairing and health care are two areas where this is true. Most citizens are presently helpless in face of malfunctions of their cars and bodies. Yet many disorders could be diagnosed and repaired by a person of average intelligence with a minimal amount of training. In both fields, to be sure, some disorders require specialized treatment, which only someone with longer training is qualified to dispense. But citizens can also learn the limits of their knowledge and, thus, know when they need to refer to a specialist.

How will citizens become self-reliant rather than hopelessly dependent on the services of others? One effective way would be through a change in socialization. Schools would teach basic skills necessary for dealing with the natural and physical environment. As in the Israeli kibbutz and the Chinese commune, the artificial split between "mind-work" and "physical-work" as well as the cleavage between city and country would diminish. Physical work would not be considered demeaning, and the narrow specialization that produces reliance on experts would decrease. In a more general way, socialism would nurture different motivations and values. Capitalist socialization encourages the search for material acquisition, makes waste a virtue, and emphasizes such values as competitiveness and obedience. Socialist socialization would encourage the search for spiritual fulfillment and stress the values of cooperation and self-reliance.

In the United States today, racial relations are geared to a dual labor market that confines most black workers to the small-capital and surplus-labor sectors: blacks still have the worst jobs, the lowest salaries, the meanest housing, and the least control over their lives and neighborhoods. In addition, they are subject to daily discrimination from sources ranging from neighborhood police officers to the dominant culture that denigrates, trivializes, or ignores the black society.

The radical outcome would strive to eliminate these expressions of inequality. For example, it would end economic arrangements that confine most blacks to the small-capital and surplus-labor sectors of the economy. In the newly organized economy, they would have equal access to all jobs. This goal cannot be accomplished simply by outlawing racial discrimination in hiring. It will also be necessary to recognize that race has been a fundamental basis of inequality for hundreds of years and that economic equalization requires direct positive measures such as compensatory programs in education, health care, and job placement.

The dominant culture has always had a virulent strain of racism that would be replaced by authentic cultural diversity. Underpinned by economic equality, this diversity would be reflected in society at large as well as in newspapers, radio and television, schools, and the entertainment industry.

Socialism would strive to overcome sexist practices and attitudes in the United States. As a first step, discrimination in the labor market would cease: women would have the same opportunity as men to attain challenging employment. Publicly provided day-care centers would enable those who chose to take jobs outside the home. In a far-reaching way, sexist attitudes and conceptions, which presently demean both women and men, would be transformed: American society would deemphasize the "machismo" virtues of domination, acquisition, and "toughness." Although the nuclear family might persist, cooperative living arrangements would be freely available for those who chose. (American communes and the Israeli kibbutz suggest the range of possibilities.)

The radical outcome would attempt to transform America's relationship to the world. Just as socialism would democratize the control and use of productive resources within the United States, so in the international sphere it would employ America's immense resources to benefit, not control, those in other countries. At the present time, a capitalist America aims at producing or maintaining stable capitalist regimes that are usually repressive and often dependent on American military and economic support. A socialist America would ally with democratic, egalitarian forces abroad rather than with undemocratic forces. Note, however, that the radical outcome would involve a cutback in wasteful consumption by Americans, who would relinquish privileges that have come with global dominance.

Socialism would not usher in a utopia where "correct" decisions would always be made and all compulsion and injustice
eliminated. Some current hardships, such as disagreeable tasks,
the social costs of industrial production, and the dehumanizing
effects of bureaucracy, would persist—albeit to a lesser degree.
New questions would arise, for example, how to allocate resources. Socialism would not signify the end of political conflict—
struggle is rooted in the human condition. But the likelihood of
meeting basic human needs equitably and reducing compulsion
and injustice would be greater under socialism than under
corporate capitalism.

It is important to correct some common misconceptions about
socialism. Socialism need not be a system of state control, in which
large corporations are taken over by government and run pretty
much as they were before, nor does it mean that an all-powerful
state and party apparatus would regulate every aspect of life and
create a drab uniformity of taste, dress, and culture. Instead,
democratic socialism would radically enlarge the sphere of citizen
participation and decision making at all levels. People would seek
individual goals and would not be mere automatons in a totalitarian
society. Indeed, under socialism, individuality and privacy could
flourish more than under present conditions of apparent cultural
freedom, where, in fact, tastes are largely rigged by the advertising, entertainment, popular music, clothing, and communications
industries.

Would the radical outcome benefit all members of the society?
Of course not. Precisely because socialism aims at abolishing
privilege, it follows that those who presently are privileged will be
deprived of their dominance. But by a democratic accounting
scheme in which everyone counts equally, most Americans will
benefit from structural change.

Let us review here, too, the possibilities for and against
socialism in America.

The arguments against its likelihood are formidable indeed. A
radical outcome, virtually by definition, is more difficult to achieve
than situations more continuous with the present. Moreover, although there is a vibrant socialist tradition in many western
societies, the history of American socialism provides a weak inheritance. There is no socialist party or movement on the immediate horizons. The Democratic party and the AFL-CIO unions
find accommodationist politics more congenial.

Further, even if a broad-based popular movement for socialism were to be developed in the United States, the radical outcome would be far from a certainty. The commanding heights of the productive apparatus, the state, the means of physical force (police, army), and institutions of socialization (media, schools, government) remain firmly in the control of the corporate complex. Challenges have not gone unmet. A far-ranging program of repression has already been mounted: police violence, expansion and rationalization of police forces, political trials, harrassment of the media, and surveillance of political opponents and potential revolutionaries. In the White House of the early 1970s, no measure was excluded from consideration—no matter how illegal or unconstitutional. Examples of actions considered or authorized by the president, drawn from transcriptions of the taped presidential conversations Nixon released in 1974 in an unsuccessful attempt to stay in office, included paying "hush money" to Watergate defendants, committing perjury, falsely invoking national security to cover up the investigation, promising executive clemency to defendants in return for their silence, and obstructing criminal investigation of the Watergate affair. While a wave of popular revulsion against official misconduct was set off by the impeachment proceedings against President Nixon, there was little mobilization to achieve substantive democracy. Moreover, indignation concerned the measures taken against established groups, not against those more fully opposed to the status quo.

The repression of radical movements would not be without support. Many Americans have—or believe they have—a stake in existing arrangements. The position of the United States as the most privileged country in the world continues to provide many Americans with benefits. Many communities are dependent for their livelihood on high military spending. Many workers fear that structural change would threaten the niche they have found for themselves in society: white-collar workers believe it is in their interest to stress what divides them from manual workers; organized labor presses for advantages over small-capital workers and the unemployed. Even those Americans with serious grievances find it hard to favor structural change.

Nevertheless, the radical outcome cannot be ruled out. The basic contradictions between capitalism and democracy can be managed for long periods; they cannot, however, be eliminated short of structural change. The fact that conflict and change are contained should not obscure the persistence of underlying tensions.

The 1960s, with their urban, black, student, and anti-Vietnam mass movements, were years of political and social turmoil. Today, the situation is one of relative quiet. This social peace is usually interpreted in conservative terms, but such is not necessarily the case. More appropriate is the *Wall Street Journal*'s observation that there is no conservative groundswell but rather that people are losing faith in government's ability to solve problems. Public opinion polls show that the majority of Americans still want national health insurance and a cleaner environment; they resent, however, paying taxes to government units that leave their problems intact. Both the loss of faith and the resentment, it should be remembered, are directed not against government per se but against people's experience of the corporate complex. A formative radical consciousness already exists, competing with other understandings. Pollster Tully Plesser, utilizing the metaphor of a herd of cattle, puts the current situation this way: The American people are "milling around, swinging in different directions, not really focused yet. Maybe they'll quiet down, but maybe they'll stampede." [21]

Even in this period of relative quiet, accommodationist struggles have continued; and each implicitly contains the seeds of a radical outcome. Wildcat strikes (the United States has more of these than any other western society) place issues of workers' control ahead of higher wages. Insurgencies within unions challenge the locked-in arrangements that tie union leaders to the corporate complex. Radical caucuses within professional associations—American Medical Association, American Economics Association, American Bar Association—challenge patterns of control within the professions and seek to overcome the distance between professional and client. The women's movement, which began as a protest against job discrimination, has developed a more total structural analysis of the subordinate place of women in American capitalism. Similarly, protest against the Vietnam war broadened into a thoroughgoing critique of militarism and the corporate complex abroad. This adds up to evidence both of increasing protest of a particular nature and of an incipient radical movement.

[21] Cited in the *Wall Street Journal*, August 4, 1974, p. 1.

There is an increasing rapidity and ease with which those sharing interests may communicate. The mass media, especially television, make it possible for individuals sharing interests within the same sector to reach each other and a much broader constituency. At the same time, the media break down the isolation of different groups. Chicanos become aware of black struggles, and both became aware of the welfare-rights movement. The media also bring authorities down to vulnerable human size. Through the media's extensive coverage of Watergate, Americans learned that "The President" and his most trusted colleagues were capable of venality, corruption, and criminal conduct.

Changes in the international and economic spheres have sharpened contradictions in the United States. During a brief period following the Second World War, the United States was in a uniquely privileged position in the world. The only major industrial power not to suffer war damage, the United States was also able—through its military, economic, and political advantages—to command a plentiful supply of raw materials on favorable terms. The result was the largest economic boom in world history.

As long as the economy continued to grow, the basic structural cleavage between capital and labor in the United States could be masked. Materially, a larger economic "pie" meant more jobs, better wages, and growing numbers of consumer goods—television sets, washing machines, and automobiles. Ideologically, an expanding economy fostered the belief that all could benefit from economic advances and that economic inequality could be redressed without political struggle.

Beginning in the late 1960s, however, this privileged situation based on international dominance became less secure. Other industrial powers (Western Europe and Japan) narrowed the economic gap separating them from the United States. United States military dominance was challenged both as a result of advances in weaponry by the USSR and by America's unsuccessful attempt to impose its will in Indochina. The era of cheap and abundant commodities—most dramatically, petroleum, but also food, fertilizer, and other raw materials—has come to an end. As a result, inflation and scarcity have developed, manifested most clearly by a slowdown of economic growth and sharply rising prices. The economic "pie" is no longer growing rapidly, and most Americans have found their "slices" getting smaller. There is no longer a plentiful supply of jobs, as both the college graduate and the high-school dropout have been discovering. Even many with good jobs find that wage hikes are more than offset by the rise in the cost of living: when inflation is at the rate of nearly 10 percent annually, a wage gain of 7 percent a year results in a loss of real wages. The dilemma is compounded by the fact that without opportunities for expansion, the tendency is for a capitalist system to stagnate.

A POSTSCRIPT

It is easy to reject the dominant outcome. The real choice for those who wish to act to shape the future is between the accommodationist and radical outcomes. Between the two, the accommodationist outcome appears to many to be the more sensible, prudent, reasonable, and responsible possibility. It would focus on what appear to be the most pressing and flagrant problems in America—racial discrimination, environmental pollution, malfeasance in government, inflation, and unemployment. For each problem it would offer a reasoned solution. It would attempt to minimize disruption by leaving American capitalism and democracy unchanged.

We have tried to apply a rigorous and demanding standard in this book, one that requires democratizing areas of human activity (such as production) ignored by the accommodationist perspective. Even if one conceded the goals of substantive democracy or socialism were impossible to attain, it would be a useful exercise to analyze the ways in which American practice falls short of the democratic ideal. An additional reason for using the standard of substantive democracy linked to socialism is to avoid complacency about the United States. The tendency toward self-congratulation, common in the United States, often functions to permit inequalities to persist or even increase. (During the 1970s, for example, income inequalities increased between the rich and poor.) By striving for the democratic ideal, one may at least achieve greater improvements or reduce antidemocratic developments. The absence of such a vision may only make matters worse.

And yet we do not agree that to be realistic requires preferring the accommodationist to the radical outcome. The accommodationist outcome may not always be the most responsible or effective choice. Politics becomes a never-ending quest for solutions to one problem after another—racial discrimination and poverty in the early 1960s, the Vietnam war later in the decade, and, after that, environmental pollution. Note, however, a distressing fact: none of these questions on the accommodationist agenda was really resolved. As political scientist Michael Parenti has pointed out, despite the accommodationist struggles of the 1960s

> things are getting worse, not better. As opposed to a decade ago, there are more, not less people living in poverty today, more substandard housing, more environmental pollution and devastation, more deficiencies in our schools, hospitals, and systems of public transportation, more military dictatorships throughout the world feeding on the largesse and power of the Pentagon, more people from Thailand to Brazil to Greece to Chicago suffering the social oppression and political repression of an American-based status quo.[22]

In a similar fashion, New Deal reforms, adopted as the result of mass pressure over the resistance of most business groups, provided government protection for corporate workers, social security benefits, and some measure of economic stability. Yet the ultimate significance of the New Deal era (one of the most fruitful accommodationist reform periods in American history) was to strengthen corporate capitalism and postpone a thorough confrontation of its inequities.

The accommodationist approach misunderstands the basic characteristics of the corporate complex. As we have seen throughout this book, the particular "ills" of American society are closely intertwined with the activities of the corporate complex. The routine operation of the corporate complex generates class inequality, the misuse of resources, and an elaborate military apparatus. However flexible the corporate complex may seem to be in particular areas, its fundamental requisite is the concentration of capital in private hands and a work force that sells its labor for a wage to those in control. This requirement sets the outer limit to accommodationist reform and accounts for the failure of accommodationist struggles. No amount of tinkering can deal with the source of America's problems—the basic cleavage between capital and labor.

[22] Michael Parenti, "The Possibilities for Political Change," *Politics and Society* 1 (November 1970): 86.

Why then does government choose to be bound to the impera-tives of corporate capitalism? Granted that government derives its revenues from corporate production. But a society does not have to be organized within a capitalist framework. Production can occur, jobs be made available, and living standards secured in a socialist economy. Indeed, as we suggested earlier, a socialist order could minimize costs and democratize benefits. In theory, then, there are no barriers to government acting as the spokesper-son for the majority and helping to bring about the radical outcome.

In practice, however, a socialist outcome can only occur as the result of struggle by a broad-based radical movement. Yet the integration of the state and corporate capitalism means that government actions are designed to prevent rather than facilitate this result. Socialist thinker and activist Michael Harrington points out, "As long as the system is dominated by private corporations and wealth, that fact will tend in the long run to make all collectivist measures discriminate in favor of the status quo."[23] In earlier chapters we have seen how government programs in housing, transportation, and education often provide more benefits for the well-off than the poor.

The job of the activist only begins with the choice of the socialist outcome. The next step is to translate that choice into action: to develop a strategy that will achieve the goal of socialism effectively and responsibly. André Gorz has suggested a strategy geared to advanced capitalist societies. It revolves around the notion of *structural reform*: the posing of demands that utilize the rhetoric and machinery of procedural democracy to stretch struc-tural limits.[24] An example would be a demand by workers in collective bargaining not simply for higher wages but for control over aspects of production that have been left solely to manage-ment, such as the speed of the assembly line, authority over firing, and wage differentials between white-collar and manual workers. This strategy counterposes a logic of need (socialism) to the logic of production for profit (capitalism). It uses the machinery of procedural democracy in order to broaden the sphere of substan-tive democracy.

Posing structural demands does not mean that they will be met. In fact, the reverse is more likely. Demands will not be conceded as gestures of good will, on the basis of superior in-

---

[23] Michael Harrington, *Socialism* (New York, 1972), p. 242.
[24] André Gorz, *Strategy for Labor* (New York, 1967), part one.

tellectual argument, or as a response to the logic of need. Too much is at stake. But it is useful to pose these demands whether or not they are met. If they are not, authorities demonstrate that they are unresponsive to demands rooted in human need and democratic imperatives. Thus they will be less able to rely on symbol manipulation and the dominant ideology to secure control. For those posing the demand, the experience is revealing. It exposes dominant myths (including the myth of consensus), and it reveals the shortcomings of a seemingly equitable order. Thus, as a result of posing the demand, more and more people become aware of the obstacles and steps necessary to overcome resistance to democracy.

The most important tools available to activists are numbers and organization. The posing of structural demands is a means both of creating mass organization and of solidifying it in struggle. Mass organization holds out the possibility of coordinating the small resources available to each member. The result may be that it is "cheaper" for authorities to grant the organization's demands than to resist and suffer the penalties. A long strike called in support of structural demands may reduce a firm's share of the market permanently or force it out of business. Mass sit-ins or boycotts of public schools may be threatened to gain a measure of community control by black parents over ghetto schools.

Should structural demands be granted as a result of these sanctions, the radical outcome has been moved that much closer. The achievement represents an incremental change in structure that results in a weakening of corporate capitalism, however imperceptible it may seem at the time. There is also an ideological and organizational result. Citizens have learned that the dominant are not invincible, that struggles may succeed. Their sense of collective power grows, just as the confidence of the corporate complex declines. Citizens are better equipped to pose further structural demands. The victory is thus not an end in itself, as it is in the accommodationist alternative, but a means to pose new demands animated by a vision of the socialist outcome that seeks to transform and overcome remaining inequalities.

Until now we have discussed the posing of structural demands and the building of radical organization in diverse arenas. These struggles are an integral part of the movement for the socialist outcome. But if they stopped at this level, however successful, at best they would represent an advanced form of the accommodationist outcome. The additional quantum leap to structural transformation will be taken only when an effective, broad-based, mass democratic movement emerges to link citizens. This development has never happened in the American past, and the difficulties ahead should not be underestimated. For this reason, we are under no illusion that socialism in America is just around the corner.

Yet if naive optimism about the possibility of socialism in America is unwarranted, so too is despair that socialism is impossible. We have seen that increasing numbers of Americans are beginning to realize the costs of living under corporate capitalism at the very time that political-control techniques are weakening. A mass radical movement could potentially recruit from a wide variety of groups: workers—both manual and white collar, in both the small-capital and corporate sectors—who face ever-greater difficulties concerning job security, wages, and conditions and control of the work process; blacks and Latin minorities, whose lot has not substantially improved despite accommodationist rhetoric; the poor, for whom government handouts are increasingly meager under inflationary conditions; women, who continue to be cast in demeaning subordinate roles; and students, who will be harder to coopt as corporate capitalism proves unable to generate an adequate number of challenging jobs. Rather than socialism representing a plot of elitist intellectuals to be crammed down the throats of the American people, the potential constituency for a socialist movement includes the immense majority of Americans.

This strategy of structural reform, then, is part of a revolutionary process: it is a patient step-by-step effort to build a new society. It is sensitive to the relation of particular struggles to overall changes in the structure of society. It rejects both a piecemeal view of reality and a simplistic view of structure that sees America being transformed in one fell swoop. Success will mean a democratic socialist America.

selected bibliography

The following bibliography indicates some of the most important work in the field. Additional works are cited in footnotes throughout the text.

*Books indicated by * are available in paperback.*

Chapter 1

*Edwards, Richard C., Michael Reich, and Thomas E. Weisskopf, eds. *The Capitalist System*. 2nd ed. Englewood Cliffs, N.J.: Prentice-Hall, 1978.
A comprehensive anthology containing a broad range of essays on the structure of the capitalist system and the functioning of capitalism in the United States.

*Mills, C. Wright. *The Sociological Imagination*. New York: Oxford Univ. Press, 1958.
A provocative critique of the social sciences that connects people's everyday lives with the social structure in which they must live.

*Pateman, Carole. *Participation and Democratic Theory*. Cambridge: Cambridge Univ. Press, 1970.
In this analysis of the role of participation in democratic theory, the author emphasizes the work of political theorist Jean Jacques Rousseau.

*Pechman, Joseph. *Federal Tax Policy*. New York: W. W. Norton, 1971.
This comprehensive study explains in nontechnical terms the nature of the United States tax system and the effects of taxation on the economy. It stresses that the tax system undergirds the existing unequal distribution of income and wealth.

*Pitkin, Hanna. *The Concept of Representation*. Berkeley: Univ. of California Press, 1967.
The most important recent statement by a political theorist on the central role played by the concept of representation in constructing a critical approach to democracy.

*Tucker, Robert, ed. *The Marx-Engels Reader*. New York: W. W. Norton, 1972.
The best available one-volume anthology of the essential writings of Marx and Engels. It also contains a useful interpretive introduction.

Chapter 2

*Bowles, Samuel, and Herbert Gintis. *Schooling in Capitalist America: Educational Reform and the Contradictions of Economic Life*. New York: Basic Books, 1976.
The book integrates theory and data concerning the functions served by schooling under capitalism (to train students to accept hierarchy and to legitimate inequalities in American life), along with a history of the conflicting purposes of educational reforms.

*Edelman, Murray. *Politics as Symbolic Action: Mass Arousal and Quiescence*. Chicago: Markham Publishing Co., 1971.

*————. *The Symbolic Uses of Politics*. Urbana, Ill.: Univ. of Illinois Press, 1964.

408

Both books are imaginative analyses of the process by which political symbols influence political behavior. Edelman stresses the manipulation of ideology and symbols to strengthen political stability.

*Roelofs, H. Mark. *Ideology and Myth in American Politics: A Critique of a National Political Mind*. Boston: Little, Brown. 1976.
A lively analysis of the dominant American ideology, which, Roelofs shows, obscures disturbing features of American reality.

Trilateral Commission, *The Crisis of Democracy*. New York: New York Univ. Press, 1975.
Perhaps the most influential statement of the right turn in the dominant ideology. The various essays in the report agree on the need to restrict participation in the name of democracy.

*Weinstein, James. *Ambiguous Legacy: The Left in American Politics*. New York: New Viewpoints, 1975.
A survey of left movements in the twentieth century, including the socialist and communist parties, the new left, and the women's movement.

Chapter 3

Commoner, Barry. *The Poverty of Power: Energy and the Economic Crisis*. New York: Knopf, 1976.
A sprightly account of how the energy crisis has been in large part a product of corporate profit maximization and government policy.

*Galbraith, John Kenneth. *The New Industrial State*. rev. ed. New York: Signet Books, 1972.
Galbraith's controversial analysis of how corporate requirements have shaped American society and politics.

*_____. *Economics and the Public Purpose*. Boston: Houghton Mifflin, 1973.
Galbraith restates his earlier argument, describes how the corporate sector coexists with and exploits the rest of the economy, and proposes reforms to tame corporate power.

Lindblom, Charles E. *Politics and Markets: The World's Political-Economic Systems*. New York: Basic Books, 1977.
An analysis of the strengths and weaknesses of market (capitalist) versus politically directed (socialist) economies.

*O'Connor, James. *The Fiscal Crisis of the State*. New York: St. Martin's Press, 1973.
O'Connor analyzes the various sectors of American capitalism, discusses the role of government in maintaining capitalism, and points to emerging contradictions in American economic and political development.

Chapter 4

*Best, Michael H., and William E. Connolly. *The Politicized Economy*. Lexington, Mass.: D. C. Heath, 1976.
Simple and comprehensive review of the theory and practice of American capitalism, focusing on the need for government to bolster a sagging system.

*Dowd, Douglas F. *The Twisted Dream: Capitalist Development in the United States Since 1776*. 2nd ed. Cambridge, Mass.: Winthrop, 1977.
Historical review of how capitalist development perverted priorities in the evolving American society.

*Lowi, Theodore. *The End of Liberalism: Ideology, Policy and the Crisis of Public Authority*. New York: W. W. Norton, 1969.
A critique of the American "interest group liberalism" system of logrolling.

*McConnell, Grant. *Private Power and American Democracy*. New York: Vintage Books, 1970.
A critical analysis of how American government is responsive to narrow private interests.

Noble, David F. *America by Design: Science, Technology, and the Rise of Corporate Capitalism*. New York: Knopf, 1977.
A study of the intertwined development of technology, management education, and engineering training in the service of emergent corporate capitalism during the early twentieth century.

Wolfe, Alan. *The Limits of Legitimacy: Political Contradictions of Contemporary Capitalism*. New York: The Free Press, 1977.
An ambitious study of the changing character of capitalist government and the contemporary crisis of political authority.
See also books by J. K. Galbraith and James O'Connor in Chapter 3 Bibliography.

Chapter 5

Aronowitz, Stanley. *False Promises*. New York: McGraw-Hill, 1973.
This study of America's working class emphasizes workers' social history, the importance of trade unions, and working class culture in an attempt to grasp the forces that shape working class consciousness.

*Averitt, Robert. *The Dual Economy*. New York: W. W. Norton, 1968.
Averitt argues that American capitalism has two distinct business sectors: a dominant center economy of large capital and a periphery economy of small-capital firms.

*Blauner, Robert. *Racial Oppression in America*. New York: Harper & Row, 1972.
The essays in this book develop the perspective that America's racial minorities are colonized minorities, sharing a colonization process and experience with Third World peoples. Blauner points out the differences in the experiences of the ethnic immigrants and blacks and stresses the themes of culture and institutional racism.

Braverman, Harry. *Labor and Monopoly Capital*. New York: Monthly Review Press, 1974.
A major analysis both of the changing class structure of the United States and of the character of work in America. More than any other recent book, this study makes clear the bases of workers' discontents.

*Brecher, Jeremy. *Strike!* San Francisco: Straight Arrow Books, 1972.
Brecher treats the neglected history of mass strikes in the United States and demonstrates that mass strikes are recurring phenomena.
See also James O'Connor, *The Fiscal Crisis of the State*, in Chapter 3 Bibliography.

Chapter 6

*Burnham, Walter Dean. *Critical Elections and the Mainsprings of American Politics*. New York: W. W. Norton, 1970.
Burnham traces the decline of the party system through analysis of turnout figures and other methods.

*Chambers, William Nisbet, and Walter Dean Burnham, eds. *The American Party Systems: Stages of Political Development*. 2nd ed. New York: Oxford Univ. Press, 1975.

Changes in the American party systems analyzed by historians and political scientists.

Nie, Norman H., Sidney Verba, and John R. Petrocik. *The Changing American Voter*. Cambridge, Mass.: Harvard Univ. Press, 1976.
Comprehensive survey of changes in the political attitudes and voting patterns of American citizens since the period when studies of voter attitudes originated.

*Pomper, Gerald. *Voters' Choice: Varieties of American Electoral Behavior*. New York: Harper & Row, 1975.
Pomper charts changes in the party preferences of different social groups.

*Sundquist, James. *Dynamics of the Party System: Alignment and Realignment of Political Parties in the United States*. Washington, D.C.: The Brookings Institution, 1973.
Sundquist presents a careful review of changing party cleavages in American history.

Chapter 7

Greenstone, J. David, and Paul Peterson. *Race and Authority in Urban Politics*. New York: Russell Sage Foundation, 1973.
An analysis of Community Action programs in five cities traces the impact of local contexts on the implementation of the War on Poverty. The study illuminates the structures of race and authority that undergird much of American political life.

*Marris, Peter, and Martin Rein. *Dilemmas of Social Reform*. Chicago: Aldine, 1973.
The authors argue that the barriers to meaningful social reform in the present political economy are enormous. Their study of Community Action programs stresses the conservatism of bureaucracy, rivalries among political and administrative jurisdictions, and the meager resources of the poor.

*Moynihan, Daniel. *The Politics of a Guaranteed Income*. New York: Random House, 1973.
A lively case study of President Nixon's Family Assistance Plan. Particularly important is the discussion of the origins of the legislation and its relationship to the urban turmoil of the 1960s.

*Piven, Frances Fox, and Richard Cloward. *Regulating the Poor*. New York: Pantheon, 1971.
Relief giving, the authors argue, arises from the need to stem political disorder during periods of mass discontent and to enforce low-wage work during periods of economic and political stability. Welfare is thus a system for regulating the poor.

*Steiner, Gilbert. *The State of Welfare*. Washington, D.C.: The Brookings Institution, 1972.
A broad survey of welfare-state programs, including public housing, food stamps, veterans' relief, and AFDC.

Chapter 8

*Barnet, Richard J., and Ronald E. Muller. *Global Reach: The Power of the Multinational Corporations*. New York: Simon and Schuster, 1974.
A wide-ranging account which documents the way that giant corporations have reshaped the world to the requirements of corporate capitalism.

Blair, John. *The Control of Oil*. New York: Pantheon Books, 1976.
A study of the roots of the energy crisis and the way that United States petroleum companies dominate the world supply of petroleum.

Block, Fred L. *The Origins of International Economic Disorder: A Study of United States International and Monetary Policy from World War II to the Present.* Berkeley: Univ. of California Press, 1977.
Block traces the rise and fall of United States dominance over other capitalist nations; he analyzes how the United States shaped international organizations to further American interests following the Second World War and studies how the balance has been shifting against the United States.

*Melman, Seymour. *Our Depleted Society.* New York: Holt, Rinehart & Winston, 1965.

*_____. *Pentagon Capitalism: The Political Economy of War.* New York: McGrawHill, 1970.

*_____. *The Permanent War Economy.* Boston: Simon and Schuster, 1974.
In these books Melman argues that the Department of Defense controls a private constituency (whose most notable members are giant military producers) favorable to military production. He traces the damaging effects on the rest of the economy.

Chapter 9

*Barber, James David, ed. *Choosing the President.* Englewood Cliffs, N.J.: Prentice-Hall, 1974.
Essays on various aspects of presidential selection, including procedures, strategy, symbolic aspects, and recent trends.

Pious, Richard M. *The American Presidency.* New York: Basic Books, 1979.
A thorough account of the attempts by presidents to stretch the constitutional limits of their power.

*Tugwell, Rexford G., and Thomas E. Cronin, eds. *The Presidency Reappraised.* New York: Praeger, 1974.
These essays challenge the earlier scholarly consensus on the value of a strong president.

Wildavsky, Aaron, ed. *The Presidency.* Boston: Little, Brown, 1969.
Essays on various aspects of the presidency.

The Presidential Transcripts. (various editions, 1974.)
The spontaneous and unrehearsed Watergate drama, as seen through transcriptions of White House tape recordings of presidential conversations.

Chapter 10

Fenno, Richard. *Congressmen in Committees.* Boston: Little, Brown, 1972.
The author looks at House and Senate committees and analyzes the effects various factors have on committee autonomy and influence in legislative deliberations.

Fiorina, Morris. *Congress: Keystone of the Washington Establishment.* New Haven, Conn.: Yale Univ. Press, 1977.
The book treats the interrelated questions of the decline of marginal congressional seats, the changing responsibilities of members of Congress, and the consequences for democratic practices and the making of public policy.

Ferejohn, John. *Pork Barrel Politics: Rivers and Harbors Legislation.* Palo Alto, Calif.: Stanford Univ. Press, 1974.
An excellent treatment of the role of Congress in managing federal programs that direct aid to specific constituencies such as dam and post office construction, urban renewal, sewage treatment plants, and highway construction. The author is particularly good in specifying the relationship between Congress and the relevant bureaucrats in the executive branch.

*Green, Mark, et al. *Who Runs Congress?* New York: Bantam Books, 1972.
A solid muckraking book by the Ralph Nader Congress Project, focuses on the themes of campaign financing, the internal control of Congress, congressional culture and norms, and relations between Congress and the executive branch.

Ornstein, Norman, ed. *Congress in Change.* New York: Praeger, 1975.
One of the best recent anthologies on the Congress. Its essays focus on the ways the institution has changed in the past decade, paying particular attention to the nature of representation, external pressures on Congress, and internal determinants of congressional behavior.

Chapter 11

*Abraham, Henry. *The Judicial Process.* New York: Oxford Univ. Press, 1968.
This introduction to the judicial process contains a first-rate treatment of the Supreme Court and judicial review and has much useful comparative material about European systems of justice.

Friedman, Lawrence. *A History of American Law.* New York: Simon and Schuster, 1973.
The finest one-volume legal history of the United States covering the eighteenth and nineteenth centuries. It treats not only such subjects as law and the economy, crime and punishment, judges and courts, and legal reform, but also the emergence of the modern legal profession, and the impact of early American practices on current legal questions.

Horwitz, Morton. *The Transformation of American Law, 1780–1860.* Cambridge, Mass.: Harvard Univ. Press, 1977.
Essential reading for an understanding of the importance of the emergence of an instrumental conception of law and of changes in conceptions of property for American economic, political, and social development.

Hurst, James Willard. *Law and Social Order in the United States.* Ithaca, N.Y.: Cornell Univ. Press, 1977.
A sensitive and literate treatment of the relationship between the law, the economy, and social change in nineteenth- and twentieth-century America. The discussion of science and technology is especially original.

*Jacob, Herbert. *Justice in America.* Boston: Little, Brown, 1972.
The best accessible treatment of the justice system as a whole. It is direct, scholarly, and lays bare the shocking conditions under which justice is dispensed.

*Richardson, Richard, and Kenneth Vines. *The Politics of Federal Courts.* Boston: Little, Brown, 1970.
The authors examine the neglected topic of lower federal courts in the United States. They trace the history of the court system, review mechanisms of judicial selection, and examine patterns of decision-making.

Chapter 12

*Gorz, André. *Socialism and Revolution.* Garden City, N.Y.: Doubleday, 1973.

*———. *Strategy for Labor.* Boston: Beacon Press, 1967.
In both books Gorz sketches a Marxist analysis of the outlines of a socialist society and how to achieve it through structural reforms.

*Harrington, Michael. *Socialism.* New York: Bantam Books, 1973.
Harrington gives a history of socialist thought and its application to American society.

Lipsky, Michael. *Protest in City Politics.* Chicago: Rand McNally, 1970.

In his examination of the rent-strike movement in New York City in the early 1960s Lipsky asks what poor people can expect to gain from protest politics. He examines their strategies and elite counterstrategies aimed at blunting protest.

*Lynd, Staughton, and Gar Alperovitz. *Strategy and Program: Two Essays Toward a New American Socialism*. Boston: Beacon Press, 1973.
Two American radicals develop a strategy and program to achieve a socialist America.

*Moore, Barrington, Jr. *Reflections on the Causes of Human Misery and Upon Certain Proposals to Eliminate Them*. Boston: Beacon Press, 1973.
A challenging study of the obstacles impeding the elimination of human misery; Moore also reviews critically but sympathetically some radical critiques of American politics and foreign policy.

Piven, Frances Fox, and Richard Cloward. *Poor People's Movements: Why They Succeed, How They Fail*. New York: Pantheon, 1977.
Through case studies of the labor movement and movements of the unemployed in the 1930s, and of the civil-rights and welfare-rights movements of the 1960s, the authors develop the argument that gains for the poor come more from disruption than from political organization.

index

Note: Page numbers in italics refer to tables or figures.

Byrd, Harry, Jr., 310
Byrd, Harry, Sr., 310

Cabinet, 272, 275–76
California, 109, 162; University of, at Davis, 344
Calleo, David P., 252
Cambodia, 237, 269
Campaign consulting firms, 172, 173
Campaign organizations, 172, 173
Canada, United States investment in, 228
Cannon, Joe, 297–98
Capital, corporate, see Corporate capital; definition of, 64; export of, see Foreign investment; and labor, structural cleavage between, 4, 118, 120, 402, 404; new sources of, 80–82; professionalization of, 79–80; rights conferred by control of, 65–68; small, see Small-capital sector; social, 183, 186, 192, 209
Capital accumulation, 62, 65, 98–100, 102, 104, 265, 278
Capital gains tax, 102, 103
Capitalism (capitalist economy; capitalist system), 8; classic era of competitive, 90–91; corporate, see Corporate capitalism; crises of, 43–44, 84, 89, 91, 96–98, 106–11, 254, 263, 291–93; crisis-prone tendencies of, 83–98, 110; definition of, 64; democracy and, see Capitalism and democracy, relationship between; expansion as essence of, 76; factory, see Factories; industrial, 113–15, 153, 191, 374–75; legal system and, 329–31, 365; New Deal and, 97, 157, 187, 340; planning in, 110–11; as private government, 61–83; production in, organization of, 4, 5, 25, 62, 64–68, 83; unstable character of, 83–98, 110; urbanism and, 372–76; values of, 30–31; welfare state and, 205–08
Capitalism, Socialism, and Democracy (Schumpeter), 3, 11–14
Capitalism and democracy, relationship between, 3–20, 65, 148; contradictions, 3–5, 20, 51, 65, 68, 295, 370–73, 392, 393, 400; standards of democracy and, 10–20; see also Capitalist democracy, paradoxes of
Capitalist class, 6, 115; origin of, 114; see also Capitalists
Capitalist democracy, 63; paradoxes of, 6–9
Capitalists, 6; corporation as, 80; see also Owners of the means of production

Carter, Jimmy (Carter administration), 110, 160, 167, 247, 250, 263, 283, 292–93, 343
Catholic Church, 378–79
Catholics, 154, 164, 378; in Congress, 306–07; immigrants, 126, 127
CBS (Columbia Broadcasting Corporation), 37
CBS/New York Times News poll, 176n
Censorship, television and radio, 38; self–, 39
Central Intelligence Agency (CIA), 55, 235, 237–40
Chamberlain, Lawrence, 299
Chambers, William Nisbet, 145n, 152n, 179n, 181n
Change, in American society, 369–71; movements for, 370 (see also Opposition movements); structural (fundamental), see Structural change
Charles River Bridge v. *Warren Bridge Co.*, 338
Chase, Salmon, 339
Chase Manhattan Bank, 81–82, 230
Checks and balances, 260
Chevigny, Paul, 355
Chicago, Illinois, 124, 357, 366, 374, 378, 382, 385
Chicago Tribune, 313n
Children, television and, 41; see also Schools
Chile, 226, 235, 238–40
China, 214, 215, 219, 230, 396
Chinese immigrants, 122, 126
Chomsky, Noam, 347n
Christoffel, Tom, 244n
Chrysler Corporation, 73
CIA, 55, 235, 237–40
CIO (Congress of Industrial Organizations), 134, 156; see also AFL-CIO
Cities, 8, 114, 153, 201–02; black migration to Northern, 163, 164, 201, 370; see also Urban political machines
Civil liberties, 16, 392; see also Freedom
Civil rights legislation, 163, 166
Civil rights movement, 53, 124
Civil War, 146, 153, 267, 339
Civil Works Administration (CWA), 186–87
Clapp, Charles, 315n
Clark, Joseph, 316
Clark, Kenneth, 204n
Clark, Ramsey, 351, 352n
Class (class divisions; class structure), 4–8, 10, 11, 112–14, 118, 120, 122–23,

Monopolies, 91, 92
Monroe Doctrine, 213
Monthly Review (publication), 108
Moore, Barrington, Jr., 153*n*
Moore, Beverly C., Jr., 80*n*
Morgan, J. P., 92–94
Morgan Guaranty Trust, 81, 82
Moynihan, Daniel P., 192*n*, 198*n*, 199–201, 307
Muller, Ronald E., 226*n*, 227*n*
Multinational corporations, 220, 223–31, 236, 239, 240, 252–55, 270
Muskie, Edmund, 307

Nakamura, Robert T., 269*n*
National Association for the Advancement of Colored People, 366
National Recovery Administration, 96
National security, 32, 270–71, 285
National Security Council, 18, 270
National supremacy, 336
NATO, 220, 235
Natural resources, *see* Raw materials
NBC (National Broadcasting Corp.), 37
Neighborhood government, 383, 384
Neustadt, Richard E., 262, 265, 268–69, 282
New Deal, 52, 95–97, 157, 186–88, 201, 217, 299, 404; Supreme Court and, 340–41, 345
New Deal coalition (Democratic Party coalition), 150, 163, 165–68, 175, 201
"New Economic Policy," Nixon's, 110
"New economics," 274
New England, 157, 164
New Frontier, 200, 201
New Haven, Connecticut, Dahl's study of politics in, 10–11
New International Economic Order, 254
New Jersey Governor's Select Commission on Civil Disorder, 365
New left, 53–55, 167
New York City, 17–18, 194–95, 355, 357, 374, 375, 377, 381–84
New York State, 362–63, 381
New York Times, 41*n*, 44*n*, 55, 61*n*, 63, 64*n*, 80*n*, 82*n*, 124–25, 134, 138*n*, 176*n*, 195*n*, 211*n*, 221*n*, 225*n*, 238*n*, 241*n*, 260*n*, 263*n*, 264*n*, 278*n*, 290, 348*n*
Newark, New Jersey, 366, 372–73, 377, 385–86
Newfield, Jack, 362*n*, 363*n*
Newspapers, 5, 37, 49, 73

Newsweek (magazine), 198
Nichols, David, 158–59, 159*n*
Nickerson, Albert, 199
Nie, Norman H., 44*n*, 45, 166*n*, 174, 175*n*, 176, 178
Nimmo, Dan, 42–43
Nixon, Richard M. (Nixon administration), 158, 164, 182, 242, 253, 260, 263, 264, 271, 279–81, 325, 349, 392; Burger Court and, 342–44; Family Assistance Plan of, 198–200; impeachment proceedings against, 269, 287–89, 400; inflation and, 109–10; Watergate affair and, 284–90, 343, 400
Noble, David F., 91
Nominating conventions, 141, 151, 160, 168–70
Nomination of presidential candidates, 158, 168–71
North, the (Northern interests), 150, 152–55, 166, 336, 339; migration of blacks to, 163, 164, 201, 370
North American Congress on Latin America, 227*n*
North Atlantic Treaty Organization (NATO), 220, 235
Nuclear power plants, 50
Nuclear weapons, 232–34
Nutter, G. Warren, 9*n*

O'Connor, James, 73*n*, 99–100, 136*n*, 183–84, 189*n*, 190, 191*n*, 192*n*, 193, 204, 309
Offe, Claus, 205, 276
Office of Management and Budget (OMB), 274
Oil, *see* Petroleum
Olney, Richard, 95
O'Neill, "Tip," 327
OPEC (Organization of Petroleum Exporting Countries), 89, 106, 222
Opinion, minority, 31; public, 26, 41–42; *see also* Political beliefs
Opinion polls, public, 170
Oppenheimer, Bruce I., 317*n*, 326*n*
Opportunities, educational, 35–37; job, 77
Opposition movements (movements for structural change), 51–56, 279, 347–51, 366, 389, 400; absence of, in United States, 6–8, 28, 29, 50, 370; socialist outcome and, 405, 407; *see also* Radical movements and groups

A 9
B 0
C 1
D 2
E 3
F 4
G 5
H 6
I 7
J 8